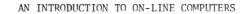
AN INTRODUCTION TO ON-LINE COMPUTERS

An Introduction to
ON-LINE COMPUTERS

W. WAYNE BLACK

GORDON AND BREACH SCIENCE PUBLISHERS
New York   London   Paris

PREFACE

   Approximately two decades ago, what has come to be called
the computer revolution started. In the last few years a second computer revolution has begun. The first revolution saw
the development of large computers capable of performing computations on a scale and complexity orders of magnitude greater
than man had been able to perform previously. This movement
continues. The second computer revolution has seen the emergence of computers to perform an entirely different function.
These are known as on-line computers. The on-line computer,
in its short existance, has already been used to direct and
control a vast variety of devices and processes, to serve individuals instead of multitudes, to automate everything from
baseball park scoreboards to spacecraft--and yet, the potential
has hardly been scratched.
   The computer of the second revolution does not differ
from that of the first so much in technical detail as in function. However, the on-line computer has often been differentiated from that normally found in the central computing facility by referring to it as the mini-computer. This is somewhat
unfortunate. Although many of the on-line computers now being
manufactured are of the desk-top variety, and in some cases
even portable, there are still many on-line systems with values
in the range from several hundreds of thousands of dollars to
the order of a million dollars. Thus, the method and purpose
of utilization are the true dividing line.
   This book is aimed at anyone who wishes to use an on-line
computer. This includes those in the fields of applied and
basic scientific research; those that want to control an industrial process; those who want to automate a task that has
reached a point of complexity that exceeds human capability;
those who are interested in learning the basic fundamentals of
the computer art.
   It is surprising, but true, that there is a dearth of material related to the on-line computer--one of the most widely
applicable tools every invented. With such a diversity of

application this book is obviously not directed to any specific professions or fields of endeavor. However, all those interested need the same basic questions answered. How does a computer actually perform arithmetic? How does one go about programming a computer? How does one get information in and out of the computer? How is the computer linked to equipment already available? What do the terms of the computer jargon mean? How does one use the standard peripheral equipment associated with computers; and how does one decode the data formats that these peripheral devices use? What is the significance of binary and octal number systems? The answers to such questions are required whether one is a college student taking a one semester course in computer usage, a scientist trying to find the means of performing an elaborate experiment, or a plant engineer wanting to automate an assembly line.

On the one hand, I hope this book starts those who desire toward the competent use of on-line computers. On the other hand, I hope it does not create another wave of "experts". The computer area is now bulging with those who have read one or two manuals or have written one or two programs and are "experts". The field could do with more competence and less "experts".

A computer is not a great and wonderous thing. It is, in fact, a rather simple device to understand. Therefore, it should not be held at arms length, or given the aura of the mysterious unknown. It is simply a tool at man's disposal. To be used properly any tool must be understood, and that is the goal of this book--to start anyone who wants toward the understanding of that breed of computer known as the on-line computer.

I have found myself in the position to write this book due to the efforts of many people. In particular, I would like to mention Mr. Russell Heath, who provided encouragement as well as the time for the early phases of the work. A book, such as this, necessarily contains material and conclusions based on experience. The reservoir of experience is not only that of the author, but of many people with whom the author has been privileged to associate. Outstanding among these are Mr. Gary Morgan and Mr. Wendell Richardson. The book has benefited directly from the following who have read and commented on the complete text: Mr. Morgan, Mr. Richardson, Dr. Clarence Tilger, and Dr. Richard Trinko. Mrs. Judith Blau executed all the illustrations.

My wife, to whom the book is dedicated, has contributed to all phases of the effort. She typed all drafts and the final copy, read the complete text, tried to keep my grammar under control, and sacrificed many social occasions.

CONTENTS

PART I
PRELIMINARIES

CONTENTS

PART II
ON-LINE COMPUTER FUNDAMENTALS

CONTENTS

PART III
ON-LINE COMPUTER UTILIZATION

CONTENTS

CONTENTS

CONTENTS

APPENDICIES

PART I

PRELIMINARIES

CHAPTER 1

INTRODUCTION

1.0 THE ON-LINE COMPUTER

1.1 What is It?

The on-line computer can be expected to have the features
found on any computer. Thus, it is not defined by its technical or economic characteristics, i.e. its speed, its size or
its cost. Instead, it is defined by the functions it performs,
and hence, it is probably best characterized by contrasting it
against other types of computers.

If one were to distribute the various kinds of computers
on a spectrum by function, then the on-line computer would lie
at one end of the spectrum and the large batch operated, central
facility would lie at the other end. Therefore, a comparison
of these two types of systems should provide the sharpest contrast. Before going on to this comparison, it is probably well
to look at what is meant by a batch operated, central facility.

In many large organizations and laboratories computing
centers have been established for doing many of the computational chores of that particular organization. The computations
performed on these machines are often done in an assembly-line
fashion, i.e. as the jobs come in they form a stream that is
fed through the computer. This is typically referred to as a
batch operation.

With this small amount of background let us now contrast
the on-line computer system with the batch operated, central
facility.

Purpose. The purpose or "reason to be" for the central
computing facility is to provide a service. In the case of
the on-line computer, the system is a tool.

Support personnel. What support personnel are required
with the two types of computer systems? The service computer
requires engineers for maintenance, professional programmers
for writing programs, and full-time operators. Except for the
largest systems, on-line computers require no full time

3

maintenance personnel and no full time operators. Full time
programmers may be needed.

Typical cost. The cost of a central facility varies from
several hundred thousand dollars to a few million dollars. On
the other hand, on-line computer systems vary from a few thousand dollars to a few hundred thousand dollars. Therefore, in
some average manner, the on-line computer system costs two to
three orders of magnitude less than the central facility.

Utilization. How many people utilize the computer system?
In the case of the central facility, a large number of people;
as high as several hundred individuals. In contrast the on-line
system will typically have one to a few individuals directly
utilizing it.

Computer availability. The central computing facility sets
as its goal the maximum availability of the system to as many
people as possible. The on-line system is maximized to make
the computer available to the experiment or control process to
which it is linked for the largest amount of time possible and
in the fastest time possible.

Operation schedule. In the service computer system the
prime (day) shift is the most desirable, and hence, the most
expensive. This precept is recognized and taken advantage of
by computer manufacturers in their lease contracts. Because
of its very nature the on-line computer system is typically
ran 24 hours a day with no differentiation made between time
periods.

Cost recovery. The cost of a service computer system is
usually recovered by charging for the services that are performed in conjunction with the computer. The cost of an on-
line computer may be recovered by the eventual marketing of a
product. In most instances, the cost of the on-line computer
is charged against the project or process of which it is a
part similar to any other piece of capital equipment.

Mobility. The service system is almost always a permanent
installation, and hence is not mobile. The on-line computer may
be permanent but can easily be mobile or semi-mobile.

Another way to define an on-line computer is on the basis
of its utilitarian aspects. Unfortunately, this has been somewhat difficult to do. The computer has emerged with such an
aura that one very simple fact has been almost lost from view.
It is just a tool! A very versatile one, but nevertheless, a
tool.

If it is a scientist using the on-line computer, it is a
tool just as his laboratory oscilloscope or voltmeter is a tool.

If it is an industrialist using an on-line computer on his
assembly line, it is a tool just as his overhead crane or his
conveyer belt is a tool.

If it is a teacher using an on-line computer to teach dif-
ferential and integral calculus, the computer is a tool just as
his blackboard is a tool.

Why is this simple fact overlooked? First, a jargon has grown up over the years in the computer sciences. Most fields do have a jargon, but the jargon usually serves as a shorthand means of communication and it is also fairly precise. Unfortunately, in the computer sciences the jargon has acted more as a cloud than as a means of communication. The jargon has often exceeded the need for a shorthand, and it does not meet the criterion of accuracy*.

A second reason for the difficulty in recognizing the computer as a tool is probably its versatility. There have been few, if any other, physical tools developed by man that have been able to accomplish so many tasks and to be used for so many purposes.

The news media must also take some of the blame for contributing to the aura that has developed around the computer technology. The persistent use of terms like "electronic brains" have greatly clouded the facts, because such terms are grossly misleading.

On-line computers are often described as those computers that control a device, a process or an experiment. They are also sometimes related as those that serve several different functions at the same time. I would agree that all of these represent on-line computer applications, but, they take too narrow a viewpoint. Again, when one thinks of the on-line computer as a tool, such limitations are removed. Then, there is no difficulty in thinking of a computer as an instrument which can be used to calibrate other instrumentation today, and serve as a super desk calculator tomorrow. Perhaps this is the key to the stumbling block. The tool has become versatile enough that it need not be dedicated to a given task. Thus, broader views must be taken to prevent the limitation of the horizons of application.

1.2   Who Uses It?

In the not too distant future large segments of the population of the United States will certainly be using on-line computers. Almost everyone will be benefiting in some direct fashion from their use. However, the present-day list of those who are

---

*A glossary of terms have been included in this book. Because these terms often are not precise, there is more than one meaning for many of them. The author readily admits that when there is any doubt the definitions given in the glossary are his own. Every attempt has been made to maintain a consistency between the definitions given in the glossary and the usage of the terms in the text.

<u>already using</u> on-line computers is quite impressive. The ex-
panding use of computer systems is substantiated by economic
forecasts which now state that the computer industry will be
the largest industry in the United States by the end of the 19
decade.

Like many advanced instruments, the computer began in the
laboratory. Although, on-line computers have been widely and
more increasingly used in the laboratory, they have long since
spread beyond that domain.

There is really little reason to try and itemize all of
those applications for which on-line computers have already bee
used. However, a short list demonstrates the wide application
and diversity of use that is already in existence.

> Laboratories of all kinds.
> Almost every new power plant.
> Patient monitoring in hospitals.
> Controlling traffic lights.
> Automated billboards.
> Oil exploration.
> Automated warehouses.
> Steelmills.
> Classroom teaching aid.
> Airline reservations.

2.0   ON-LINE COMPUTER TRENDS

2.1   The Recent Past

On-line computers are a comparatively new phenomenon. The
have enjoyed a rapid growth in the last five years. What has
happened is astounding. For example, in this period of time th
speed of the average on-line computer has changed by approximately a factor of five from about five or six microseconds per
memory cycle time to approximately one microsecond. Also, duri
this same five year period, the cost of on-line computers has
decreased by approximately a factor of three. So, at this poin
in time, about one third as much buys approximately five times
more capability. Needless to say, with these dramatic changes
the accomplishments and applications of on-line computers have
been rapidly changing.

There are other important trends. For example, the reliability of the on-line computer has greatly increased, the delivery time has decreased to the point that many are purchasabl
on an off-the-shelf basis, and there has been a large prolifera
tion of manufacturers which provide a large spectrum of compute
models to choose from.

The price of the basic computer now ranges from something
less than $5,000 to perhaps $250,000. The physical size of on-
line computers has also been decreasing and the upshot of all

these trends is that the truly portable, desk-top computer is
a reality and is being built on an everyday basis. This is
vividly demonstrated by the computer in the photograph of Fig. 1.
The footrule indicates this to be a rather small device--yet,
it is a full blown computer. As a point of comparison Fig. 2
shows an on-line computer system of a more intermediate size.
Note that the computer of Fig. 1 is a part of this bigger system-
-it can be seen between the two Teletype units.

In some sense the trends in on-line computers have been so
dramatic that until recently they have literally left the art
of the computer peripheral* behind. In the past it has not been
uncommon for on-line computer systems to have peripherals which
cost more than the computer itself. Fortunately, this trend
has begun to abate and considerable effort has been put into
making economical peripherals for on-line computers.

The trends have also resulted in some dramatic changes in
the applications of on-line computers. In their infancy on-line
computers would seldom have been used in any application where
a conventional device could have met the specific requirements.
This was simply because the computer was more expensive than
conventional devices. Therefore, computers tended to be used
only in rather exotic applications where no other device could
meet the stringent requirements. However, with the economic
trends that have taken place, the on-line computer is in many
cases now quite competitive with conventional devices. In fact,
there are numerous instances where using an on-line computer is
the most economic approach to a given problem.

2.2 Conjectures on the Future

In the case of the hardware (equipment), there will un-
doubtedly continue to be an unabated advance. However, the
present state-of-the art of computer hardware is quite sufficient for many as yet untapped applications. Therefore, I
think there can be little doubt, that the next spurt of activity will be the application of on-line computers to many new
domains.

In the area of computer peripherals, a major hurdle remains. That is the ability to easily move peripheral equipment
from one computer to another computer. To be able to do this
requires a standardization of the electronics that link

---

*Peripherals are those devices attached to the basic computer.
 Examples are magnetic tape units, card readers, displays, etc.

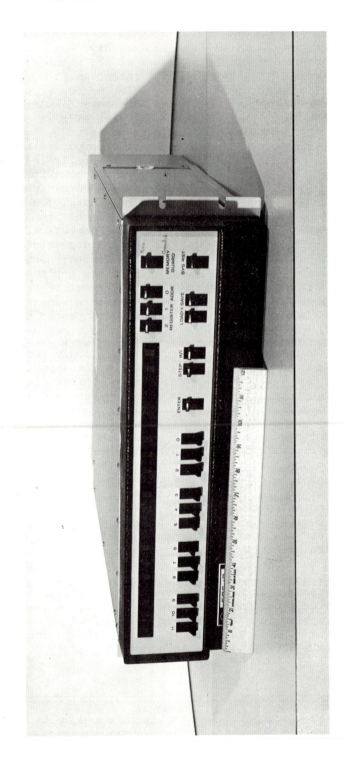

Fig. 1.   One of the smaller on-line computers currently being produced.

Fig. 2.   An intermediate-size on-line computer system.

peripheral devices to the basic computer*. Only recently has
progress been made in this area. This is discussed in more detail in the chapter "Computer Interfaces". There is a significant side benefit that results from the standardization of
computer interfaces; a large reduction in cost.

In the case of the computer software (programming), there
are two major needs to be fulfilled in the future. The first
is for less programming. Although the flexibility of computers
derives from the ability to reprogram them, at present, too much
time is spent in programming the computer. Advances in the computer hardware can do much to satisfy this problem. This is
currently beginning to be seen in what might be described as
functional peripherals, i.e. peripherals that are more naturally
engineered and designed to perform a specific function. When
the peripheral directly performs the function then the hardware
has assumed much of the load that has been born by the programming
in the past.

The second major need in the computer software of the future is easier programming. There is a sizeable requirement
for a programming language that is well suited to on-line application. This is a large order to fulfill and to date there has
been much talk but little real progress.

---

*This linking electronics is usually referred to as the inter-
 face between the peripheral and the computer.

As the on-line computer assumes its rightful position as a very general tool, a fundamental question must be answered--what is the role of the on-line computer in the larger scheme of things? There is a tendency to act as if the computer can literally do anything, even to the assumption of human faculties The computer can certainly replace some of the more mechanical human functions but there has been little to demonstrate that it can assume human faculties. The answer lies in a fundamental theory of information--a yet to be delineated theory in a new, and largely unrecognized, fundamental science.

3.0   THE ORGANIZATION OF THIS BOOK

This section might more appropriately be entitled something like the "Assumptions Upon Which This Book Have Been Organized". However, that is a rather long title.

3.1   The Learning Sequence

The total on-line computer system is made up of both the equipment and the software that makes it operate. It is not really possible to discuss either without knowing something of the other. Thus, the author faces a teaching dilemma which is discussed further in the chapter "Computer Organization I".

One fact must be kept in mind. This book is directed to the user of on-line computer systems. Therefore, the basic question to ask is what sequence of presentation is best from the user's viewpoint.

With this in mind the book is organized in a manner that is in keeping with the author's experience in teaching others what might be classed the computer art. This experience has indicated that the average person first wants to know something about programming the computer. <u>Not, how does a computer actually work</u>. After the initial curiosity has been satisfied, the practicalities of the situation demand that the new user find how to get information in and out of the computer in order that his newly written program can actually be executed. At this point, the novice has before him some cryptic notations, and is wondering how they can be reduced to something meaningful for the computer. The computer can only digest binary numbers. It, therefore, becomes necessary to learn about assembler programs (or compiler programs).

Once the use of the assembler (or compiler) is mastered then the programs can be reduced to a form that permits execution. But it is a rare occasion indeed, when a program runs error free the first time. With the class of computers being considered, it is about this time that the new user finds himself sitting in front of the computer console wondering where he went wrong.

Now the thought processes turn to the questions: how does
the computer actually perform arithmetic?; what do those instructions mean precisely?; what would have been a better way to write
the program?; and perhaps, the first thoughts of how does the computer itself function?

Having agonized through the writing and debugging of the
first few programs, one's thoughts turn to seriously considering
how the computer functions. If the trail has been pursued this
far, then it is inevitable that the question will be asked; how
does one connect the computer to other devices? And, going on
to ever greater heights what about such things as real-time computing and time-sharing of computers? At this point one is no
longer a novice.

It is along the lines of the preceding narrative that this
book is organized. A real attempt is made to meet the almost
impossible goal of giving a continuity from chapter to chapter,
while at the same time trying to keep the information in each
chapter independent enough to allow a reader to turn to a given
chapter and satisfy his curiosity about the subject dealt with
therein.

3.2   The Choice of a Computer Model

When discussing the subject of programming computers it
is essential that examples of computer programs be given. As
an author, one has two choices:
    1)   Invent a set of computer program instructions for a
fictitious computer, or
    2)   Choose to use the instruction set of an existing com-
puter.

In the first case, there is a real difficulty of defining
an instruction set that "rings true". There is also the danger
of inventing an instruction set which contains instructions that
are not feasible from the engineering standpoint. Finally, any
computer instruction set that is invented will tend to resemble
the set of some computer that the author has actually programmed.

In the second case, there is the difficulty of finding an
existing computer with an instruction set that might be considered representative. In addition, there is the difficulty of
implied commercialism and the endorsement of specific equipment.

The present author feels that the perils of the second case
are somewhat less than those of the first, and that the balance
is significantly tipped when one considers the advantages to
the reader.

Having decided to use the instruction set of an existing
computer, one faces a decision that is almost as difficult:
which computer to use as a model? The decision was made to use
the PDP-8 computer, which is manufactured by Digital Equipment
Corporation. This actually is a family of several computers,
all of which use the same programming instruction set.

This computer was chosen for the following reasons:

1) It is one of the computers that the author has had considerable experience programming and has also had the opportunity to teach several other individuals how to program.

2) It is a simple computer both organizationally and in its programming aspects. The instruction set is small and contains instructions which can be found as a subset of the instruction sets of many other computers.

3) For several years Digital Equipment Corporation has published and widely distributed a small paperback book entitled "Small Computer Handbook" which is primarily devoted to the PDP-8 family of computers.

4) There have probably been more computers of the PDP-8 family built and installed than any other on-line computer.

5) It will probably be built for some years to come.

CHAPTER 2

NUMBER SYSTEMS

1.0 INTRODUCTION

It is perhaps worthwhile to make a few opening remarks a-
bout why a chapter on number systems is necessary. The answer
is that almost all of the computers on the market today use binary numbers internally, and the assumption is that most people
are not facile at using binary numbers. But this immediately
raises the question: why are computers organized in such a way
that they use binary arithmetic and binary numbers? The answer
is related directly to the fact that almost all of the devices,
devices here meaning electronic and mechanical, that are used
in present-day computers are of a binary nature. The majority
of all the devices associated with the computer, and the electronics of the computer itself, are dependent on processes that
are bistable. Electronic gates have two stable states, magnetic
cores can be magnetized in two directions, magnetic tapes and
magnetic surfaces, such as are used in drums and disks, can be
magnetized in two directions, switches are either open or closed,
etc. In every case there are two stable states, and it is obvious that an arithmetic should be used that employs two integers,
i.e. binary arithmetic. Then the two states of all these examples can be chosen, by convention, to correspond either to a
"0" or a "1".

Presumably, we now have good reasons for the need to become facile with binary arithmetic, let us go on and touch on
the subject of octal and hexadecimal number systems. If computers operate with binary arithmetic, why is it necessary to
know anything other than decimal and binary number systems?
As will become evident in some of the examples, the manipulation of binary numbers becomes very cumbersome. Because binary numbers are so cumbersome, it is helpful when working outside the machine itself, to have at hand some other way of handling numbers which are easily converted back to binary. For this
reason, it has become common to use either octal or hexadecimal
arithmetic because these number systems require much less manipulation of fewer digits. It should be pointed out that one

rarely has to know both the octal and the hexadecimal number
systems. It is necessary to know only one of these systems
if only one manufacturer's computers is involved. The computer
manufacturer normally determines whether one uses octal or hexadecimal with a particular computer. Although either octal or
hexadecimal number systems may be used with any binary computer
the manufacturer will choose one of the systems, which results
in all manuals for the computer being printed in one of the two
notations. Thus, as a practical matter, the computer user must
work in the number system chosen for the manuals.

Summing up this chapter has been inserted for two reasons:
first, the utilization of a computer usually represents the fir
real exposure to non-decimal systems, and second, most of the
on-line computers on the market today require facility in at
least two non-decimal systems, either binary and octal, or binary and hexadecimal.

The final question that might be asked is; what depth of
understanding is required of non-decimal systems? There is no
unique answer to this question because it depends almost entire
upon the circumstances of each individual. Obviously, for the
person who is only going to make cursory use of the computer,
an in-depth understanding is not required. However, for the
person who is going to be using the computer daily, and is going to be programming it extensively, the better the understand
ing of number systems he has and the more facility he has in
using them, the better off he will be. This is because an unde
standing of number systems will be quite helpful whether the
computer user is writing a program for the computer, assembling
a program for the computer or trying to get a program to run on
the computer. An understanding of number systems is particular
useful in trying to test or implement special devices that have
been added to a computer. It is almost always the case that
binary numbers will be inspected for intermediate results. Tha
is, there are always numbers in a test which are of interest at
the time of the test, but are rarely of interest after that
point. Therefore, there will never be any special provision
to convert them to decimal numbers in the programs.

Because an in-depth understanding of number systems is important, and since a relatively small investment of time is required to become facile with number systems, this chapter will
attempt to give a sufficient coverage of the subject for anybod
using on-line computers.

2.0 HOW NUMBER SYSTEMS EVOLVED

An understanding of number systems can, in general, be obtained by simply reviewing the concepts of the decimal number
system. This does mean looking at some of these concepts in
a little more general light including the concepts of borrowing
and carrying when doing computation; and it would also include

a very good understanding of what is meant by the base of a number system. These concepts can be obtained in a natural way by a short review of the history of number systems, which is not too surprising, since this history just represents the evolvement of man's thinking about number systems.

There are three distinct number systems that can be identified in the history of man: the mark or slash system, the alphabetic system, and the position or place-value system. In each case more than one culture has used the number system. Table I gives an example of each of the three number systems and a culture which used these systems.

The first column of Table I is an example of the mark or slash system, in this case the Egyptian Hieroglyphics system, which is the oldest of the three systems, and represents nothing more than a simple counting procedure. In this system every number has associated with it a symbol that is unique to that number in the sense that each number's symbol is unlike the symbol for any other number. However, the way the symbol is written is not unique. For example, look at the symbol for the number twelve. It can be written in any of the three following ways: ∩II I∩I II∩ .
For future reference, look also at the symbol associated with the number twenty-one. This, too, can be written in any of three ways as follows: ∩∩I ∩I∩ I∩∩

Another important consideration of any numeration system is; how does one do computation? With a mark or slash system it is an extension of the counting procedure. Returning to the Egyptian Hieroglyphic system, if one wanted to add ten and four, it would simply mean writing down the symbols for ten and four and then doing a simple counting. In other words, adding is completely analogous to having two groups of objects, collecting the objects into one group and counting all the objects. Likewise, subtraction would be carried out by putting two groups of objects together and removing the group to be subtracted. In this type of system multiplication and division would have no real meaning other than repeated additions and subtractions. It is also very hard to establish the concept of a fraction in this type of system. The Egyptians did make an attempt to the extent that they devised special symbols for the fractions. This was done by placing an oval-shaped symbol above the ordinary symbols, e.g. the fraction one-half would be the symbol for two with this oval-like structure drawn above it.

Turn now to the alphabetic system. This system is illustrated in column two of Table I and as indicated there, it was used by the Ionian Greek culture. Of course, the Greeks used the Greek alphabet, but for purposes of clarity, the modern-day alphabet has been substituted. This system has two advantages over the mark and slash system: by using the alphabet a sense of order has been given to numbers, and an economy of writing has been achieved. For example, the number twenty is now represented by one symbol, namely K, while in the Egyptian

Table I.   Examples of a mark or slash numeration
system, an alphabetic numeration system,
and a position or place value numeration
system.

Egyptian Hieroglyphic	Ionian Greek with Present Day Alphabet	Modern
I	A	1
II	B	2
III	C	3
IIII	D	4
IIIII	E	5
IIIIII	F	6
IIIIIII	G	7
IIIIIIII	H	8
IIIIIIIII	I	9
∩	J	10
∩∩	K	20
∩∩∩	L	30
∩∩∩∩	M	40
∩∩∩∩∩	N	50
∩∩∩∩∩∩	O	60
∩∩∩∩∩∩∩	P	70
∩∩∩∩∩∩∩∩	Q	80
∩∩∩∩∩∩∩∩∩	R	90
9	S	100
99	T	200
999	U	300
9999	V	400
99999	W	500
999999	X	600
9999999	Y	700
99999999	Z	800
999999999	–	900

system, the number twenty was represented by two symbols. The
alphabetic system has all the disadvantages that the mark and
slash system did as far as computations are concerned, for additions and subtractions are still done by grouping the symbols
together and doing a simple counting. An added disadvantage is
that the number of symbols are greatly limited, in fact, the
Greeks had to extend their original alphabet. At the time this
system was being used, the Greek alphabet had twenty-four letters
in it. To get the necessary twenty-seven letters to reach the
symbol for nine hundred, the Greeks had to use three symbols
from more ancient times. In one sense, this shortage of symbols
represented an advantage, for in order to get around the problem,
the Greeks started repeating symbols. That is, after the symbol
for nine hundred, it was customary to again use the symbol for
one. To this extent, position meant something in the Greek notation, for after one got beyond nine hundred, a symbol was re-
used with a distinguishing slash or mark to indicate its greater
value.

This brings us to the modern-day numeration system. Because
we are all aware of the characteristics of the modern-day system,
there is no need to elaborate on them here. But, it is worthwhile to compare the modern-day numeration system with the earlier
systems just reviewed. Again, referring to Table I, it can be
seen that a greater efficiency has been made of symbols, because the modern-day system requires only ten symbols regardless
of the size of the number to be written. The modern-day system
has another advantage over the more ancient ones: the position
of the symbol in the number takes on meaning. This is easily
illustrated in the previous example using the numbers twelve
and twenty-one with Egyptian Hieroglyphics. Unlike the hieroglyphic case twelve and twenty-one in the modern-day system
consist of exactly the same symbols the only difference being
that the position of the symbol in the written number has meaning. Another very important concept is required by giving the
position of the symbol meaning, namely zero. If the position
of the symbol is to have meaning, it is necessary to also have
a method of indicating when there is no value in a given position. In the cases of the slash and alphabetic systems, zero
is implied, but never made explicit. In these cases zero is
indicated by a true null, i.e. the complete absence of any
symbols.

Another important result of giving value to the position
of the symbols is that it now permits computation. These computations can be set down or outlined in exact detail as to
how they are to be done. In fact, it is interesting to note,
at this point, a definition for the term, algorithm. Algorithm
is a term originating from the name of a ninth-century Arabic
scholar, al-Khuwarizmi. It initially indicated a class of
arithmetic in which Arabic numbers were used by al-Khuwarizmi.
in his publications. Modern usage of the term has come to mean
any mathematical operation in which arabic numerals are used

in corresponding algebraic operations. Thus, the arabic number
themselves take on the connotation of being able to compute. A
we shall see, the term algorithm has now taken on a considerabl'
broader meaning in the world of electronic computers. This a-
bility to compute and also the attachment of value to position
provides a means of defining the concept of a fraction.

With the concept of the fraction we have now arrived at
a modern-day repertoire of symbolism and manipulations. Armed
with this historic viewpoint of number systems, we will now
proceed to look at the modern-day number systems in more detail

3.0   THE CONCEPT OF BASE

Suppose that you are watching a sporting event and it is
desired to keep track of the scores made by one team. A very
simple way to do this would be to mark a vertical slash on a
piece of paper for each score made. If a large number of score
were made, this would soon become a cumbersome method of keepin
account of the scoring. The notation could be simplified by
the following procedure: suppose that on every fifth score a
horizontal slash is made through the previous four scores. Thi
would group the notation into blocks of five, which would be
considerably easier to keep track of than the original method.
In fact, this is a method of keeping track of various kinds of
events which is common in everyday life. What has been devised
is a mark and slash numeration system quite analogous to that
of the Egyptian Hieroglyphic system in Table I. We have also
constructed what might be called a tally; in this case, a symbo
that stands for five events. This is precisely what the Egyptians did. To indicate every tenth event they invented a new
symbol, which was not nearly so cumbersome as the one we have
devised for five. In the case of the Egyptians, a symbol or
tally was invented for ten events, one hundred events, one
thousand events, and so forth.

Now the concept of base* can be defined. The base of a
number system is the smallest tally of the system. In our accounting of scores we chose a base of five, but the Egyptians
preferred to collect their objects or numbers in groups of ten.
Therefore, their numeration system was on a base of ten. Referring to Table I, the Ionian-Greek numeration system had a
base of ten as does our modern numeration system. Considerable
literature can be found on various bases and why the base ten
seems to enjoy a preference, and as far back as Aristotle, this
has been ascribed to the fact that we have ten fingers. Howeve
there have been many cultures that have used other bases; for

---

*The term base is often used interchangably with the term radi×

example, the bases two, three, four, twelve and sixty. The
Babyalonians used the base sixty, which has, at various times,
been ascribed to astronomical origins. However, doubt has been
cast upon this origin.

What then is the ideal base? The answer is that there is
no ideal base. Arguments can be given for several different
bases, and none of them are overwhelming, but it is interesting
to note that good arguments can be given for why the base eight
or the base twelve are superior to the base ten.

Carrying our original thinking a little further, what happens if the concept of a place-value notation is combined with
the concept of a base. In terms of symbology, there is an immediate result. If one chooses the base ten with a place-value
notation, then only ten symbols are required to represent all
numbers. Thus, the base directly determines the number of u-
nique symbols required and this fact plays an important role in
the choosing of a base. It has little influence on whether the
base eight, the base ten, or the base twelve is chosen, but in
the case of the base sixty it is difficult, and cumbersome, to
have sixty unique symbols. Some of the ancient cultures complicated their choices of bases even further. The Ionic-Greek
numeration system used the base ten for the integer numbers,
but used the base sixty for fractions.

Return again to the coupling of the concept of base and
the concept of place-value notation. This coupling results in
a unique number of symbols required for any given base. It also
uniquely determines the positional value of a symbol. To illustrate, what is precisely meant by the number 249 is as follows:
$$2 \times 100 + 4 \times 10 + 9 \times 1.$$
Examining this number one sees that the position of each symbol
is directly associated with a unique power of the base. Writing
this explicitly, we have the following;
$$2 \times 10^2 + 4 \times 10^1 + 9 \times 10^0 .$$
The concept of a base is a simple one. It is nothing more
than a way of grouping entities, whether real or abstract. The
difficulty of switching bases, for most individuals, does not
lie in a difficulty of understanding the concept of base, or
the conversion between bases, or other topics yet to be covered.
The difficulty lies with those things that are normally memorized
by rote and the difficulty of separating the concept of a number
and the symbol that represents it. This should become clear as
we proceed.

4.0 REPRESENTING A NUMBER ON AN ARBITRARY BASE

We have now seen how the mark and slash numeration systems
and the alphabetic systems have culminated in our modern-day
numeration system. The relationship between place value notation and the concept of a base have also been stressed. From
this point on we will restrict ourselves to the modern-day

system. Return to the example of the number 249 written in
the base ten and extend it in the following way: what is meant
by the symbol 249.168? In the base ten, it is

$$2\times100 + 4\times10 + 9\times1 + \frac{1}{10} + \frac{6}{100} + \frac{8}{1000}$$

which can be rewritten in terms of the powers of ten as

$$2\times10^{2} + 4\times10^{1} + 9\times10^{0} + 1\times10^{-1} + 6\times10^{-2} + 8\times10^{-3}.$$

To make these remarks more comprehensive, a generalized notation is needed. Examining the expansion of 249.168 in powers
of ten, it can be seen that such an expansion can be written
in the following way:

$$N_{10} = \sum_{n=\infty}^{-\infty} a_n 10^n. \tag{1}$$

The subscript ten indicates that the number N is being written
on the base ten. Equation 1 demonstrates how to write any number on the base ten. But, how would one proceed to write any
number on any base? Remembering the discussion of base and the
relation of place values to the powers of the base, it should
be apparent that the most general expression for writing any
number on any base is:

$$N_{B} = \sum_{n=\infty}^{-\infty} a_n B^n. \tag{2}$$

Where B now indicates the base on which the number is being
written.
    Equation 2 is deceivingly simple, because the notation
leaves a lot unsaid. First turn to the left-hand side of the
equation. To understand the full significance of the symbol
N_B, two important terms need to be defined; number and numeral.
These terms are related, for a numeral is used to represent a
number. This can be illustrated by examining the fingers of
both hands. A modern person would represent the fingers of both
hands with the numeral 10, but from Table I, the Greek would
have represented his fingers by the numeral J. From this illustration it can be seen that number has an absolute sense
while numeral is relative, and can even have double meaning.
Summing up, the N_B of Eq. 2 is a numeral which represents a
number on the base B.
    Turn now to the right-hand side of Eq. 2. Referring back
to the expansion of 249.168 in powers of ten, the characteristic
of the coefficients a_n can be deduced. First, the coefficients
are always integer and take on the values

$$0 \leq a_n < B - 1.$$

Examining this range of values, it follows that the coefficient
a_n can always be represented by the symbols of the base in

question. It can also be seen that the coefficients are always positive, (unless the number being represented is negative, in which case all the coefficients are negative).

To further elucidate the right-hand side of Eq. 2 look at two examples:

$$11_{10}=1_{10}\times10_{10}^{1} + 1_{10}\times10_{10}^{0} \tag{3}$$

$$13_8=1_{10}\times8_{10}^{1}+ 3_{10}\times8_{10}^{0}. \tag{4}$$

In Eq. 3 a number is represented by the numeral 11, base ten, expanded on the base ten. In Eq. 4 a number is represented by the numeral 13, base eight, expanded on the base eight. First notice that the numeral representing the base should have its base specified, and that Eqs. 3 and 4 nicely illustrate the difference between numeral and number. If we sum up the terms on the right-hand sides of these two equations we see that they both add to eleven on the base ten. Thus, the numeral eleven on the base ten and the numeral thirteen on the base eight both represent the same number. Next, note the difference in Eqs. 3 and 4. In Eq. 3 the numerals on both sides of the equal sign have been expressed in the base ten, but in Eq. 4 the numeral on the left-hand side of the equation is expressed on the base eight while the numerals on the right-hand side of the equation are expressed in base ten. What would Eq. 4 look like if both sides of the equation were expressed on the base eight? It would be

$$13_8=1_8\times10_8^{1}+ 3_8\times10_8^{0}. \tag{5}$$

Eq. 5 illustrates how difficult it is for us to escape from the base ten notation of our everyday lives. For in Eq. 5 the subscripts are still expressed on the base ten. The numeral eight does not exist in a base eight system. However, it would be somewhat confusing to use a different notation.

By generalizing Eq. 5 a general expression can be arrived at, which is another way of expressing Eq. 2. That is:

$$N_B= \sum_{n=\infty}^{-\infty} a_n10_B^{n} \tag{6}$$

where n is understood to also be expressed in the base B.

Return now to Eq. 2. What is really meant by this expression? The normal meaning is that the numeral on the left-hand side of the equation represents a number in the base B, while the right-hand side of the equation is the expansion representing that number with all numerals expressed in the base ten. With a proper understanding of the concepts of a number and of a numeral, and the help of Eqs. 2 and 6 it is

now possible to represent any number with a numeral on any
base expanded on any base.

5.0   IMPORTANT CONCEPTS

     Because of the normal difficulties encountered in working
with bases other than the base ten, a review will be given at
this time of the important concepts. One of the most important
concepts that must be firmly fixed in mind is the meaning of a
number. As has already been mentioned, the meaning of a number
is absolute. Because a number can be represented in several
different ways, it is seen that if one pursues the true meaning
of a number to its limit, it is inevitable that the number will
be related to a group of objects or entities. This, of course,
is just another way of saying that the meaning of a number is
absolute. Once a number has been pursued to this logical conclusion of associating it with a group of entities, one is in
a position to reverse the thought processes back to the everyday usage of number. To manipulate these entities it is more
convenient to arrange them in some basic building block groups.
These groups may again be collected into larger groups and so
on. Having established these conventions, one now has a base;
namely the smallest group. There is still an important requirement that has not been met; a symbolism to represent these individual entities and groups. What is an efficient method of
establishing these symbols? As we have seen, one efficient
method is to only invent as many symbols as there are entities
in the basic group or base. However, to be able to use such a
limited number of symbols requires the establishment of two
more concepts. That of zero and place value. If a numeral
takes on value due to some established order of its position,
then the minimal number of symbols can be used. This immediately requires a symbol or a concept for those positions in
which there is no value, i.e. zero. It has been shown that
the value of the place or position of a number in modern-day
numeration systems is directly related to a power of the base.
     What are the relationships between different bases? Suppose
an individual has been raised in a culture where the base ten
is used. If this individual were to count his fingers out loud,
the sequence would go as follows: one, two, three, four, five,
six, seven, eight, nine, and ten. But, now consider another
individual in a culture which uses the base eight. He would
count his fingers out loud in the following manner: one, two,
three, four, five, six, seven, ten, eleven, twelve. Both individuals are considering the same number, but they have used
different numerals to represent this number. The difference
between the concept of a number and a numeral to represent
that number cannot be over-emphasized because it is one of the
basic sources of difficulty in translating from one base to
another. This is probably because the normal individual is

raised in an environment with one base and therefore associates one numeral with one number. Thus, in the example above, one individual almost instinctively associates ten with the number of fingers on his hands whereas the other individual, in a similar manner, would associate twelve with the number of fingers on his hands. It is, therefore, important to realize the necessity of specifying the meaning of a numeral, i.e. what base the numeral is expressed on. Because it is normally difficult to work in bases other than ten, for computational accuracy it is often wise to work in the base ten as much as possible. This can be done, in many cases, through the use of a formalism like that of Eq. 2.

Turn now to some specific number systems. If the concepts of base, number and numeral have been clearly fixed in mind, these number systems should not present any great difficulty.

6.0   THE BASES TWO, EIGHT AND SIXTEEN

It is difficult to resist pointing out that if we were accustomed to using the base eight, the title of this section would have been "The Bases Two, Ten and Twenty". Having taken this last opportunity to emphasize the importance of the difference between numeral and number, let us proceed on to these three specific bases*. First, look at Table II. This table shows the first thirty-two integers of the bases two, ten, eight and sixteen. One of the things that becomes immediately apparent is that new symbols have been used with the base sixteen. As mentioned before, the number of symbols required is equal to the magnitude of the base. Because the decimal number system has an insufficient number of symbols, it is necessary to choose additional symbols to complete the total for the base sixteen. The typical practice is to choose the letters, A through F, thus, we have, to a partial extent, returned to the system of the Ionian-Greeks. However, concept of place value has been added. The base sixteen is normally the most difficult to become accustomed to of the bases presented in Table II and the necessity of adopting these new symbols is probably the major reason. For it is necessary to not only become accustomed to using these new symbols but because they are letters of the alphabet, they take on a double meaning. Also, there is no standardized way of pronouncing these letters when used as numerals. Although there have been recent suggestions for sounds to be attached to these numerals to avoid this difficulty, the suggestions have not been widely accepted.

---

*The number systems with the bases two, eight, and sixteen are referred to as the binary, octal, and hexadecimal number systems.

Table II. Numerals representing the first 32_{10} numbers
in the bases ten, two, eight, and sixteen.

Base Ten	Base Two	Base Eight	Base Sixteen
0	0	0	0
1	1	1	1
2	10	2	2
3	11	3	3
4	100	4	4
5	101	5	5
6	110	6	6
7	111	7	7
8	1000	10	8
9	1001	11	9
10	1010	12	A
11	1011	13	B
12	1100	14	C
13	1101	15	D
14	1110	16	E
15	1111	17	F
16	10000	20	10
17	10001	21	11
18	10010	22	12
19	10011	23	13
20	10100	24	14
21	10101	25	15
22	10110	26	16
23	10111	27	17
24	11000	30	18
25	11001	31	19
26	11010	32	1A
27	11011	33	1B
28	11100	34	1C
29	11101	35	1D
30	11110	36	1E
31	11111	37	1F
32	100000	40	20

Table II also serves to emphasize a point that was made earlier. Scanning the column under the base two it becomes apparent how very cumbersome the binary system is to work with. Already, at the thirty-second integer (base ten), six binary integers are required to represent the number. As was also pointed out earlier, this is the major reason for utilizing another base such as the base eight or base sixteen.

To clarify the notation for each of these number systems, recall Eq. 2 and use it to expand the number twenty-nine (base ten) in each of these systems. The following shows the resulting expansions:

$$29_{10}= \sum a_n 10^n = 2\times10^1 + 9\times10^0$$

$$29_{10}=11101_2= \sum a_n 2^n = 1\times2^4 + 1\times2^3 + 1\times2^2 + 0\times2^1 + 1\times2^0$$

$$29_{10}=35_8= \sum a_n 8^n = 3\times8^1 + 5\times8^0$$

$$29_{10}=1D_{16}= \sum a_n 16^n = 1\times16^1 + D\times16^0 .$$

It is perhaps necessary to recall that Eq. 2 was written with the summation limits of infinity to minus infinity. This is only done to write this expression in the most general case. It is, of course, understood that all higher terms with a co-efficient equal to zero are not written. For example, one does not normally write twenty-nine to the base ten in the following way:

$$29_{10}=\ldots + 0\times10^3 + 0\times10^2 + 2\times10^1 + 9\times10^0 + 0\times10^{-1} + 0\times10^{-2} +\ldots$$

Having taken this general look at the bases two, eight and sixteen, attention will now be given to how computation is performed in these bases.

7.0   COMPUTATION IN THE BASES TWO, EIGHT AND SIXTEEN

Normally, the first confrontation with arithmetic in a non-decimal system requires a detailed review of those operations that are normally performed in doing computations on the base ten. Specifically, such operations as the concept of borrowing or carrying when doing addition and subtraction. In the process, it is also found, that a proper understanding of these operations applies not only to the base ten but to any arbitrary base. With these thoughts in mind, it has been decided that the approach to be taken here will be to first give the cookbook rules for performing operations and examples of these operations. Following the cookbook presentation will be a more general and formal development of why the rules work. As is true with so many things, there is no substitute for actual practice and it is perhaps only after some practice that the appetite is whetted enough to attempt to find a fundamental understanding of what is being done.

7.1 Addition

How is addition normally performed? By memory: which is to say, that addition is a fundamental process and one cannot develop a formalism for finding the sum of two numbers. By this it is meant that if one wants to add two plus two, there are only two means available: either one counts fingers or some other objects, or one remembers that two plus two equals four. Thus, we have all at some time committed the decimal addition table to memory. There is no short-cut. The same statements apply equally well to doing addition in other bases. For example, to perform additions efficiently in the octal number system it is necessary to commit the octal addition table to memory. The addition tables for the bases two, eight, ten and sixteen may be found in Appendix I.

Let us approach addition by examining in detail the addition of two decimal numbers. Shown below is the addition of the numbers 18 and 16.

$$
\begin{array}{r}
1 \\
18 \\
\underline{16} \\
34
\end{array}
$$

The rules state that the first step is to add the integers in the right-most column. The rules state that if the sum of the column is greater than nine, the excess is to be carried to the next column to the left; in this case, one. We then add the left-most column to get three for the answer of thirty four. The rule can be stated in a more general way, as follows: if the sum of a given column exceeds the value of the base minus one, the excess is to be carried to the next column to the left.

In the example above a one is carried to the left-most column, however, it can be seen that ten has been added to the final answer. This makes sense. If we were to expand 18 and 16 according to Eq. 6, the left-most column of the addition example becomes the coefficients of 10^1. Of course, the rule of carrying is progressive. If the addition of succeeding columns again results in a number greater than nine, the excess is carried to the next left-most column.

With this re-stating of the rules in mind, turn to an example of octal addition.

$$1$$
$$15_8$$
$$14_8$$
$$\overline{31_8}$$

From the octal addition table of Appendix I, it can be seen that five plus four is equal to eleven which is greater than seven on the base eight, therefore, the excess is to be carried to the next left-most column. In this case, this is equivalent to adding 10_8 to the final answer. To further illustrate these rules three example additions in the binary, octal and hexadecimal number systems respectively are given below:

$$10110_2 \qquad 146_8 \qquad 7A2B_{16}$$
$$\underline{00111_2} \qquad \underline{771_8} \qquad \underline{B2F6_{16}}$$
$$11101_2 \qquad 1137_8 \qquad 12D21_{16}$$

Turn now to a more formal development of the rules of addition. Again using the expression given in Eq. 2 the summation of two numbers of the base B is as follows:

$$X_B = \sum a_n B^n + \sum b_n B^n = \sum (a_n + b_n) B^n .$$

Suppose that in the term n=N

$$a_N + b_N \geq B,$$

we can then write

$$a_N + b_N = B + C_N .$$

Where $C_N < B$ because we know that $a_N + b_N < 2B$.

The Nth term can now be written as

$$(a_N + b_N) B^N = (B + C_N) B^N = B^{N+1} + C_N B^N .$$

By collecting corresponding elements the Nth and (N + 1)th terms become

$$X_B = \ldots (a_{N+1} + b_{N+1}) B^{N+1} + (a_N + b_N) B^N + \ldots$$

$$= \ldots (a_{N+1} + b_{N+1}) B^{N+1} + (B + C_N) B^N + \ldots$$

$$= \ldots (a_{N+1} + b_{N+1} + 1) B^{N+1} + C_N B^N + \ldots$$

Thus the rule of carrying has been demonstrated. This is
seen in the latter expression where the sum multypling one
power of the base has exceeded the magnitude of the base and
that the excess over the base has been carried to multiply the
next higher power of the base. This has increased the magnitude of the answer by the base to the N plus one power.

7.2   Subtraction

There are two methods of performing the subtraction operation. The first method to be examined can be approached in
a manner quite similar to that with which we have just approached addition. As in the case of addition, there is no substitute for memorizing the addition tables for it is from the
addition tables that we also learn how to subtract. If we
want to find the result of subtracting two from nine, we can
ask, nine is equal to what quantity plus two; writing this in
algebraic notation we have $9=X+2$. By examining the addition
table one can determine the value of X. However, knowing the
addition table is not enough. Just as in addition where it is
necessary to learn how to carry, in subtraction it is necessary
to learn how to borrow. Turn again to a specific example in
the base ten:

$$\begin{array}{r} 2 \\ \cancel{3}2 \\ -17 \\ \hline 15 \end{array}$$

In examining the right-hand column we see that seven is greater
than two. The rules for subtraction say that in this situation
we are to borrow from the next column to the left reducing the
value of the top number there by one and adding ten to the top
number in the right-hand column. Now subtract seven from twelve
to get five. In borrowing from the left-most column, we have
really reduced the final answer by ten. We can re-phrase the
rule for borrowing, in the following way: when subtracting
one number from another and the number to be subtracted is the
larger, go to the next column to the left and reduce it by one
and add the value of the base to the right-hand column. With
this restatement of the rule of borrowing look at the same example in the octal number system:

$$\begin{array}{r} 3 \\ \cancel{4}3_8 \\ -24_8 \\ \hline 17_8 \end{array}$$

In the right-hand column four is greater than three; therefore,
go to the left-hand column, reduce its value by one and add the
value of the base, in this case 10_8, to the right-hand column.
In the right-hand column we now have thirteen minus four which

is equal to seven. In borrowing from the left-hand column, the
final answer is reduced by the amount of 10_8. To further illustrate borrowing, three examples are given below of subtraction
in the bases two, eight and sixteen respectively.

$$110101_2 \qquad\qquad 756_8 \qquad\qquad 3A9F_{16}$$
$$\underline{-011011_2} \qquad\qquad \underline{-677_8} \qquad\qquad \underline{-2D8E_{16}}$$
$$110010_2 \qquad\qquad 57_8 \qquad\qquad D11_{16}$$

Now that the rules for subtraction have been given, a
more formal approach will be developed to see how these rules
come about. By using Eq. 2 the subtraction of two numbers can
be written in the following way:

$$Y_B = \sum a_n B^n - \sum b_n B^n = \sum (a_n - b_n) B^n.$$

Now suppose that in the Nth term we have $b_N > a_N$.

We know that $a_N < B$, $b_N < B$

and we also know that $|a_N - b_N| < B$

from these conditions $a_N - b_N + B < B$

With this information $a_N - b_N + B = C_N$ where $C_N < B$.

Using these relationships the following manipulations on the Nth
term and the Nth plus one term can be performed.

$$Y_B = \ldots (a_{N+1} - b_{N+1}) B^{N+1} + (a_N - b_N) B^N + \ldots$$

$$= \ldots (a_{N+1} - b_{N+1}) B^{N+1} + (C_N - B) B^N \ldots$$

$$= \ldots (a_{N+1} - b_{N+1} - 1) B^{N+1} + C_N B^N + \ldots$$

Examining these last equations the rules for borrowing have
been demonstrated. The value one has been removed from the
multiplier of the B^{N+1} term and the value of the base , B, has
been added to the B^N term.
    The second method of performing the subtraction operation
is through the use of complimentary arithmetic. How is the
complement of a number defined? The answer is that there is
more than one complement defined for any given number. There
are commonly two complements that are used. In Appendix I
Tables of Complements for the integers in the binary, octal,
decimal and hexadecimal number systems are given. For the
moment, let us confine our attention to the ones, sevens,

nines and fifteens complements given in these tables. Examination will show that these complements are formed by finding a number which when added to the desired integer sums to the value of the base minus one. For the purposes of this discussion, let us call the ones, sevens, nines and fifteens complements the base-minus-one complements. How are these base-minus-one complements formed for numbers larger than the basic integers? To illustrate this look at the following examples:

$$\text{Number} \qquad 29_{10} \qquad 11101_2 \qquad 35_8 \qquad 1D_{16}$$

$$\text{Base-1 Complement} \quad 70_{10} \qquad 00010_2 \qquad 42_8 \qquad E2_{16}$$

In the top row are numbers in the decimal, binary, octal and hexadecimal systems respectively. In the second row, directly below each of these numbers is its respective base-minus-one complement. Examining these numbers in conjunction with the Complements Tables of Appendix I it can be seen that the base-minus-one complement is simply formed by writing down the base-minus-one complement of each individual integer in the number.

How can base-minus-one complements be used to perform the subtraction operation? Suppose the negative of a number is defined to be its base-minus-one complement, and attempt to perform a subtraction by using this complement. For example, take the case of thirty-two to the base ten minus twenty seven to the base ten. First of all, it can be seen that the base-minus-one complement of twenty-seven (base ten) is seventy-two (base ten). Now add thirty-two and the base-minus-one complement of twenty seven. One obtains the following:

$$
\begin{array}{r}
32_{10} \\
72_{10} \\
\hline
104_{10}.
\end{array}
$$

This certainly does not give the correct answer. However, if we define what is called an end-around-carry, the proper answer is found. This is illustrated below:

$$
\begin{array}{r}
32_{10} \\
72_{10} \\
\hline
04_{10} \\
1_{10} \\
\hline
05_{10}
\end{array}
$$

In this example we have been working with two digit numbers. It is seen, that the significance of the end-around-carry is to take any digit in excess of the original number of digits and add it to the right-most digit of the answer.

Why should such a scheme as adding the base-minus-one complement and utilizing the end-around-carry give the subtraction operation? To find out first remember that normally

$$Y_B = \sum a_n B^n - \sum b_n B^n = \sum (a_n - b_n) B^n. \tag{7}$$

Now define $\bar{b}$=base-minus-one complement of b.

Using this definition, the sum of a number with the base-minus-one complement of another number can be written as

$$Y'_B = \sum a_n B^n + \sum \bar{b}_n B^n = \sum (a_n + \bar{b}_n) B^n. \tag{8}$$

From the definition of the base-minus-one complement one can write
$$\bar{b}_n = B - 1 - b_n.$$

Make this substitution into Eq. 8 and perform the following manipulations:

$$Y'_B = \sum (a_n + B - 1 - b_n) B^n \tag{9}$$

$$= (a_N + B - 1 - b_N) B^N + (a_{N-1} + B - 1 - b_{N-1}) B^{N-1} + \ldots + (a_1 + B - 1 - b_1) B^1$$

$$+ (a_0 + B - 1 - b_0) B^0 = (a_N - b_N) B^N + B^{N+1} - B^N + (a_{N-1} - b_{N-1}) B^{N-1} + B^N - B^{N-1}$$

$$+ \ldots + (a_1 - b_1) B^1 + B^2 - B + (a_0 - b_0) B^0 + B - 1$$

$$= B^{N+1} + (a_N - b_N) B^N + (a_{N-1} - b_{N-1}) B^{N-1} + \ldots + (a_1 - b_1) B^1 + (a_0 - b_0 - 1) B^0 \tag{10}$$

Having performed the addition, the application of the end-a-round-carry says to subtract the <u>coefficient</u> of the highest term and add it to the lowest term. When we perform this operation on Eq. 10 we get the following:

$$Y''_B = (a_N - b_N) B^N + (a_{N-1} - b_{N-1}) B^N + \ldots + (a_1 - b_1) B^1 + (a_0 - b_0) B^0$$

$$= \sum (a_n - b_n) B^n$$

This result is identical to Eq. 7 demonstrating that adding the base-minus-one complement of the number to be subtracted and utilizing the end-around-carry is equivalent to a direct subtraction.

One final question remains to be answered. If the base-minus-one complement is defined to be the "negative" of the number complemented, then the sum of a number and its base-minus-one complement should equal zero. Look at the following example:

$$27_{10}$$
$$\underline{72_{10}}$$
$$99_{10}$$

This shows that the sum of a number and its base-minus-one complement does not equal zero. This result can also be easily shown by substituting $a_n=b_n$ into Eq. 9 giving the following example:

$$Y'_B = \sum (B-1)B^n \qquad (11)$$

This result does not prevent us from using base-minus-one complements to do subtraction. It does mean that one more convention has to be adopted. In base-minus-one arithmetic it is necessary to define both a plus zero and a minus zero. The zero as we normally know it is to be taken as the plus zero and the result of adding a number to its base-minus-one complement, as in Eq. 11, is to be taken as a minus zero. Suppose that one is working with numbers composed of four integers, regardless of base, then minus zero according to Eq. 11 would be:

1111 in binary,
7777 in octal,
9999 in decimal, and
FFFF in hexadecimal.

It is very important to specify the number of integers that one is working with. To emphasize this, let us again take the example of 27_{10}, but work with four integers, and add it to its base-minus-one complement. The base-minus-one complement of 0027_{10} is 9972_{10}, and adding these two numbers gives

$$0027_{10}$$
$$\underline{9972_{10}}$$
$$9999_{10}.$$

Although it may seem awkward at this point to work with 0027 rather than 27, we will find later that the registers in most computers are of a fixed length and handling numbers in this fashion will be quite natural.

In summary, the base-minus-one complements of numbers can be used to perform the subtraction operation if two conventions are defined: 1) the end-around-carry, and 2) both positive and negative zeros.

Let us now return to the tables of Appendix I, and examine the two's, eight's, ten's and sixteen's complements. Examination of the tables will show that the base complement is formed by first obtaining the base-minus-one complement and then adding one. To further illustrate this, look at the following examples of a number and the corresponding base-minus-one complement and base complement in the decimal, binary, octal and hexadecimal number systems respectively.

Number	29_{10}	11101_2	35_8	$1D_{16}$
Base-1 Complement	70_{10}	00010_2	42_8	$E2_{16}$
(Plus One)	$+1_{10}$	$+1_2$	$+1_8$	$+1_{16}$
Base Complement	71_{10}	00011_2	43_8	$E3_{16}$

The top row of numbers are those to be complemented. The second row of numbers gives the base-minus-one complements of those in the first row and finally the fourth row of numbers gives the base complement of the top row of numbers. It is to be emphasized that the base complement is formed by determining the base-minus-one complement of the whole number and adding one.

Pursuing the original course, can the base complement be defined to be the negative of a number for use in a subtraction operation? Look at a trial subtraction $(32_{10}-27_{10})$:

$$
\begin{array}{r}
32_{10} \\
73_{10} \\
\hline
105_{10}
\end{array}
$$

This gives the wrong answer, and it can also be seen that defining an end-around-carry will give the wrong answer. Noting that this example is composed of two-digit numbers, it can be seen that the right answer would be obtained if all digits in excess of two were ignored, that is, if the digit one is discarded.

It has been shown that the base complement of a number can be used for the subtraction operation if all digits in excess of the number of original digits are ignored. Development of a more general formalism should demonstrate this to be true. Let us write down the following expression:

$$Y_B' = \sum a_n B^n + \overline{\sum b_n B^n} \tag{12}$$

Where the bar over the second summation is to indicate the base complement. Using the definition of the base complement and its relationship to the base-minus-one complement we can write the second summation in the following way:

$$\overline{\sum b_n B^n} = 1 + \sum \overline{b}_n B^n$$

Making this substitution into Eq. 12 results in the following:

$$Y_B' = 1 + \sum a_n B^n + 1 + \sum \overline{b}_n B^n = 1 + \sum (a_n + B - 1 - b_n) B^n \tag{13}$$

Expanding and recollecting the terms we have the following:

$$Y_B' = B^{N+1} + (a_N - b_N)B^N + \ldots + (a_0 - b_0)B^0 = B^{N+1} + \sum (a_n - b_n)B^n \qquad (14)$$

Comparing Eq. 14 and Eq. 7 it can be seen that the subtraction operation can be performed by adding the base complement of the number to be subtracted and ignoring any digits in excess of the original number of digits.

We must again ask the question "Does a number added to its base complement give zero?". Look at the following example:

$$27_{10}$$
$$73_{10}$$
$$\overline{\quad 100_{10}}$$

When using the base complements, zero is obtained when a number is added to its complement, provided all digits in excess of the number of original digits are ignored. This can be demonstrated by substituting $a_n = b_n$ into Eq. 13 to get the following:

$$Y_B' = 1 + \sum (B-1)B^n = 1 + \sum (B^{n+1} - B^n) = 1 + B^{N+1} - 1 = B^{N+1}$$

We now have three methods of performing subtractions: what might be called the normal method, the method using base-minus-one complements and the method using base complements. Examples are given below using each of these three methods in the decimal, binary, octal and hexadecimal systems respectively.

Normal	Base-1 Complement	Base Complement
125_{10}	125_{10}	125_{10}
-49_{10}	950_{10}	951_{10}
$\overline{76_{10}}$	$\overline{075_{10}}$	$\cancel{1}076_{10}$
	$\quad\hookrightarrow 1_{10}$	
	$\overline{076_{10}}$	
1011_2	1011_2	1011_2
-0101_2	1010_2	1011_2
$\overline{110_2}$	$\overline{0101_2}$	$\cancel{1}0110_2$
	$\quad\hookrightarrow 1_2$	
	$\overline{110_2}$	

Normal	Base-1 Complement	Base Complement
452_8	452_8	452_8
-127_8	650_8	651_8
323_8	$\lceil 322_8$	$\not{1}323_8$
	$\hookrightarrow 1_8$	
	323_8	

$7BCD_{16}$	$7BCD_{16}$	$7BCD_{16}$
$-2A4F_{16}$	$D5B0_{16}$	$D5B1_{16}$
$517E_{16}$	$\lceil 517D_{16}$	$\not{1}517E_{16}$
	$\hookrightarrow 1_{16}$	
	$517E_{16}$	

The rules for the three methods of subtraction can be summarized as follows:

1. Normal subtraction requires the use of borrowing. To borrow go to the next column to the left, subtract one from that column and add the value of the base to the original column.

2. In the base-minus-one complement method of subtraction, any excess digits must be added to the first column; this is called the end-around-carry. It is also necessary to adopt a convention whereby plus and minus zero are two different numbers.

3. In the base complement method the only necessary convention is to ignore excess digits. For example, if two three-digit numbers are used in a subtraction, then all digits in excess of the three right-most digits in the answer are to be ignored.

Of course, the reason for entering into the subject of subtraction by complementary arithmetic is because most computer manufacturer's use complimentary arithmetic. Of the computers presently on the market, some use one's complement arithmetic and some use two's complement arithmetic. Electronically, it is simpler to use one's complement arithmetic, because it is easy to convert the contents of a register to its one's complement by simply enterchanging the zeros and one's of the binary number. Also, the end-around-carry, electronically speaking, is indicated simply by the overflow of a register and it is very easy on the overflow to add one to the right-most bit of the register. However, in the two's complement case one extra operation is involved. After the one's complement is taken, the overflow must be ignored and the value one must be added to the register.

From the programming viewpoint, it is perhaps easier to use two's complement arithmetic and the reasons for this will become apparent in later chapters. Suffice it to say for now, that most of the increment instructions in computers presently on the market are two's complement increment instructions. (An increment instruction is an instruction that adds one to the contents of a register). The difficulty arises because it is often found that even though a particular computer performs one's complement arithmetic, its increment instructions are two's complement. It should be noted that the present trend seems to be toward computers that perform two's complement arithmetic.

7.3 Multiplication and Division

There are two ways of doing multiplication and division in a computer. In the first, multiplication is simply done by repeated additions and division is done by repeated subtractions. For example, the answer to five times three can be found by adding three fives or by adding five threes. Likewise, the answer to twenty-nine divided by three can be found by repeatedly subtracting three from twenty-nine until a value less than three remains. At this point one has a quotient plus a remainder. Remember that subtraction by complements is actually done with an addition operation. Thus, addition, subtraction, multiplication and division can be done in a computer with only the addition operation.

The second method of doing multiplication and division in a computer is to build additional electronics that perform multiplication and divisions. In this case a multiplication or division is performed by giving the computer a specific command; whereas, in the first method one actually has to write a small program to do a multiplication or division. A survey of the on-line computers on the market today would show that some do not have circuitry for doing multiplication and division, but it would also be found that most of these do provide this circuitry as an option at additional cost. Two advantages are to be found in using multiply and divide circuitry. The first advantage is convenience; as mentioned above, it is only necessary to give a command to do a multiply or divide whereas in the alternative a program has to be written. The second advantage is speed. Electronic circuitry can do a multiply or divide in a much shorter time than the computer can execute a small program to perform the same operation.

Learning how to do multiplications and divisions in non-decimal number systems is quite analogous to learning how to do additions and subtractions. First of all, one must commit to memory the multiplication table. For this purpose the multiplication tables for the binary, octal, decimal and hexadecimal number systems have been included in Appendix I. Similar to the case of subtraction, the multiplication tables are used to learn how to divide. For example, to perform the division

nine divided by four, we can ask four times what plus a constant is equal to nine and we know that the constant is less
than four. Writing this algebraically we have: 4X+C=9. Of
course, the constant is the remainder.

Keeping with the idea that only practice will make for
proficiency in handling numbers in the non-decimal system, the
following examples of multiplication and division in the decimal, binary, octal and hexadecimal systems respectively are
given.

Examples of Multiplication

Decimal

```
  24              15              17
   5              12              25
 120              30              85
                  15_             34_
                 180             425
```

Binary

```
 11000           1111           10001
   101           1100           11001
 11000           0000           10001
 0000            0000           00000
11000_           1111           00000
1111000          1111_          10001
                10110100        10001___
                              110101001
```

Octal

```
  30              17              21
   5              14              31
 170              74              21
                  17_             63_
                 264             651
```

Hexadecimal

```
  18               F              11
   5               C              19
  78              B4              99
                                  11_
                                 1A9
```

Examples of Division

Decimal

```
       4                    5                  14
   8)35                 15)87              12)168
     32                   75                 12
      3                   12                 48
                                            48
                                             0
```

Binary

```
         100                     101                      1110
1000)100011            1111)1010111           1100)10101000
     1000                    1111                   1100
      011                   11011                  10010
                            1111                   1100
                            1100                    1100
                                                    1100
                                                       0
```

Octal

```
       4                    5                  16
  10)43                 17)127             14)250
    40                    113                 14
     3                     14                110
                                            110
                                              0
```

Hexadecimal

```
       4                    5                   E
   8)23                  F)57               C)A8
     20                    4B                 A8
      3                     C                  0
```

8.0   CONVERSION OF A NUMBER TO ANOTHER BASE

There are several different ways of approaching the conversion of a number from one base to another base. The way in which the conversion is done usually depends upon the context. For example, one converts a number from one base to another in a manual computation in a different way than writing a program to do the same conversion within a computer. Or there are relationships that exist between some bases that allow conversio to be made so easily that the conversion can be made by visual inspection. Since there are several different methods for converting from one base to another, one wants to use the most expedient under any given circumstance. Therefore, three different methods of converting a number from one base to another base are presented: a computational method, a tabular method and a visual method.

8.1 Computation   Methods

If a formalism can be developed which gives a set of rules for computing the representation of a number on one base from its representation on another base, then this is certainly the most straightforward way of converting a number from one base to another. Such a formalism exists. The following are the rules for converting a number from one base to another base.

1.   To convert an integer whole number from one base to another, divide the integer number by the value of the base to which the transfer is to be made. Set aside the remainder, and divide the resulting quotient by the value of the new base. Again, set aside the remainder. Repeat this process until a quotient of zero is obtained. At this point, write down the remainders in the reverse order, i.e. make the last remainder the left most integer of the converted number. This is the representation of the number on the new base.

2.   To convert a fraction from one base to another base multiply the fraction by the value of the new base and keep the integer portion of the result. Next remove the integer portion of the result and multiply the remaining fraction by the value of the new base and again keep the integer portion of the result. This operation is carried on repeatedly until the fractional portion of the result is zero or the desired accuracy is obtained.

3.   If a number has both an integer and fractional portion, split the number into its integer part and its fractional part, then apply rules one and two to the integer and fractional parts respectively. When this has been done sum the results.

4.   All computations must be carried out in the base in which the number was originally represented.

Because these rules are much easier to grasp by looking at examples, the following sample computations are given:

INTEGER WHOLE NUMBERS:

Convert	Divisions	Remainders

168_{10} to base 8

$$\begin{array}{r} 21 \\ 8)\overline{168} \end{array} \quad \begin{array}{r} 2 \\ 8)\overline{21} \end{array} \quad \begin{array}{r} 0 \\ 8)\overline{2} \end{array}$$

Remainders: 0, 5, 2

Answer: $168_{10}=250_8$

168_{10} to base 16

$$\begin{array}{r} 10 \\ 16)\overline{168} \end{array} \quad \begin{array}{r} 0 \\ 16)\overline{10} \end{array}$$

Remainders: 8, A

Answer: $168_{10}=A8_{16}$

$1A7_{16}$ to base 10

$$\begin{array}{r} 2A \\ A)\overline{1A7} \end{array} \quad \begin{array}{r} 4 \\ A)\overline{2A} \end{array} \quad \begin{array}{r} 0 \\ A)\overline{4} \end{array}$$

Remainders: 3, 2, 4

Answer: $1A7_{16}=423_{10}$

462_8 to base 10

$$\begin{array}{r} 36 \\ 12)\overline{462} \end{array} \quad \begin{array}{r} 3 \\ 12)\overline{36} \end{array} \quad \begin{array}{r} 0 \\ 12)\overline{3} \end{array}$$

Remainders: 6, 0, 3

Answer: $462_8=306_{10}$

49_{10} to base 2

$$\begin{array}{r} 24 \\ 2)\overline{49} \end{array} \quad \begin{array}{r} 12 \\ 2)\overline{24} \end{array} \quad \begin{array}{r} 6 \\ 2)\overline{12} \end{array} \quad \begin{array}{r} 3 \\ 2)\overline{6} \end{array} \quad \begin{array}{r} 1 \\ 2)\overline{3} \end{array} \quad \begin{array}{r} 0 \\ 2)\overline{1} \end{array}$$

Remainders: 1, 0, 0, 0, 1, 1

Answer: $49_{10}=110001_2$

101011_2 to base 10

$$\begin{array}{r} 100 \\ 1010)\overline{101011} \end{array} \quad \begin{array}{r} 0 \\ 1010)\overline{100} \end{array}$$

Remainders: 3, 4

Answer: $101011_2=43_{10}$

FRACTIONAL NUMBERS:

Convert	Multiplications	Integer Portion
0.752_{10} to base 8	$0.752 \times 8 = 6.016$	6
	$0.016 \times 8 = 0.128$	0
	$0.128 \times 8 = 1.024$	1

Answer: $0.752_{10} \cong 0.601_8$

0.752_{10} to base 16	$0.752 \times 16 = 12.032$	C
	$0.032 \times 16 = 0.512$	0
	$0.512 \times 16 = 8.192$	8

Answer: $0.752_{10} \cong 0.C08_{16}$

0.524_8 to base 10	$0.524 \times 12 = 6.510$	6
	$0.510 \times 12 = 6.320$	6
	$0.320 \times 12 = 4.040$	4

Answer: $0.524_8 \cong 0.664_{10}$

$0.D3A_{16}$ to base 10	$0.D3A \times A = 8.444$	8
	$0.444 \times A = 2.AA8$	2
	$0.AA8 \times A = 6.A90$	6

Answer: $0.D3A_{16} \cong 0.826_{10}$

0.53_{10} to base 2	$0.53 \times 2 = 1.06$	1
	$0.06 \times 2 = 0.12$	0
	$0.12 \times 2 = 0.24$	0
	$0.24 \times 2 = 0.48$	0
	$0.48 \times 2 = 0.96$	0
	$0.96 \times 2 = 1.92$	1

Answer: $0.53_{10} \cong 0.100001_2$

0.11010_2 to base 10	$0.11010 \times 1010 = 111.110100$	7
	$0.110100 \times 1010 = 1000.001000$	8
	$0.001000 \times 1010 = 1.010000$	1

Answer: $0.11010_2 \cong 0.781_{10}$

If one is uncomfortable about the answers that result from these conversions, it is always possible to convert back to the base ten. For example,

$$177.413_8 = 1 \times 64 + 7 \times 8 + 7 \times 8^0 + 4/8 + 1/64 + 3/512 = 127.521_{10}$$

$$1A7_{16} = 1 \times 16^2 + 10 \times 16 + 7 \times 16^0 = 423_{10}$$

Because the rules given in the first part of this section result in the integers in the new base sometimes coming in what might be called the normal order and sometimes in the reverse order, it is particularly important to see how these rules come about. First, let us develop rule one. Again, utilizing Eq. 2 an <u>integer</u> <u>number</u> can be represented in the following way:

$$I_A = \sum_{n=\infty}^{0} a_n B^n$$

Where A is the original base and the number is to be represented on the new base B. Rule one says to first divide by the value of the new base. This gives us:

$$\frac{I_A}{B_A} = \ldots a_4 B^3 + a_3 B^2 + a_2 B^1 + a_1 + \frac{a_0}{B} \qquad (15)$$

Examining Eq. 15 the last term on the right-hand side is a fraction and all other terms are integers. Therefore, a_0 is the remainder of the division. Rule one says to again divide the quotient of the first operation by the value of the new base. Carrying out this operation gives the following:

$$\frac{1}{B_A}\left(\frac{I_A}{B_A} - \frac{a_0}{B_A}\right) = \frac{1}{B}(\ldots + a_4 B^3 + a_3 B^2 + a_2 B + a_1)$$

$$= \ldots + a_4 B^2 + a_3 B + a_2 + \frac{a_1}{B} \qquad (16)$$

Examining Eq. 16 the last term on the right-hand side is again a fraction and all other terms are integers, and therefore, the remainder of this division is a_1. Repeating this procedure once more we get:

$$\frac{1}{B_A}\left(\frac{1}{B_A}\left(\frac{I_A}{B_A} - \frac{a_0}{B_A}\right) - \frac{a_1}{B}\right) = \frac{1}{B}(\ldots + a_4 B^2 + a_3 B + a_2)$$

$$= \ldots + a_4 B + a_3 + \frac{a_2}{B} \qquad (17)$$

From Eq. 17 the last term on the right-hand side is fractional while all others are integer and the remainder is a_2. From Eqs. 15, 16 and 17 it can be seen that repeated applications of the rule gives the coefficients for the integers in the new base. It is important to note that the coefficients do appear in what might be called a reverse order. That is, the first coefficient to appear is the one just to the left of the point, or in other words, the coefficient of the base to the zeroth power.

Turn now to rule two. Again using Eq. 2 a fractional number can be represented in the following way:

$$F_A = \sum_{n=-1}^{-\infty} a_n B^n$$

Rule two states that we should first multiply the fraction to be converted by the value of the new base. This would give us,

$$F_A x B_A = B(a_{-1} B^{-1} + a_{-2} B^{-2} + a_{-3} B^{-3} + a_{-4} B^{-4} + \ldots)$$

$$= a_{-1} + a_{-2} B^{-1} + a_{-3} B^{-2} + a_{-4} B^{-3} + \ldots \tag{18}$$

Now we are to set aside the integer portion of the result. Looking at Eq. 18 the first term on the right-hand side of the equation is integer while all other terms are fractions; therefore, the integer portion is the coefficient a_{-1}. Having removed the integer portion, multiply the remaining fraction by the new base. Performing these operations on Eq. 18 gives:

$$B_A (F_A x B_A - a_{-1}) = B(a_{-2} B^{-1} + a_{-3} B^{-2} + a_{-4} B^{-3} + \ldots)$$

$$= a_{-2} + a_{-3} B^{-1} + a_{-4} B^{-2} + \ldots \tag{19}$$

Again keep the integer portion, which is the coefficient a_{-2}. From Eqs. 18 and 19 it is obvious that repeated applications of these rules will successively bring forth the coefficients on the right-hand side of the equation and give the fraction on the new base. Also note that the fraction's coefficients appear in what would be a normal order, i.e. the first fraction to appear is the one nearest the point, the coefficient a_{-1}. It is also important to realize that the operations in general can be performed an infinite number of times when working with fractions. This is because a fraction on one base is not always representable on another base with a finite number of terms.

Finally, look at rule three. If one writes the expansion of a number on a base in its most general form, it can then be split between two expansions that represent the integer portion of the number and the fractional portion of the number as follows:

$$N_A = \sum_{n=\infty}^{-\infty} a_n B^n = \sum_{n=\infty}^{0} a_n B^n + \sum_{n=-1}^{-\infty} a_n B^n = I_A + F_A$$

Thus, a number can be broken into its integer portion and into its fractional portion and these portions treated individually with rules one and two.

Rule four stated that computations must be carried out in the original base. This is amply demonstrated by examining the left-hand sides of Eqs. 15 and 18. This is merely stating the fact that within a given computation, one cannot conveniently mix the bases of the numbers.

8.2 Tabular Methods

Although the methods of the last section permit the conversion of a number represented on any base to any other base regardless of its magnitude, this is sometimes a laborous process, particularly, if several numbers are to be converted. Another method is to have available conversion tables, in which one simply looks up the number represented on the proper base and finds the equivalent on another base. Appendix II has tables giving conversions between the octal, decimal and hexadecimal number systems. The binary number system is not included, for, as we shall see, this is easily converted to either octal or hexadecimal numbers which can then be converted in the tables.

The tables that have been described above might be called long-form tables because entries are on a one-for-one relationship. However, it is often convenient to have what might be called short-form tables available. Appendix III has such a set of short-form tables; again for the octal, decimal and hexadecimal number systems. Instructions on how to use these tables are also to be found in Appendix III. The main advantage of short-form tables lies in the fact that if one is willing to do a small amount of computation, the conversion tables can be condensed into a small space that can be conveniently kept at a computer console or other places where such conversions might be made.

8.3 Visual Methods

There are relationships that exist between some bases that allow conversions to be done by examination, in particular, the relationship whereby one base is equal to another base raised to some power. As an example of this, consider the base eight and the base two. Eight is, of course, two raised to the third power. How can a conversion be made from octal to binary or

from binary to octal by inspection? Look at the binary number
110101110000 and break it into groups of three bits starting
from the right-hand side and then progressively label the members of each group one, two, and four. This gives the following:

4	2	1	4	2	1	4	2	1	4	2	1
	1	1	0	1	0	1	1	1	0	0	0	0

Now take each group of three bits individually and multiply the
bit by the number above it and sum the multiples. The result
from the left to right is the integers, six, five, six, and
zero. By using one of the previous conversion methods it can
be proven that $110101110000_2 = 6560_8$. Thus, the method outlined will convert a binary number to its octal equivalent.
Because the coefficients are always zero or one, it is not
really necessary to multiply each bit by four, two or one but
simply to add those combinations of these three numbers that
appear above non-zero bits.

   A method has just been demonstrated that will let us, by
inspection, convert binary to octal and by reversing the procedure convert octal to binary. What about conversions between
binary and hexadecimal numbers? We first note that sixteen is
equal to a power of two, namely four. Taking a cue from the
binary-octal conversion, return to the same binary number and
break it into groups of four bits starting from the right-hand
side. Label these bits progressively one, two, four and eight,
which gives the following:

8	4	2	1	8	4	2	1	8	4	2	1
1	1	0	1	0	1	1	1	0	0	0	0

Again, multiply each bit in a grouping by the number above it
and sum these numbers within each four bit group. This time
write down the resulting integers in hexadecimal notation
which gives from left to right the integers D, 7 and zero. If
we again use our previous methods it can be shown that:

$$110101110000_2 = D70_{16} = 6560_8.$$

Thus, by breaking a binary number up into groups of four bits,
starting at the right-hand side, we can visually convert to
hexadecimal. By using the reverse procedure a hexadecimal
number can be converted to its binary equivalent.

To further clarify these procedures look at the following examples:

Binary	Octal

421 421 421 421

| 000 001 010 011 | 0123 |
| 100 101 110 111 | 4567 |

Binary	Hexadecimal

8421 8421 8421 8421

0000 0001 0010 0011	0123
0100 0101 0110 0111	4567
1000 1001 1010 1011	89AB
1100 1101 1110 1111	CDEF

Although all of the discussion to this point has dealt with integer numbers, visual method works equally well for fractions, the only difference being that the groupings of the bits must now start from the left-hand side. Below are severa examples in which fractions occur.

$$0.111\ 001\ 110_2 = 0.716_8$$
$$0.1010\ 0010\ 1100\ 0011_2 = 0.A2C3_{16}$$
$$10\ 110\ 001\ 100.001\ 100\ 101\ 111_2 = 2614.1457_8$$
$$10\ 1111\ 0011.0100\ 01_2 = 2F3.44_{16}$$

Following our normal procedure, turn now to a more formal development of the visual method of conversion. Suppose that a number on the base A is to be converted to the base B, where $B=A^m$. From these facts it is possible to write the following relationships:

$$N = \sum_n a_n A^n = \sum_p b_p B^p \tag{20}$$

Stated in a different way the problem is to find the integers b_p on the new base in terms of the integers a_n on the old base Let us start by expanding Eq. 20 and remembering that $B=A^m$, then

$$N = a_0 A^0 + a_1 A^1 + a_2 A^2 + a_3 A^3 + \ldots = b_0 A^0 + b_1 A^m + b_2 A^{2m} + b_3 A^{3m} + \ldots \tag{21}$$

Now collect the terms on the left-hand side of Eq. 21 in the following manner:

$$N=(a_0A^0+a_1A^1+\ldots+a_{m-1}A^{m-1})+(a_mA^m+a_{m+1}A^{m+1}+\ldots+a_{2m-1}A^{2m-1})+$$

$$(a_{2m}A^{2m}+a_{2m+1}A^{2m+1}+\ldots+a_{3m-1}A^{3m-1})+\ldots \tag{22}$$

Equation 22 can now be further modified by removing certain powers of A from the respective groupings,

$$N=(a_0A^0+a_1A^1+\ldots+a_{m-1}A^{m-1})A^0+(a_mA^0+a_{m+1}A^1+\ldots+a_{2m-1}A^{m-1})A^m+$$

$$(a_{2m}A^0+a_{2m+1}A^1+\ldots+a_{3m-1}A^{m-1})A^{2m}+\ldots \tag{23}$$

By comparing Eq. 23 with Eq. 21 we have the desired result,

$$b_0=a_0A^0+a_1A^1+\ldots+a_{m-1}A^{m-1}$$

$$b_1=a_mA^0+a_{m+1}A^1+\ldots+a_{2m-1}A^{m-1}$$

$$b_2=a_{2m}A^0+a_{2m+1}A^1+\ldots+a_{3m-1}A^{m-1} \tag{24}$$

....

From Eqs. 24 it can be seen that to convert a number from the base A to the base B, where $B=A^m$, that one should

1) start at the point and break the integers of the number on the base A into blocks of m integers,
2) multiply the integers within each block by A^0, A^1, ..., A^{m-1} respectively,
3) and sum these multiples within each block.

Now look at a specific example, the conversion of a number written in binary to the same number written in octal. Using Eqs. 24 we can immediately write

$$b_0=a_02^0+a_12^1+a_22^2=a_0+2a_1+4a_2$$

$$b_1=a_3+2a_4+4a_5 \tag{25}$$

....

Likewise for a binary to hexadecimal conversion where m=4,

$$b_0=a_0+2a_1+4a_2+8a_3$$

$$b_1 = a_4 + 2a_5 + 4a_6 + 8a_7 \tag{26}$$

. . . .

Comparing Eqs. 25 and 26 with the numerical examples of visual conversions given at the first of this discussion, it can be seen why the methods outlined there worked.

Three methods have been given now for converting a number represented on one base to its representation on another base. Because numbers within a computer are almost always in binary, the readout devices on the computer are normally in binary. Thus, the contents of a memory location or of a register within the computer are normally read out on a binary register where lights indicate the status of the various binary bits. For the same reason, numbers are almost always manually entered into the machine through a series of switches where the switches represent the status of the binary bits. An example of a binary light register is given in Fig. 1. The circles there represent the lights. Those lights that are lit are darkened, those light that are not lit are open circles. If a light representing a bit is lit, that bit is equal to 1; if not lit, that bit is equal to zero. By examination it can be seen that the contents of the register represented in Fig. 1 is the binary number 1110-10101001 and this is, by visual methods, the octal number 7251

Figure 2 shows a switch register which might be used to manually enter information into the computer. In this case, the convention choosen is that a switch up corresponds to a binary 1, and a switch down corresponds to a binary 0. It can be seen that the contents of the switch register are exactly the same as the contents of the light register in Fig. 1, i.e. octal 7251.

Figures 1 and 2 give a concrete example of why it is necessary to have a number system other than the binary number system to work with. The contents of these registers can be quite easily handled, in an uncumbersome way, in either octal or hexadecimal number systems. If one wanted to know the decimal value of the contents of these registers, the normal procedure would be to read them out visually in either octal or hexadecimal numbers and then convert to decimal by either the computational or tabular methods that have already been discussed.

9.0 SUMMARY

Because of the nature of electronic circuitry and mechanical devices, computers normally use the binary number system internally. But, the binary number system is cumbersome to

Fig. 1.   Example of a light panel indicating
          the contents of a binary register.
          The darkened circles indicate lights
          that are lit and correspond to a bi-
          nary one. The open circles are lights
          that are not lit and correspond to a
          binary zero.

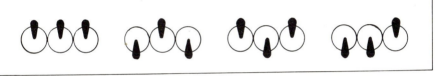

Fig. 2.   Example of a switch register that might
          be used to manually enter information
          into the computer. A switch in the up
          position corresponds to a binary one,
          and a switch in the down position cor-
          responds to a binary zero.

use, so outside the computer itself other number systems are
normally used. For convenience sake and the ability to do
visual conversions these other number systems are normally
chosen to be of bases that are equal to some power of two.

In order to lay a firm foundation for number systems, a
short history of number systems has been given. This was primarily to fix the concepts of base, numeral, number, and place
value notation. Utilizing these concepts a method was then
developed that permits a number to be represented on any base.
This development highlighted the significance of knowing the
concept of a numeral and the concept of a base. At this point,
particular attention was paid to the bases, two, eight and sixteen, because almost all modern-day computers use at least two
of these number systems.

Detailed examples have been given on how one proceeds to
do the arithmetic operations, add, subtract, multiply and divide in any number system. Since numbers entered or extracted
from a computer are almost always converted to another base,
several methods have been given for converting a number represented on one base to that same number represented on another
base.

    This chapter is of particular importance because a facili
with numbers in non-decimal systems is fundamental to almost
everything else that will be done in the remainder of the book
Although the formalisms developed in this chapter have paid
particular attention to the binary, octal and hexadecimal number systems, they are applicable to any number system.

PART II

ON-LINE COMPUTER FUNDAMENTALS

CHAPTER 3

COMPUTER ORGANIZATION I

1.0 THE HARDWARE-SOFTWARE TOTALITY

To really be competent in the use of on-line computers it
is necessary to become knowledgeable in both the area of computer hardware (equipment) and computer software (programming).
Unfortunately, from the standpoint of introducing a newcomer to
the subject, one is faced with a situation that is akin to the
chicken and the egg. It is not really satisfactory to introduce computer hardware first followed with subject matter on
programming. It is equally bad to start with programming; for
it is the hardware-software totality that really adds up to an
on-line computer system. Of course, this is just another way
of saying that the programming and the hardware are not two independent entities.

To illustrate the hardware-software totality refer to
Fig. 1 which displays the components of the totality. In passing
from one end of this diagram to the other the spectrum of the
computer totality is traversed. At the left-hand end one is
completely immersed in electronic hardware, while at the right-
hand end and working towards the center one is completely associated with computer programming. Many of the books that have
been written about computers approach the subject from either
one of the two ends, but rarely traverse the whole spectrum
as is attempted in this book. A book written from the engineering standpoint typically starts from the left of the diagram
and perhaps proceeds up to/or through the fourth block labeled
"Computer Organization". On the other hand, a book written
from the programming standpoint typically starts from the right
hand side and reaches to/or through the block labeled "Computer
Organization".

Now examine the blocks of Fig. 1 in more detail. On the
far left-hand side are those components that actually go to
make up a computer system. These would be typified by resistors,
capacitors, transistors, and integrated circuits. Later it will
be demonstrated that these can be developed into what are called

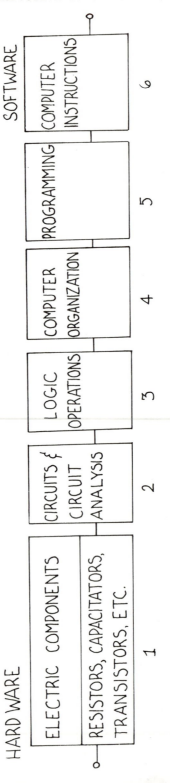

Fig. 1.   The spectrum of contributing elements that constitute the hardware-software totality of an on-line computer.

logic lines and modular cards which are used to construct computers.

Moving on to block 2 we come to "Circuits and Circuit Analysis". Once the electric compondents have been assembled to form circuits one can look at these individual circuits and analyze how they perform and operate.

In block 3 consideration is given to how these circuits are combined to perform what are called logic operations. Digital logic circuits are the basic functional units of a computer.

In block 4, under "Computer Organization", the major subunits of a computer are examined and consideration given to how they are interconnected and interrelated.

In block 5 the programs that are actually written for a computer are represented and which as a body represent the programming for that computer.

Finally, in block 6 are individual computer instructions which are joined to form computer programs.

Looking at the spectrum again it can be seen that there are several analogies between hardware and the software. The individual computer instructions might be thought of as being directly analogous to the electric components on the left-hand side of the spectrum of the totality. Just as the electric components are assembled into circuits which might be thought of as subunits of the computer, likewise, the computer instructions may be assembled together into blocks of instructions that form programming subunits. In the case of the hardware, these circuits or subunits are then combined to provide different logic operations. Similarly, the computer program subunits are combined to form the programming of the computer. Finally,' these hardware and software subunits combine to comprise the operating computer with the programming controlling the hardware subunits.

Although this book attempts to cover a large portion of the spectrum shown in Fig. 1, considerable thought has brought the author to the conclusion that it is not mandatory to consider blocks 1 and 2 of Fig. 1. This is primarily based on two facts. First, many books have been devoted to the subjects of blocks 1 and 2 and anything said here would be repetitious; and secondly, I do not personally feel that an understanding of circuits and circuit-components is an absolute necessity for coming to grips with the hardware-software totality. Another factor is that by taking this approach and only considering blocks 3 through 6 of Fig. 1, the present book can be almost completely independent from the type of circuitry that is used at this point in time. Such independence is particularly important in a field that is changing as rapidly as the one under discussion. A few years ago the circuits and circuit analysis portion of a book such as this would have addressed itself to the use of vacuum tubes. A few short years later in the same book blocks 1 and 2 would have addressed themselves to the use of transistors. Two or three years

ago, or perhaps less, such a book would have addressed itself
to integrated circuits. The same book of the early 1970's
would address itself to the large scale integration of circuits.
The important point is that no matter what components were
being used to construct the circuits, through the complete history of computers, components have always been combined to form
the same logical operations. Therefore, the logical operations
themselves, at least until the present time, have been essentially
independent of the circuit components used.
Returning now to the problem of how to begin a discussion
of the hardware-software totality, a compromise has been made.
This chapter will take an initial step in the direction of hardware by giving an introductory discussion of computer organization. However, after this the discussion will switch to programming (software) and then later return again to a more detailed discussion of computer organization. It is hoped that
this will be a more satisfactory approach than entering into
a discussion of either programming or hardware and completing
the discussion of that topic before returning to the companion
topic.
The discussion of this chapter will concern itself primarily with the basic computer. However, a short introduction is
given to peripheral devices that are attached to the basic computer. In Part III of the book a complete chapter is devoted
to several of the peripherals that may be attached to on-line
computers. These do not by any means represent the entirety of
peripherals that might be attached to a computer but hopefully
do represent some of the more common ones and some of those that
will become important in the future.

2.0 THE BASIC COMPUTER

What is the basic computer? Typically, a computer system
might be thought of as the basic computer plus its peripherals.
Peripherals will be explored further. For the moment, suffice
it to say that examples are printers, keyboards, and cathode-
ray tubes. Although there are a literal infinity of peripherals
that can be attached to a computer, the basic computer might be
thought of as the smallest stand-alone programmable unit.
The basic computer may be broken into the four major subunits illustrated in Fig. 2 within the confines of the dotted
line. Of these subunits the memory modules are the basic storage unit of a computer. It is here that both the computer programs and any data associated with these programs are stored.
Another subunit of the basic computer is the data channels.
These provide a high-speed path for data to flow in and out of
the memory modules.
A third subunit of the basic computer is the central processing unit; often abbreviated to CPU. Main frame is another
term that will often be heard. This expression is somewhat

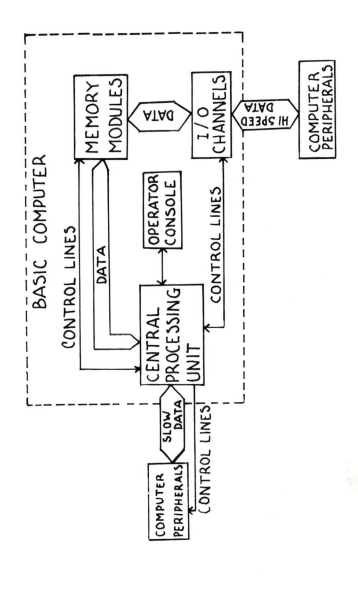

Fig. 2. A functional diagram of an on-line computer system. For the present purposes the basic computer is defined to be those portions within the dashed lines, and is made up of the memory modules, the central processing unit, the operator console, and the I/O channels.

synonymous with CPU but is more commonly used in connection
with computers at large central computing facilities. There
is some ambiguity of usage making it necessary to define what
will be meant by CPU here. The definition that will be taken
is a rather broad one. Essentially, the CPU will be defined
as everything in the basic computer but the data channels, the
operator console, and the memory modules. On many computers
this is equivalent to defining the CPU as the control section
plus the arithmetic section. However, in other computers of
recent design the definition of the CPU is not quite so clear-
cut. This will become evident in the chapter "Computer Organization II" in the discussion of synchronous and asynchronous
computers.

The final element in the basic computer is the operator's
console. The operator's console is simply an assortment of
lights and switches by which the user controls the computer.
It is here that the machine would typically be started and
stopped and various other manual control functions performed*.

Turn now to a more detailed discussion of each of these
elements of the basic computer.

2.1 Memory Modules

One way to look at a computer memory is to think of it as
a large array of storage elements each of which represents one
binary bit i.e., each element either contains a zero or a one.
Typically, these memory elements are small donut shaped objects
referred to as magnetic cores. They may be magnetized in two
different directions. Therefore the direction of the magnetization represents either a zero or a one.

These binary elements are in turn grouped into larger arrays of bits. For example, the total array of bits in a memory
might be subdivided into sixteen bit groups. These sixteen bit
groups would represent memory words (computer words). In some
computers the bits might also be grouped into elements which
are smaller than the computer's memory words. A typical example in many current machines consists of eight binary bits
or memory elements. These eight bit groups are typically referred to as bytes.

The words within the computer memory each have a label.
Suppose that a memory contains 4096 words. Then each word
(location) of the memory can be thought of as having a label
between 0 and 4095. These labels are usually referred to as

---

*Some on-line computers have consoles that may be placed at
some spot remote from the computer. In a few instances the
console may even be offered as an option on the assumption
that the user may want to provide his own external controls.

memory addresses. Thus, to mention a memory address specifically identifies a unique word within the computer's memory.

To illustrate a typical organization of a computer memory
assume a 4096 word memory where each word consists of 16 bits.
Then, it is easy to calculate that the memory is composed of
65,536 memory elements (bits) which have been divided into
4096 sixteen bit groupings (words). Each of these 16 bit words
is labeled with an address between 0 and 4095.

Normally on-line computers have memory modules which permit the total amount of memory to be expanded. For example, a
machine might be delivered with a 4096 word module. At some
later time another 4096 word module might be purchased to expand the core. Typically, these expansions can be added to at
least 32,768 words of memory.

Magnetic core memories are usually referred to as being
random access memories. This means that any memory word may be
addressed directly without recourse to looking at any other memory words. This is made possible by the address labels. In
other words, it is possible to put data into any memory location
or extract data from it by specifying its address. Hence, random accessing of the magnetic core memory.

It is important to note that the memory will accept only
binary numbers. Although there have been a few computers that
have taken slight variations on this statement, almost all the
current on-line computers use binary memories. The upshot is
that whether one is storing numbers or alphameric characters
they must be in the form of binary numbers. The alphabet, for
example, represents part of what are normally called alphamerics.
The letter A cannot be stored in a computer memory until it has
been converted to some binary number that is to represent the
letter A.

As indicated by Fig. 2, there are normally two paths that
binary numbers (data) may take in going to and from the computer
memory. One of the paths is through the CPU and the other is
via the data channels.

2.2 Data Channels

The data channels provide a direct means of passing binary
data back and forth between the computer's memory and a peripheral device attached to the channel. Typically, peripherals
that generate small amounts of data or have slow data transfer
rates are connected to the computer via the CPU, while peripherals with fast and/or large amounts of data are linked to
the computer via the data channels.

The data channels are specifically designed to pass large
blocks of data back and forth between the computer memory and
peripheral devices. This typically is understood to mean the
transfer of large blocks of data to or from consecutive locations in the computer's memory, which permits the blocks of

data to be transferred with as little intervention from the computer program as possible.

The expression data channels (plural) has been used here because some computers have parallel channels going into the memory. This means that a method has to be devised to let the memory either select one of the channels or to be able to sample each of the channels in some cyclic fashion. This sampling of channels in a cyclic fashion is often referred to as multiplexing.

Data channels on larger computer systems can become quite sophisticated. In fact, some large computer systems have small computers which act as data channels.

2.3 Central Processing Unit

As the term implies, the CPU is the heart of the basic computer. In a broad sense it is the control center of the computer. When a computer is to be used the desired computer program is typically loaded into the basic computer memory. When put into execution this program may then be thought of as directing the actions of the computer. Although the computer is under the direction of the computer program stored in the memory, it is the CPU which extracts the individual instructions or steps of the program from the memory one at a time, decodes them, and then instigates the necessary action. Thus, although the program may be thought of as directing or commanding the computer the CPU is the instrument by which these directions are implemented.

The CPU also typically contains the arithmetic section of the computer. Therefore, it is within the CPU that all the arithmetic is performed as directed by the steps in the computer program. The arithmetic section of the computer may vary from a very simple one-register device to rather sophisticated hardware that will perform floating point arithmetic (which in essence is doing arithmetic and keeping account of the decimal point location).

Another major function of the CPU relates to peripheral devices. The computer will typically control, to some degree, all peripheral devices attached to it. These controls are effected by signals which normally emanate from the CPU. Likewise, when the peripheral device wants to get the attention of the computer, it often does this by notifying the CPU.

2.4 Operator Console

In the typical on-line computer the operator's console will simply be a panel containing an array of switches and lights. The computer operator uses this control panel to monitor the actions of the computer and to determine the status

of the computer at various times. These monitoring functions
and status determinations are normally made via the lights provided on the console panel. The lights indicate information
about the state of the computer to the operator typically via
binary numbers. The operator also uses the console to control
the operation of the computer. Usually the switches are used
to perform these control actions.

In order to get a better feel for what might be done with
the operator console, consider some of the typical features
found on computer operator consoles. An almost universal function found on operator consoles is a switch or two switches
which start and stop the computer. To start a computer really
means to start the execution of a program in the computer's
memory. The stop function is used to stop the execution of the
program, and is often performed by the computer program itself.

The switches on the operator console can be used to designate any address in the computer's memory. Once the address has
been selected it is possible to read via the indicator lights
the contents of that memory location. The switches may be used
in a similar manner to select any memory address and to deposit
a binary number into that location. Sometimes the switches and
lights may be used to examine the status of the computer and
perhaps the status of certain peripherals.

3.0 COMPUTER PERIPHERALS

In a sense, peripherals are what on-line computers are all
about. On-line computers are not primarily computational devices; although the on-line computer may undertake quite long
and complex computations to perform its task, the ultimate end
of the task is not to arrive at a numerical result. On-line
computers are to be thought of as tools in the laboratory, in
industry, in universities and wherever else they might be found.
As might be expected then, on-line computers are built in a
manner which the manufacturers hope will make it very easy to
attach peripheral devices to them. Because of this design objective there are almost an infinity of peripheral devices that
may be attached to an on-line computer. Table I has been inserted to show a smattering of the large number of devices that
have been attached to on-line computers. These do not by any
means represent all such devices, but will perhaps give a feeling of both the breadth of peripheral devices and the areas of
application which have been exploited.

Certain computer peripherals are offered by computer manufacturers which may be classified as standard peripherals. A-
mong these are magnetic tape transports, magnetic disks and drums,
paper tape punches and readers, and printers. But a large number
of the devices that are attached to computers are not standard
products. In fact, any new application of an on-line computer
is likely to mean that it is to be attached to a non-standard
device.

Table I. A short list of devices that have been attached
          to on-line computers.

Magnetic tape units.
Mechanical plotters.
Digital volt meters.
Punched card readers.
Type setting machines.
Aircraft simulators.
Analog-to-digital converters.
Digital-to-analog converters.
Mercury relay pulsers.
RAND tablets.
Oscilloscope displays.
Television displays.
Magnetic drums and disks.
Nuclear accelerators.
Nuclear reactors.
Electric power plants.
Steel mills.
Telecommunication systems.
Printers.
Character readers.
Spacecraft.
Building heating/cooling systems.
Larger computers.
Biological studies.
Mass transit systems.
Ticket reservations for airlines and
    public events.
New York Stock Exchange transactions.
Library card files.
Aircraft guidance systems.

To attach any peripheral to a computer, it is necessary to
build a block of electronics (hardware) which electrically
couples the peripheral device to the on-line computer. This
block of electronics is normally referred to as the interface
for that computer peripheral. The word controller is often used
interchangeably with the word interface. It can be seen that
the term interface is appropriate since it does act as the interfacing element between the computer and the peripheral device.
The word controller is equally appropriate because the interface generally acts as the controlling element for the peripheral
device. The relationship between the basic computer, the peripheral interface, and the computer peripheral is shown schematically in Fig. 3.

As shown in Fig. 3 there are two primary functions that
may be performed by the computer interface. The first is what
is often referred to as the hand shaking function. The hand

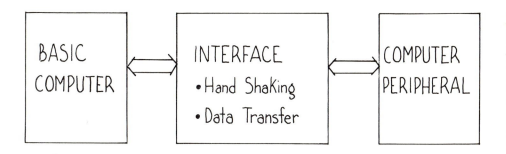

Fig. 3.   The relationship between the basic computer, the peripheral interface, and the computer peripheral.

shaking function can be illustrated by using a childhood experience.   Remember the days when as small children in class we would raise our hand with the prescribed number of fingers extended?   The teacher, upon seeing our hand and noting the number of fingers, would recognize our request.   Upon her nod of approval we would leave the room and perform the necessary action.   This sequence of events is in direct analogy to the hand shaking function of the peripheral interface.   The peripheral catches the computer's attention with the appropriate electronic signals, the computer recognizes the request and approves the action, and then the desired action takes place.

Another function performed by the interface is to act as a path between the computer peripheral and the basic computer for data transfers.   These transfers may be bidirectional, i.e., either in or out of the computer.

There will be no attempt here to describe individual computer peripherals.   A later chapter is completely devoted to several of the most common computer peripherals and those that the author feels will play a significant role in the near future.

CHAPTER 4

COMPUTER INSTRUCTIONS

1.0   DEFINING COMPUTER INSTRUCTIONS

It will be seen as this discussion develops that one cannot really consider computer instructions and the direction of
computers without becoming involved in a discussion of computer
programs and computer languages. For this reason a first attempt
will be made here to define computer instructions and give a
feeling for computer programs. This will then lead into the
next section which will develop the concept of a computer language.

The action of the computer is determined by arrays of binary bits that are held within its memory and registers. Some
of these binary arrays are generated by the computer itself
for housekeeping purposes, and others are inserted in the computers magnetic core memory registers by the user. These latter arrays are predominantly computer instructions and constitute
a computer program. These binary instruction arrays direct the
computer in every action that it takes. The most important point
to remember is that these instructions will always reside in the
memory in a binary form*. Thus, no matter what other form an
instruction may take, it will always, in the last analysis, be
converted to a binary number and placed in the computer's magnetic core memory.

It has just been implied that computer instructions may
actually take several different forms. The most basic of these
instructions are referred to as machine or assembly language
instructions. To properly discuss these various forms or levels
of instructions, it is necessary to introduce the concept of the
computer language.

---

*There are computers on the market which store instructions in
 a non-binary format. However, these are rarely used as on-
 line computers and will not be considered here.

65

2.0 THE CONCEPT OF A COMPUTER LANGUAGE

There is often a good deal of confusion about computer languages on the part of persons first learning how to utilize a computer. This stems, primarily, from a difficulty of understanding the hierarchy of the computer languages and computer instructions that can exist. As one might guess, a computer language, in the simplest of terms, is composed of computer instructions. Thus, a computer language might be said to be composed from one particular kind or form of computer instruction. The hierarchy of computer languages and instructions that have been developed relates directly back to the fact that the computer can only interpret instructions in a binary format. In fact, if one looks at the hierarchy of computer languages and instructions in a historical way, it becomes rather obvious why these developments have taken place.

When some of the first digital computers were built, they were programmed in what is often called binary or absolute instructions. To make the concept of programming in binary or absolute instructions more concrete, turn to a specific example of a program written in binary or absolute for the PDP-8 computer

```
111 010 000 000 ------/ Zerø the accumulatør register
001 001 000 000 ------/ Add cøntents øf memøry løcatiøn 100
                        tø the accumulatør register
001 001 000 001 ------/ Add cøntents øf memøry løcatiøn 101
                        tø the accumulatør register
011 001 000 010 ------/ Depøsit the cøntents øf the accumu-
                        lator in memøry løcatiøn 102
```

In this example each of the binary numbers represents a specific instruction to the PDP-8 computer. In the right-hand column immediately following the slashes is a description of what each instruction does. The program takes two numbers, one from memory location 100 and the other from 101, adds them together, and stores the result in memory location 102. It is immediately obvious that writing programs with binary numbers is a very unwieldy process with several disadvantages. For example, it is difficult to remember the different kinds of instructions when they are expressed as binary numbers. There is considerable labor in just writing the numbers themselves. The binary notation is not suggestive in any way. Although a program may have been written today and is perfectly understandable to the writer, it is a good bet that in a week or in a month the same array of binary numbers would be essentially meaningless without a complete review.

Many of the disadvantages associated with writing in binary code may be overcome if one can in some conceptual way attach labels or mnemonics to each of the computer instructions. The advantages to be obtained by using mnemonics is probably best illustrated by returning to our original example. The following is exactly the same program for the PDP-8 computer, however, this time it has been written using the mnemonics as developed by Digital Equipment Corporation for this computer.

CLA   /Zerø the accumulatør register
TAD   A   /Add cøntents øf memøry løcatiøn 100
             tø the accumulatør register
TAD   B   /Add cøntents øf memøry løcatiøn 101
             to the accumulator register
DCA   C   /Depøsit the cøntents øf the accumulatør
             in memøry løcatiøn 102

Typically, mnemonics are chosen to be as suggestive as possible in describing the computer operation that results from the issuance of the associated instruction. In the example above, CLA stands for clear the accumulator register. The command, TAD stands for a two's complement addition, and the instruction, DCA stands for deposit the contents of the accumulator and clear the accumulator. If the mnemonic names are suggestive enough, then writing a program becomes much easier in terms of routing ones thought processes and it is also much easier to refer back to the program at some later time and understand what the program was to accomplish. This little program written with the mnemonic notation is an example of an assembly language program and thus these instructions are normally referred to as machine or assembly language instructions.

Although a method has now been developed which makes the task of writing programs considerably easier, it must be kept in mind that although the instructions themselves are now in an easier format, they are not in a format that the computer can understand. As mentioned earlier, all instructions, when entered into the computer's memory, must be in a binary format. How are these assembly language instructions to be converted to a binary format? The solution to this problem, like the solution to many programming problems, is a program. The manufacturer of a computer delivers with the computer, a program called an assembler. The primary purpose of an assembler is to read programs that have been written with assembly language instructions and convert them to the appropriate binary numbers. This definition of an assembler will suffice until a complete discussion of assemblers is taken up in a later chapter.

It has now been shown that mnemonic or assembly language instructions form the basis for an assembly language. It is very important to note that the assembly language is completely computer dependent. That is, every manufacturer has a different set of assembly language instructions for his particular computer and hence, the programs written in the assembly language for his computer will not run on any other computer.

This now brings us to a position to consider what are commonly referred to as higher-level languages. Returning to the history of computer program development, we have already seen that assembly languages are machine dependent. It became obvious in the development of computer programming that it would be highly desirable to have computer languages which were independent of the computers themselves. That is, computer programs could be written in this higher level language and would be operable on many manufacturers' computers. Of course, what this really means is that the higher level languages are composed of a class of computer instructions which are computer independent. An instruction given in such a language would have the same resulting action on any computer in which the program is ran.

Let us again turn to the original example and see what the program would look like in a higher level language. In this case, it is most appropriate that we would choose FORTRAN as our higher level language. First, FORTRAN is one of the most common or standardized languages presently in use; secondly, it is scientifically oriented, i.e. it was designed primarily to do scientific computations. The following is our earlier example written in FORTRAN.

$$C = A + B$$

It can be seen that this represents an even greater simplification, and the language itself is even more suggestive, i.e., more English-like. However, the same problem exists that arose in the case of the assembly language. The computer will not understand FORTRAN instructions; they must again be converted to a binary format. Again, the solution is a program, and, in this case the program is called a compiler. Therefore, any manufacturer that supplies FORTRAN with his computer, will supply a FORTRAN compiler. This compiler will take the FORTRAN statements when they are read into the computer and convert them to assembly language instructions whence they can then be converted to binary instructions. Thus, we see the origin of higher level languages which are also sometimes called compiler languages. It should also be obvious at this point, that there can be many other compiler languages besides FORTRAN. In each case the language has usually been designed to serve some special purpose or class of problems. As has already been mentioned, FORTRAN was primarily designed for scientific uses. Another language called COBOL was primarily designed for business applications, and requires an entirely different compiler.

It should be apparent at this point, that although a compiler language per se may be computer independent, the compiler associated with that language is not. This is obvious because the compiler must take the compiler language instructions and reduce them to the binary instructions associated with that particular computer. As we have already seen, each manufacturer's computer has a different set of assembly language instructions.

Therefore, whenever a new computer is designed, a compiler for any higher level language has to be written specifically for that computer.

This development of a hierarchy of languages has, at the present time, even advanced to the state where there are now available programs for computers that are called compiler compilers. The object of these programs are to generate compilers for new computers in their own assembly language.

Higher level languages will not be discussed in detail in this book. This decision has been made primarily for two reasons. First, there are a large number of books dealing with the higher level languages such as FORTRAN. Secondly, these languages are designed to be, as we have seen, computer independent. This book primarily addresses itself to those matters directly associated with the computer itself. One exception has been made--the last chapter deals with a sub-set of the higher level languages called the conversational languages. There has been comparatively little written about these languages and they play a rather special role with computers that are used for on-line applications.

3.0   RELATIONSHIP OF PROGRAM INSTRUCTIONS AND THE COMPUTER

All of the following discussion will be confined to assembly language instructions. However, it has already been shown that all other classes or forms of instructions are eventually reduced to this form, and therefore, the present approach remains completely general.

3.1   The Concept of a Register

Although this will not be an attempt to actually give a description of a computer register at the circuit level, it is highly important to have the concept of a register fixed firmly in mind*. Almost any operation or action that takes place in a computer or in its peripheral equipment will be in some way or another associated with a register or registers.

A register can be described by both its attributes and its functions. One of the most important attributes of a register is its length, which is normally specified in detail. For example, the PDP-8 memory registers are 12 bits long, and thus most of the other registers in this computer are also 12 bits in length. The significance of the length should be immediately

---

*Registers are discussed in further detail in the chapter "Computer Organization II".

obvious from the previous discussions of Number Systems--the
number of bits in the register will directly determine the
largest binary number that may be stored in that register. In
a 12-bit register the largest integer number that may be store
is 4095_{10}. This has direct implication in terms of what are
called overflows. If a 12-bit register contains all binary
ones, that is 4095_{10}, adding one more to the register will result in an overflow. The register, at that time, will have as
its contents zero.

Computer registers may also be classified as to their
function. As an example, most computers have memory-buffer
registers. These registers function as the name implies. Tha
is, data being transferred to and from the magnetic core memory is buffered (passes through) these memory buffer registers
Another very important register is the accumulator register,
which plays a central role in taking information to and from
the computer and often in performing arithmetic functions. A
detailed description of the various kinds of registers and
their functions is given in the chapter "Computer Organization
II".

Registers may also be classified as to their construction
of which there are typically two kinds. One is normally referred to as a hardware register, which is a register that has
been built from electronic circuitry, typically flip-flop circuits*. The hardware register differs from the magnetic core
or memory register, in which each bit in the register is repre
sented by a magnetic core element. Typically, the constructio
of a hardware register is more expensive than the magnetic cor
register, while on the other hand, the hardware register is
normally faster than the magnetic core register.

Registers may also have different capabilities. For example, some registers may have the ability to be complemented.
That is, upon a given computer instruction the contents of the
register is replaced by its one's or possibly two's complement
Accumulator registers typically have more capabilities than
other registers in the computer.

We will normally consider registers to be of a binary for
By construction this is normally true, with each bit or portio
of the register being binary. However, for conceptual purpose
one can often think of a register as being octal, hexadecimal,
etc. For many purposes it is advantageous to have a pictoral
representation of a register such as Fig. 1. This particular
register contains the following number: 001010011100_2 or
1234_8. This now brings us to a point where the interaction of
computer instructions and computer registers can be considered

*Discussed in the chapter "Computer Organization II".

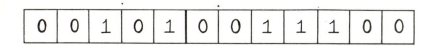

Fig. 1. Conceptual representation of a computer register.

3.2 Computer Instructions and Registers

Considerable emphasis has been given to the concept of a computer register in the preceding section because of the very intimate role that registers play with computer instructions. Almost all assembly language instructions relate directly to either hardware or memory registers. In many instances, a single assembly language instruction may involve both hardware and memory registers. Returning to our earlier example, there was an instruction TAD A. This instruction had the following specific action: take the contents of a memory register, which we have called "A" and add it to the contents of the accumulator register, which is a hardware register. Although only the memory register "A" and the accumulator register are explicitly involved, several other registers in the computer have been utilized executing this one instruction. For example, the contents of memory register "A" have actually been moved to the memory buffer register prior to entry into the accumulator register. Likewise, the memory address register has been involved and also the program counter register, which will be taken up later.

Perhaps this one example will impress on the reader the intimate relationship between computer registers and computer instructions. It is very important to realize that there is a direct one-to-one relationship between a machine language or assembly language instruction and the action taken by the computer, and that in general the action taken by the computer will be via registers. It is also important to note that this is in general true only of assembly language instructions. Referring back to the earlier FORTRAN program example, it should be clear that a computer instruction given in a higher level language will result in several actions being taken by the computer and that these actions are not necessarily unique. They would not be expected to be unique because of the differences that might arise in various manufacturer's compilers.

4.0 TYPES OF INSTRUCTIONS

As we have seen, there are several levels of computer instructions. The most basic of these is the machine or assembly language instructions, which may in turn be broken down into

several types or classes. The categorizing of assembly language instructions into classes is not entirely unique. The way
that they may be categorized can vary from manufacturer to manufacturer. However, examination shows that with the computers
of interest here, most manufacturers assembly language instructions can be broken into three types: memory reference, gener
and input/output (I/0). These three types of instructions are
discussed, and in each case a format is presented and discusse
As will be pointed out in individual cases, the details of the
format can vary from manufacturer to manufacturer.

4.1 Memory Reference Instruction

The labeling of this type of instruction may be taken som
what literally in defining its action. In general, a memory
reference instruction will either result in a number being deposited in the computer memory, withdrawn from the computer
memory, compared with the computer memory or determine a memory location. In most computers, the time to execute a memory
reference instruction is equal to the computer memory cycle
time. A memory cycle time is usually taken to be the time it
takes to read the contents of a particular memory location and
write back into that location the original contents. Hence,
the memory cycle time is composed of a read cycle and a memory
cycle both of which must be executed to carry out a memory reference instruction. Figure 2 portrays the memory reference instruction as it would typically exist in a memory or hardware
register. It can be seen that the bits of the register have
been broken into three separate blocks; the op code block, the
modification bits block, and the address bits block. Although
the memory reference instructions of most computers can be described in terms of these three blocks, the particular arrange
ment of the blocks within the register varys from manufacturer
to manufacturer.

4.1.1 Op Code

Op code is an abbreviation of the expression, operation
code. It defines the kind of memory reference instruction,
e.g. subtraction, addition, etc. The op code block occurs in
all three types of computer instructions. If, in a particular
computer, the op code block contains N bits, then the maximum
number of unique instructions that can be performed are 2^N.
However, this does not mean that the machine is limited to thi
number of instructions; only that there are 2^N unique instructions which may be subdivided into more instructions. This wi
become clear as other types of instructions are discussed.

Op Code	Modification Bits	Address Bits

Fig. 2.   A typical format for a memory reference instruction.

4.1.2   Address Bits

This block of bits completely or partially specifies the address in memory or some portion of the memory. It is important to make this distinction because this block often does not specify a specific (absolute) address within the computer's memory. However, this group of bits is always used in the determination of the memory address that is to be utilized. Specific examples are given with the PDP-8 computer which should clarify the role that this block of bits plays.

4.1.3   Modification Bits

In most computers the modification bits serve two functions: one, they can modify or change the significance of the address bits, and/or two, they can specify register action. The register actions include incrementing or decrementing index registers, register to register transfers and comparison between registers. Address modification includes specification of memory pages, direct and indirect addressing and specification of other registers that may contain a portion of the address. All of these concepts will be further discussed.

4.1.4   Memory Paging

Returning to Fig. 2 it can be seen that the number of bits which are assigned to the address block automatically determine the number of memory locations that may be directly addressed. If the address block contains ten bits, then it is possible to address directly zero through 1023 addresses. Because most computers that are used for on-line applications typically have word lengths in the neighborhood of 16 bits, the number of bits that may be assigned to the address block definitely present an addressing limitation. It is certainly desirable to address more than a few thousand memory locations. This problem is typically solved by using a technique called memory paging. In a memory paging scheme the address block specifies the address on the current page, where current page pertains to that portion of the memory in which the computer is presently

executing instructions. If the address block specifies only
the location on a current page, some means must be devised to
determine the remainder of the total address. There are several ways of doing this, one of which is to utilize some of
the modification bits. Another is to use an entirely different
register in the computer, such as an index register to contain
the remainder of the address.

It is important to realize that pages are not usually physical. If a computer program is executing instructions in its
memory sequentially, and a page boundary is encountered, execution of the program will not halt. The program will continue
to execute across the page boundary. The memory pages simply
determine what memory locations may be addressed by an instruction in some particular location of the computer's magnetic
memory. This can be further amplified by noting that some
machines do not use fixed pages. Fixed is used here in the
following sense: A fixed page machine would divide the computer's memory into pages of equal length. Suppose that the
page length is N memory words, then the memory locations zero
through N-1 will constitute page zero and the memory locations
N through 2N-1 will constitute page one and so forth. In this
scheme, instructions located on any page may address any other
location on that page and hence the reference to fixed pages.
Now turn to a non-fixed or floating page scheme. In this particular scheme it is arranged so that a page is always defined
in reference to the memory location that the current instruction is being executed from. Assume a computer with a page
length of 512 words and assume that the instructions in location M is being executed. In a typical floating page scheme,
an instruction in location M is able to address any other location from M to M + 255, and any location from M-256 to M.
Thus, in this particular scheme, the page is floating, i.e. can
be thought of as moving along with the program as sequential
instructions are executed. In most paging schemes the computer
can address both the page on which the current instruction is
located and page zero.

It should also be mentioned that paging schemes are used
for other purposes than to avoid word-length limitations. In
computer systems that have large word lengths, it is not necessary to go to a paging scheme to be able to address large
quantities of core memory; however, it is advantageous to go
to paging schemes in such computers for several other reasons.
Among these is memory protection. In other words, one can
assign certain blocks or pages of memory in which most users
may not operate. The pages in this case are somewhat physical,
in that the hardware can actually recognize the page boundaries
and prevent the use of given pages. A paging scheme is useful
in some machines also to provide easy means of memory alloca-
tion when more than one program can reside in the computer's
memory at any given time.

Another utilization of memory paging is coming into common practice which is connected with what is often referred to as virtual memory. In virtual memory schemes not only the computer's magnetic core memory is divided into pages, but auxiliary storage devices, such as magnetic disks and magnetic drums, are also divided into pages. These auxiliary storage devices are then integrated into the computer system in such a way that the computer user is unaware, when addressing a page, whether that page currently resides in the computer memory or on some other device. Such a system gives the user the illusion of having almost limitless storage space to work with.

4.1.5 PDP-8 Memory Reference Instructions

Considerable clarification of the discussion of memory reference instructions to this point may be had if one considers a specific computer. The PDP-8 has a magnetic memory with words that are 12 bits in length. All of its instructions are also 12 bits in length. Fig. 3 shows the bit arrangement for a PDP-8 memory reference instruction. The length of these

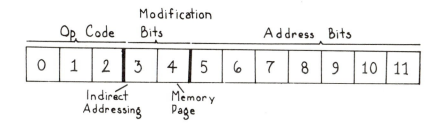

Fig. 3.   The organization of a PDP-8 memory reference instruction.

various bit blocks immediately specifies several things about this computer. Because the op code is assigned three bits, only eight unique operation codes are available. Of the eight op codes in the PDP-8, six are memory reference instructions*. These are as follows:

Op code 000 is the instruction AND. This performs the logical <u>and</u> between a specified memory location and the accumulator register.

---

*The PDP-8 instruction set is given in Appendix IV.

Op code 010 is the instruction ISZ. This instruction
increments a specified memory location by one and
then skips the following computer instruction if
the increment has caused the memory location to
overflow to zero.

Op code 011 is the instruction DCA. This instruction
deposits the contents of the accumulator register in
a specified memory location and then zero's (clears)
the accumulator.

Op code 100 is the instruction JMS. This instruction
is the jump to subroutine instruction. This type of
instruction allows the program to leave its current
sequence of action to execute other instructions and
then return to the original sequence. It will be
further amplified later.

Op code 101 is the instruction JMP. This instruction
is the jump instruction and allows the sequence of execution of instructions in a program to be altered.

Turning now to the address block shown in Fig. 3, it can
be seen that seven bits are available for addressing. Therefore, it is possible to only address 2^7 or 128_{10} memory words.
The PDP-8 uses a fixed page concept. Page zero is the memory
locations zero through 127, page one is the memory locations
128 through 255, and so forth. An instruction on any given
page can address any other location on that page or on page
zero.

Turn now to the modification block in the diagram of Fig.
3. Bit four specifies the memory page. If bit four is equal
to zero, the address in the address block is taken to be on
page zero. If bit four is equal to one, the address is taken
to be on the page where the current instruction is being executed.

To clarify this paging concept, return to our earlier example and expand on it considerably. Fig. 4 contains the expanded information. In the first column the memory location
where each instruction or piece of data is stored is shown in
octal. The second column indicates the page on which that particular memory word is located. The third column gives the
octal value of the address within the page (the page address).
The fourth and fifth columns give the binary and octal contents,
respectively, of the memory location in question. The three
right-most columns show the program as it would typically be
written with assembly language instructions. The first of these
last three columns is the tag column. This is simply a means
of giving a particular memory location an abstract name. The
second of these columns, the operations column, gives the instruction and its address. Finally, the last column is the

Memory Location (Octal)	Page (Octal)	Page Location (Octal)	Binary Contents	Octal Contents	Tag	Operation	Comment
20	0	20	000 000 000 001	0001	A,	1	
21	0	21	000 000 000 011	0003	B,	3	
400	2	0	111 010 000 000	7200		CLA	/CLEAR THE AC
401	2	1	001 000 010 000	1020		TAD A	/ADD A TØ THE AC
402	2	2	001 000 010 001	1021		TAD B	/ADD B TØ THE AC
403	2	3	011 011 101 000	3350		DCA C	/DEPØSIT AC IN C
404	2	4	111 100 000 010	7402		HLT	/HALT
550	2	150	000 000 000 000	0000	C,	0	

Fig. 4. The expansion of an earlier program example to illustrate the principles of addressing in a computer with paged memory.

comment column and is provided to further clarify the contents
of the previous two columns.

This program would start execution at memory location
400_8. The instruction contained there is CLA, which clears the
accumulator register and is therefore independent of any memory address. The next instruction is TAD A. This instruction
directs the computer to obtain the contents of the memory location labeled A and add them to the contents of the accumulator which is currently zero. For further clarification, let
us examine the binary representation of this instruction.
Fig. 5 shows the instruction TAD A. The first three bits
specify the instruction to be a TAD instruction. The first
bit of the modification block is zero, which indicates direct
addressing. (We will return to direct and indirect addressing
later). The second bit of the modification block is zero specifying the page to be page zero. Because page zero extends
from location zero to location 200_8, A does, indeed, fall on
page zero. Finally, the address given in the last seven bits
is equal to 20_8. Thus, when the computer executes this instruc
tion, it goes to location 20_8 on page zero, obtains its contents, which is one, and adds them to the accumulator which
contains a zero. Therefore, after TAD A has been executed, the
accumulator register contains one. The computer executes the
instruction TAD B next in exactly the same manner and at the
end of this instruction the content of the accumulator is four.
The next instruction to be executed is DCA C. Fig. 6 shows
this memory reference instruction broken down into its various
bit blocks. The op code block indicates this to be a DCA instruction. The first bit of the modification block indicates
direct addressing, and the second bit of the modification
block is a one indicating "this page". What is "this page" in
the present case? Note that the instruction currently being
executed is located in memory location 403_8. This memory location is on page two which extends from location 400_8 through
location 577_8. Further note that the address block has as its
contents 150_8. Remembering that the modification bits have
indicated the current page ("this page"), which has been determined to start at 400_8, we add 150_8 to 400_8 and obtain 550_8.
Thus, the location labeled C is actually memory location 550_8.*
When the computer executes DCA C the content of the accumulator
register, which is now 4, is deposited in location 550_8. Finally, the program executes the instruction in location 404_8
which is a halt. This instruction stops program execution.
Return for a moment to the instruction DCA C. Suppose that
this instruction had been located in memory register 603_8
rather than 403_8. Following the arguments given in reference

---

*This is often referred to as the absolute location or address
i.e. location C is the absolute location 550_8.

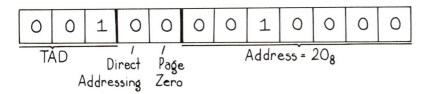

Fig. 5.   A breakdown of the instruction TAD A from the
          example of Fig. 4.

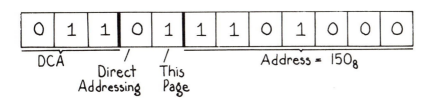

Fig. 6.   A breakdown of the instruction DCA C from the
          example of Fig. 4.

to Fig. 6, it can be seen that the number four would have been
deposited in location 750_8 instead of location 550_8.

4.1.6   Indirect Addressing

The example of the last section stills leaves open the
question of how one addresses a location on a page other than
the current page. This is accomplished by indirect addressing.
Referring again to Fig. 3 the first bit of the modification
block is labeled "Indirect Addressing". In the previous examples this bit has always been set to a zero, indicating direct addressing.

Now consider the case where this bit is equal to one and
indicates indirect addressing. Indirect addressing allows the
computer to use the entire contents of a specified memory location as an address. For example, if the instruction TAD I A
were given, the contents of location A can be used as an address*. That is, the computer goes to location A with contents,

*TAD I A is read, "TAD indirect A".

say, N. Then it takes the content of location N and adds it
to the accumulator register.

In some computer systems it is possible to do multi-leve
indirect addressing. In our example, if the computer goes to
location N and again finds a bit indicating indirect addressi
it takes the content of location N as the address and adds th
contents of this new location to the accumulator register and
so forth.

To further clarify the concept of indirect addressing,
turn again to an example using the PDP-8 computer. Before ex
amining Fig. 7 in detail, look at what the program shown ther
does in a general way. The program starts execution in memor
location 20_8. The first operation is to clear the accumulato
register. The second instruction takes the contents of the
memory location F and adds them to the accumulator. The thir
instruction deposits the contents of the accumulator, indirectly, into memory location G. Finally, the fourth instructi
halts the execution of the program. Now return to the second
instruction TAD F. The location labeled F is memory location
110_8 which is on the same page as the instruction that references it. Also, note that location 110_8 contains the value
12_8, therefore, when the second instruction has completed execution the value 12_8 will be in the accumulator register.
Now move on to the next instruction. The contents of the accumulator are to be deposited indirectly in the location labe
G. First, note that G is at location 111_8 which is on the sa
page as the DCA instruction. Remember that in the execution
of an indirect instruction the content of the address block i
that instruction is to be taken as a location at which the ad
dress will be found. Therefore, the content of the location
labeled G, 647_8, is utilized as an address. The execution of
the DCA instruction results in the value 12_8 being placed in
location 647_8. This illustrates how a memory location on a
page different from that of the instruction being executed ma
be addressed in a paged computer.

Although indirect addressing is a necessity to provide
the ability to address other pages, it also serves other useful functions. In the course of writing many programs, it
often becomes useful to manipulate the address at which certa
quantities are to be stored. Indirect addressing provides a
perfect means for doing this by permitting a number which is
to be used as an address to be located in a memory register
separate from that of the instruction. With the address so
placed in a memory register it is possible to manipulate it
with any of the memory reference instructions in the computer
repertoire. For example, it can be incremented, decremented
or replaced with some completely arbitrary value that results
from a computation.

As was pointed out above, many computers have the capability of multi-level indirect addressing. This capability
is not available on the PDP-8. However, the example of Fig.

Memory Location (Octal)	Memory Contents (Octal)	Assembly Language		
		Tag	Operation	Comment
20	7200		CLA	/CLEAR THE ACCUMULATØR
21	1310		TAD F	/ADD F TØ THE ACCUMULATØR
22	3711		DCA I G	/DEPØSIT INDIRECT G
23	7402		HLT	/HALT
110	12	F,	12	
111	647	G,	647	
647	12			

Fig. 7. An expanded program example to illustrate the principle of indirect addressing.

can serve to illustrate how multi-level indirect addressing is
accomplished. A bit in the modification block is assigned to
indirect addressing for each word contained in memory. In the
example of Fig. 7 there would have to be a bit which is to be
interpreted as an indirect addressing bit in memory location
111_8. If this were so, the computer, upon arriving at location 111_8, and detecting an indirect addressing bit to be set,
then proceeds to memory location 647_8. Suppose the indirect
bit in location 647_8 is not set, then the content of 647_8 is
used as an address.

4.2 Generic Instructions

This type of instruction has been called generic, but it
might just as easily have been called a class of unclassified
instructions. The instructions that fall in this class are of
a very general nature in that they direct the computer in many
diverse actions. A large majority of this type of instruction
are utilized in connection with computer hardware registers.

4.2.1 General Formats

A format used by many computer manufacturers for generic
instructions is shown in Fig. 8. The generic instruction is
often only broken into two blocks of bits; the op code block
and a second block of bits which specify the action that the
computer is to perform. Because the op code block normally
does not have more than five or six bits contained within it,
the action block can represent a large number of individual
actions.

Some manufacturers prefer to further break the action block
down into a class of action and an action to be performed within that class as shown in Fig. 9. Figure 9 indicates how the
action block might be broken into two individual blocks for the
skip class of instruction. From this example, the skip shown
is skip on zero accumulator. This means that if the accumulator
register contains zero when this instruction is executed, the
next instruction in the program is to be skipped. Typically,
there is a skip on a non-zero accumulator, or a positive accumulator, or etc. Many computers also have skip instructions
involved with other hardware registers in the computer and in
some instances skips associated with memory registers.

The literature describing computers often indicate large
numbers of instructions for that particular computer. Even
very small computers are sometimes quoted as having as high as
200 instructions. This is perhaps somewhat misleading in that
the large bulk of these instructions are often made up of the
generic type of instruction.

OP CODE	ACTION TO BE PERFORMED

Fig. 8.   Typical format for the generic type instruction.

OP CODE	SKIP	SKIP ON ZERO ACCUMULATOR

Fig. 9.   An example of how a generic type instruction might
be further subdivided.

4.2.2 PDP-8 Generic Instructions

The format for PDP-8 generic instructions is shown in
Fig.10. As is indicated the op code for a generic instruction
in the PDP-8 is seven. In this particular computer the action
block is not further subdivided, leaving nine bits from which
to construct various generic instructions.
Table I shows a few random examples of generic instructions for the PDP-8. A list of PDP-8 instructions may be found
in Appendix IV.

Table I.   A few examples of generic instructions
in the PDP-8 Computer.

Mnemonic	Octal Code	Action
CLA	7200	CLEAR (SET TO ZERO) THE ACCUMU-LATOR.
SZA	7510	SKIP THE NEXT INSTRUCTION IF THE ACCUMULATOR IS ZERO.
HLT	7402	HALT THE PROGRAM.
DVI	7407	DIVIDE.

4.3 Input/Output Instructions

This third and last type of instruction controls all the
interactions between the computer and its peripheral devices.
Because these instructions are directly related to the devices
that are attached to the computer, an itemized list of I/O instructions for a particular computer will differ in almost every

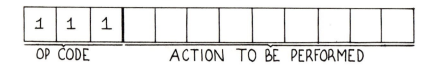

OP CODE   ACTION TO BE PERFORMED

Fig. 10.   Format of a PDP-8 generic type instruction.

case, even when the computer is of the same manufacturer. Actions initiated by I/O instructions may cause the transfer of
information from peripheral devices to the computer, transfers
of information from the computer to peripheral devices, transfe
of control signals from the computer to devices, and feedback
signals from the peripheral devices to the computer. I/O instructions often are the source of more difficulty to computer
novices than the other two types of instructions. This is prob
ably due to the fact that the proper usage of I/O instructions
requires a knowledge of what the computer and the peripheral
device both do when an instruction is issued. In addition,
with many devices, timing is of the utmost importance. I/O
instructions often must be given in the proper sequence, and
often must wait for some appropriate length of time before continuing on to the next instruction.

4.3.1 General Formats

The general format of I/O instructions used by most computer manufacturers is shown in Fig. 11. In this case as in
the case of the last two types of instructions, the ordering
of the various blocks within the register word is not unique
from manufacturer to manufacturer. However, most manufacturers
have their I/O instructions broken into the three major blocks
shown in Fig. 11.
As always, the first block shown is the op code block and
specifies this to be an I/O instruction. The second block of
bits is the device selection block. This grouping of bits eith
determines which device the computer is to select or which devi
is asking for the computer's attention. The action block determines which action is to be taken in connection with the device selected. Once a device selection has been made, there
are usually several legitimate actions that might be initiated.
Returning to the device block, this is an appropriate time
to comment on the number of devices that can be attached to a
computer. The first limitation results from the number of bits
that have been designated for the device selection block.

OP CODE	DEVICE SELECTION	ACTION

Fig. 11. A typical format for an I/O instruction.

However, this is not usually the practical limit of the number
of devices that may be attached to the computer. For example,
it is not uncommon to see literature on a computer stating
that 256 devices may be attached to that particular computer.
This normally means that the device selection block of the I/O
instruction for the computer contains eight bits. However, it
is a rather rare occasion when 256 devices could actually be
attached to a computer and effectively used as a practical
matter, the number of devices that may be linked to a computer
depends almost entirely on how fast the computer can serve the
needs of each device. Many devices are fast enough to occupy
the time of the whole computer. Other devices are rather slow
and a large number of such devices may be attached to one computer.

4.3.2 PDP-8 I/O Instructions

Fig. 12 shows the format for PDP-8 I/O instructions. A-
gain the op code block is three bits in length and the op code
for the I/O instructions is six. The device selection block
is made up of six bits, therefore permitting a theoretical
limit of 64 devices to be attached to this computer.

To expand on the use and operation of I/O instructions
turn to a specific example of a PDP-8 I/O instruction for the
teleprinter. The instruction to be examined is TLS. In essence,
the issuance of this particular instruction will cause a character to be taken from the accumulator of the PDP-8 and printed
on the teleprinter, which is the printing mechanism of a Teletype terminal*. The octal representation of this particular
instruction is 6046_8.

Figure 13 shows the TLS command as it would appear in one
of the computer registers. The op code block contains a 6 indicating that this is an I/O instruction. The device selection
block contains an 04 indicating that the teleprinter on the
PDP-8 is device four. Finally, the action block contains a
six which in this case results in one character being printed
from the accumulator register as explained above.

---

*Teletype is a registered trademark of the Teletype Corpora-
  tion.

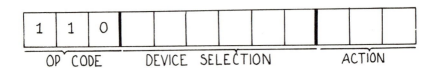

Fig. 12. Format of the I/O instructions for a PDP-8.

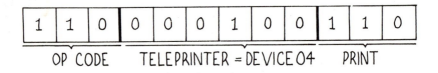

Fig. 13. Breakdown of the TLS instruction for a PDP-8 computer.

It should be pointed out that the device number which appear
in a device selection block does not necessarily have a one-to-
one correspondence with an actual device. This is due to the
fact that there may not be enough bits in the action block to
specify all the actions that are desired for one device. Therefore, one actual peripheral might have more than one device
number assigned to it in order that enough action codes may be
made available.

5.0 HOW THE COMPUTER INTERPRETS INSTRUCTIONS

Now that all the three types of computer instructions have
been discussed it is possible to consider how the computer actually goes about interpreting an instruction and executing the
action indicated by that instruction. It is not the intent to
describe this interaction in minute detail in terms of the
electronic circuitry. However, in the broader sense one is
describing what the electronic circuitry does.

The execution of an instruction by a computer normally
takes place in some integer multiple of memory cycle times. It
is not often apparent to the user, but each of these memory cycle
is further broken into sub-units of time. Thus, although a computer instruction may be executed in one memory cycle time, several sub-events have taken place during the execution of the
instruction. Typically, the first sub-unit of time will be used
to read the instruction from the computer's memory and place

it in an appropriate hardware register. Once in the hardware register, the instruction is examined by the computer to determine which operation code occurs in the op code block. This determines the type of instruction that the machine is to execute. Once the type of instruction has been determined, the computer can branch to several different courses of action based on the type of instruction which has been identified. For example, if the instruction is an I/0 instruction, then the computer might identify from the device block which device is involved and proceed to the action block to determine what appropriate action should be taken. If the instruction was a memory reference instruction, the computer would determine which type of memory reference instruction and obtain the necessary information concerning the memory address to complete the required action.

Of course, these descriptions of the action taken by the computer when interpreting an instruction are generic in nature. The specific details vary greatly from computer to computer. As an example, many computers have what are called double-word instructions, i.e. two memory words are used for such instructions. In terms of our example these instructions would require more memory cycle times and the involvement of more than one memory location. There are many, many other variations.

CHAPTER 5

PROGRAMMING

1.0 WHO SHOULD PROGRAM?

Asking who should program the computer may seem irrelevant. However, it is a very important question, and one that is often heatedly argued. The purpose here is not to decide this question in every case but attempt to provide some insight. It is felt that this is necessary because like so many other things in the aura of computers, it is not always argued objectively.

The types of people which might be associated with an on-line computer, and have reason to program it, might be broken into three categories: the professional programmer, the knowledgeable user, and the inexperienced user. In this instance professional programmer is taken to mean a person who has had formal training and spends most of his time programming computers. The knowledgeable user is one who spends a reasonable percentage of his time programming computers and is probably involved in the application of the computer. Finally, the inexperienced user is the person who rarely programs the computer but often uses it.

The central question of who should program the computer arises because the new user often has to determine which category he is to fall in, i.e. how much programming should he do. It is largely a matter of choice. The arguments on this subject range from one extreme to the other. Some would argue that professional programmers cannot be effective with on-line computers because of their lack of knowledge concerning those things for which the computer is being used. At the other pole, some would argue that professional people, who use the computer should not have to learn how to program. In my opinion, both arguments could be corrent in the different situations. In other words, because on-line computers are used in such widely differing environments, the decision as to who should program the computer may be entirely different because of the respective environments. Yet, the computer equipment used in two different cases might be identical. Therefore, it is my contention that if the environment is taken into consideration along with

some facts that may be stated on the subject, it is a fairly
straightforward decision to decide who should program the
computer.

Some of these facts are as follows: to use any tool well
one must know something about it. In the applications discussed in this book, computers certainly are in the category
of a tool. Anyone who uses a computer should know enough
about this particular tool to use it well. If an elementary
knowledge is not obtained, there is no basis on which to decide whether the job being performed by the computer is being
done well or even being done right.

A limited knowledge of application programming is not hard
to obtain. Application programming is taken to mean those programs that are written for the computer to actually perform
the on-line task to which it has been assigned. Examples of
application programs might be simple arithmetic operations,
those instructions which permit control of equipment by the
computer--e.g., the opening and closing of valves--, and the
turning on and off of experimental equipment.

It takes a genuine talent and considerable experience to
be able to write good systems programming. By systems programming it is meant those programs that are pertinent to the
operation of the computer itself. Examples of systems programming would be assemblers and monitors.

When a computer is utilized in a new application the person that has been associated with that application in the past
has an insight into the problem that nobody else can have. If
this person does some of the coding, particularly the application coding, a significant improvement can result. For example,
in the very act of coding, the arrival at a branch point in a
program can be more significant to such a person. He may have
only considered one branch prior to the actual coding, but the
other branch may be very significant in terms of faultless operation of the computerized operation, and may even provide insight into a problem.

Programs change constantly. This fact is significant in
several different ways. To assume that a few weeks or months
of programming will suffice with no further programming needs
once the computer is delivered, is usually a false assumption.
Although, there are certainly instances where such assumptions
can be reasonably made in on-line applications, in the more
typical case programming continues for some time, if not in-
definitely. The very nature of programming and the flexibility
of computers means that new ways of approaching the problem
and improving it constantly present themselves. Therefore, in
many programming applications, it is wise to assume that a con-
tinual programming effort will be going on. This, of course,
may be at a level of activity considerably below the initial
activity upon receiving and implementing the computerized system.

It has definitely been shown in my own experience, that professional programmers can program sophisticated on-line computer applications working in association with the people who use the equipment. In this case, the environment is particularly important. I personally feel that this approach to solving the programming problem can only succeed if the user of the computer and the professional programmer are in a close-working relationship. In fact, this usually means working in a close physical proximity. If the programmer is removed to some other part of the organization, different from that of the user, the situation can be extremely difficult.

To some extent, the itemization of the facts above is a mute question. In those applications where new college graduates normally are associated with the computer system, it must be kept in mind that more and more graduates know how to program. Admittedly, this is usually in a higher level language, like FORTRAN, but the transition is not that difficult to make, and the experience is certainly applicable to on-line programming.

If facts like those stated above are taken into account, a close analysis of the environment in which the computerized on-line system is to be installed will normally indicate who is to program the computer. As mentioned before the environmental factor is extremely important. In fact, in many cases the environmental factor alone will determine who should program the machine without any other options at all. If the on-line computer system is being installed in a very small organization that has no professional programmers and will be used by a relatively small group of people, there is no choice about who shall program the computer. However, if the computer is being installed in a large laboratory, such as those the Atomic Energy Commission or the National Aeronautics and Space Administration maintains, then all possibilities may be available and the question probably falls back on how manpower is to be utilized.

2.0 WHAT PROGRAMMING LANGUAGE?

What language the computer should be programmed in is almost as heatedly debated as the question of who should program. As with most things in the computer field, this is not a dormant situation. Therefore, the discussion of the subject is broken into the present situation and what the situation will possibly be in the future.

2.1 The Present Situation

At present, the choice of programming languages available for on-line computers falls primarily between the higher-level languages, particularly FORTRAN, and the assembly languages of the computers. Answering the question about what language to use is much like answering the question about who should program the computer. Again, some facts may be stated on the subject, and these taken into consideration with the environment in which the computer is to be used often answer the question in a direct manner. If the question of what programming language is raised prior to purchasing the equipment another factor enters. As we shall see, the choice of language has direct implications on the extent of the equipment to be purchased.

Some of the facts in this instance are as follows:

Higher-level languages such as FORTRAN are easier to use but not to learn. There can be no doubt that the majority of problems may be programmed more quickly in a higher level language than in assembly language. However, it is a myth that FORTRAN or many of the other higher-level languages are easier to learn than the typical assembly language.

Assembly languages are more efficient of computer time and magnetic core memory than higher level languages. Because compilers for higher-level languages cannot generate assembly language code as efficiently as a programmer, it naturally follows that the higher-level languages require more memory space, which in turn means that they will typically run slower than the equivalent assembly language programs.

It is easier to directly control special peripherals with assembly language coding. This is a particularly important fact because by the very nature of on-line computers they are not normally connected to what most computer manufacturers term standard peripheral equipment. Higher-level languages have commonly been written to handle only such devices as magnetic tape, punch card equipment, and plotters.

It must also be remembered that most of the standardized higher-level languages were written for what is termed a batch operation. Namely, a computing center to which jobs are submitted and ran in an assembly-line fashion. Therefore, one can expect that the programming for the peripherals in the higher-level languages is rather restricted in the way in which it may be used.

The programming of non-standard peripherals in FORTRAN is becoming easier. Some of the manufacturers are beginning to supply FORTRAN compilers which allow FORTRAN coding to be directly linked with assembly language coding. This permits some parts of the program to be coded in FORTRAN, while other parts may be programmed in assembly language. This is quite significant because coding for special peripherals may be written efficiently in assembly language, while other portions may be quickly written in a higher-level language.

What conclusions may be drawn in terms of the programming language to use? As mentioned earlier, the use of higher-level languages has direct implications on the equipment requirements.

Because FORTRAN and other higher-level compilers are not as
efficient at producing assembly language code as the programmer,
it naturally follows that more memory space will be required
if FORTRAN is to be used. The FORTRAN and other higher level
languages will also require additional memory space for coding
that must be resident in memory when higher-level languages
are being ran in the computer.

This discussion of memory space requirements is particularly important. A new user of on-line computers should not
be fooled into thinking that he is going to buy a very small
computer system with say 4096 words of memory and use FORTRAN.
This is not to say that the many computers with 4096 words of
memory that are advertized to have FORTRAN do not work. FORTRAN
is there and it does work. However, because of the memory requirements for FORTRAN, so little room is left in the memory
for actual applications programming that few problems may be
considered.

Of course, the other side of the coin is: that if assembly language programming is chosen, then one must be prepared
to spend more time writing and making the coding operational
in the normal case.

If the computer is of an intermediate size, then it is
often possible to use a mix of languages. A little common
sense indicates that if the computer system is capable of realistically handling a higher-level language, such as FORTRAN,
then each particular program that is to be written should be
looked at in the light of what language it can best be programmed in.

2.2   The Future Situation

It should be noted that the bulk of the arguments given
above against higher-level languages primarily stem from the
fact that none of the standardized higher-level languages
presently in existence were designed for on-line computer application. There is, of course, much merit in designing and
providing higher-level languages which are directly suited for
use in on-line applications. There has been considerable discussion of how such a language might be devised and implemented.
Such discussions normally refer to this type of programming
language as a control language.

A control language will suffer from the same problems as
the other higher-level languages in terms of memory space. In
other words, with the state of the programming art as it now
stands, a specifically designed control language will require
more space and often more execution time than a carefully written assembly language program. However, it would presumably
solve one of the major problems of the other higher-level languages in that it could directly control non-standard peripheral devices in an easy manner.

The need for such a control language is obvious. Why
hasn't one been provided? One of the primary problems is to
obtain agreement on what the control language should be. As
noted earlier, although a higher-level language should be independent of the computer on which it is executed, the compilers
themselves are strictly machine-dependent. Therefore, in order
to obtain a working control language, it is necessary to standardize on what the language should do and to have compilers
for that language widely distributed for all manufacturers'
computers. Although many languages have been written over the
years, probably less than half a dozen have become standardized.
Realistically speaking, it is not feasible to ask a computer
manufacturer to provide a compiler for a language which is not
standardized because of the extremely large amount of effort
that goes into writing the compiler.

It is easily concluded that a standardized control language is highly desirable. The day will arrive when such a
language is available, but many obstacles lie in its present
path and considerable time may be required.

3.0 SYSTEMS SOFTWARE

What is systems software? Here systems software is defined to be those programs that are directly connected with the
operation of the computer itself, as differentiated from those
programs which are used to apply the computer to a specific
task. Another somewhat more crude definition would be: most
of the software supplied by the computer manufacturer is systems
in nature, while most of the programming developed by the typical user is application in nature. In the following discussion
systems software typically provided by computer manufacturers
is enumerated.

3.1 Program Development Tools

Some of the most important systems software provided by
any computer manufacturer deals with the development of programs by the user. In writing a program and making it operational there is a development cycle that is almost always ad-
herred to. Once the program has been committed to a coding
sheet, the cycle goes in the following manner: 1) The program
is edited. If the program has just been written, editing will
be simply putting it in a form which can be read into the computer. In very small systems this might mean punching it in
paper tape. On larger systems it might mean transferring the
data from a keyboard to a magnetic disk or magnetic tape.
2) The second step in the cycle is to assemble the edited program. The program is read from the medium on which it has been
edited, e.g. paper tape, magnetic disk, etc. and read into the

assembler program to convert it to binary code. 3) Once the
program has been assembled, it is normally loaded in its binary
form into the computer and an execution attempted. In most
cases the program will not execute properly on the first trial.
Determining why the program does not execute properly is the
"debugging" portion of the cycle. After errors have been found
the cycle begins again when the programmer returns to the edit
stage to modify the program to take account of the errors. This
is again followed by an assembly and a debug stage to insure
that the program does indeed work. As might be guessed, it
doesn't always and the cycle is repeated.

The edit-assemble-debug cycle is a very important one and
is taken up extensively in the next chapter.

Computer manufacturers typically provide program development tools to be used for the edit-assemble-debug cycle. These
tools may be provided as three separate programs--an editor,
an assembler, and a debugging program--or they may be combined.
For example, the editing and assembling functions may be combined into one program.

3.2 Utility Programs

Utility is being used here to denote programs that permit
the user of the computer to carry out functions that are almost
universally and frequently needed on a computer. This definition should become self-evident as examples are enumerated below.

3.2.1 Mathematics Package

Almost all on-line computer manufacturers provide software which permits common mathematical operations to be performed. At first this may seem like a very unusual statement;
one of the primary purposes for building a computer is to have
the ability to do computation. However, if the discussions on
the concept of a register are recalled, it should be obvious
that the computer register, whether magnetic core or hardware
registers, are only capable of handling integer numbers. More
accurately stated: most registers can only handle positive
integer numbers, i.e. there is no provision made to keep account of sign or fractions. Therefore, a method must be provided which permits arithmetic to be performed with numbers
that have fractional and integer portions and which may carry
a positive or negative sign.

The normal way of providing these functions is to provide
a programming package, i.e. a mathematics package. It is true
that some computers are provided with hardware which permits
such arithmetic to be done directly in the computer without
writing programs. However, at present, this must be classified

as special hardware, since few computers used for on-line purposes have this as standard equipment. It is also true that
this type of equipment is becoming more common, and will probably become a common feature in the future with the advent of
integrated circuitry and large scale integration.

Mathematics packages almost universally use floating
point arithmetic. Floating point arithmetic is a way of performing computations which takes advantage of scientific notation. In other words, all numbers involved in the computation are broken into two portions: the mantissa and the exponent. For example, the number 238.3 may be written in scientific or floating point notation as 0.2383×10^3. Here the mantissa is 0.2383 and the exponent is 3. More abstractly, this
can be written as
$$\pm M \times 10^{\pm E}.$$
There are two primary reasons for using floating point notation in mathematical computations: 1) floating point notation permits very large and very small numbers to be written
in a compact manner, and 2) computations performed using this
notation allow the same number of significant figures to be
easily carried throughout a computation, regardless of the
magnitude of the number. Both characteristics lend themselves
very nicely to the restrictions of the computer because memory
word-lengths are normally fixed. Floating point notation allows
the maximum amount of information to be packed into one computer
word since the storing of insignificant zeros is not required.
Because the registers in most computers are inherently integer
in nature, it can be very difficult to keep track of the decimal point as computations proceed; floating point notation
greatly simplifies this problem.

Turn now to more specific details of floating-point computations in computers which do not have floating-point hardware, i.e. when the computations must be performed by programming. First, it must be noted that in the examples above,
decimal notation has been used. As always, any numbers residing in the computer must be in a binary format. In the example
above, both M and E were expressed in the base ten. With the
same general notation, the number in the computer appears as
follows:
$$\pm m \times 2^{\pm e}.$$
Where in the computer the exponent, e, is expressed as a power
of 2, and both it and the mantissa, m, are expressed on the
base 2. Having established the notation, what conventions are
chosen to actually store a number in floating point notation
in a computer's registers or its magnetic memory? Fig. 1 shows
a possibility. Here the left-most bit is reserved for the sign
bit of the mantissa. This is followed by a block of bits
which contain the mantissa, which in turn is followed by a single
bit for the sign of the exponent, and finally, by a block of bits
which are the exponent. Normally the convention is followed
that if a sign bit is zero, the sign is plus and if the sign

Fig. 1. A typical format for storing a floating point
         number in one memory word of a computer. An
         S indicates a sign bit.

bit is one the sign is negative. This follows rather naturally from using 1's or 2's complement arithmetic, because the
left-most bit will automatically be a one if the number is
negative.
     It is well to pause at this point and consider the number
of bits required in the mantissa and in the exponent to do
reasonable sized calculations. Suppose that it is desired to
carry six significant figures of accuracy in the mantissa and
that numbers up to plus or minus 10^{38} be accommodated. A
little arithmetic leads one to the following conclusions. In
order to handle six significant figures, twenty binary bits
will be erquired in the mantissa, and to handle magnitudes up
to 10^{38} will require that the exponent have seven bits. In
addition, two bits will be required to tally the sign of the
mantissa and of the exponent. It follows that a total of twenty-
nine bits will be required. The majority of on-line computers
presently in use have the order of sixteen bits per word. A
few machines have twenty-four bit word lengths and a small mi-
nority exceed this word length.
     One concludes that most of the on-line computers presently
being used cannot do floating-point computations of sufficient
accuracy by restricting the floating point format to be one
word in length.
     The PDP-8 floating point format is shown in Fig. 2. Be-
cause the PDP-8 has only a 12 bit word length, it is necessary
to go to a format in which three twelve bit memory words correspond to one floating point number. The first word is the
exponent and its sign, the second word is the sign of the mantissa and the high order bits of the mantissa, and the third
word is the low order bits of the mantissa. Thus, the mantissa
is twenty three bits in length and the exponent can go as high
as ±2047. This permits an accuracy of between six and seven
significant figures to be carried in the mantissa, and allows
numbers up to approximately $10^{\pm617}$ in magnitude. It is understood that the decimal point always stands to the left of the
mantissa.
     Because floating point numbers require three memory words
per number in the PDP-8, any mathematical operation requires
the manipulation of at least three memory locations. This

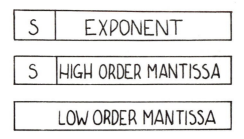

Fig. 2.   This is the format used with the PDP-8 computer for
storing floating point numbers.   Each block represents one twelve bit PDP-8 memory word.   If the top
word were the Nth memory word, then the middle and
bottom words would be the N+1 and N+2 words in memory.
An S indicates a sign bit.

makes it necessary to create a floating point accumulator.
What this means is that three specific magnetic-core memory
locations are set aside and called the floating point accumulator.   These three registers are thought of conceptually as
one thirty six bit register for doing thirty six bit floating
point computations.   All floating point computations are done
utilizing this fictitious accumulator.
     We have seen that in most on-line computers the register
lengths are not sufficient to allow floating point computations
within one word, and therefore, some multiple word format must
be used.   In the floating point program packages supplied with
many computers different orders of precision are made available.
These are often referred to as single and double precision computational packages.   This is somewhat misleading; for example,
double precision does not always refer to two words being used
per floating point number.   Also, double precision does not
always mean twice the precision of single precision, e.g., if
single precision arithmetic is performed with six significant
figures, it does not follow that double precision is twelve
significant figures.
     Many floating point packages provide input and output ca-
pability.   This is especially desirable because the conversion
from a floating point decimal number to a floating point binary
number and vice versa is a rather difficult task and is not for
the novice programmer.   This creates a need for a means of entering decimal numbers via a keyboard or other device, the programming to convert them to floating point binary, and the means
to go the reverse route out of the computer.   This can be expanded somewhat to allow the entry of the numbers to be floating
point or non-floating point with conversion to floating point
within the computer and the inverse on output.   It has become
standard on all computers that floating point numbers be input
and printed in the following format:

$$\pm 0.\text{XXXXXXE}\pm\text{XX}$$

This is just scientific notation with the understanding that the capital "E" is to be thought of as 10. Then we have from left to right sign, mantissa, E standing for 10, sign, and the exponent of 10.

It should be obvious that the execution times of the common mathematical operations--addition, subtraction, multiplication and division--become significantly longer when these operations are done in floating arithmetic as compared to integer arithmetic. In fact, it is not atypical for these common operations in floating point to take the order of a hundred-fold more time than in integer arithmetic.

Beside the normal operations of addition, subtraction, division and multiplication in floating point, most mathematical packages provide other computational functions. For example, one can normally obtain the logrithmns of numbers to powers of 10 and the powers of e. Also, the transcendental functions are normally available such as sine, cosine, arc tangent, etc.

In referring to mathematical software, the word package has been used rather loosely. The mathematical functions may be provided in different ways by different manufacturers. Everything may be supplied in one inseparable package. That is, a complete block of programming which supplies all the normal functions of addition, subtraction, multiplication and division along with logrithmns, etc. This particular approach has the disadvantage that the whole package has to be loaded into the computer even though one might want only to calculate logrithmns. Another approach is to provide the floating point package as a series of subroutines. This overcomes the just mentioned disadvantage by permitting one to load and call only those subroutines that are required.

3.2.2 Device Linking

Anyone with programming experience on small on-line computers knows one of the most frequent and frustrating requirements is getting from one device or medium to another. As an example one may have data on a paper tape and desire to transfer this data to a magnetic tape. This involves reading the data on the paper tape into the computer and having the computer write the same data on the magnetic tape. This is not as simple as it might appear. The format of the data on the paper tape is almost certainly different than that which would be written on the magnetic tape. For example, the paper tape might be in ASCII code and the information to be written on the magnetic tape in BCD code. Also, the control of the two devices by the computer is quite different.

Although performing this operation is rather straightforward, with no unknown quantities, it is quite frustrating to be in the middle of another job and find that this capability is not available. This means programs have to be written and checked out before the original job can be finished.

More and more manufacturers are providing systems software which allows such device linking to be accomplished or provide a framework of software which makes it very easy for the user to program the necessary functions. If the software is provided, all one needs is a user's manual. If a framework such as a monitor system is provided, it is necessary to write programs which are often referred to as device handlers or device drivers. Each device driver communicates with one specific device. The framework of the monitor system makes application programming essentially device independent in such cases.

The range of software that is provided by various manufacturers for device linking varies from nothing to some systems that are quite good. Whenever a machine is being purchased, particular attention should be paid to this portion of a systems software. Very large quantities of time can be consumed in writing device linking software because the user does not usually approach the problem in a general enough way, and ends up with a multitude of small programs to do very specific jobs.

3.2.3 Loaders

A loader is a program which allows the computer to read other programs in from peripheral devices. Suppose that a program is available on a paper tape and it is desired to load it into the computer for execution. Further, suppose that the paper tape is to be read in through a Teletype unit on the computer. A program must be provided which controls the Teletype paper tape reader, reads the information from the paper tape, and loads it into the appropriate locations in the computer memory. The program that performs this operation is known as the loader. Loaders can vary a great deal in their complexity and what they can do.

Because the loader is itself a program, one can realistically ask; how does the loader get into the computer memory? This problem is usually solved by actually having a series of loader programs. Suppose that a user is preparing to run a computer which has nothing in its magnetic core memory? The user certainly does not want to go through a long and laborious procedure to load his program and bring the system into operation. In the simpler computers the user must manually enter instructions into the computer memory via the console switches. Because sophisticated loader programs may require several hundreds of memory locations, it is certainly not desirable to have to manually enter the complete loader. This problem is

normally solved by first loading manually a boot-strap loader.
The boot-strap loader is a loader to input a more sophisticated
loader, hence, the name boot-strap. In fact, it is not atypical
to boot-strap to the final loader through two loaders, i.e. a
boot-strap, intermediate loader, and then finally the most
sophisticated loader.

Loaders may be implemented in different ways. In the example above the boot-strap loader was placed in the computer
core manually through the console switches. The intermediate
loader could then be read into the computer from a peripheral
device by this loader, and then a final loader read in from a
peripheral with the intermediate loader. Loaders may also be
put into the computer memory by means of special hardware built
into the computer. Then the boot-strap loader is placed in
memory by simply pushing a button on the computer console. This
saves a great deal of time over the manual method and is much
more accurate. In the manual method the loader program must
be entered through the switches in a binary manner leaving considerable possibility for error. Hardware oriented boot-straps
may also be automatic in execution. That is, when the button
on the computer console is pushed, the boot-strap loader is
automatically placed in the computer's memory, and execution
started. This execution eventually brings in the most sophisticated loader, and it then appears to the user as if the push
of the button has resulted in complete readiness of operation
of the computer.

The complexity of the final loader which is used to input
programs and other coding can vary a great deal. Even in the
simpler cases the loader normally checks the information being
read for parity and other types of errors.

It is very useful in computer programming if subprograms
can be written and assembled separately from any other coding
that might make use of these subprograms. The primary difficulty in implementing such a scheme is to find a way by which
information may be communicated from the subprogram to other
coding. In order that another portion of coding may make use
of a subprogram, it is often necessary to pass information to
the subprogram. If the two programs are not assembled at the
same time, the communication links are normally established by
the loader at the time the two programs are loaded. A loader
that can establish communication links between programs as it
loads them is called a linking loader.

Subprograms may be used with a great deal more facility
if they can be loaded into different locations of the computer
memory each time they are loaded. This, then, makes it possible
to use these subprograms, without new assemblies, with entirely
different main programs. Complete libraries of subprograms
may then be constructed, and the subprograms called from the
library as needed. Loaders which are capable of reading the
same program into different memory locations on successive
loads are called relocatable loaders.

Several observations may be made about these more sophisticated types of loaders. They can operate on complete program
or program packages or subprograms. A good example of a subprogram is a subroutine which is elaborated on in detail later
in this chapter. Loader programs must be strongly correlated
to the assembler for the computer. This is discussed in more
detail in the next chapter. Loaders greatly simplify the use
of the computer and the development of programs. As always in
the computer game the price that is paid for the increased
sophistication is in terms of more memory space and computer
overhead. It is a price that any computer user wants to pay.

3.3 Monitors

The discussion taken up here will be more in the nature
of an overview on the subject of monitors rather than a detailed accounting of monitors. In general, a monitor (also
called an executive program and an operating program) is provided to make the use and programming of the computer considerably easier. This is accomplished not only in making day-to
day usage of the computer at the console easier but presumably
in the writing of programs and the development of programs.
Two of the more important functions that are performed by most
monitor systems are communications and the monitoring of I/O
devices. By communications, I mean the ability of the user to
communicate with the computer. With most monitor systems this
is typically done via a keyboard. Once the computer has been
started the typical monitor system does not require the user t
use the console switches from that point on. The complete con
trol and running of the computer is done via the keyboard. Th
includes such functions as manipulation of files on bulk stora
devices, loading of programs, execution of programs, etc.
The second important function, the monitoring of I/O devices, includes such capabilities as controlling the periphera
devices, logical assignment of the devices, etc. These are th
capabilities in monitors that allow device linking as describe
earlier. Peripheral control must be considered in almost ever
program that is written. Therefore, in a well-written monitor
system, enough flexibility is built in to allow the manipulati
of the peripherals in about any way desired. If the monitor
system does not provide this broad flexibility, the user tends
to write many small programs, all of a specific nature. It
should also be emphasized that the writing of sophisticated
monitor programs is not in the domain of the novice programmer
The writing of good monitor systems requires very talented individuals.
Referring back to boot-strap loaders in connection with
computers ran under monitor systems; the boot-strap loads and
begins the execution of the monitor system itself. From this
point on the monitor controls the computer.

The phrase "real time monitor" is often encountered. This is a very nebulous phrase because the phrase "real time" is also nebulous. Normally, it would mean that a monitor system has been provided which can react to the peripheral devices on their own time scale. In other words, the monitor system executes fast enough to keep up with the fastest peripheral on the computer.

Several things may be mentioned about monitor systems for on-line computers. Monitor systems are not standard on all computers by any means. Some computers are supplied with no monitors at all. In the case of the very small computers, particularly those with only four thousand words of memory, general monitor systems are not usually feasible. If a monitor system has any general degree of sophistication, it requires so much of a four thousand word memory that little of significance can be done with what remains. This is not to say that small specialized monitor systems cannot be written for computers with small memories. Specialized is being used here in the sense that the monitor is directed at some particular application of the computer system.

4.0   GENERAL PROGRAMMING CONCEPTS

It would be far more satisfactory if this particular section could be entitled "The Theory of Programming". Unfortunately, there is no general theory of programming. This is one of the most formidable problems that faces the computer sciences of the present day.

Elaboration should help make the point; there are those that disagree. Take the situation of a programmer about to begin the writing of a program. Although he may have many years of experience in programming, there is nothing in his background that permits him to approach the present problem with a theory or guide on how to solve the problem. He has in his past experience developed a bag of tricks which he can apply to specific parts of the problem as it progresses. There are, however, no general guidelines which will lead him through the problem to its solution. As a result, large amounts of manpower are wasted in the programming of computers in both the repetition of problems that have been solved before and in the necessary hit-and-miss approach to solving new problems.

I would hope that the future would see a development of a body of theory that will do for programming what quantum mechanics has done for physics and chemistry. It does not at all seem inconceivable to me that the problem will be solved by a new mathematics. It is unfortunate, I think, that in the past the usual approach to finding a solution for a programming problem is to write a program. We have seen this in the historical development of going from absolute code to assemblers to compilers, and now to compiler compilers.

Until the day of the programming theory arrives we can only speak in broad terms of concepts and good practices in teaching programming. The only other alternative is to write a very detailed and encyclopedic description of how to do specific problems. This certainly is not within the realm of this an introductory book on the subject.

Throughout this discussion of programming concepts example programs are written in assembly language. Nevertheless, these same concepts apply equally well to programming in higher-level languages.

4.1   Program Modularity

4.1.1   General Modularity

The word modularity is greatly overworked. It is, therefore, appropriate to define what is meant in the present text by modularity. Program modularity will be defined as:

The writing of a program in such a way that sharply definable portions of it may be used intact elsewhere in the same program, or in an entirely different program.

In certain instances this might be extended to programs themselves, i.e. a complete package of programs in which each program is sharply defined. This criterion would be met for example if a package of programs is written to accomplish a specific task, and the programs may be used individually.

There are several advantages to be accrued from writing programs in a modular fashion. One is that the program may be easily modified later. This must not be overlooked; for it is a rare program, indeed, that ever actually reaches completion. This does not imply that the program is unusable; it does mean that a working version is finished and in operation, but the user or the programmer has seen a newer, or better, or faster way of writing the program. Once this new version is written and executed, similar ideas again occur and the process goes on in ad finitum. In fact, if such a process does not take place to some degree one can only conclude that the programmer is not taking advantage of the inherent flexibility provided by the computer.

A second advantage is that a program which has been written in a modular fashion may have the modules removed from it and substituted into another program. This can save large amount of time and duplication of effort. If a specific task has been performed as a sub-portion of one program, it only makes sense that the sub-portion should be written as a small module which may be lifted in its entirety and placed in another program to execute the same task. In programming an on-line computer system one will eventually build up a library of modules which

often permit the programmer to put together a program to do an
entirely new operation by simply assemblying modules that have
been written in the past.

Another important advantage of writing the program in modular fashion is that considerable memory space may be saved in
the computer. Suppose that an operation is being programmed
which will require some sub-task to be executed many times.
The obvious thing to do is to write a program module to do this
particular task and enter it into the computer's memory only
once, and provide a means of executing it from anywhere else
in the main program.

Perhaps a common experience will exemplify some of the
arguments that have been advanced for modularity. Assume a
small on-line computer system which has as one of its peripherals a Teletype unit. It is a certainty that the time will
come when somebody will want to enter numbers into the computer
from the Teletype keyboard. Specifically, this means that a
program must be written which will read decimal numbers from
the Teletype keyboard, convert them to binary, and store them
in the computer memory. Novice programmers often write the
reading of the Teletype keyboard and the decimal-binary conversion in such a way that it becomes scattered throughout the
first portions of the larger program. But the need to read
decimal numbers into the computer is a very general one and
will occur again and again. Hence, on the next occurence the
programmer discovers that although he has in effect solved the
problem once, the appropriate code is scattered through his
original program in such a way that it is not recoverable. If
the reading of the Teletype keyboard had been written as one
module, and the decimal-to-binary conversion as another module,
these modules could be used in the future innumerable times in
other programs bearing no relation to the first program.

It has been mentioned that if a task must be performed many
times within a program, considerable memory space may be saved
if the coding to perform that one task occurs only once. This
leads us to the subject of the next section.

4.1.2 Subroutines

In writing programs it is often found that there are tasks
which need to be performed repeatedly. Also, the modularity of
a program may be greatly increased if certain portions are made
independent from the remainder of the program. Obviously, both
these needs could be satisfied if there was a way to write a
subprogram and execute it at any time desired. In order to execute such a subprogram from anywhere in the main program a
method of linking the main program to the subprogram must be
found. That is, as the execution of the main program occurs,
it must be possible to interrupt the program flow and exit to
another portion of the program, the subprogram, and then return

to the original flow of the main program. Such subprograms
are called subroutines.

To better clarify the meaning of a subroutine and how it
may be used, turn to some examples. Suppose that eight numbers
are to be added together for a grand total, and that the value
of a parameter called A is to be added to each number. As a
result, there will be nine totals; the grand total and the total
of A added to each of the eight individual numbers. Fig. 3
shows how this program might be written for the PDP-8 computer.

Before examining the program of Fig. 3 in detail, there
are some conventions that should be mentioned. In all of the
program examples given in this chapter, the program is shown
as it would appear in the computer prior to execution. This
must be specified because some quantities change value as the
program is executed.

The convention will be to put slashes through the letter
0. In coding it is always necessary to have a means of distinguishing zeros and 0's. With mechanical printers these two
characters may be made easily distinguisable, but in hand-written code they are usually difficult to distinguish. It should
be mentioned that on many small computer systems teleprinters
are supplied which put slashes through the zeros rather than
the letter o. The slashing of the letter o has been chosen
here because this is the convention that is almost universally
used in the higher-level languages such as FORTRAN.

Throughout this chapter all programming examples will be
shown in specific memory locations. These programs do not have
to reside in the exact memory locations shown. Primarily, the
assignment of memory locations allows an easy means of identifying each computer instruction to facilitate discussion of the
program.

Turn now to the program of Fig. 3. Starting at memory location 307, memory space has been assigned for the nine original
numbers, and for each of the answers that will be obtained from
the program. The nine original numbers are the variable A,
which is in location 307, and the eight numbers in locations
311 through 320. Location 310 has been assigned the tag name
TØTAL, and is the location where the grand total of the eight
numbers will be stored. In locations 321 through 330 are variables called TØT1 through TØT8. These eight locations are
where the values of NUM1+A, NUM2+A, ..., NUM8+A respectively
will be stored.

The program begins execution at memory location 200. The
first instruction clears the accumulator. This is done to insure that the second instruction loads the value of NUM1 in the
accumulator. In location 202 is an instruction which adds the
value of TØTAL to the first number. Note that the value of
TØTAL prior to execution of the program is zero, as it must be,
or the grand total computed will be erroneous. TØTAL plus NUM1,
is stored back in TØTAL. The value now residing in location
310 is the value of NUM1. In location 204 NUM1 is again

Memory Location (Octal)	Tag	Operation	Comment
200		CLA	/CLEAR AC
201		TAD	NUM1	/GET 1ST NUMBER IN AC
202		TAD	TØTAL	/ADD TØ GRAND TØTAL
203		DCA	TØTAL	/SAVE NEW GRAND TØTAL
204		TAD	NUM1	/GET 1ST NUMBER AGAIN
205		TAD	A	/ADD A
206		DCA	TØT1	/SAVE NUM1+A
207		TAD	NUM2	/GET 2ND NUMBER IN AC
210		TAD	TØTAL	/ADD TØ GRAND TØTAL
211		DCA	TØTAL	/SAVE NEW GRAND TØTAL
212		TAD	NUM2	/GET 2ND NUMBER AGAIN
213		TAD	A	/ADD A
214		DCA	TØT2	/SAVE NUM2+A
.	.	.	
.			
.	.	.	
253		TAD	NUM8	/GET 8TH NUMBER IN AC
254		TAD	TØTAL	/ADD TØ GRAND TØTAL
255		DCA	TØTAL	/SAVE NEW GRAND TØTAL
256		TAD	NUM8	/GET 8TH NUMBER AGAIN
257		TAD	A	/ADD A
260		DCA	TØT8	/SAVE NUM8+A
261		HLT		/END ØF EXECUTIØN
.		.	
.		.	
307	A,	XXXX	/ADDRESS CØNTAINING A
310	TØTAL,	0	/ADDRESS CONTAINING GRAND TØTAL
311	NUM1,	XXXX	/1ST NUMBER
312	NUM2,	XXXX	/2ND NUMBER
.	.	.	
.	.	.	
320	NUM8,	XXXX	/8TH NUMBER
321	TØT1,	0	/WHERE NUM1+A WILL BE STØRED
322	TØT2,	0	/WHERE NUM2+A WILL BE STØRED
.	.	.	
.	.	.	
330	TØT8,	0	/WHERE NUM8+A WILL BE STØRED

Fig. 3. A program which has as its input the eight numbers, NUM1 through NUM8, and the constant parameter A. The purpose of the program is to find the grand total of the eight numbers, and the eight individual totals NUM1+A, NUM2+A, ..., NUM8+A.

brought to the accumulator. During the next instruction A is
added to this, and in location 206 the total, NUM1+A, is deposited in location 321. In 207 NUM2 is brought into the accumulator and then the value of TØTAL is added to this. Becaus
TØTAL previously equalled NUM1, the sum now in the accumulator
is NUM1+NUM2. This sum is then deposited back in TØTAL. Execution of the instruction in 212 again brings NUM2 into the
accumulator. The following instruction adds A to this, and the
following instruction, in location 214, will cause NUM2+A to
be stored in location 322.

     The series of operations that have just been described is
performed eight times, after which TØTAL equals NUM1+NUM2+...
+NUM8, and NUM1+A, NUM2+A, ...,NUM8+A is stored in locations
321 through 330 respectively. At this point, the program executes the instruction in location 261, which is a halt, and
the computer stops.

     The manner in which the program of Fig. 3 has been writter
is very wasteful of memory space and energy. Essentially, the
same coding has been repeated eight times; the coding in the
locations 201 through 206 is very nearly the same as the coding
in 207 through 214 and so forth. A subroutine is needed which
performs the basic operations of this problem; the adding of
the numbers to form the grand total, and the adding of the valu
A to each individual number.

     In the program of Fig. 4 the previous program has been moc
ified by incorporating a subroutine. The memory spaces 236
through 247, and the memory spaces 270 through 277 have again
been reserved for the numbers that will be computed and the
parameters that are used in the programming. How does this
program obtain the desired results? As before, the first instruction clears the accumulator, and the next instruction brir
NUM1 into the accumulator. In location 202 is a jump to subroutine instructions, i.e. the JMS ADD. Look now at the series
of instructions from 250 through 257, which form the subroutine
called ADD. In the instruction of 251 the contents of the accumulator are stored in a location called TEMP. Remember that
in location 201 an instruction brought the value of NUM1 into
the accumulator. Therefore, the value of NUM1 has just been
deposited in location TEMP. The next instruction to be execute
is that of 252, which brings back into the accumulator the valu
of TEMP. To this is added TØTAL which is zero at the beginning
of the program. Next, the instruction in location 254 deposits
the current grand total back in the location 237. TEMP is aga
brought into the accumulator and to this is added the value A.
At this point, the program returns to the location 203 where
the value of NUM1 plus A is deposited in location 270. The instruction of 204 brings NUM2 into the accumulator, and the nex
instruction again jumps to the subroutine ADD. ADD adds NUM1
to the grand total, adds A to NUM1, and returns to location 20
where NUM2+A is deposited in location 271. This procedure wil
be repeated eight times until the program encounters the instr
tion of 231 which halts the computer.

Memory
Location

(Octal)	Tag	Operation		Comment
200		CLA		/CLEAR AC
201		TAD	NUM1	/GET 1ST NUMBER
202		JMS	ADD	/JUMP TØ SUBRØUTINE ADD
203		DCA	TØT1	/SAVE NUM1+A
204		TAD	NUM2	/GET 2ND NUMBER
205		JMS	ADD	/JUMP TØ SUBRØUTINE ADD
206		DCA	TØT1	/SAVE NUM2+A
.		.	.	
.		.	.	
226		TAD	NUM8	/GET 8TH NUMBER
227		JMS	ADD	/JUMP TØ SUBRØUTINE ADD
230		DCA	TØT8	/SAVE NUM8+A
231		HLT		/END ØF EXECUTIØN
.		.	.	
.		.	.	
236	A,	XXXX		/ADDRESS CØNTAINING A
237	TØTAL,	0		/ADDRESS CONTAINING GRAND TØTAL
240	NUM1,	XXXX		/1ST NUMBER
241	NUM2,	XXXX		/2ND NUMBER
.	.	.		
.	.	.		
247	NUM8,	XXXX		/8TH NUMBER
250	ADD,	0		/ENTRY/EXIT ADDRESS
251		DCA	TEMP	/TEMPØRARILY SAVE NUMBER
252		TAD	TEMP	/GET NUMBER IN AC
253		TAD	TØTAL	/ADD TØ GRAND TØTAL
254		DCA	TØTAL	/SAVE NEW GRAND TØTAL
255		TAD	TEMP	/GET NUMBER AGAIN
256		TAD	A	/ADD A
257		JMP I	ADD	/JUMP INDIRECT TØ ADD
260	TEMP,	0		/TEMPØRARY STØRAGE ADDRESS
.	.	.		
.	.	.		
270	TØT1,	0		/WHERE NUM1+A WILL BE STØRED
271	TØT2,	0		/WHERE NUM2+A WILL BE STØRED
.	.	.		
.	.	.		
277	TØT8,	0		/WHERE NUM8+A WILL BE STØRED

Fig. 4.   Another program to calculate the grand total NUM1
+NUM2+...+NUM8, and the eight individual totals
NUM1+A, NUM2+A,..., NUM8+A. In this example the
computations have been accomplished with a considerably shorter computer code by utilizing a subroutine.

Several things are to be noted in comparing the programs
of Fig. 4 and Fig. 3. First, both programs accomplish exactly
the same objective. Next, in the program of Fig. 4 the instru-
tions to perform the two basic additions of this example are
written only once in the form of the subroutine ADD. This has
saved considerable memory space. In the program of Fig. 3,
sixty eight decimal locations were required to contain the program and all the related numbers. In the program of Fig. 4
fifty three decimal locations were required to do exactly the
same job. Thus, fifteen decimal locations have been eliminate
for a savings of approximately twenty-two per cent. Most important, the means has been provided in the main program, i.e
that portion of coding from 200 through 231, to repeatedly
leave the mainstream of the program, execute the subroutine
ADD, and return to the appropriate place in the main subrouti

Turn now to a detailed examination of the mechanics of ho
one may leave the flow of a main program, execute a subroutine
and return to the main program. To accomplish this feat, thre
types of operations must be possible. These are:

1. The ability to jump to the location of the subroutine

2. The ability to transfer quantities or arguments to
    the subroutine from the main program, and to also
    transfer arguments from the subroutine to the main
    program.

3. The ability to return to the appropriate place in
    the main program after exiting from the subroutine.

It is well to itemize these capabilities before talking
about the specific mechanics of any given computer, because
the entry, the exit, and the transferral of arguments to and
from subroutines differ from computer to computer. However,
in every case the three operations must be available even
though they are achieved in different ways. It is important
to fix clearly in mind the three required operations to be
able to understand the use of subroutines.

To get a detailed look at how the three operations are
accomplished in a particular computer, return to the program
of Fig. 4. For the purpose of illustration, assume that the
program has just executed the instruction of 202. The execution of this instruction provides the mechanism for the first
operation: the ability to jump to the first location of the
subroutine ADD.

There are actually several ways of accomplishing the
second operation. In the program of Fig. 4 the transferral of
arguments involves the transferral of the appropriate number
to the subroutine and the transferral of the original number
plus the value of A from the subroutine back to the main program. In this particular example argument transferral has

been accomplished via the use of the accumulator register.
Note that prior to executing the instruction in location 202,
the value of NUM1 had been placed in the accumulator. Because
the execution of a JMS instruction does not change the accumulator, the value of NUM1 still resides in the accumulator when
the program arrives at location 251. Thus, the argument NUM1
has been transferred from the main program to the subroutine.
Likewise, after the computer executes the instruction of 256,
the value of an argument is residing in the accumulator. The
jump instruction in location 257 does not alter the contents
of the accumulator. Therefore, when the program arrives back
at location 206 the total of a number plus A is still in the
accumulator and may be deposited wherever desired. The program
has accomplished transferral of an argument, namely the number
plus A, from the subroutine back to the main program.

As already mentioned, there are several ways of transferring arguments back and forth from subroutines. In the example just discussed, this was done by using the accumulator
register. If only one argument is to be transferred, the accumulator register or some other register in the computer, such
as an index register, are probably the best means of transferring one argument. A detailed example of another method of
transferring arguments is taken up later.

How does the PDP-8 computer satisfy the third requirement
for subroutines: the ability to return to the appropriate
place in the main program after executing the subroutine. Before entering into this discussion, it is necessary to discuss
one register in the central processing unit of the PDP-8 computer. This register is called the program counter.

The primary purpose of the program counter is to keep
track of the next instruction that is to be executed in a program. The instructions in a program are largely executed in
sequential order. However, in some instances there is a departure from this sequential program flow. We are now considering such an instance in the form of a subroutine.

Return to the example of Fig. 4. When the computer executes the instruction in location 200 the program counter contains the number 201. Likewise, when the computer executes
the instruction in location 201 the program counter contains
202. Similarly when the computer begins execution of the instruction in location 202, the program counter will contain
203. However, when the JMS instruction in location 202 is
executed, the computer proceeds to location 250; the first instruction of the subroutine ADD. When the program arrives at
location 250 the program counter contains 203. The JMS instruction is designed so that the content of the program counter
is deposited in the first location of the subroutine--location
250 now contains 203. After the program counter is deposited
in location 250, it is modified, as part of the JMS instruction,
to contain 251; therefore, the first instruction executed after
the JMS instruction of location 202 is the instruction of

location 251. When the instruction of 251 is executed the
program counter contains 252. Hence, the instructions of the
subroutine are executed sequentially until the program arrives
at the location 257. The instruction of 257 says jump indirec
to ADD, which is location 250. Remembering our earlier discussions, the JMP indirect means that the program is to actua
jump to the location that is contained in 250. The JMS instru
tion caused the contents of the program counter, 203, to be de
posited in location 250. Therefore, the jump instruction of
location 257 causes the computer to jump to location 203 which
is the appropriate point to return after having departed from
the stream of the main program. As a result of the JMP instru
tion the program counter now contains 204.

The departure and return to the stream of the main progra
is accomplished by depositing the contents of the program cour
in the first location of the subroutine, and then replacing th
contents of the program counter with the location of the secor
instruction in the subroutine. This is done automatically by
the computer. For this specific computer the programmer must
remember that the first location of the subroutine is to be
left unused to allow for the deposit of the program counter,
and that the exit from the subroutine is accomplished by a
jump indirect instruction to the first location of the subroutine.

Now that the operations necessary to accomplish the prope
execution of subroutines, and how these mechanisms are implemented in a specific computer are known, return to the discussion of argument transferral to and from subroutines. In
the program of Fig. 5 our example problem of adding eight numbers for a grand total and adding a constant to each individua
number has been reprogrammed in a third way. Although this
particular program requires more memory and would require more
time to execute than the program of Fig. 4, it has been includ
to give a thorough discussion of another method of transferrin
arguments.

Before discussing the actual execution of the program in
Fig. 5 look at the differences in constants and other tagged
locations. Note that in location 303 through 312, some new
tags have been inserted, and that the contents of these tagged
locations are the locations of the totals of the individual
numbers with the constant A (TØT1, TØT2,...,TØT8). For exampl
the contents of location 303 would be 325, the address of TØT1
Also note that tagged locations have been inserted throughout
the main program and are called ARG1 through ARG16.

The central theme of this program is the same as that of
Fig. 4, i.e. a jump is made to a subroutine called ADD to perform the two basic additions of the example. However, this
time the subroutine ADD takes the numbers and adds them to a
grand total, and in each case, adds the parameter A and deposi
the total in its appropriate location; all within the subrouti
In order to accomplish this the subroutine must know the value

Memory Location (Octal)	Tag	Operation		Comment
200		CLA		/CLEAR AC
201		TAD	NUM1	/GET 1ST NUMBER
202		DCA	ARG1	/STØRE IN THE FIRST ARGUMENT
203		TAD	LØC1	/GET THE ADDRESS ØF TØT1
204		DCA	ARG2	/STØRE IN THE SECØND ARGUMENT
205		JMS	ADD	/JUMP TØ SUBRØUTINE ADD
206	ARG1,	0		/ARGUMENT ØNE
207	ARG2,	0		/ARGUMENT TWØ
210		TAD	NUM2	/GET THE SECØND NUMBER
211		DCA	ARG3	/STØRE IN THE FIRST ARGUMENT
212		TAD	LØC2	/GET THE ADDRESS ØF TØT2
213		DCA	ARG4	/STØRE IN THE SECØND ARGUMENT
214		JMS	ADD	/JUMP TØ SUBRØUTINE ADD
215	ARG3,	0		/ARGUMENT ØNE
216	ARG4,	0		/ARGUMENT TWØ
.	.	.		
.		.		
.	.	.		
262		TAD	NUM8	/GET 8TH NUMBER
263		DCA	ARG15	/STØRE IN FIRST ARGUMENT
264		TAD	LØC8	/GET THE LØCATIØN ØF TØT8
265		DCA	ARG16	/STØRE IN SECØND ARGUMENT
266		JMS	ADD	/JUMP TØ SUBRØUTINE ADD
267	ARG15,	0		/ARGUMENT ØNE
270	ARG16,	0		/ARGUMENT TWØ
271		HLT		/END ØF EXECUTIØN
.	.	.		
.	.	.		
303	LØC1,	TØT1		/ADDRESS ØF TØT1
304	LØC2,	TØT2		/ADDRESS ØF TØT2
.	.	.		
.	.	.		
312	LØC8,	TØT8		/ADDRESS ØF TØT8
313	A,	XXXX		/ADDRESS CØNTAINING A
314	TØTAL,	0		/ADDRESS CØNTAINING GRAND TØTAL
315	NUM1,	XXXX		/1ST NUMBER
316	NUM2,	XXXX		/2ND NUMBER
.	.	.		
.	.	.		
324	NUM8,	XXXX		/8TH NUMBER
325	TØT1,	0		/WHERE NUM1+A WILL BE STØRED
326	TØT2,	0		/WHERE NUM2+A WILL BE STØRED
.	.	.		
.	.	.		
334	TØT8,	0		/WHERE NUM8+A WILL BE STØRED
.	.	.		
.	.	.		
350	ADD,	0		/ENTRY/EXIT ADDRESS
351		TAD I ADD		/GET NUMBER

(Fig. 5 Continued)

Memory Location (Octal)	Tag	Operation		Comment
352		TAD	TØTAL	/ADD TØ GRAND TØTAL
353		DCA	TØTAL	/SAVE NEW GRAND TØTAL
354		TAD I	ADD	/GET NUMBER AGAIN
355		TAD	A	/ADD A
356		DCA	TEMP1	/SAVE NUMx + A TEMPØRARILY
357		ISZ	ADD	/SET UP STØRAGE ADDRESS FØR TØT
360		TAD I	ADD	/GET THE ADDRESS ØF TØTx
361		DCA	TEMP2	/SAVE ADDRESS TEMPØRARILY
362		TAD	TEMP1	/GET NUMx + A
363		DCA I	TEMP2	/STØRE NUMx + A IN TØTx
364		ISZ	ADD	/SET PRØPER RETURN LØCATIØN
365		JMP I	ADD	/RETURN
366	TEMP1,	0		/TEMPØRARY STØRAGE LØCATIØN 1
367	TEMP2,	0		/TEMPORARY STØRAGE LØCATIØN 2

Fig. 5.   Yet another program to calculate NUM1+NUM2+...
+NUM8, and NUM1+A, NUM2+A,...,NUM8+A. In this
example the subroutine has been written in
another manner to illustrate a method of argument transferral that does not utilize the
accumulator.

of the current number and the location in which it is to deposit the value of the number plus A.

Now turn to the actual execution of the program. The fir
instruction to be executed is that of location 200. This clea
the accumulator so that the second instruction can put NUM1 in
the accumulator. The third instruction deposits the value of
NUM1 in location 206. The instruction of 203 fetchs the location of TØT1 and this is deposited in 207. Location 207 now
contains 325. When the jump to subroutine instruction of 205
is executed the program counter has 206 as its contents. Ther
fore, when the program arrives at the first location of the su
routine ADD the number 206 is deposited in location 350. The
next instruction to be executed is that of location 351. When
the instruction in 351 is executed it puts the contents of location 206 in the accumulator. Remember that the value of NUM
was placed in 206 prior to jumping to the subroutine. The execution of the TAD in 352 adds the value of NUM1 to the grand
total and 353 deposits it in the location labeled TØTAL, i.e.
location 314. Location 354 again contains TAD indirect ADD,
and again results in NUM1 being placed in the accumulator. Th
instruction in location 355 adds the value of A to the value o
NUM1. The instruction in location 356 temporarily saves this
total, and the next instruction changes ADD to contain 207.
The instruction of 360 gets the address of TØT1, and the next

instruction stores it in TEMP2. The instruction of 362 retrieves
NUM1+A. Prior to jumping to the subroutine the contents of 207
was set to be 325; thus, we finally see that the execution of
the instruction in 363 results in the deposit of NUM1 plus A
in location 325. The instruction in 364 again increments the
location ADD, changing location 350 to now contain 210. Therefore, when the instruction in location 367 is executed the program jumps to location 210, which is the proper place to continue the mainstream of the program.

Reviewing what has happened in the execution of the first
portion of the program in Fig. 5, we see that the instructions
in 200 through 204 were executed sequentially at which point
the program branched to the subroutine ADD. Unlike our previous example, the program did not return from the subroutine
ADD to the location following the JMS instruction but instead
returned two locations later to 210. Also the transferral of
arguments to the subroutine has taken place in an entirely different way. First, two arguments were transferred to the subroutine, and secondly, these were not transferred via the accumulator. The programmer in this case has set a convention
that the arguments to be transferred to the subroutine follow
the JMS instruction. Normally, the return from the subroutine
would be to the location following the JMS, making it necessary,
by the ISZ instructions in the subroutine, to modify the contents of the location ADD so that the return will be to the desired place, i.e. location 210.

Following the execution of the program a bit further it
can be seen that the execution of the instructions in location
210 and 211 result in the value of NUM2 being placed in location ARG3. Likewise, the execution of the instructions in 212
and 213 result in the location of TØT2, 326, being deposited in
ARG4. The program again jumps to the subroutine ADD which results in the value of NUM2 being added to the grand total and
the value of NUM2 plus A being deposited in location 326. A-
gain, modification of the location ADD, which contains 215 at
the beginning of the sequence results in a value of 217 at the
end of the subroutine ADD, continuing the stream of the program
as desired.

Not only does the example of Fig. 5 show a different method
of transferring arguments to and from subroutines; it makes
another important point. Namely, that if one keeps clearly in
mind the three operations that must be performed to properly
leave the mainstream of the program, to execute a subroutine,
and to re-enter the mainstream, it is possible to take liberties with these operations. This has been done in the present
case by incrementing the first location of the subroutine ADD.
The manner in which the modification of these operations may
take place have been shown here in a specific example for a
specific computer. However, if the operations are clearly
understood, it is possible to perform similar modifications
for any computer.

4.1.3 Program Loops

A program loop is just a means by which certain portions of a program may be executed repeatedly. In fact, it is comm for the program itself to compute the number of times that th loop is to be executed. As in the case of the subroutine, th ability to loop programs is quite valuable in saving memory space within the computer.

To illustrate how a program loop might work and how the concept of looping may be used, return to the program of Fig. Examination will show that location 201 through location 230 contain essentially the same coding repeated eight times. Co siderable savings of memory space and programming effort coul be made by writing a program loop. This has been done in the program of Fig. 6.

In the program of Fig. 6 note that the constants and oth tagged values are the same as those of the program in Fig. 4 and, in addition, there are three new tagged locations. The first new tag, in location 221, contains the address of NUM1, 224. The second in location 222 contains the location of NUM1+A, 234. The third tag, CNTR, contains a minus 10 octal which is the 2's complement of eight on the base 10. Also no that the subroutine ADD is identical to that of Fig. 4.

Execution of the program starts at location 200. Again, the first instruction clears the accumulator register. The next instruction places the contents of location 224 in the accumulator, i.e. the value of NUM1. The next instruction jumps to the subroutine ADD which adds the value of the curre number to the grand total and finds the value of the current number plus A. This latter sum is in the accumulator when th program returns from the subroutine and is deposited in loca- tion 234 by the instruction in location 203. The instruction of 204 adds one to the value in 221; therefore, the current value in location 221 is 225, the location of NUM2. The inst tion of 205, likewise, adds one to the contents of 222, which is then 235. Next, the instruction of location 206 adds one the location tagged CNTR. CNTR then equals minus seven octal

One must remember that the ISZ instruction not only adds one to the contents of a memory register, but after adding on checks to see if the contents are zero. If the contents are zero, the next instruction is skipped; if not, the next instr tion is executed. Since, the contents of CNTR are not zero, at this time, the instruction in location 207 is executed. Tl instruction jumps the program back to location 201.

At this point, the program loop has been executed once. In the second pass through the loop the instruction of locatio 201 brings the value of NUM2 into the accumulator. The JMS tc ADD determines the two desired totals, TØTAL+NUM2 and NUM2+A, and the return is to location 203 where the second total is saved in location 235. The instructions of 204 and 205 again add one to the pointers for the number and total locations.

Memory Location (Octal)	Tag	Operation		Comment
200		CLA		/CLEAR AC
201	START,	TAD	I NUMLØC	/GET NEXT NUMBER
202		JMS	ADD	/JUMP TØ SUBRØUTINE ADD
203		DCA	I TØTLØC	/SAVE NUMx+A
204		ISZ	NUMLØC	/ADVANCE NUMBER PØINTER
205		ISZ	TØTLØC	/ADVANCE TØTx PØINTER
206		ISZ	CNTR	/IS THIS EIGHTH NUMBER
207		JMP	START	/NØ, REPEAT LØØP
210		HLT		/YES, END EXECUTIØN
⋮		⋮		
217	A,	XXXX		/ADDRESS CØNTAINING A
220	TØTAL,	0		/ADDRESS CØNTAINING GRAND TØTAL
221	NUMLØC,	NUM1		/ADDRESS ØF NUM1
222	TØTLØC,	TØT1		/ADDRESS ØF TØT1
223	CNTR,	-10		/NEGATIVE 8
224	NUM1,	XXXX		/1ST NUMBER
225	NUM2,	XXXX		/2ND NUMBER
⋮	⋮	⋮		
233	NUM8,	XXXX		/8TH NUMBER
234	TØT1,	0		/WHERE NUM1+A WILL BE STØRED
235	TØT2,	0		/WHERE NUM2+A WILL BE STØRED
⋮	⋮	⋮		
243	TØT8,	0		/WHERE NUM8+A WILL BE STØRED
⋮	⋮	⋮		
250	ADD,	0		/ENTRY/EXIT ADDRESS
251		DCA	TEMP	/TEMPØRARILY SAVE NUMBER
252		TAD	TEMP	/GET NUMBER IN AC
253		TAD	TØTAL	/ADD TØ GRAND TØTAL
254		DCA	TØTAL	/SAVE NEW GRAND TØTAL
255		TAD	TEMP	/GET NUMBER AGAIN
256		TAD	A	/ADD A
257		JMP	I ADD	/JUMP INDIRECT TØ ADD
260	TEMP,	0		/TEMPØRARY STØRAGE ADDRESS

Fig. 6.   A modification of the program of Fig. 4 which eliminates redundant coding by making use of a program
loop. The program loop runs from memory location
201 through memory location 207.

The next instruction increments CNTR, which now contains the
value minus six octal. Because CNTR is not zero, the instruction of 207 is executed and the second loop of the program is
complete. The program loop will be executed repeatedly until
the execution of ISZ CNTR in the eighth loop causes the contents of CNTR to become zero. When this happens the instruction in 207 is skipped and the instruction in 210 halts the
program.

The program of Fig. 6 is considerably shorter than that
of Fig. 4 and requires considerably less programming effort.
In fact, we have now gone from our original example of Fig. 3,
where 68 decimal locations were required, to the 47 decimal
locations of Fig. 6 for a savings of about 31 percent in memory space.

Because the locations tagged NUMLØC and TØTLØC in Fig. 6
now keep track of the locations of the eight individual numbers
and the sums of these numbers with the constant A, it is not
really necessary to have the tags NUM2 through NUM8 and the tags
TØT2 through TØT8. In other words, with the present method it
is only necessary to know the first location of each of these
two lists, for the program assumes that the numbers of these
lists are in sequential locations.

With the example program of Fig. 6 we have progressed from
the program of Fig. 3, where essentially eight identical operations were performed by repeatedly writing the code; to the
program of Fig. 4, where considerable savings were made by introducing a subroutine. Finally, in the program of Fig. 6 the
program has been reduced to one small loop which executes the
subroutine eight times with the appropriate arguments. These
three programs not only illustrate how certain techniques such
as subrouting and looping may be used to save both labor and
memory space, but they also illustrate how the same goals may
be accomplished with entirely different programs. Although the
two original programs are wasteful of memory space, all of the
programs attain the desired goals and give the same answers.

4.1.4   Branch Tables

Several ways of making programs more modular have been
explored. In particular, subroutines are program modules which
can be substituted into any program and executed without change.
However, there are often situations where under prescribed conditions it is desired to take specific action, but because of
the nature of the actions that are to be performed, subroutines
may not provide the proper program flow. As an example of this,
assume an on-line computer controling an experimental process.
The program is to be written in such a way that all commands
to the computer are given via a keyboard. Further, assume that
there are four commands which may be given: SETUP, GØ, STØP,
and PRINT. The command SETUP is to be given at the beginning

of an experiment to establish the experimental parameters and
other control conditions. Giving the command GØ starts the
acquisition of data, and giving the command STØP stops the acquisition of data. The command PRINT causes the experimental
results to be output on a printing device.

How might such an arrangement be accomplished? For the
moment, leave this particular example and turn to a much more
specific example. Suppose we again have the eight numbers
NUM1, NUM2 through NUM8, and that each may only take on the
four values from zero to three. Further, it is desired that
the computer program take a different action for each value;
e.g., if NUM1 has a value of zero, then a different action is
taken by the program than if NUM1 has a value of three.

The program of Fig. 7 shows a way that such a scheme could
be accomplished. First, look at location 425, which is tagged
NUMLØC. This contains the location of NUM1, 431. In the next
location is CNTR which contains a negative eight. In location
427 is a tag called PNTR which contains 456. Location 430 has
a tag called PØINT, which contains zero prior to the execution
of the program. Locations 431 through 440 contain the eight
numbers of interest. Finally in locations 456 through 461 are
four jump instructions to various other points in the program.
The termination of one of these jumps has been included in the
example. This is CASE3 which starts at location 542.

The program first executes the instruction in location 400,
which is the usual clear the accumulator. The next instruction
brings the value of NUM1 into the accumulator. Instruction 402
adds NUM1 to the contents of PNTR. The instruction of 403 saves
this sum, NUM1+456, in the location PØINT. Remember that the
values of the numbers NUM1 through NUM8 may only take on integer values between zero and three. Therefore, some value between zero and three has been added to the contents of PNTR.
Returning to the execution sequence, the instruction in location 404 causes the program to jump to some location between
456 and 461. For example, if the value of NUM1 is zero, the
execution of the instruction in location 404 results in a jump
to location 456. In 456 is another jump instruction, which
diverts the program to CASE1.

Suppose that the value of NUM1 had been two, then the execution of location 404 results in a jump to location 460, which
has in turn a jump to CASE3. Now suppose that CASE3 is to set
a control variable and also to complement another constant
called VARI. Accordingly, the first instruction in CASE3 is to
zero the parameter called CØNTRL. Next, the 2's complement of
the parameter VARI is determined and deposited back into the
same location. Then in location 546 a jump instruction causes
the program to return to location 405. There the contents of
location 425 are incremented to become 432. In location 406
the contents of CNTR are incremented, and the program jumps
back to the location START for a second loop. This second loop
branches to one of the four cases depending on the value of NUM2.

Memory Location (Octal)	Tag	Operation		Comment
400		CLA		/CLEAR AC
401	START,	TAD I	NUMLØC	/GET NEXT NUMBER
402		TAD	PNTR	/ADD 1ST BRANCH LØCATIØN
403		DCA	PØINT	/SAVE BRANCH PØINT
404		JMP I	PØINT	/GØ TØ THE BRANCH TABLE
405	ENTER,	ISZ	NUMLØC	/ADVANCE TØ NEXT NUMBER
406		ISZ	CNTR	/IS THIS LAST NUMBER
407		JMP	START	/NØ, REPEAT LØØP
410		HLT		/YES, END EXECUTIØN
.	.	.		
.	.			
.	.	.		
425	NUMLØC,	NUM1		/ADDRESS OF NUM1
426	CNTR,	-10		/NEGATIVE 8
427	PNTR,	JMPØNE		/1ST ADDRESS ØF BRANCH TABLE
430	PØINT,	0		/PØINTER TØ PRØPER BRANCH
431	NUM1,	XXXX		/1ST NUMBER
432	NUM2,	XXXX		/2ND NUMBER
.	.	.		
.	.	.		
.	.	.		
440	NUM8,	XXXX		/8TH NUMBER
.	.	.		
.	.	.		
.	.	.		
456	JMPØNE,	JMP	CASE1	/1ST ENTRY ØF BRANCH TABLE
457		JMP	CASE2	/2ND ENTRY ØF BRANCH TABLE
460		JMP	CASE3	/3RD ENTRY ØF BRANCH TABLE
461		JMP	CASE4	/4TH ENTRY ØF BRANCH TABLE
.		.		
.		.		
542	CASE3,	DCA	CØNTRL	/SET CØNTRL=0
543		TAD	VAR1	/GET VAR1
544		CIA		/TAKE 2'S CØMPLEMENT
545		DCA	VAR1	/STØRE CØMPLEMENTED VAR1
546		JMP	ENTER	/RETURN TØ MAIN LØØP
.		.		
.		.		

Fig. 7.   This program illustrates another method by which
computer coding may be made modular. In this
example modularity is attained by the branch
table residing in memory locations 456 through
461.

In the program of Fig. 7 a series of numbers are examined, and depending on their value a branch is made to a specific set of coding such as CASE3. The appropriate branch is determined by the manipulation of the contents of PØINT. The locations 456 through 461 constitute the branch table.

By using the branch table approach it has been possible to obtain modularity even though the action of the program prior to any specific loop is unknown. The modularity comes about because each case of the example is written as a separate set of executable code, all of which re-enter the main program by the instruction JMP ENTER. Thus, it is possible to remove these modules and put them into other programs or to change the action of any of these modules within a given program.

Returning to our original example of experiment control; it can now be seen that as a command is received from the Teletype terminal, it is defined as being either the SETUP, GØ, STØP, or PRINT command and a branch table would be utilized to cause the computer to go to the appropriate module of coding to carry out the desired action. Using the branch table technique it is very easy to add other commands by adding further jump instructions in the branch table and corresponding program modules. Also, it is possible to set up several branch table entries for future expansion by adding do-nothing loops. Suppose that there were only three cases when the program of Fig. 7 was written, but it was desired to allow for a fourth case for future expansion. Then instead of the instruction JMP CASE4 in location 461 one could put the instruction JMP ENTER. Thus, a computation could be made which would result in the main program loop jumping to location 461, but the JMP ENTER there would immediately bring the program back to location 405 creating a do-nothing loop.

4.2 Program Initialization

Program initialization is a cardinal rule that is almost always violated when a beginner writes his first few computer programs. What is meant by program initialization? If a program has been properly initialized, it may be executed as many times as desired without reloading the program into the computer. Return to the program of Fig. 6. This and the other program examples that have been presented are not properly initialized. This is the reason for specifically mentioning that the listings of the programs represented the state of the computer prior to the execution of the program. To illustrate, examine what the state of the program of Fig. 6 would be, had it been executed once. If the program is to execute properly, it is assumed that the instruction of location 201, in the first loop, loads the value of NUM1 into the accumulator. However, if the program has already been executed once, the value of NUMLØC has been incremented eight times. Therefore, if the program is

executed a second time; the instruction of 201 in the first
loop would actually load the contents of location 234. Of
course, this is completely erroneous. Similarly, for the instruction in location 203; TØTLØC, has been incremented eight
times during the first execution of the program. Therefore,
during the first loop of the second execution, the value of
NUM1 plus A would be deposited in location 244, again giving
an erroneous result.

Before the first execution the value of CNTR is set to a
negative eight, but on the eighth loop of the first execution
the value of CNTR is incremented to zero. Therefore, if the
program were executed a second time, the first loop would increment CNTR to one, the second loop would increment CNTR to
two, etc. Because the PDP-8 is a 12 bit word length machine,
this means that the value of CNTR would have to be incremented
2^{12} times before becoming zero, or 4096 loops. As we have just
seen, the first loop of the second execution would deposit
NUM1 plus A in the location 244. If the loop were actually
executed 4096 times, values would eventually be deposited in
location 250 and the following locations, thereby destroying
the subroutine ADD.

Looking at the value of TØTAL it has already been mentioned
that a correct grand total is not computed if the value of this
variable is not zero at the beginning of execution. It would
not be zero at the beginning of a second execution because the
grand total found during the first execution would still reside
in location 220.

It can be seen that if the program of Fig. 6 were to be
executed a second time, several disastrous results would occur.
The wrong numbers would be used for NUM1 through NUM8, the grand
total would be wrong, and the sum of each individual value with
the parameter A would be deposited in the wrong locations. Also
we have seen that the number of loops executed would be entirely
wrong and in fact would be such that the subroutine ADD would
be obliterated within the memory of the computer.

What must be done to properly initialize the program of
Fig. 6 should now be obvious. The appropriate instructions
must be inserted at the beginning of the program to correct all
of those difficulties that have been enumerated above. These
instructions must be inserted in such a way that the program
may be executed as many times as desired, giving exactly the
same result each time and not destroying itself in the process.
The program of Fig. 6 has been rewritten in Fig. 8 with the
proper initialization.

In order to properly initialize the program it is necessary to add some new variables. These are NUMPT, TØTPT, and
MIN10. The need for these should become apparent as the execution of the program is discussed.

The execution of the program is to start at location 200.
As always the accumulator is cleared to zero. The instructions
in location 201 and 202 place the address of NUM1, 240, in the

Memory Location (Octal)	Tag	Operation		Comment
200	INIT,	CLA		/CLEAR AC
201		TAD	NUMLØC	/GET LØCATIØN ØF NUM1
202		DCA	NUMPT	/INITIALIZE NUMBER PØINTER
203		TAD	TØTLØC	/GET LØCATIØN ØF TØT1
204		DCA	TØTPT	/INITIALIZE TØTAL PØINTER
205		TAD	MIN10	/GET NEGATIVE 8
206		DCA	CNTR	/INITIALIZE CØUNTER
207		DCA	TØTAL	/INITIALIZE GRAND TØTAL TØ ZERØ
210	START,	TAD I	NUMPT	/GET NEXT NUMBER
211		JMS	ADD	/JUMP TØ SUBRØUTINE ADD
212		DCA I	TØTPT	/SAVE NUMx+A
213		ISZ	NUMPT	/ADVANCE NUMBER PØINTER
214		ISZ	TØTPT	/ADVANCE TØTx PØINTER
215		ISZ	CNTR	/IS THIS EIGHTH NUMBER
216		JMP	START	/NØ, REPEAT LØØP
217		HLT		/YES, END EXECUTIØN
.	.			
.	.			
230	A,	XXXX		/ADDRESS CØNTAINING A
231	TØTAL,	0		/ADDRESS CØNTAINING GRAND TØTAL
232	NUMLØC,	NUM1		/ADDRESS ØF NUM1
233	TØTLØC,	TØT1		/ADDRESS ØF TØT1
234	CNTR,	0		/LØØP CØUNTER
235	NUMPT,	0		/NUMBER PØINTER
236	TØTPT,	0		/TØTAL PØINTER
237	MIN10,	-10		/NEGATIVE 8
240	NUM1,	XXXX		/1ST NUMBER
241	NUM2,	XXXX		/2ND NUMBER
.	.	.		
.	.	.		
257	NUM8,	XXXX		/8TH NUMBER
260	TØT1,	0		/WHERE NUM1+A WILL BE STØRED
261	TØT2,	0		/WHERE NUM2+A WILL BE STØRED
.	.	.		
.	.	.		
267	TØT8,	0		/WHERE NUM8+A WILL BE STØRED
.	.	.		
.	.	.		
305	ADD,	0		/ENTRY/EXIT ADDRESS
306		DCA	TEMP	/TEMPØRARILY SAVE NUMBER
307		TAD	TEMP	/GET NUMBER IN AC
310		TAD	TØTAL	/ADD TØ GRAND TØTAL
311		DCA	TØTAL	/SAVE NEW GRAND TØTAL
312		TAD	TEMP	/GET NUMBER AGAIN
313		TAD	A	/ADD A
314		JMP I	ADD	/JUMP INDIRECT TØ ADD
315	TEMP,	0		/TEMPØRARY STØRAGE ADDRESS

Fig. 8.   This program is a modification of the program in Fig. 6. In the present case coding has been added at the beginning of the program to properly initialize the necessary parameters. This makes it possible to re-run the program an arbitrary number of times and still obtain the correct results.

location NUMPT. In a similar manner, the instructions of 203
and 204 place the address of TØT1, 260, in location TØTPT. The
instructions in locations 205 and 206 place the 2's complement
of decimal eight in the location CNTR. Finally, the instruction
of location 207 sets the value of TØTAL equal to zero. The execution of location 210 brings the value of NUM1 into the
accumulator. Next, the program jumps to the subroutine ADD,
which adds the value of NUM1 to TØTAL and returns with the value
of NUM1 plus A in the accumulator. Execution of 212 deposits
the latter sum in location 260. The instructions in locations
213 through 215 increment NUMPT, TØTPT, and CNTR respectively.
In the first seven loops through the program the instruction
in 216 is executed, jumping the program back to location 210.
Upon the eighth loop the execution of ISZ CNTR in location 215
causes location 216 to be skipped and the computer halts at 217.
        Note that the variables NUMPT, TØTPT, and CNTR are incre-
mented, in this new version of the program but that their values
are initialized each time the program is re-executed. NUMPT
and TØTPT have been added to the program so that they might be
incremented and the addresses of NUM1 and TØT1 could be preserved in the locations 232 and 234. Likewise, the variable
MIN10 has been created to permanently preserve the value of
negative eight.
        In going from the program of Fig. 3 through the several
versions that culminated in the program of Fig. 8, we now have
a realistic program that can be ran on a small computer. The
program of Fig. 8 has been optimized in terms of memory space
and in terms of programming effort. It has also been properly
initialized so that it may be run as many times as desired with
correct results in each computation.

        4.3 Program Input

        Until this time, no mention has been made of how the eight
numbers were placed in the locations tagged NUM1 through NUM8,
nor how the constant A had been placed in the computer memory
prior to the execution of the example programs. Actually, the
numbers can be placed within the computer magnetic core memory
in any number of ways; Teletype keyboard, paper tape, magnetic
tape, magnetic disk etc. The actual mechanism, i.e. actual
programming, to place numbers into the computer memory from
some peripheral device is not covered here, but is covered
later. This section is devoted to good practices that should
be used in putting numerical values and other control information into an on-line computer.
        Many times the entering of information into a computer
prior to execution of a program is not done in a proper manner
or with proper documentation. Suppose that a program requires
three numbers to be read into the computer prior to the actual
execution of the program. There is a strong temptation to

simply have a keyboard or other device await the user to input
these numbers. Because of the very nature by which a program
operates,these numbers must be placed in the computer in a
proper sequence, i.e. the computer expects the numbers in the
order in which the program was coded to accept them. Too often
this is not documented in any way. It is up to the user to
remember what numbers, and in what order they are to be fed
to the computer. With a small amount of effort a much better
approach can be realized by having the program conduct a dialogue, i.e. the computer prints directions which ask the user
for the next variable or number to be read in.

If such a dialogue is established, the program becomes
much more useful; any person who desires to use the program
needs no assistance from anyone else. Also, it is certainly
true that even the person who originally wrote the program will
forget, with the passage of time, what order variables are to
be entered, and in what format. These two reasons alone make
it worthwhile to take the time to write program inputs with a
proper dialogue.

A keyboard with a printing device such as a typewriter or
a Teletype terminal is an ideal peripheral to enter information into the computer. Entering numeric and alphameric values
through a keyboard is natural. Also, with such a device it is
always appropriate to have any alphanumeric that is entered
through the keyboard to be echoed (printed) on the printer,
which provides documentation for later use. If the computer
is used on an experiment or an on-line control process, this
listing may be used at any later time to verify that the right
values were entered.

Anticipation of human errors is one of the primary considerations to keep in mind when writing the input portion of
a program. All too often, the program is written as if the
input will always be entered in exactly the right formats and
with exactly the right values. If no anticipation has been
made of human errors then the only recourse upon committing an
input error is to restart the program from the beginning. To
repeatedly start the program after having gone most of the way
through the input procedure is a very frustrating experience.
Therefore, at every point the programmer should anticipate
what errors might be made in the input process, and allow a
recovery procedure which only requires the user to back up one
step in the input sequence. Also, it is often possible to
check the input for validity. In many cases numeric information may be restricted to a certain range of numbers. In such
instances, it is perfectly feasible to have the program check
the magnitudes of the numbers as they come in, and output error
messages if the acceptable range has been exceeded.

The format of the input information must take account of
the purpose of the program. For example, if a program has
been designed to set up a piece of equipment or a process controlled by the computer, then it is often desirable to put

automatic recycling of the input into effect so that certain parameters of the equipment linked to the on-line computer may be adjusted. An input dialogue could tell the user to set a certain knob on a piece of equipment; this action could then be followed by the computer reading back a parametric value controlled by the knob. It might be appropriate after reading back the value which resulted from the adjustment of the knob, to ask the user if he would again like to adjust the knob again or to continue on with the input dialogue.

On the other hand, if the program input dialogue is for a normal run, rather than a setup, it is not appropriate to continue to recycle the user back and ask him questions about continuing or repeating certain processes.

Once a program has completed execution, a factor that is not required or necessary, but which is often a convenience is to have the program recycle back to the input dialogue rather than halt. If the program is left on a halt, the user must restart it again from the computer console or other appropriate device. However, if the program is automatically recycled back to the beginning, and the first question of the input dialogue is asked, the program is again ready for immediate execution.

Return again to the example computation of Fig. 8 and assume that all input to the computer is to be via a Teletype keyboard, and that the appropriate coding to read the Teletype information has been added. Then the example below illustrates how the dialogue might appear on the teleprinter. All the text underlined was entered by the user, all other text was printed by the computer. The time sequence in this example would go as follows:

A=30.1 ↓
NUM1=85.9 ↓
NUM2=64.7 ↓
NUM3=10.9 ↓
NUM4=5.75 ↓
NUM5=35.8 ↓
NUM6=25.2 ↓
NUM7=77.8 ↓
NUM8=1.33 ↓

When the program execution was started, the computer immediatel typed A= and paused. At this point the user typed on the Teletype keyboard 30.1 ↓. (The down arrow(↓) is used here to indicate carriage-return, because the carriage return is not a printing character). As soon as the user struck the carriage return key the carriage returned, a line feed* is supplied,

---

*The carriage return on a Teletype unit only returns the carriages it does not roll the carriage to the next line. The line-feed character rolls the carriage to the next line. Ther fore, the carriage return character plus the line-feed charact is equivalent to the normal carriage return on a typewriter.

and the computer printed NUM1=, and again paused. At this
point the user entered through the Teletype keyboard 85.9).
In this manner the computer sequentially asked for each variable by name, and the user supplied a value at each pause.
In an actual situation the computer program should be written
to ask for the variables by more descriptive names. Although
the name A may be the name of a specific variable in the program, it is better to ask for it in more descriptive terms in
the input dialogue. For example, if A is really a control
pressure, then the dialogue should read CØNTRØL PRESSURE=.

To illustrate how a recovery process might be used, return again to the example input for the example of Fig. 8 and
suppose that the nature of the process limits the values of all
numbers to be less than ninety. Then, an input might go as
follows:

.
.
.

NUM7=97.8)   TØØ LARGE, NUM7=77.8)
NUM8=1.33)
.
.
.

Upon reaching the value of NUM7 the computer has typed NUM7=,
and the user has entered 97.8) . The user has committed an
error for a number in excess of 90 has been entered. The computer program, upon checking the value determines this fact
and types back: TØØ LARGE, NUM7=. This permits the user to
re-enter 77.8) . From this point the dialogue continues as
it would in the normal case. The important point is that if
the user, after typing the value 97.8, realized he had committed an error, and the program did not check or allow recovery procedures; the only recourse would be to restart the
program and again enter the value of A and all other numbers
up through NUM7. Needless to say, this is a time consuming
and frustrating experience.

Another example of a recovery procedure for numeric input is to provide a means for the user of correcting errors
which he himself·detects. Returning to the example dialogue
suppose one had the following instance: NUM2=65 ← 4.7)
Here the user has started to enter the value of NUM2, and
after entering the digit five, realizes he has committed a
typographical error. Assume the input dialogue for this particular program provides for "erasure" of errors by striking
the RUBOUT key. When the RUBOUT key is struck, the program
types the backarrow symbol to indicate an erasure has taken
place. Thus, in the example, the user has erased the five and
replaced it with a four; finally, entering for NUM2 a value of
64.7.

Even if all input to the computer program is not done via
a keyboard, a dialogue on the Teletype terminal is still a
very useful procedure. Returning again to the example of Fig.
8, suppose that the number A is to be entered by the keyboard,
but the program expects the values NUM1 through NUM8 to be
supplied on a punched paper tape. That is, these numbers are
to be read into the computer from a punched paper tape through
the Teletype paper tape reader. In this case the Teletype
dialogue might appear as follows:

A=30.1)
PLACE PAPER TAPE IN READER AND HIT START.
NUM1=85.9
NUM2=64.7
.
.
NUM8=1.33

What has happened in this particular example? After the execution of the program has begun, the computer typed A=, and
the user supplied the value 30.1 from the Teletype keyboard.
At this point the computer printed a message telling the user
to mount the paper tape--which contains the values of NUM1
through NUM8--in the paper tape reader and hit start on the
reader. As the values are read from paper tape, they are
printed on the printer which gives a hard copy listing of those
numbers that were actually read from the paper tape. This example illustrates how information might be read from any peripheral device with special instructions supplied by the printer.

In summary, good input procedures can be attained by
thinking through the whole input situation thoroughly and trying
to anticipate errors. When planning an input dialogue, it is
desirable to try to put oneself in the position of someone who
has never run the program before, and who does not know anything about the coding logic of the program. The anticipation
of errors and the provision for recovery from such errors can
not be over-emphasized. It is only human nature to commit
such errors and a good deal of frustration can be avoided if
the recovery from errors is not difficult.

4.4 Good Practices

There are many good practices and working habits that can
be developed in programming. Most are of the common-sense category. Because programming is a very logical art, it naturally
follows that good organization is paramount. This means good
organization in many aspects of computer programming; debugging
at the computer console, obtaining up-to-date and properly
marked listings, up-to-date source media, and frequent reviews
of the whole program procedure.

What is presented here is not an exhaustive expose' of
good programming habits and practices, but rather a few examples of good programming practices which should suggest the
tenor of approach.

One good example of a desirable programming habit is in
the choosing of tag names. Too often the naming of tags is
done in a rather loose or haphazard manner which can lead to
problems in all stages of the program development from the
actual coding to the debugging and execution. It is very helpful to have a prescribed way of naming tags. My own practice
is to take the first four letters of the subroutine or program
that I am writing and follow these with a number. If I had
written a program named READØT the tags in the program would
be READ1, READ2, READ3, and so forth. This particular approach
helps reduce the possibility of many problems that can occur.
First, by using at least four letters of the program name plus
a number the possibility of giving two tags the same name is
highly unlikely. Furthermore, since the tags end in numbers
which would normally increase sequentially as the program proceeds an easier facility of scanning the listings is obtained.
There are certainly many other equally good methods of naming
variables in the program. The important goal is to establish
a practice which will give some organization to the way tags
are named, and thereby avoid the more common errors of redundantly named tags and difficulties of scanning program listings.

In reference to tags, it is particularly useful to use descriptive names in the case of constants. Many programs require
several constants for program initialization and computation.
These may be easily identified and located in the program if a
consisten way of naming them is established. For example, positive constants may be preceeded with a P and negative constants
with an M. Thus, P1 would indicate a constant whose value is
positive one, and M10 would indicate a constant whose value is
negative 10. Similarly, if the value of pi should occur in a
program, it would most appropriately be called PI.

In programming with assembly languages, it is often difficult to resist the temptation to modify instructions as the
program proceeds. Although there are situations where this is
perfectly acceptable and the best way of accomplishing a desired end; in general, it is not a good programming practice.
To illustrate this look at an example program written in two
different ways: one which makes use of instruction modification and one which does not. The computation to be performed
in the example program is to take the values of the eight numbers NUM1 through NUM8 and add them to obtain a grand total.

First look at the program of Fig. 9 which performs the desired computation without instruction modification. The program starts execution at location 500. The instructions in
501 through 504 are the initialization portion of the program
and simply set the address of NUM1 and the counter to negative
eight. Starting at location 505 is a loop to add each of the

Memory
Location

(Octal)	Tag	Operation		Comment
500	INIT,	CLA		/CLEAR AC
501		TAD	NUMLØC	/GET LØCATIØN ØF NUM1
502		DCA	NUMPT	/INITIALIZE NUMBER PØINTER
503		TAD	MIN10	/GET NEGATIVE 8
504		DCA	CNTR	/INITIALIZE CØUNTER
505	START,	TAD I	NUMPT	/GET AND ADD NEXT NUMBER
506		ISZ	NUMPT	/ADVANCE TØ NEXT NUMBER
507		ISZ	CNTR	/LAST NUMBER
510		JMP	START	/NØ, REPEAT LØØP
511		DCA	TØTAL	/YES, SAVE GRAND TØTAL
512		HLT		/END EXECUTIØN
513	NUMLØC,	NUM1		/ADDRESS ØF NUM1
514	NUMPT,	0		/NUMBER PØINTER
515	MIN10,	-10		/NEGATIVE 8
516	CNTR,	0		/LØØP COUNTER
517	TØTAL,	0		/GRAND TØTAL
520	NUM1,	XXXX		/1ST NUMBER
521	NUM2,	XXXX		/2ND NUMBER
.	.	.		
.	.	.		
527	NUM8,	XXXX		/8TH NUMBER

Fig. 9.   A program to calculate the sum NUM1+NUM2+...+NUM8.
This is to be compared with the program of Fig. 10
which performs the same calculation, but utilizes
the technique of instruction modification.

numbers to the grand total. In this program computation of the
total has been accomplished in a slightly different way. The
first time through the loop the instruction in location 505
adds the value of NUM1 to the accumulator, which contains a
zero. The next instruction advances the pointer and the next
instruction increments the loop counter. If the loop has not
been passed through eight times, the program jumps back to
START. It must be remembered that neither the ISZ or the JMP
instruction modifies the accumulator. Therefore, each time
the program passes through the loop a new value is added to
the accumulator. Upon the eighth pass through the loop, the
program will skip from location /507 to 511 and deposit the
contents of the accumulator in TØTAL, which then contains the
grand total of the eight numbers.

Now turn to the program of Fig. 10 which performs the
same computation, but uses instruction modification. In this
version of the program initialization takes place in location
501 through 504. The instructions in 501 and 502 take the
instruction TAD NUM1 and deposit it in location 505. The

Memory Location (Octal)	Tag	Operation		Comment
500	INIT,	CLA		/CLEAR AC
501		TAD	INSTR	/GET TAD INSTRUCTIØN
502		DCA	START	/DEPØSIT
503		TAD	MIN10	/GET NEGATIVE 8
504		DCA	CNTR	/INITIALIZE CØUNTER
505	START,	0		/LØCATIØN ØF VARIABLE TAD INSTRUCTIØN
506		ISZ	START	/INCREMENT ADDRESS BITS
507		ISZ	CNTR	/LAST NUMBER
510		JMP	START	/NØ, REPEAT LØØP
511		DCA	TØTAL	/YES, SAVE GRAND TØTAL
512		HLT		/END EXECUTIØN
513	INSTR,	TAD	NUM1	/TAD INSTRUCTIØN FØR INITIALIZATIØN
514	MIN10,	-10		/NEGATIVE 8
515	CNTR,	0		/LØØP CØUNTER
516	TØTAL,	0		/GRAND TØTAL
517	NUM1,	XXXX		/1ST NUMBER
520	NUM2,	XXXX		/2ND NUMBER
.	.	.		
.	.	.		
526	NUM8,	XXXX		/8TH NUMBER

Fig. 10. A program which illustrates the technique of instruction modification. With each execution of the program loop starting at location 505, the instruction
in location 505 is modified by the ISZ instruction
in location 506.

instructions in location 503 and 504 places a minus eight in
the loop counter. Now remembering that the instruction TAD
NUM1 has been put in location 505, the first pass through the
loop will bring the value of NUM1 into the accumulator. The
instruction in 506 increments the contents of location 505.
Thus, the instruction of 505 has been modified. Remembering
the right-most bits of a memory reference instruction in the
PDP-8 are the address bits; incrementing the instruction in
505 means that the address portion of the instruction has been
advanced by one. Therefore, the next execution of the instruction in 505, on the second pass through the loop, causes the
value of NUM2 to be added to the accumulator. On each succeeding pass through the loop, the address bits will be incremented
causing succeeding values of the numbers NUM1 through NUM8 to
be added to the accumulator. On the eighth pass, the program
skips from location 507 to 511 and deposits the grand total of
the eight numbers in TØTAL.

In the example program of Fig. 10 program modification
has been carried out in two ways. First an instruction has

been placed in memory location 505 in the initialization portion of the program. Second, on each succeeding pass through
the loop the address bits in the instruction of 505 have been
modified.

Comparing the programs of Fig. 9 and Fig. 10, it can be
seen that no advantage has been gained by modifying instructions. Each program requires exactly the same amount of memory space. In terms of execution time the program of Fig. 10
actually executes slightly slower than the program of Fig. 9.
However, if a coding error had been made in the program of
Fig. 10, considerable difficulty in finding the error could
be experienced because of the constant instruction modification in each loop of the program.

Other good programming practices are often related to a
particular computer. For example, if a computer uses paged
memory, then it is always a good idea to leave a few memory
locations on each page. One of the primary reasons for doing
this is to allow for errors that may be found in the debugging
process; then there are spare locations on each page for additional coding to correct the errors. Many other examples could
be mentioned in terms of special registers and special instructions that might occur in any given computer.

In summary, it can be said that good programming practices
usually result from common sense, and an effort to efficiently
organize from start to finish the whole procedure of writing a
program and making it run.

4.5 Flow Charting

Flow charting is a method of diagramming programs with
specific symbols to indicate how the flow of the program proceeds. The actual use of flow charting and the symbolisms are
neither completely standardized, but are becoming more so with
the passage of time. Fig. 11 shows some of the more common
flow chart symbols.

The technique of flow charting may be used in several different ways. In very simple programs there is probably no
reason to use a flow chart, (also called a flow diagram) but
in complex programs there can be no doubt that the construction
of a flow chart should be the first step of the programming
procedure. In many cases a flow chart can and should be a
part of the final documentation. To illustrate some of the
foregoing remarks return to the program of Fig. 8. After the
programmer has given some thought to how he might want to write
the program, the flow chart of Fig. 12 would be a typical result. With this flow chart in front of him, he would then proceed to write the code which would result in the program of
Fig. 8.

Now turn to the flow chart of Fig. 13. This is again a
flow chart which describes the program of Fig. 8. However, it

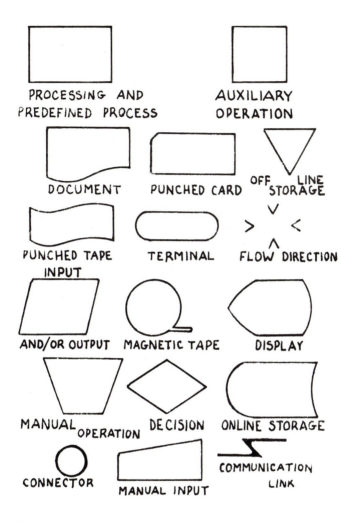

Fig. 11.   Some of the more commonly used flow charting
           symbols.

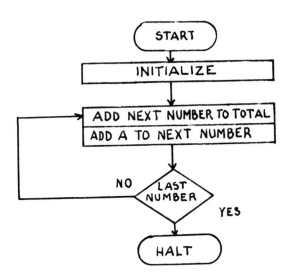

Fig. 12.   A flow chart for the program of Fig. 8.   This is
           exemplar of the type of flow chart that might be
           constructed prior to the actual coding of the
           program.

is probably more akin to the flow chart that would be drawn
up after the program has been coded and tested.   In the flow
chart of Fig. 13 actual variable names of the program occur
and recognition that the program includes a subroutine.   Also,
a flow chart for the subroutine itself has been drawn up.

A flow chart can vary a great deal in detail and approach
even for the same program.   The flow chart that is drawn up
prior to the actual coding of the program will probably be of
a simple nature.   However, the flow chart that is drawn up
after the program has been completed will be more detailed and
more closely parallel the actual coding.   Of course, this
latter flow chart should be the one that is included with the
final documentation of the program.

These two simple examples should illustrate the use of
flow charts.   Further examples will occur throughout the book
as specific programs are encountered.

4.6   Documentation

In this discussion we are going to look at documentation
from three different aspects: the value of documentation,

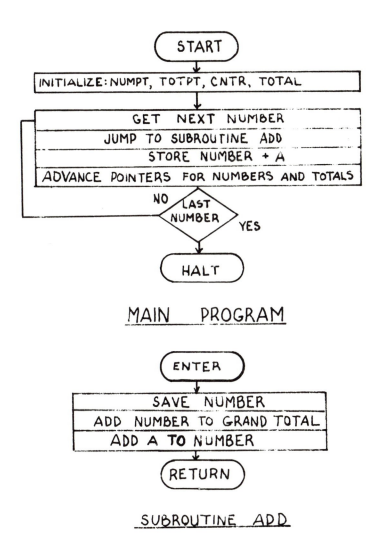

MAIN   PROGRAM

SUBROUTINE ADD

ig. 13.   Another flow chart of the program in Fig. 8.
          This typifies the flow chart of a program that
          has been completed, and would be suitable for
          documentation.

and documentation for both programmers and users. It might at
first seem strange that documentation for programmers and doc
umentation for users should be broken into two different categories. However, a little thought and experience shows that
the type of documentation needed in these two different cases
is, for the most part, entirely different.

4.6.1 Value of Documentation

In computer programming documentation is almost universally abused. In general, there is too little documentation
and what exists lacks in quality. A direct consequence of th
general situation is that programs are too closely tied to th
individuals who develop and write them. There are many insta
of large project efforts which have practically come to a sta
still; or even worse, had to be redone because the individual
responsible for the programming of the associated computer
system has not done an adequate job of documentation, or has
left the institution in the middle of the job.

Even a tiny on-line computer installation with one perso
supplying all the programming needs a complete documentation
of the programs. This is required, if for no other reason th
programming is an art which contains a multitude of minutia a
details. Although the programmer may often feel, upon the co
pletion of a program, that its details have been burnt into h
mind forever by the rigors of actually making it run, the exa
opposite is true. If the programmer is not associated with t
program for a few weeks, he will tend to forget many of the d
tails. If these details are not documented, he will have tro
returning to the program and modifying it, and he or other pe
who use the program will find many frustrations in trying to
it operate.

Documentation is commonly thought of as a specific write
up describing the program and perhaps how it is to be used.
the contrary, the documentation of a program is more than a
write-up. For example, documentation should include the late
listing of the program, and this should be dated to prove tha
it is the latest listing of the program. There should also b
a correspondingly labeled paper tape, magnetic tape or other
medium that the program has been placed on for storage. The
listing and the source tape should correspond.

Thus, the primary value of documentation is the savings
of time and labor. As indicated this savings of time and lab
even extends to the person who originally wrote the program.

4.6.2 Programmer Documentation

As has already been mentioned, there are at least two ty
of documentation that should be considered for every program.

One for the programmer and one for the user. The documentation for the programmer should be comprised of at least an up-
to-date, and dated listing of the program, an up-to-date, and
dated source and object version of the program, a flow diagram,
and a write-up describing the program.

It is well to stop at this point and define what is meant
by the source version and the object version of the program.
The source version of the program is the program in its mnemonic
form just as the programmer has written it on a coding sheet.
This might be on any one of several different media such as
paper tape, magnetic tape or punched cards. The object version
of the program is the actual binary code that has resulted from
the assembly of the program. Again this might exist on paper
tape, magnetic tape, punched cards or other media.

Turn now to a more detailed discussion of each of the four
entitles that comprise programmer documentation. It is absolutely mandatory that an up-to-date listing of the program be
available, and that this listing be accurate. Often a print-out
of a program is available with certain modifications marked on
it in pencil. Such marked up versions of the program listing
are not adequate documentation. There is no guarantee that
what resides in the computer memory corresponds to the marked
up listing. All too often a slip has been made somewhere and
the marked modification has not been made in the computer memory, or a change has been made in the computer memory without
the listing being modified. The only way to insure that the
contents of the computer memory correspond to what is on the
program listing is to have the listing printed from the computer
memory.

One of the most valuable sources of documentation to a
programmer is a properly commented listing. In all the example
programs that have preceeded, there has been a comment added to
every instruction for the sake of clarity. Although a comment
per instruction is not normally necessary, a listing should be
commented to whatever degree is necessary to make absolutely
clear what is happening in the program. In many instances a
properly commented listing is probably the most valuable piece
of documentation that can be provided for a program from a programmer standpoint. All too often lengthy programs are written
with no comment at all. Even the person that writes such a program finds he has difficulty returning to it and understanding
it at some later time.

In analogy to up-to-date and accurate listings it is also
absolutely necessary that up-to-date and accurate object and
source versions of the program exist. It is not an uncommon
occurrence to have an object version of the program which is
not quite up-to-date, i.e. does not contain the latest changes.
When the program is loaded a few changes must be made via the
computer console or the keyboard to properly modify the program
so that it will run. This has obvious disadvantages. Even the
original programmer will often forget to make the necessary

modifications after loading the program. Needless to say, a
person who did not write the program may not even be aware
that modifications are necessary, and waste large amounts of
time trying to make the program run.

As mentioned earlier, simple programs may not require fl
charts. However, programs with any complexity at all require
flow chart for complete documentation. In most instances it
relatively easy for one programmer to follow another programm
coding if he has available a well-commented listing and a sat
isfactory flow diagram.

Finally, every program should have a write-up. This is
of even the smallest of programs although the write-up in suc
instances may be quite easy. Because it is comparitively eas
to have a listing of a program, and to have an object and sou
for the program, this type of documentation is somewhat automatic. Of course this does not mean that this form of documentation cannot fall behind and not be up-to-date. On the
other hand, there is nothing automatic about the write-up of
the program. As a result, the write-up is probably the most
neglected portion of program documentation. Consequently, th
should be two goals established for the write-up of programs.
First, make the writing up of programs a habit. Two, the wri
ing up of the program should be made as painless as possible.

Little need be said about getting into the habit of maki
write-up's except, perhaps, the desirability of making the wr
up as soon as possible after the completion of the program.
the other hand, to make the write-up as painless as possible,
a standard form helps considerably in easing the burden. A
standard form insures that the essential pieces of informatio
are recorded with the least effort, and also provides a uni-
formity in the write-up's which can be particularly helpful
on large projects. To give an example of how this might go,
the form of Fig. 14 shows a format which has been successfull
used. Figure 14 includes the name of the program (which is p
sumably the one that occurs on any object version and listing
of the program), the name of the programmer or programmers,
and the date the program was completed. A version number and
a revision number much like those in engineering drawings is
included. This is to insure that the latest version of the
program and write-up is being used. A block of entries just
below the version and revision number is used for filing purposes. This includes the type of computer for which the program was written, the type of program, a number for the progr
and a year, month, date, version, and revision entries. This
type of format is amenable to filing the programs in a computerized file and extracting them as desired.

Next on the form is the space for the type of program.
Some example types are data analysis, device handler, and u-
tility. The next blank indicates whether the program is a ma
program or a subroutine.

PROGRAM NAME:		DATE:	VERSION	REVISION				
PROGRAMMER:	COMPUTER	TYPE	NUMB	Y	M	D	V	R

TYPE OF PROGRAM_____
            (Data Analysis, Device Handler, Utility, Etc.)

MAIN PROGRAM OR SUBROUTINE_____

COMPUTER WRITTEN FOR _____

PERIPHERALS REQUIRED _____
              _____

PROGRAMMING SYSTEM_____
              (PAL, FAST, MACRO 9, MAP, FORTRAN IV, Etc.)

SUBROUTINES REQUIRED
      (NOT CONTAINED)_____
              _____
              _____
              _____

GLOBALS_____
      _____

NUMBER OF CORE LOCATIONS _____

              (Specify Octal, Decimal, Etc.)

ABSOLUTE OR RELOCATABLE_____

              LOADING PROCEDURE

Fig. 14.   This is an example of a form that might be
           used to provide programmer documentation for
           a program. This would normally be the first
           sheet of the program documentation, and attempts
           to obtain all the routine information that is
           needed.

The next entry names the computer for which the program
was written because in the larger laboratories and industrial
organizations several different manufacturers' computers may
be used. The next entry asks what peripherals are required.
Again, at larger installations several computers of the same
model may be available but may have different peripheral devices attached to them. Therefore, the peripherals may limit
the computer systems on which the program can be run. The next
entry asks for the programming system, or the language in which
the program was written. The programming system is followed
by the subroutines that are required but not contained in the
object version of the program. (It is a very frustrating experience to load a program and find that it will not execute
because other subroutines must be supplied.) The next entry
asks for any globals* that the program uses. Globals are used
in computer systems which have a linking loader capability. A
linking loader can load programs that have been written entirely
separately, and the globals provide a mechanism for communications between the linked programs.

The next entry is for the number of magnetic core locations required by the program in the computer's memory. The
final entry asks whether the program is absolute or relocatable.
This line has been provided because in some computers the programs may be written in either an absolute or relocatable form.
In an absolute form they must be located in specific memory
locations. In a relocatable form they may be loaded into arbitrary locations in the computer memory. Finally, a blank
section is left for loading procedures. This is necessary because there are many details that can go into the proper loading of a program including the media on which it is stored,
and if a monitor is used, what loader is needed.

The form of Fig. 14 is not normally a complete write-up
of the program. It is meant to include those details that are
always relevant. Normally the form is considered to be only
the first page of the program write-up, and would be followed
by further details and discussions of the program in question.

4.6.3 User Documentation

Here, the word user is to be taken literally. Even a professional programmer will have occasion to use the programs
written by other programmers. In this situation a programmer
is a true user because he does not know, or does not care to
know, the actual details of how the program is written but only
what he needs to do to use the program.

---

*Globals are discussed in more detail in the chapter "Editing,
Assembling, and Debugging".

Because of its nature, user documentation is primarily concerned with instructions on how to utilize and run any particular program. It would not normally deal with the details of how the program was written. User documentation should consist of an object version of the program, a user write-up of the program, and perhaps a flow chart. However, the flow chart in this case is entirely different in nature than the flow chart that would be provided with the programmer documentation.

The write-up for user documentation probably should be more appropriately labeled a "User's Manual". A user's manual is even more difficult to get properly prepared than a programmer write-up because it is not susceptible to a form. Another difficulty is that user write-up's typically are written by programmers who can only do a good job by putting themselves in the shoes of the user who knows nothing about programming, and may not even know anything about the computer. This is, of course, a difficult request.

Some entries that might be included in a user's manual are:

1. How to start the computer and load the program.
2. A description and instructions of any equipment settings that need to be made for the proper operation of the computer system.
3. A general explanation of the philosophy of operation of the program.
4. Explanation of any keyboard commands or hardware controls that have to be exercised. It is often a good idea to also include a summary of such commands or hardware controls which can be quickly referred to at the computer console.
5. A complete description should be given of how and in what form input/output is achieved by the program.

These guidelines can be amplified by referring to an actual user's manual. Fig. 15 is the table of contents of the user's manual in question. This particular manual describes a package of four programs that were written for the analysis of data from a specific kind of spectrometer in nuclear physics. Each of the four programs performs a specific step in the analysis of the data.

The first section of the user's manual gives a short description of each program in the package. The names of the programs are DRMCON, PKLOC, EDIT, and ANAL. The second section of the manual is devoted to a description of how the package of programs is to be used. This might be called a procedure's section.

The third section is related to data pertaining to the spectrometer systems. This section enumerates data that must be supplied to the program package which describes the equipment that was used to take the experimental data. From this data equipmental effects may be removed from the experimental results.

Table of Contents

Fig. 15.   This is the table of contents from
           an actual user's manual for a package
           of programs written to analyze exper-
           imental data.

In section 4.0 a philosophy of the programming system is
given. This section describes what is expected of the user.
For example, that he is to obtain certain magnetic tapes for
his own use. It also describes where specific data is stored
at any given time in the computer system. This particular
computer system had a magnetic drum, and the information in
section 4.0 describes what data resides on the drum and what
data resides in the magnetic core memory at any given time.
    Section 5.0 gives specific details about the program pack-
age. Section 5.1 tells how to load the program package and
initialize the computer. Each of the sections 5.2 through 5.5
give details on how to use each program in the package. Section
5.6 tells how to list specific information related to the experimental data. Section 5.7 summarizes how much experimental
data may be stored on the computer's magnetic drum. Section 5.8
tells the user how to delete experimental data from the drum.
Finally, section 6.0 is simply a blank page on which the user
may make notes and comments for his own purposes, and also for
the programmers who will provide future versions of the programs.
    A useful comment can be made about the lay-out of this
user's manual. Note that in each section the pages are numbered
consecutively starting at one. By numbering the pages in this
manner the manual becomes more modular; if a major modification
in the program is made--say section 2.0 has to be completely
rewritten--then it is possible to simply rewrite section 2.0,
insert it and have an up-to-date manual.
    It has already been mentioned that flow diagrams may be
helpful for user documentation. Figure 16 gives an example of
a flow diagram that might be supplied with the user's manual
which has just been described. The flow chart indicates that
the user must first initialize the computer. Data is then
written on the computer's drum. Next, the user calls one of
the four programs from the package and executes it. Here, several alternatives are available. The user may wish to call another program from the package and execute it. He may be finished using the computer at this point, or he may want to delete
data from the drum. If data is deleted from the drum, he may
either be finished or he may wish to write additional data on
the drum.
    The flow diagram for the user documentation is entirely
different from that of the programmer documentation. In the
case of the user documentation, the emphasis is on the mechanics
of running the computer and the program and does not, in general,
dwell on any details of how the programs themselves are put together. When many decision points are available in a large program package, a flow diagram can be particularly useful.
    The important thing to be emphasized in constructing user
documentation is to write it from the viewpoint of the uninitiated. Assume that the eventual user will have no familiarity
with the program and no familiarity with the computer. User
write-up's often leave out the first steps. For example,

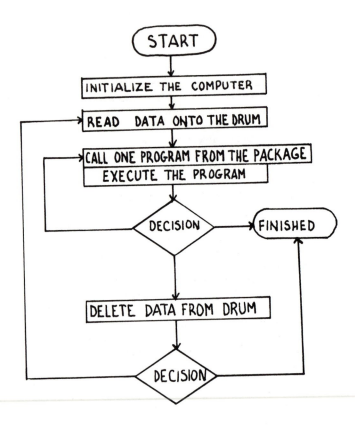

Fig. 16. A flow diagram for user documentation.
In this case the diagram instructs the
use on the proper sequence of using the
program package described in connection
with Fig. 15.

write-up's assume that the program is in the computer and that the user knows something about the switches of the console or the use of a keyboard. In fact, the program may not be in the computer, and the computer may not even be running. Furthermore, the user may not know how to turn the computer on, let alone, load the desired program. Therefore, it is not at all facetious for a user's manual to begin with instructions on how to turn the computer on.

CHAPTER 6

EDITING, ASSEMBLING AND DEBUGGING

1.0 THE DEVELOPMENT OF PROGRAMS

Prior to this chapter the mechanics of writing a program have been looked at in detail. The writing of the program really amounted to the commitment to paper of the mnemonic statements constituting the source program. This chapter concentrates on the mechanics of actually developing the source code that has been written on paper into something that runs in the computer.

1.1 The Edit-Assemble-Debug Cycle

The edit-assemble-debug cycle has already been described to some extent in the previous chapter. In short, the edit-assemble-debug cycle is the process that takes the program from a hand-written code to correctly operating binary code.

Turn to Table I which describes the steps that typically go into the edit-assemble-debug cycle. In preparing Table I it has been assumed that the program has already been placed on some computer medium. That is, the statements written on the programming sheet have been transferred to some medium such as paper tape, magnetic tape, a disk, drum, etc.

As this discussion develops, we will see that in the case of step two of Table I there is more than one means of editing the source program. In step three the word store is to be taken literally. One would often think of "store" as the placing of information in magnetic core memory and on disks or drums. It can also and will mean, in this case, storage on such media as paper tape. Likewise, in step six, store may take on the same general connotation. In step six memory map is meant to be a complete listing of the contents of memory when the computer program has been loaded into the computer. In other words, a memory map consists of a minimum of two pieces of information. One piece of information is the memory location and the second is the contents of that memory location.

Table I.   Steps typically involved in the edit-assemble-debug cycle.

<u>EDIT</u>

1. Load editor program and source program into computer.
2. Edit source program.
3. Store new source program.

<u>ASSEMBLE</u>

4. Load assembler program and source program into computer.
5. Assemble source program.
6. Store object program, and print source program, memory map, and supplementary information.

<u>DEBUG</u>

7. Load object program into computer.
8. Attempt to execute program. If not successful, debug

The supplementary information consists of symbol tables, assembler diagnostics and similar data, all of which are explained later in this chapter. Step eight represents the debugging operation which can be done in more than one way. Finally, the arrows of Table I indicate the edit-assemble-debug cycle. The arrow going from step six to step one indicates that errors have been found in the assembly process requiring one to immediately go back to the edit phase to correct these errors. If no errors are found in the assembly, then one proceeds to step eight where errors are probably found in the debug operation and the return is made to step one to again edit out these errors.

There are many facets to the accomplishment of the steps in Table I, and also many ways to implement each step. Regardless of how the implementation is brought about the computer peripheral equipment plays a very decisive role in the efficiency of the edit-assemble-debug cycle.

It is important to know that program development at the on-line computer itself is not always necessary. If the on-line computer user has access to a central computing facility then to a large extent program development for the on-line computer may be done on the other computer facility. Computer facilities other than the on-line computer facility will be referred to as off-line computers. Utilizing an off-line computer facility for the program development of an on-line computer often alleviates many problems.

In the following two sections on-line program development
and off-line program development are discussed. It must be
realized that all of the program development need not take
place on either the on-line facility or the off-line facility.
There are a number of choices available as illustrated in
Fig. 1. The whole edit-assemble-debug cycle may be done completely at the on-line computer. Another path that one might
choose is to edit and assemble the computer programs on the
off-line computer and then debug them on the on-line computer.
If a simulator program is available on the off-line computer,
then the program may be taken through the complete cycle off-
line. As shown in Fig. 1 there are other possible combinations.

1.2   On-Line Program Development

To provide a better understanding of what the edit-assemble-
debug cycle is like on an on-line computer we are going to look
at two extreme cases. In the first case, it is assumed that
the on-line computer has only one peripheral that can be used
for program development. This one peripheral will be a Teletype
terminal. In the second case, a system is assumed which is
equipped with optimal high-speed peripherals.
Before going on to the first case, it is necessary to look
at a Teletype unit in more detail for those who do not have a
familiarity with this device. Future chapters describe the
programming of Teletype terminals and other detailed consideration. Here the concern is with the physical appearance and
general use of the unit. In Fig. 2 a photograph of a Teletype
unit is provided. There are several different models available,
but all have considerable similarity with the one shown here.
First, it should be noted that the Teletype terminal has a keyboard and printing device that is very similar to a typewriter.
Shown on the left side of the keyboard and printing unit is
paper tape equipment which includes a unit to read paper tape
and a unit to punch paper tape. (Paper tape equipment is optional). Suffice it to say, at this point, that characters
are represented on paper tape by holes that are punched by the
paper tape punch*. Whenever a paper tape is fed through the
reader unit these holes are sensed and the characters thereby
interpreted and placed in the computer memory. One other important aspect of Teletype units is that most of the models
provided with on-line computer systems have a speed of ten
characters per second. The paper tape punch, the paper tape
reader, and the printer all operate at this speed.

---

*Physically the paper tape used is a long strip of paper one
  inch wide.

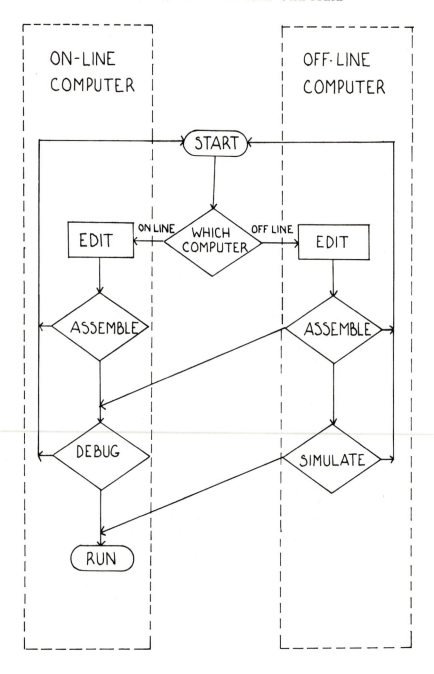

Fig. 1.   A flow chart showing the possible combinations of performing the edit-assemble-debug cycle on either the on-line computer, or the off-line computer, or both.

Fig. 2.   An ASR 33 Teletype unit.   This photograph provided
courtesy of the Teletype Corporation.

Now remember that in the first case outlined above the
Teletype unit is the only program development peripheral available on the computer system. This automatically means that
the source version of programs and the object versions of programs are stored on paper tape, and hence, the whole operation
of the on-line computer system is centered around the utilization of paper tapes.

Table II gives in some detail the steps, speeds, and time
required to complete the edit-assemble-debug cycle on a computer
system equipped with only a Teletype unit. The first column
describes the step that is being performed. The second column
gives the speed at which the step is executed. Finally, in
column three an estimate is given of the magnitude of the time
that elapses during the step. These elapsed times can vary a
great deal depending on the length of the program that is being
developed.

Several specific comments may be made about the steps of
Table II. In steps two, three, and four, variations may take
place. For example, if the computer system being used has a
very small amount of magnetic core memory, then the memory in
many cases will not be large enough to hold both the editor
program and the source version of the user's program. In these
instances a mechanism is usually set up by which the source
version of the program may be broken into several segments,
each of which fit into the computer's memory with the editor
program. This results in a subcycle between steps two, three,
and four. That is, one reads a segment of the source program
from paper tape, edits this segment of the program, and then
punches the new segment of the program on paper tape. At this
point one cycles back to step two, and starts work on the next
segment of the source program.

In steps six, seven and eight, it has been assumed that
the computer system is provided with a two-pass assembler. The
significance of a two-pass assembler is explored in more detail
later in the chapter. At this point it is only necessary to
know that a two-pass assembler actually requires, as indicated
in Table II, that the source program be read into the computer
twice in succession. Step eight indicates an optional pass
three. This step is required if a listing, a memory map, and
supplemental information are to be obtained. The reason is
that in pass two the object version of the program is punched
on paper tape. It is impossible to list the program on the
teleprinter at the same time the object paper tape is being
punched because of a mechanical linkage between the Teletype
punch and printer unit. The printer unit only accepts ASCII
code* while the object version of the program is usually in

---

*The USA Standard Code for Information Interchange. See the
 Glossary and Appendix V.

Table II. The steps, speeds, and times required to complete
           the edit-assemble-debug cycle on a computer system
           equipped with only a Teletype unit.

Step	Speed	Magnitude of Elapsed Time
EDIT		
1. Read editor program from paper tape.	10 cps**	Minutes
2. Read source program from paper tape.	10 cps	Minutes
3. Edit the source program from TTY* keyboard.	Human	Minutes to Hours
4. Punch new source program on paper tape.	10 cps	Minutes
ASSEMBLE		
5. Read assembler program from paper tape.	10 cps	Minutes
6. Pass 1 of assembly: read source program from paper tape.	10 cps	Minutes
7. Pass 2 of assembly: read source program from paper tape and punch object program on paper tape.	10 cps	Minutes
8. Pass 3 of assembly (Optional): read source program from paper tape and print source program, memory map, and supplementary information.	10 cps	Minutes to Hours
9. Read object program from paper tape.	10 cps	Minutes
10. Attempt to execute the program. If not successful, debug.	Human	Minutes to Hours

*TTY stands for Teletype unit.
**cps stands for characters per second.

some binary code. This means that during the punching of an
object tape, jibberish is printed on the teleprinter because
the characters are not ASCII. Hence, the requirement that a
listing must be obtained separately from the punching of the
object tape.

Several overall comments may be made about program development on a computer system with only a Teletype unit. First,
quite a number of steps are involved in one edit-assemble-debug cycle. It can also be noted from the third column, that
a large amount of time elapses in one cycle. A very important
point to note is that of the ten steps only two are dependent
on the speed of the human user. This immediately indicates that
the other eight steps should be optimized and made as fast as
possible. From the second column it can be seen that virtually
nothing can proceed faster than the ten character per second
speed of the Teletype unit.

Turn now to the second case of on-line program develop-
ment--the case where fast devices are attached to the computer
system for program development. In this particular case we
will not be specific about the peripherals used. It is assumed
that there are bulk memory storage peripherals available, such
as disk, drum or magnetic tapes (all of these devices are described in the chapter "Computer Peripherals"). For a printing
device a peripheral that is equivalent to a printer which can
print at least one hundred, 80 character lines per minute is
assumed. It is also assumed that a Teletype unit is attached
to the computer system. This is not at all unrealistic since
Teletype units are almost universally supplied with on-line
computers. However, in this case the keyboard and printer of
the Teletype unit are all that will be utilized in program development. The Teletype printer is primarily used to display
what has been typed on the Teletype keyboard while the fast
printer is used for program listings and other more voluminous
text.

Table III again summarizes steps, speeds, and times required to complete the edit-assemble-debug cycle on the computer with the faster peripherals that have just been described.
Of course, in this case the second column can only give magnitude of speed because several different peripherals are permitted in the system.

Again, several specific comments may be made about individual steps in the edit-assemble-debug cycle. In steps one,
two, and four note that all program storage is on the bulk
memory peripheral. In step three it is assumed that the editing is being done from the Teletype keyboard, for the keyboard is still the most eminently suited device for carrying
out editing operations. Note that in step six a two-pass assembler is still assumed. However, the two assembler passes
become one step in the present system so far as the user is
concerned because the assembler automatically executes both
pass one and pass two from a bulk memory device as it needs
them.

Table III. The steps, speeds, and times required to complete
the edit-assemble-debug cycle on a computer system
equipped with a high speed bulk storage device(s)
and a fast printing device.

Step	Magnitude Of Speed	Magnitude of Elapsed Time
EDIT		
1. Read editor from bulk memory.	1,000 to 20,000 cps.**	Seconds
2. Read source program from bulk memory.	1,000 to 20,000 cps.	Seconds
3. Edit the source program from TTY* keyboard.	Human	Minutes to Hours
4. Write new source program on bulk memory.	1,000 to 20,000 cps.	Seconds
ASSEMBLE		
5. Read assembler programs from bulk memory.	1,000 to 20,000 cps.	Seconds
6. Pass 1 and pass 2 of assembly; write object program on bulk memory.	1,000 to 20,000 cps.	Seconds
7. Print source program, memory map, and supplementary information.	125-1,200 cps.	Minutes
DEBUG		
8. Read object program from bulk memory.	1,000 to 20,000 cps.	Seconds
9. Attempt to execute the program. If not successful, debug.	Human	Minutes to Hours

*TTY stands for Teletype unit.
**cps. stands for characters/second.

What overall comments may be made in this second case u-
tilizing faster peripherals? First of all, the speeds of the
peripherals themselves are from 100 to 1,000 times faster than
the Teletype unit given in the first case. The elapsed time
for the edit-assemble-debug cycle is perhaps 100 times shorter.
The reason that this factor is not equivalent to the increase
in the peripheral device speeds is because of user interaction
during the edit-assemble-debug steps. The edit-assemble-debug
cycle can go from the order of hours to complete one cycle in
the case of a system with only a Teletype unit to a few minutes
in a system with the faster peripherals.

One point must be stressed in the second case. With a
fast printing device the user can enjoy the advantages of a complete listing. Because the printing device is fast, it is possible to print almost any information desired that is associated
with the assembly. In the case with only the Teletype unit a
complete memory map, source program listing, and supplementary
information may require literally hours to print for a lengthy
program. A printing device with the speeds indicated in the
second case could do the same printing operation in minutes.
It should also be pointed out that the speeds mentioned for the
printing device in the second case are about the minimum that
one can find among the faster printers. Some printers may be
an order of magnitude or more faster than the speeds mentioned
here.

It should be noted that there are still only two steps
that depend upon human speed.

What conclusions can be drawn from these two example cases?
The most obvious one is that the addition of faster bulk storage
and fast printing devices can dramatically improve the execution
of the edit-assemble-debug cycle. However, is it justifiable
to add these peripherals for program development, if they are
not required for the on-line process? This is a very important
point because fast printing devices and fast bulk storage devices can easily cost as much or more than the computer itself.

Another problem that often occurs with on-line computers
and their associated program development is the amount of time
available for the program development. If the computer is
attached to an experiment or a process that runs twenty-four
hours a day, there may be virtually no computer time available
for program development.

There are two approaches to solving these problems. One
approach is to go to a foreground-background operation. This
is a type of operation where the computer might be controlling
a process and at the same time be doing program development.
In this case the control of the process is a foreground operation while the program development is a background operation.
Essentially, it means that whenever the computer is not required
for the process control, it spends its time, in the background,
on the program development phases. The other, and often more
feasible approach, is to develop programs on an off-line computer

1.3   Off-Line Program Development

If an off-line computer facility, such as a computing center, is available different methods of developing software become possible. Program development on off-line computers often lifts the major restrictions that are associated with typical on-line computers. The central computing facility usually has enough peripherals to satisfy any needs that may arise in on-line program development. Fast printing devices, magnetic tape, bulk storage, and so forth are normally available on such computer systems. Also, large computing systems typically have much more magnetic core memory than on-line computing systems which lifts many restrictions associated with assemblers and other program development software.

There are two separate enterprises that may be undertaken on the off-line computer system. One is to develop an off-line assembler. Here an off-line assembler is defined to be an assembler program that is executed in the off-line computer system but assembles binary object code for the on-line computer system. This should become clear as the discussion develops. The other development that may be undertaken is to construct a simulator. This is a program which executes on the off-line computer system but simulates the operation of the on-line computer system. Both the off-line assembler and the simulator are taken up in further detail later in this chapter.

It has been mentioned previously that a keyboard makes an ideal device for interactive editing. However, interactive keyboards and editor programs are not common at central computing facilities. If an interactive capability is not available at the off-line computing facility, then punched cards make the best medium for non-interactive editing of source programming. Normally, one on-line computer instruction is punched per card; thus, it is very easy to edit the source program by simply removing cards with computer instructions that have been modified and repunching them, or inserting more than one card where it is necessary, or to delete more than one card. Punched card equipment and the facilities for handling punched cards are almost universally found at central computing facilities.

Table IV presents the steps, speeds and times required to complete the edit-assemble-debug cycle utilizing an off-line computer facility. Again, several specific comments may be made. Step one now represents the edit portion of the cycle. Step three indicates a two-pass assembler. It is still advantageous in many ways to implement a two-pass assembler on the off-line computer facility even though it might have ample memory to implement a one-pass assembler. In step five the final storage of the object program must be on a medium that is available to the on-line computer. If the on-line computer system has a Teletype unit as its only program development device, then the off-line computer system must punch the object

Table IV. The steps, speeds and times required to complete
the edit-assemble-debug cycle utilizing an off-
line computer facility.

Step	Magnitude of Speed	Magnitude of Elapsed Time
EDIT		
1. Punch cards and place in card deck.	Human	Minutes
ASSEMBLE		
2. Read assembler program and source program from punched cards.	500-1000 cps*	Minutes
3. Execute pass 1 and pass 2 of assembly.	Microseconds/ operation	Seconds
4. Print source program, memory map, and sup-plementary information.	125-1200 cps	Minutes
5. Store object program on a medium compatible to on-line computer.	**	**
DEBUG		
6. Load program into off-line computer.	**	**
7. Execute program in off-line computer, and obtain diagnostics.	Microseconds/ operation	Minutes
8. Load program into on-line computer.	**	**
9. Attempt to execute pro-gram. If not successful, debug.	Human	Minutes to Hours

*cps. stands for characters per second.
**Dependent on medium used.

code on a paper tape. Steps six and seven are taken when a
simulator program is available. Step seven would be a very
nice step to execute interactively, i.e. execution with the
user as an observer to the events and with some control over
the off-line computer facility to change the course of events
as the on-line program is simulated. However, few off-line
computer facilities have this interactive capability. If a
simulator program is not available then the user skips directly
from step five to step eight. Steps eight and nine are the
loading of the object program into the on-line computer and the
execution of it to see that it executes properly. Even though
the program may have been successfully simulated in the off-
line computer system, it is necessary to make a trial execution in the on-line computer system. Reasons for this are
taken up later.

     As in the previous examples of program development, there
are still only two human steps involved in the edit-assemble-
debug cycle. In the present instance it is important to note
that all of the steps except one, eight, and nine are executed
by personnel other than the user in a typical instance; usually
computer operators. Therefore, in the present case it is interesting to note that those steps which are primarily dependent on human speed are executed by the actual user of the on-
line computer; representing a great efficiency of time from the
user's standpoint.

2.0 ON-LINE EDITORS

     Only on-line editors are discussed here. The type of ed-
itor needed to edit source programs is referred to as a text
editor. Editing facilities generally available at off-line
facilities tend to concentrate on file handling capability*.
For this reason editors commonly available at off-line computing
centers are not applicable. Also, it has been amply demonstrated
in the preceding that an interactive capability is extremely
important with editors, and also not generally available at off-
line computing facilities.

2.1 Purpose

     Generally the on-line editor program is used to first place
a newly written source program onto some computer medium such

---

*A specific grouping of information written on a magnetic tape,
 disk, or other storage as a separate entity is usually referred to as a file. For example, a file might consist of a
 complete program.

as paper tape, magnetic tape, etc. Then, during the course of
the edit-assemble-debug cycle the editor is used to correct
errors that are found in the program.

The editor has features built in to make the edited output appear in the format that the on-line computer requires
for its assembler. However, it must be remembered that the
editor knows nothing about the assembler and should not be restricted in any way from handling any character that can be
typed on the keyboard. For this reason, one of the applications
that on-line editor programs can often be used for is text
editing.

2.2   Definitive Characteristics

What would be an ideal editor? An ideal editor would be
able to find any character or group of characters in a text,
e.g. a program, and modify or replace them with any other arbitrary number of characters. Instantly. Furthermore, the
ideal editor would be able to do this in any length of file.

This definition simultaneously defines what an ideal editor is and implies what the difficulties are. Normally the
smallest unit of information in a file is one character. Therefore, we are asking that the editor be able to search out any
piece of information, i.e. any character in the file. Furthermore, having found the specific character, that character may
be modified or replaced with one or more characters. In replacing a character with more than one character, the file is,
in effect, spread apart and an arbitrary string of characters
inserted. From the computer standpoint this is somewhat difficult. In our ideal editor we have also asked for the ability
to look for patterns because we want to be able to look for
strings of specific characters. Thus, the editor must be able
to take an arbitrary string of characters and match them with
all other strings of characters in a file to see if a match
can be made.

It is particularly stringent to say that the editor shall
be able to search and perform replace operations instantly.
Even though these operations are being done at computer speeds
there are so many operations to be performed that the length of
time required may be quite large even on the human scale of
time. Also the length of the file has obvious implications in
the file handling capability of the editor itself and the bulk
storage requirements. Even the shortest of source program files
has several hundred characters in it.

In view of the above discussion, what should one look for
in an editor, and hence from the user's viewpoint, what should
be offered in the editor for an on-line computer system.

1) What is the smallest piece of information that the editor can handle? If the smallest piece of information is not
a character, but perhaps a whole line of the source program,

then the amount of manual labor is greatly increased in the
editing process because of the decreased search and replace
capabilities that automatically result.

2)   What are the file handling capabilities of the editor?
Can the program source file be read from more than one peripheral device? What are the size restrictions on the length of
the files? Is it possible to link different files into one
file or, on the other hand, to be able to separate one file
into several files?

3)   What is the largest block of information that the editor can act on at any given time? Ideally, the editor should
be able to have the complete file at its disposal. If the file
is on a magnetic tape and only one line of the source program
is read into the computer memory at any given time, then only
this line can be edited. Therefore, if it is desired to edit
a line that is far removed from the current one, a lengthy
magnetic tape operation may be involved. Of course in the limit, the size of the block of information that the editor may
act on is dependent on the amount of memory that is left in
the computer after loading the editor program. Therefore, a
definite trade-off exists between the functions that can be
built into the editor and the length of the source file, i.e.
the size of the editor versus the block size that the editor
may handle.

Having looked at some of the macroscopic features of editors, turn now to some microscopic features.

2.3   Typical Features

We are now going to discuss several features that may appear
in editors. It should be noted that although an editor should
ideally be able to manipulate individual characters the nature
of a source program is still to be line-oriented, i.e. each line
normally represents one computer instruction. Therefore, even
in a text editor that can deal with individual characters, many
features can be found for manipulating complete lines (instructions) of the program.

1.   Text Modification. Text modification is the very heart
of the editor program. All other features are simply aides to
this end. Text modification as defined here includes such operations as appending text to existing text, deleting text, inserting text, and the replacement of text with other text.

2.   Error Recovery. It is highly important that an on-line
editor program provides the user with the ability to recover
from errors that he has made at the keyboard. Often error recovery includes the capability to restart a whole line. If the
user has typed several characters in a line, the easiest way to
recover may be to simply restart the line. On the other hand,
if a typing error has occurred which only affects the last character typed then it is desirable for the editor to have a

feature which permits the user to "erase" the last character.
Of course, it is impossible for the erase operation to physically erase the printed character from the typewriter page, but
the character is removed from the computer memory.

3. _Orientation_. In most editing operations the user does
not have the whole program in view on the typewritten page before him. Also when a program is being heavily edited its appearance changes rapidly. In such situations, the user needs
capability to know at any given time where he is located in
the program, and an easy means of getting anywhere else in the
program. One way to provide this capability in the editor program is to either number the different lines of the computer
program or consider them to be numbered. The user can then
say, "go to line ten", for example. It is also convenient to
have features in the editor program which permit the user to
specify that the editor move to any given tag in the program.
Also, it is quite useful to be able to go to the top (the first
line) of the program or to the bottom (the last line) of the
program.

4. _Format Aids_. Assembler programs often require rather
strict formats for the source programs. For example, a program
is often formatted into various fields made up of individual
columns. The tags may be in one field, the operator another
field, the address in a third field, and finally the comment
in a fourth field. However, almost all on-line computers are
supplied with Teletype units which do not have tabulation features on them. Tabulation must be supplied within the editor
program. Typically the user strikes a designated Teletype key
and the editor program causes the teleprinter to "type" spaces
until it arrives at the first column of the next field.

5. _Search Capability_. In order to be able to move about
easily in a program that is being edited, the editor program
needs a good search capability. This search capability would
include the ability to search out specific lines, specific tags,
and specific strings of characters.

6. _File Handling_. It is desirable that the editor have
several file handling capabilities. It should for example have
the ability to open a file and to close a file. To open a file
means that the editor program may operate on and modify the
file. On the other hand, after a file has been closed, it should
be impossible to modify that file. The editor program should
have the ability to read, write, and add to a file; the ability
to link separate files; and the ability to separate one file into
other files. The user should also have the choice of whether
the modified file shall replace the old file; otherwise file
handling can become quite cumbersome.

2.4 Peripheral Equipment and Codes

From the preceding discussions it should be apparent that
the utility of an editor depends as critically on the peripheral

devices available, as the features built into the editor program itself. Remember the extreme example of a small computer
with only a Teletype unit for program development. The slow
speed of a Teletype unit, the handling of paper tape, and the
lack of sufficient buffer space in the computer memory made
the situation difficult; not the lack of sophistication in the
editor.

Ideally, one would desire enough magnetic core memory in
the computer to hold not only the editor program but the largest
of source programs. This is obviously impractical from a cost
standpoint. The alternative is to have the portions of the program that cannot be stored in the computer memory to be stored
on bulk storage media. After the magnetic core memory of the
computer itself, the best storage medium is probably magnetic
disk or magnetic drum because information may be accessed randomly and rapidly. Magnetic disks and drums are considerably
cheaper than magnetic core memory. The next best bulk storage
medium is probably magnetic tape. However, magnetic tape is
not randomly accessible and hence, not as rapid as magnetic
disk or drum. Therefore, user's attempting to edit from magnetic tape find themselves being considerably slowed by the re-
action time of the magnetic tape equipment. After magnetic
tape, the least desirable medium to edit from is probably paper
tape.

It is also important that editors have some device independence. By this it is meant that the editor should be able
to access and handle files on different peripheral devices. If
a computer system has a disk as a peripheral, it is most dis-
turbing to find that the editor program provided only operates
with paper tape.

Editors are, by necessity, oriented around a specific character code*. For example, if paper tape is being used, a certain pattern of holes punched in the paper tape might represent
the letter A. Another pattern would represent the letter B, etc.
Most on-line computers supplied with Teletype units use the ASCII
code. The primary reason is that the Teletype unit itself uses
this code and is built mechanically around this code.

The ASCII code requires eight binary bits to represent one
character**. Therefore, the patterns just mentioned are made

---

* It is important to note that the word code is used with a dual
  meaning. In this case the word code has been used as a representation of characters such as the alphabet and the numbers.
  Previously, the word code has been used in phrases, such as computer code, meaning instructions that the user has written for
  the computer.
**Strictly speaking the ASCII code only requires seven bits to
  be uniquelly defined, but an eighth bit is often added, usually
  for designating parity. This is fully illustrated in Appendix
  V.

up of permutations of these eight bits. The editor must be
designed to manipulate these eight bit entities. In many manufacturer's computers eight bit groupings are referred to as
bytes. Thus, common references to byte-oriented computers,
meaning computers that have hardware specifically designed to
handle eight bit groups of data. The handling of the ASCII
character set in byte-oriented computers is rather straightforward. However, if a computer does not have a word length
which is a multiple of eight bits then packing schemes must be
devised: the packing of more than one ASCII character in one
computer word. If a computer has a sixteen bit word length,
then two ASCII characters nicely fit into one word.

3.0 ASSEMBLERS

The assembler program is certainly one of the most important items of software that the manufacturer provides with a
computer. It is probably also one of the least understood.
For this reason the following discussion enters into the rudi-
mentary details of how an assembler operates.

3.1 Purpose

The basic purpose of an assembler program is to convert
the instructions that make up a source program to binary numbers that the computer may operate upon. This is a deceivingly
simple statement. Although this is the primary function of an
assembler, many periphery functions are added to the assembler
program. Primarily these periphery functions stem from three
sources: convenience, the addressing scheme of the computer,
and the sophistication of the loader program that is supplied
with the computer. From the conceptual standpoint the primary
advantage of an assembler is to allow the user of a computer
to write his program with mnemonics rather than in an absolute
(binary) code. It also allows him to tag locations and think
in terms of these tags rather than of absolute memory addresses.

3.2 Rudiments of Assembler Operation

It would be easy to write a complete book on the subject
of how assemblers work and how assembler programs are written.
The purpose here is not to cover the topic so exhaustively but
to attempt to convey a basic understanding of assemblers. No
attempt is made to describe how to write an assembler.

It is important to keep in mind that when one talks of
program assembly there are actually two programs within the
computer. One is the assembler program itself which is being
executed, and the other is the user's source program which is
being assembled, i.e. acted upon by the assembler program.

There are two major types of assembler programs. One is referred to as a one-pass assembler and the other is referred to as a two-pass assembler. The terms one-pass and two-pass may be taken rather literally. The one-pass assembler requires that the user's source program be read into the computer once. The two-pass assembler requires that the user's source program be read into the computer twice. The two-pass assembler is probably the most prevalent and is the one discussed in the following example.

A convention for format is usually established for the source code. The format to the right of the vertical line in Fig. 3 is a typical assembler format. The first field contains the tags. The second field contains the operation and the third field contains addresses. Finally, the fourth field contains any comment that the programmer might want to add. Once a format is chosen, then the assembler program, with a few exceptions, automatically knows that anything that occurs in the tag field is a tag, anything that occurs in the instruction field is an instruction and so forth. In the example of Fig. 3 the four fields have been blocked off by putting them in specified columns. Some assemblers simply separate the fields with spaces or some other form of punctuation.

Typically the assembler controls the reading of the source program from storage devices. The reading operation may bring only one instruction (one line of the source program) into the computer at a time. The assembler then operates on this individual line, i.e. assembles this one line. The assembly process usually involves the breaking of the line into the individual fields and then taking an action that is appropriate to each column. In the first pass (the first reading of the source program) the assembler builds tables or dictionaries. The number and types of tables is related to the sophistication of the assembler. The more sophisticated assemblers have more tables.

In the present example of Fig. 3 there will be a system symbol table, a pseudo-instruction table and a user symbol table. The system symbol table is permanently built into the assembler program, and is always in the computer's memory along with the assembler program. This permanent symbol table defines the instructions that are associated with the computer in question. Fig. 4 represents a portion of the permanent symbol table; that portion which is needed to assemble the program of Fig. 3. As shown in Fig. 4 the permanent symbol table contains each of the computer's instructions and the binary equivalent of the instruction. The equivalents are shown in Fig. 4 as octal numbers for convenience.

Pseudo-instructions and the pseudo-instruction table are defined and discussed later.

A user symbol table is built each time a user's source program is assembled, and therefore, is not permanently resident in the assembler program. The user symbol table is similar in construction to the permanent symbol table, and contains

Line	Tag	Operation	Comment
		Instruction Address	
1	*200		
2	/A PRØGRAM TØ ADD A SERIES ØF NUMBERS		
3	/WRITTEN BY W. W. AUTHØR. SEPT.6, 1969.		
4		/INITIALIZE	
5		CLA	
6		TAD NUMLØC	
7		DCA NUMNEX	
8		TAD NN	
9		DCA CNTR	
10		/START MAIN PRØGRAM	
11	START,	TAD I NUMNEX	/ADD NEXT NUMBER
12		ISZ NUMNEX	
13		ISZ CNTR	/LAST NUMBER
14		JMP START	/NØ, ADD ANØTHER
15		DCA TØTAL	/YES, SAVE GRAND TØTAL
16		HLT	/HALT
17	NUMLØC,	NUM1	/LØCATIØN ØF 1ST NUMBER
18	NUMNEX,	0	/LØCATIØN ØF NEXT NUMBER
19	NN,	-5	/NUMBER ØF NUMBERS
20	CNTR,	0	/LØØP CØUNTER
21	TØTAL,	0	/GRAND TØTAL
22		DECIMAL	
23	NUM1,	6	/1ST NUMBER
24		25	/2ND NUMBER
25		2	/3RD NUMBER
26		11	/4TH NUMBER
27		7	/5TH NUMBER
28	$		

Fig. 3.   A sample program written for the purpose of demonstrating how assembler programs function.   The program is in the format in which it would be written
with the exception that a left-hand column has been
added which contains line numbers.   These line numbers serve no purpose other than to facilitate the
discussion of the program.

INSTRUCTION	OCTAL EQUIVALENT
CLA	7200
TAD	1000
DCA	3000
ISZ	2000
JMP	5000
HLT	7402

Fig. 4.   A portion of a permanent symbol table that would be
stored within the assembler program.

those symbols defined by the user. In this case the numeric
values associated with the symbols no longer refer to the
binary representation of an instruction but to the address in
memory at which the symbol is located. The amount of memory
space required by the user's symbol table is not to be taken
lightly. It is possible for the user's symbol table to contain several hundred to a few thousand entries. This leads
to a trade off between the amount of available memory allotted
for the user symbol table and the assembler program itself.

Turn now to an example of how an actual program might be
assembled. The program is written with PDP-8 instruction and
with some PDP-8 assembler conventions. However, we will not
restrict ourselves here to the methods actually used in the
PDP-8 assembler, but will assume general assembler features to
serve our purposes. Thus, this example is to be thought of as
only the way an assembler might operate and not as a description of a specific assembler. The example program is that of
Fig. 3.

It is important to ask what the situation is at this point
in time. First, the assembler program has been loaded into the
computer. Secondly, the source program as shown in Fig. 3 to
the right of the vertical line, exists on a paper tape, magnetic
tape or some other storage medium. The column of numbers to
the left of the vertical line has been added for convenience of
discussion.

When the assembler is put into execution it immediately
turns to line one of the source program. The asterisk in the
tag column of a source program is an instruction to the assembler. In this case, the instruction tells the assembler that
the object program is to be loaded starting at the memory location two hundred (octal). The assembler takes account of
this fact by virtue of a memory location which it uses as a
location counter. The use of the location counter is quite
similar to the hardware program counter that has been previously described*. The purpose of the location counter is to allow
the assembler program to keep track of what computer memory location it is presently working with. These memory locations
are those that the program will be loaded into after it is
assembled. Thus, the example program of Fig. 3 will be loaded
starting at memory location octal two hundred. What has really
happened is: the assembler upon encountering the asterisk has
set the location counter to the value of two hundred.

The assembler next goes to line two of the source program.
The slash character is another instruction to the assembler
program. In this instance the assembler knows that the slash
indicates everything which follows on that particular line is

---

program counters were discussed in the section on subroutines
of the chapter "Programming".

a comment. Therefore, the assembler ignores line two of the source program and for the same reason ignores lines three and four. Note that the slash can be used in any field. Comments do not advance the location counter, and do not result in any binary code in the object version of the program. Allowing comments to be scattered throughout the program provides one of the best possible means of documenting programs.

The assembler program turns next to line five of the sour program. Because the entry of this line is in the instruction field, the assembler immediately goes to its permanent symbol table, a portion of which has been shown in Fig. 4. The assem bler methodically compares the contents of the instruction fie with each entry in the left-hand column of Fig. 4. A match will be obtained for the entry marked CLA. Depending upon the sophistication of the assembler, either no action is taken at this point, or a note may be made that the symbol of line five is in the permanent symbol table. No use is made of the octal equivalent 7200 of the CLA instruction in this first pass. Th location counter is incremented to the value 201.

When the assembler program reads line six it again finds something in the instruction field, goes to the permanent symb table, and repeats the operation of line five. Upon finding the symbol NUMLØC, the assembler returns again to the permanen symbol table, but of course, does not find this symbol there. NUMLØC is then placed in the left-hand column of the user symb table. At this time no entry is made in the right-hand column of the user symbol table because the assembler does not know in what memory location the symbol NUMLØC is located. After operating on line six, the location counter is incremented to 202. The user's symbol table at this time appears as follows:

                    NUMLØC   ----

The assembler continues to lines seven, eight and nine in turn, and proceeds in exactly the same manner as in line six. After operating on each line the location counter is increment After line nine, the user symbol table appears as follows:

                    NUMLØC   ----
                    NUMNEX   ----
                    NN   ----
                    CNTR   ----

The location counter now contains 205.

When the assembler program comes to line 10 it identifies the line as being a comment. Therefore, no assembler action i taken, and the location counter is not incremented.

When the assembler program reaches line 11 it finds an entry in the tag column for the first time. By virtue of the fact that the entry occurs in the tag column, and is followed by a comma, the assembler immediately knows that the contents of the column is a user defined symbol. In other words, writi a tag in this column is equivalent to declaring a symbol. The

ssembler adds START to the left-hand column of the user's
symbol table and puts the number 205, the current value of the
location counter, in the right-hand side of the symbol table.
The symbol table at this time appears as follows:

NUMLØC	----
NUMNEX	----
NN	----
CNTR	----
START	0205

s before, the TAD in the instruction field is identified in
he permanent symbol table. No further action is taken on this
pass. Likewise "I", standing for indirect address, is also
gnored on this first pass. The assembler in looking at the
ddress column of line 11 again finds that the symbol NUMNEX
s not in the permanent symbol table, but upon comparison finds
hat it is already in the user symbol table. Therefore, no
urther action is taken on this symbol. The slash of the last
ield is again recognized as the beginning of a comment and the
est of line 11 is ignored.

The assembler proceeds in the same manner until line 17.
t line 17 NUMLØC is located in the tag field so the assembler
oes to the user symbol table where NUMLØC is already entered.
t this time the assembler is able to add the corresponding
alue 213 in the right-hand column of the user's symbol table,
here 213 is the current value of the location counter. The
ssembler goes on to the instruction column of line 17 and finds
here the symbol NUM1. Comparison shows that NUM1 is in neither
he permanent symbol table or the user symbol table; therefore,
he symbol NUM1 is added to the user's symbol table.

When line 18 is read by the assembler program the value 214
s added to the user symbol table in the spot corresponding to
he symbol NUMNEX. Upon looking at the contents of the instruc-
ion field it finds the value zero. Because this is a numeric
alue it can be ignored on the first pass.

In line 22 the assembler finds the word DECIMAL in the op-
ration field. Comparison shows this to be in the assembler's
seudo-instruction table; that is, DECIMAL is a pseudo-instruc-
ion to the assembler. It is called a pseudo-instruction be-
ause it is an instruction to the assembler and results in no
bject code being produced. In this particular case, the pseudo-
nstruction DECIMAL tells the assembler that all numeric values
hich follow are to be considered as decimal numbers rather than
ctal numbers. Likewise, there is a pseudo-instruction ØCTAL
hich tells the assembler that all following numbers are to be
nterpreted as octal numbers. When the assembler is started
t is assumed that the ØCTAL pseudo-instruction is in force.

In a manner similar to what has already been indicated,
he assembler proceeds to line 28 where it encounters the dollar
ign. In this particular assembler the dollar sign indicates
he end of program. At this point the assembler has completed

the first pass. The user symbol table now appears as shown
in Fig. 5.

At this point the second pass of the assembler may beg
What course of action is taken at this point depends on the
peripheral devices that are on the computer system. If the
source program is on paper tape, the user must reload the p
tape into the reader. If the source program is on magnetic
tape the assembler program would probably automatically rew
the magnetic tape back to the beginning of the source progr

The primary purpose of the second pass through the ass
is to generate the binary object code (binary version of th
program). Depending upon the peripherals that are availabl
a listing of the program may or may not be obtained on the
pass of the program. As we have already seen, if the listi
device is the Teletype unit and the program is to be punche
the paper tape punch of the Teletype unit, then it is impos
to simultaneously obtain the object paper tape and the list
of the program. It is also important to note that the rest
ing of the assembler for the second pass does not destroy a
of the tables. The permanent symbol table, the user's symb
table, and the pseudo-instruction symbol table are still in
computer memory.

When pass two begins the assembler again starts with l
l of the source program. As already indicated, the *200 in
cates that the program is to be eventually loaded starting
memory location 200. The location counter is set equal to
and binary code will be generated for the object version of
program indicating that the program is to be loaded startin
location 200. Assume that a listing is being produced on t
second pass of the assembler. Then at this time the assemb
also lists on the teleprinter, *200, just as it appears in
It is also assumed that the listing contains a memory map,
the memory locations and the octal contents of those locati
for this program.

As explained previously, lines two, three and four cau
no assembler action. Although no object code is generated
lines two, three, and four are printed. After the assemble
comes to line five on the second pass it immediately goes t
the permanent symbol table, matches the instruction field o
line five with CLA, and then generates the binary equivalen
of 7200 for the object program. The assembler then lists t
number 200 in the first column followed by 7200 in the seco
column, followed by the CLA instruction just as it appears
line five of the source program. (See Fig. 6) The first t
columns are a portion of the memory map indicating the memo
location 200 will contain the octal number 7200 when this p
gram is eventually loaded in the computer.

When the assembler program reaches line six on the sec
pass it will, similar to line five, find that the octal equ
lent of the TAD instruction is 1000, but will not punch oct
code at this point. The assembler continues on to the addr

SYMBOL	LOCATION
NUMLØC	213
NUMNEX	214
NN	215
CNTR	216
START	205
TØTAL	217
NUM1	220

Fig. 5. The user symbol table for the example program.

column and finds in the user's symbol table that NUMLØC corresponds to the memory location 213. How are these two numbers, 1000 and 213, to be combined to form a final binary instruction for the computer? There is more than one way that this may be accomplished. It depends somewhat on the memory reference instruction format for the computer in question. For this example the two components of the instruction are added together. It is necessary to recall the PDP-8 memory reference instruction format*, and to isolate the various bits in the instruction. We already know that the instruction TAD corresponds to the octal value 1000 (INST=1000). We also know that the absolute address that corresponds to the symbol NUMLØC is 213. However, for the memory reference format it is necessary to find the page address portion of the absolute address 213. This may be done by isolating the right-most seven bits of the binary equivalent of 213. These last seven binary bits equal octal 13. Remember one page on the PDP-8 computer is 128 decimal locations which corresponds to seven binary bits, i.e. $128=2^7$.

Again referring to the memory reference format there are bits corresponding to indirect addressing and to the current page indicator. In this instance the addressing is direct; therefore, the indirect address bit is a zero. This may be represented by IA=0000. In this instance the current page bit is one. This may be represented by PA=0200. Therefore the assembled word is equal to INST+IA + PA + PAGE=1000 + 0000 + 0200 + 0013 to equal octal 1213. The assembler program writes the binary equivalent of 1213 in the object version of the program.

The assembler program proceeds in the same manner with lines seven, eight, and nine. For example, line nine results in the following computation: INST + IA +PA + PAGE = 3000 + 0000 + 0200 + 0016 = 3216.

---

*See PDP-8 Memory Reference Instruction in the chapter "Computer Instructions".

Memory Location (Octal)	OCTAL Contents	Tag	Operation		Comments
		*200			
		/A PRØGRAM TØ ADD A SERIES ØF NUMBERS			
		/WRITTEN BY W.W. AUTHØR. SEPT. 6, 1969.			
		/INITIALIZE			
200	7200		CLA		
201	1213		TAD	NUMLØC	
202	3214		DCA	NUMNEX	
203	1215		TAD	NN	
204	3216		DCA	CNTR	
		/START MAIN PRØGRAM			
205	1614	START,	TAD I	NUMNEX	/ADD NEXT NUMBER
206	2214		ISZ	NUMNEX	
207	2216		ISZ	CNTR	/LAST NUMBER
210	5205		JMP	START	/NØ, ADD ANØTHER
211	3217		DCA	TØTAL	/YES, SAVE GRAND TØTAL
212	7402		HLT		/HALT
213	0220	NUMLØC,	NUM1		/LØCATIØN ØF 1ST NUMBEF
214	0000	NUMNEX,	0		/LØCATIØN ØF NEXT NUMBF
215	7773	NN,	-5		/LØCATIØN ØF NUMBERS
216	0000	TØTAL,	0		/GRAND TØTAL
		DECIMAL			
220	0006	NUM1,	6		/1ST NUMBER
221	0031		25		/2ND NUMBER
222	0002		2		/3RD NUMBER
223	0013		11		/4TH NUMBER
224	0007		7		/5TH NUMBER
		$			

SYMBØL TABLE

CNTR	216
NN	215
NUM1	220
NUMLØC	213
NUMNEX	214
START	205
TØTAL	217

Fig. 6.   An example of how the assembler output might appear.
The example includes a memory map (columns one and
two), the listing of the program, and a listing of
the symbol table.

Line 10, being a comment line, is ignored by the assembler.
However, a listing of the line is produced.
The assembler comes to 11, but this time no action is taken
on the symbol START, since START has been identified and cataloq

in the first pass. The assembler moves on to the instruction
and address field of line 11. Using the numbers corresponding
to TAD in the permanent symbol table and NUMNEX in the user's
symbol table it performs the following computation:
INST+IA+PA+PAGE=1000+0400+0200+0014=1614. The binary equivalent of 1614 is then written in the object version of the program.

Lines 12 through 16 are assembled in a manner similar to
other lines already described.

The assembler in line 17 ignores the symbol NUMLØC as it
previously ignored START. It then finds NUM1 in the user's
symbol table and determines that the number 220 is to be associated with NUM1. Therefore, the object version of the program contains the binary equivalent of 220.

The assembler proceeds to line 18 where it encounters the
value zero in the instruction field. Numeric values are taken
literally; therefore, the binary equivalent of zero is written
in the object version of the program.

The assembler proceeds to line 19 and operates in a fashion
similar to that of line 18 except the constant has a negative
value. The two's complement of five is determined and the binary equivalent of 7773 is written in the object version of
the program.

Lines 20 and 21 are treated in a similar fashion.

Because of the pseudo-instruction DECIMAL in line 22, no
assembler action is taken with respect to the object version
of the program. However, the numbers that follow are interpreted as decimal numbers. The assembler still produces binary
numbers for the object program. The object code produced for
lines 23 through 27 is the binary equivalents of octal 6, 31,
2, 13, and 7 respectively.

At line 28 the assembler interprets the dollar sign as the
end of program completing pass two. The result of pass two is
an object version of the program on some medium such as paper
tape, magnetic tape, etc, and a listing of the program and a
memory map. The memory map and the listing appear as shown
in Fig. 6. The first two columns of Fig. 6 constitute the
memory map. It can be seen that the right-hand side of Fig. 6
corresponds exactly to the original source program. Also, note
that a symbol table has been added at the bottom of Fig. 6.
This is the symbol table as it was contained in the computer
memory except the symbols have been placed in alphabetical
order. Many other forms of printed information may be printed
with the listing after an assembly.

The value of a memory map, source listing, and other information, such as symbol tables, cannot be over-emphasized. This
listing is one of the most important pieces of documentation
associated with a program. It is also, by far, the most useful
piece of information that can be utilized when the program is
loaded into the computer and an execution attempted.

Other important functions of assemblers are yet to be discussed. One of the more important is the ability of assemblers

to detect certain errors and print error messages which are
normally referred to as assembler diagnostics. The assembler
diagnostics may be printed in either pass one or pass two, or
both. Which pass, to some extent, depends on how the assemble
program is constructed.

Suppose in Fig. 3 that the programmer had omitted line 17
Then NUMLØC is an undefined variable. That is, the variable
NUMLØC appears in the body of the program (line 6), yet no-
where will NUMLØC be assigned a specific memory location. The
assembler can detect this. For example, at the end of pass
one, as we have described it, the assembler could look through
the user's symbol table and discover that no memory address
has been found which corresponds to the symbol NUMLØC. Therefore, the assembler could print a diagnostic to the effect
that NUMLØC is an undefined variable. A very useful feature
is to have the assembler automatically assign memory locations
to undefined variables.

Another commonly committed error which the assembler can
detect is that of the doubly defined variable. For example, i
line five of Fig. 3 had been written as follows:

                    START,   CLA

The assembler would find the symbol START, and enter it into
the user symbol table with the corresponding location 200. Ho
ever, later on in processing line 11 the assembler would again
find the symbol START and go to the user symbol table only to
find START had already been assigned a memory location.

Assemblers can also find what are described as syntax
errors. One example of a syntax error is misspelling. For
example, a user intending to write the instruction TAD might
instead write TDA. Another example might be in the misnaming
of variables. It is common with assembler programs that variables must start with a letter of the alphabet; it is not cor
rect to start a symbol name with a number, a dollar sign or
other miscellaneous symbols.

In addition to the listing as given in Fig. 6, diagnostic
messages are often printed by the assembler pointing out speci
errors that have been made in writing the source program.

As might be guessed, many other features may be incorpora
into assembler programs. We will see more as this discussion
progresses. There are also many refinements that may be added
in the actual writing of assembler programs. For example, if
the user's symbol table becomes very large, then it is bene-
ficial to use special table search routines which minimize the
amount of time that the assembler program spends in looking up
quantities in the symbol table.

With the knowledge that has now been presented, it might
be well to redefine what an assembler program is. It could be
as follows: the basic process performed by the assembler is
the substitution of numeric values for symbols, both system

d user symbols, according to associations found in the sym-
l tables.

3.3 Assemblers, Loaders, and Addressing

The result of an assembly is an object program which has
en written on some medium such as paper tape, magnetic tape,
c. Once this assembly has been completed the next step is
load the object program into the computer and attempt an
ecution. The loading of the object program into the computer
mory is accomplished with a loader program. Furthermore,
e program must be loaded into memory locations specified by
ther the original source program or, if the program is relo-
table, loaded relative to some address specified by the loader.
the program is to be loaded into specific memory locations,
e. the program is written in what is called absolute code,
en the original coding has specified the address. In Fig. 3
is was done in line one with the *200. If the computer's
ftware system provides for a linking loader capability, then
mmunications must be set up between the various programs that
e loaded into the computer memory.
It is obvious that the object code (object version of the
ogram) must contain more than the binary representation of
e original mnemonic instructions; it must also have informa-
on for the loader program. If the program is an absolute
ogram, which is the simplest case, then actual memory address-
must be provided on the object version of the program. If
e program is relocatable, then the object version must con-
in information about relative addresses. Likewise, if the
ader is a linking loader, all the necessary information to
able the loader to set up the communications between programs
st be contained on the object version of the program.
To accomplish the assembler program-loader program commun-
ation a specific format is usually set up for the object pro-
am. For example, with the PDP-8 assembler the convention is
 punch a special character in the object paper tape indicating
at the information to follow is an address. If this special
aracter is not present, then the information on the paper tape
 to be understood as binary number to be loaded into succeed-
g memory locations. The object paper tape corresponding to
g. 6 would have a representation as follows: special char-
ter, 200, 7200, 1213, etc. The special character indicates
at the following unit of information is an address. There-
re, 7200 will be placed in memory address 200, 1213, in 201,
d so forth.

3.4 Typical Features

In the following several features often found in assembler
ograms are discussed. Most of the features mentioned are not

essential to the process of converting mnemonic instructions
to binary object code. They, for the most part, make the assemblers easier to use. All of these features could be found
in both off-line and on-line assemblers.

3.4.1 Pseudo-Instructions

Pseudo-instructions are interspersed throughout the sourc
versions of the program. The purpose of pseudo-instructions :
to guide and direct the assembler program during the course o𝟋
the actual assembly. The pseudo-instruction itself is in no
way converted to object code. Several examples of pseudo-instructions have already been encountered in the program of
Fig. 3; the asterisk, the slash, and DECIMAL are all pseudo-
instructions. Pseudo-instructions are also referred to as
pseudo-operations.

3.4.2 Macro-Instruction

Assemblers that have the capability of handling macro-in
structions are often referred to as macro-assemblers. Macro-
instructions may take two forms. The first is an instruction
which the assembler automatically expands into several micro-
instructions. Suppose that our hypothetical assembler for th
PDP-8 computer has a macro capability. Further suppose the
mnemonic for one of the macros is LAI which is to stand for
"load a variable in the accumulator and increment the accumulator by one". The following is a set of instructions that
contains the macro-instruction LAI.

```
            .
            .
        TAD Y
        DCA X
        LAI A
        DCA Z
            .
            .
```

When this particular sequence of instructions is operated upo
by the assembler program the object code that is generated wi
correspond to the following instruction sequence.

```
            .
            .
        TAD Y
        DCA X
        CLA
        TAD A
```

```
                        IAC
                        DCA Z
                         .
                         .
```

ne assembler upon encountering the macro LAI has expanded this
ne macro-instruction into several micro-instructions which
erform the action corresponding to the definition of the macro-
nstruction. Every time the assembler encounters an instruc-
ion of the form LAI VAR where VAR is any defined variable name,
ne object code equivalent to the instructions CLA, TAD VAR,
AC will be inserted.

Assemblers that have a macro capability normally recognize
oth system and user defined macros. The macro LAI used in the
xample would probably be a systems macro. However, the assem-
ler could have a procedure whereby the user defines his own
acros. Again, once the user has defined a macro the assembler
nserts a specific set of micro-instructions for the macro
verywhere that it is encountered in the source program.

The second form of macro-instruction is associated with a
ultiple operation. For example, in the PDP-8 computer there
s a generic instruction format which is shown in Fig. 7. De-
oding from Fig. 7 it can be seen that the octal equivalent of
ne instruction CLA is 7200 and that the octal equivalent of
ne instruction IAC is 7001. The structure of the PDP-8 com-
uter is such that the two instructions can be combined and
xecuted in the same length of time that it normally takes to
xecute either one of the instructions individually. Corres-
onding to this multiple operation there is an instruction
alled CIA. CIA is a macro-instruction that combines the CLA
nstruction and the IAC instruction. When the PDP-8 assembler
ncounters this particular macro-instruction it produces the
inary code equivalent to octal 7201. This combining of gen-
ric instructions is sometimes referred to as micro-coding.

3.4.3 Globals

Some computer software systems provide the capability of
ssembling program segments at different times and then linking
hese segments at the time the programs are loaded into the
omputer's memory. As has often been pointed out, lines of
ommunications must be set up at the time these programs are
oaded by the linking-loader program. The assembler program
ust in turn provide information to the linking loader to make
his communication between program segments possible. This is
one by the use of globals. Globals are sometimes broken in
o two classes: external globals and internal globals.

Perhaps the concept of a global can best be illustrated
y an example. In Fig. 8 two programs are shown. One is re-
erred to as the MAIN program and the other as a subroutine

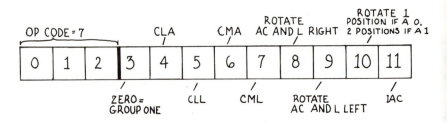

Fig. 7.   A generic instruction format of the PDP-8 computer.
By setting more than one of the bits it is possible
to have more than one action executed at one time.

<u>MAIN PROGRAM</u>

```
        CLA           /CLEAR AC
        TAD    A      /GET A
        TAD    B      /A+B
        DCA    C      /SAVE A+B
        JMS    SUB    /GØ TØ SUBRØUTINE
        TAD    D      /GET D
        TAD    E      /ADD E
          .
          .
A,      XXXX
B,      XXXX
C,      0
D,      0
```

<u>SUBROUTINE</u>

```
SUB,    0
        TAD    C      /GET C
        TAD    Sl     /ADD Sl
        DCA    D      /SAVE C+Sl
        JMP I  SUB    /RETURN
Sl,     XXXX
```

Fig. 8.   An example program to aid in the definition and use
of globals. If the program MAIN and the program SUB
are assembled at different times, it would be necessa
to declare the names of the programs, MAIN and SUB,
globals and also the variables C and D. Most assemb
use a pseudo-operation to make such declarations.

SUB which is used by the program MAIN. Suppose that these
two programs had been assembled at different times. We will
assume that our hypothetical PDP-8 assembler has a linking
loader output and can make use of globals.

When the program MAIN is loaded it is necessary for it
to know where the subroutine SUB is located in memory so that
it can access it. Likewise, when the subroutine SUB is loaded
it needs to know where the variables C and D are located in
the computer memory.

With reference to the program MAIN the subroutine tag SUB
would be an external global, i.e. it is a global that is referenced in the current program (MAIN) and defined in another
program (SUB). Similarly the variables C and D would be defined as internal globals because they are defined in the present program (MAIN) and referenced by another program (SUB).

In a similar manner from the standpoint of the subroutine
SUB, SUB is defined as an internal global. The variables C
and D are external globals in the program SUB.

By means of a pseudo-operation the tags SUB, C, and D are
identified as globals. In other words, a declaratory statement must be made within the source coding that these are global variables.

3.4.4   Literals

Assemblers that have the ability to handle literals eliminate the need for defining constants by symbolic means. This
can be illustrated by the following example.

TAD   P2

.

.

P2,   2

Here the variable P2 has been defined symbolically, i.e. there
is an instruction, the TAD instruction, that references the
variable P2. Later in the program the variable P2 is defined
or declared and given the value two.

Suppose that parentheses are used to define a constant,
i.e. a literal, then we might have the following.

TAD   (2)

The parentheses indicate to the assembler program that the
value two is to be assigned a location. This second example
is exactly equivalent to the first example: a constant with
the value of two has been placed in a memory location referenced by the instruction TAD. In the second case the assembler
decides what memory location is to contain the constant two,
while in the first case the programmer has assigned the memory
location containing two.

The word constant is being used somewhat liberally here.
For example, one could also have an instruction of the form,

TAD   (ISZ A)

which would be equivalent to the symbolic definition,

TAD   I1
.
.
I1,   ISZ   A

Literals relieve much of the bookkeeping of the programmi
process and therefore eliminate many errors. Using assemblers
which require the literals to be symbolically defined, it is a
common occurrence to forget to declare the memory assignments
or to duplicate memory assignments. However, in the case of
an assembler with literal capability this is not necessary, an
the errors are eliminated.

3.4.5 Default Conditions

Default conditions are situations whereby the assembler
attempts to correct or compensate for errors that have been
made in writing source programs. A default condition implies
that when a particular error is made a specific step is taken
by the assembler to correct the error. Several examples shoul
clarify the concept of default condition.
1) Suppose that the instruction TAD A occurs in a source
program but that A is never defined anywhere in the program.
Then the default condition for this particular case might spec
that the assembler assign a location for the symbol A. Of cou
if the symbol A was meant to represent a constant then the assembler fix will not work. However, if the symbol A is a variable that is to be computed then the assembler will have compensated for the error.
2) Suppose that in the program of Fig. 3 the programmer
never entered *200. Then there is no specified address for th
loader to start loading the program. In this case the default
condition would probably specify that the assembler always
assign a starting address for each program or might even be
sophisticated enough to check to see if one has been specified
3) Another example is the instance where a programmer ha
defined a symbol more than once. In this case the assembler
might arbitrarily select the first occurrence of the symbol as
the correct one and assign all other locations accordingly.
Assigning the variables in this way will certainly not be righ
but object code is generated and the program can often be debugged before the error is corrected in the source version of
the program and another assembly made.

3.5 Peripheral Equipment Considerations

If a two-pass assembler is utilized, only moderate amounts of magnetic core memory are required for the assembler program itself. However, memory shortages can develop in assembling programs that require large user symbol tables.

Input and output are major problem areas. Returning a-gain to the extreme case of the computer with only a Teletype unit as input/output; what operations are required of the Teletype unit?

1) The Teletype unit must read the source tape for pass one.

2) The Teletype unit must read the source tape for pass two. During this pass the Teletype punch will probably also be required to punch the object paper tape.

3) If a listing and memory map is desired then the tele-printer is required to read the source tape a third time. It has already been indicated in Table II that the execution of these steps can take an hour or more.

Three peripheral devices are typically required to per-form an assembly: one to read the source version of the pro-gram, one to write or store the object version of the program, and one for listing the source program and the memory map. It is desirable to be able to perform an assembly in the order of seconds and certainly no longer than minutes. Ideally, this means that the source and object peripheral devices must be capable of operating at several hundred characters per second, and that the printing device can print with speeds of one hun-dred lines of print per minute or more.

3.6 Off-Line Assemblers

The considerations of the previous sections have presented a two-pronged dilemma. To efficiently assemble source programs on an on-line computer higher speed peripherals are required. The first prong of the dilemma is that the application for which the on-line computer is used may not require these high speed peripherals. The second prong of the dilemma is that high speed peripherals often cost as much or more than the computer itself.

One alternative to acquiring high speed peripherals to serve only in the capacity of program development is the use of an off-line computer facility. However, this is not possible if an assembler program is not available which executes on the off-line facility and outputs object code for the on-line facil-ity. At the present time the user will normally have to write such an off-line assembler to be able to make use of an off-line facility.

One of the primary reasons for inserting the description of how an assembler works in this chapter was to show that the

writing of an off-line assembler for a small on-line computer
is not the awesome task that it is often considered to be.
Minimal assemblers may be written for off-line facilities that
require only a few hundred program statements in the FORTRAN
language.

There is more than one approach to the writing of an off-
line assembler. One is to write the assembler in some higher-
level language like FORTRAN or PL/I (Programming Language One).
The PL/I language is specifically mentioned here because it
has the capability to manipulate individual binary bits in an
easier fashion than most higher-level languages, and is, therefore, particularly apropos for writing assemblers.

A second approach is to write the off-line assembler in
the assembler language of the off-line computer. This can be
particularly useful if the off-line computer facility has a
macro capability in its assembler. With a macro capability it
is possible to define the instructions of the on-line computer
as macros to the assembler of the off-line computer. This also
makes the off-line assembler somewhat universal in that it may
be modified to assemble programs for different on-line computers
by inserting new sets of macros to describe new instructions.

In either of these approaches source programs for the off-
line assembler are usually put on punch cards, read into the
off-line computer, assembled with the off-line assembler which
outputs object code to a medium that is acceptable to the on-
line computer. To summarize some of the advantages that are to
be gained by developing programs for on-line computers at off-
line computing facilities are:

1) The off-line facilities almost always have peripherals
of the type required to efficiently assemble programs.

2) If program development is carried on at off-line facilities, the on-line computer can spend more time at the task
for which it has been chosen. This is sometimes referred to as
more on-stream time.

3) Off-line facilities offer the possibility of adding
many more periphery functions to assemblers. For example, much
more complete listings, diagnostics, and other printed materials
of the type required to efficiently assemble programs.

4) Programs can grow in size without concern for the size
of the symbol table.

One encouraging trend is that the manufacturers of on-line
computers are beginning to supply off-line assemblers. This
trend will probably increase in the future.

4.0   DEBUGGING

Debugging is the activity required to make a program execute correctly after a successful assembly has been achieved.
It must be emphasized that although a program has been assembled
correctly it does not follow that it will execute correctly.
The assembler will have removed syntax and other errors, but

it cannot detect logic errors in the programming. Hence, the
need for actually sitting down at the on-line computer and
attempting to make the assembled program execute properly.

4.1 At the On-Line Computer

In many instances debugging is done at the on-line computer. However, there are two approaches that may be taken
in debugging programs at the on-line computer itself. One is
via the computer's console and the other is with programming
aids.

4.1.1 Via the Console

In this approach the assembled program is loaded into the
computer memory and then execution is attempted. If the program does not execute properly, then the user often modifies
certain portions of the program so that it runs in steps. This
can be done by placing halts at appropriate places in the program. This type of debugging activity is one in which the
programmer attempts to find out why the computer program is
doing what it <u>is</u> rather than what he thinks it <u>should</u>.
During the debugging, the program is often modified
(patched), via the console indicators, in an attempt to make
it run. In this type of debugging the programmers only means
of input to the computer is via the console switches, and his
only means of output is via the console indicator lights.
It should be obvious that this is a very time-consuming
and inefficient method of debugging. It is also error prone.
Unfortunately, it is often the predominate means of debugging.

4.1.2 With Programming Aids

In this method of debugging additional programs are read
into the computer memory along with the object version of the
user's program. The purpose of these debugging programs (aids)
is to allow the user to perform via the keyboard and the printer
those actions that he would perform at the console by the console
debugging method. As with any programming effort, debugging
aids in the forms of programs can vary from being very simple
to extremely sophisticated.
If no programming aids are available, the user should take
it upon himself to write a small program to be used in debugging.
To illustrate how small a job this is turn to the flow diagram
of Fig. 9. Before looking at the diagram in any detail a verbal
description of how the program works is in order. The author
has called the program PATCH. PATCH performs only one basic
function; that of replacing the contents of a specific memory

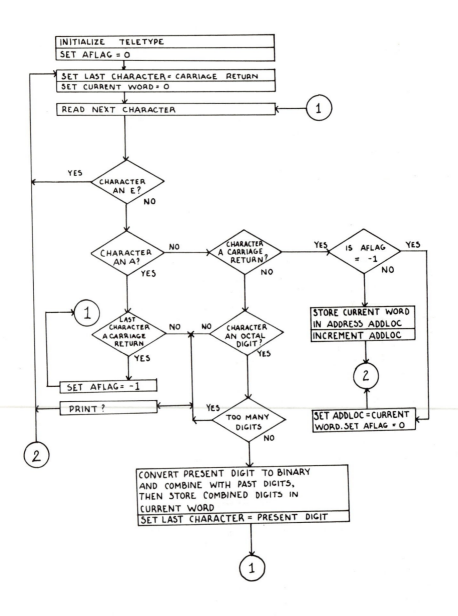

Fig. 9.   A flow diagram of a program called PATCH. The purpose
          of PATCH is to permit the on-line computer user to
          change the contents of the computer memory locations
          from the Teletype keyboard during the course of debuggin
          programs.

location with whatever binary number the user desires. If the
user wants to place a new binary number in the octal location
100, he starts the program PATCH, and then at the keyboard types
A100, carriage return. This informs PATCH that the number to
follow is to be placed in memory location 100. The user then
types, in octal, the new contents of location 100. If the user
types another octal number followed by a carriage return, it
is automatically stored in memory location 101. Thus, numbers
can be stored in succeeding memory locations as long as needed.
To move to another area of memory the user again types the
letter A followed by the desired memory address. Besides this
basic function of modifying the contents of the computer
memory, PATCH has a few error detection conditions. If the
user starts to type an entry and discovers an error, it is only
necessary to type the letter E. As can be seen from the flow
diagram of Fig. 9 this immediately initializes PATCH, and it
will be awaiting the next command. PATCH also checks to see
that the letter A is preceded by a carriage return. This prevents the user from typing an A in the middle of a command.
The program also checks to see that the numbers entered are
the octal integers. The only characters that are acceptable
to PATCH are E, A, carriage return, and the octal integers
zero to seven. Whenever an error is committed a question mark
is printed and PATCH automatically returns to the initialized
state awaiting a new command.

A small effort is required to write the program PATCH. A
version of this program written for the PDP-8 computer requires
approximately 155 octal memory locations. It is well worth the
effort to write and implement this program rather than use a
console debugging technique. Even though the program is very
simple, it can greatly increase the efficiency with which debugging may be carried out.

The program PATCH as outlined here has been written from
the viewpoint of a computer system that does not run under a
monitor program. However, it can be implemented under a monitor with only slightly more effort.

Some on-line computer manufacturers supply debugging aids.
These tend to be more sophisticated than PATCH. One of the
primary differences between the debugging aids provided by
manufacturers and PATCH is that these debugging programs control the running or execution of the user's program. PATCH,as
it has been set up in our example, does not control the execution of a user's program. It is used by starting the execution
of PATCH each time the user wants to modify his own program.
The user program must then be restarted without any control
from PATCH.

Some of the features that can be found in the more sophisticated debugging programs are the following:

1)   The automatic insertion of break points. Break points
are usually halts. In other words, this feature allows the
user to insert a halt anywhere in the program he desires.

2) Control of the starting point of execution. Often when debugging a program it is desirable to start execution of the program at some point other than the normal starting point.

3) Loads user program. This feature allows the debugging program to load the user program, i.e. the debugging program contains a loader.

4) Examination and modification. This is the feature that forms the basis of the PATCH program. It permits the user to ask for the contents of any computer location within his program, and then to modify that location if desired.

5) Insertion of patches. Oftentimes an error is found in a program which must be corrected by the insertion of one or more statements in the flow of the program. It is desirable to insert these statements as a patch to see if they will work correctly. This then means a jump from the flow of the program to some other portion of unused computer memory where the patch is placed and then a jump back to the main flow of the program. This feature is often supplied in debugging programs via a command structure.

6) Search Operations. A very useful feature to have in debugging programs is the ability to search for different character strings. For example, to be able to search for tags, variable names and so forth.

7) Symbol definition. Some debugging programs provide the facility for actually inserting new symbol names. Thus, new tags and new variables can be defined and referred to symbolically within the patches and other code that are generated with the debugging program. It is also desirable for the debugging program to recognize the symbols of the original program.

4.2 Off-Line Computers

Programs may be written for off-line computer facilities which simulate the operation of an on-line computer. Via this simulation program it is then possible to execute off-line and debug a program that has been assembled for the on-line computer. Simulation of the on-line computer's instructions is straightforward. One simply sets aside memory registers in the off-line computer which may be used for the functions that are provided by the hardware registers of the on-line computers. For example, a memory location might be called accumulator, another program counter, another index register, and so forth.

Peripherals are more of a problem. The problems concerning peripheral simulation are of two types. First, the off-line computer facility may not have the same peripherals as the on-line computer. The on-line computer might have as a peripheral an analog-to-digital converter which would not be available on the off-line computer system. Even if the off-line computer system has the same type of peripheral it may not operate in exactly the same manner as one on the on-line computer. For example, both the on-line and off-line systems might have magnetic tape transports attached to them. However, the operating characteristics of the two different tape transports might differ markedly.

The second type of difficulty that can be experienced with a peripheral is that the sequence of computer instructions which apply are often critical. The sequence of the instructions is critical in the sense of timing. Within a certain elapsed time it may be necessary to follow one instruction with another in order that the peripheral may perform properly.

Thus, a program may not be completely debugged even if it is successfully run under simulation, and hence, one should not expect to be able to do one hundred per cent of the debugging at an off-line computer under simulation. However, in terms of time spent in the debugging process certainly a large percentage may be completed at the off-line facility. Simulators, like off-line assemblers, are particularly important if large on-stream time is required of the on-line computer.

To my knowledge, no on-line computer manufacturer is currently providing a simulator. I would hope to see a large growth in this area in the future.

CHAPTER 7

COMPUTER ORGANIZATION II

1.0 DIGITAL LOGIC

1.1 General Comments

What is digital logic? The term is often used in a somewhat generic way to refer to the circuitry of a computer. More
appropriately, it might be thought of as a way of grouping computer circuitry. One might think of resistors, transistors and
electronic components as raw materials from which computer circuits are assembled. However, in the case of the computer, the
circuit is of a somewhat different nature than is found in many
other types of electronics. The typical computer circuit performs what is called a logical operation. This means the circuit reacts with a single prescribable action to an input signal. This action constitutes the logical operation. These
logical operations are digital in nature, i.e., the execution
of the operation results in a discreet condition. As an example of a discreet condition a certain point in the circuit
might be at one of two possible voltages, but will never occupy
the voltage range between these two discreet levels. These two
discreet levels then represent digital binary information.
The logical operations to be defined here are unique in
the actions taken by the circuits. However, there is little
uniqueness in the construction of the circuits to perform these
logical operations. This can be well illustrated by looking
at the history of computer logic. In the very earliest of computing devices, the logical operations were performed using re-
lays in the logic circuits. Some time after this the same operations were accomplished by circuits using vacuum tubes.
These were followed by logic circuits using transistors and
then logic using integrated circuits. It is even possible to
perform logical operations mechanically and fluidly. Thus,
although the same logic operations have been performed throughout the history of computing devices, the circuits themselves
were built with entirely different components and with different
circuit techniques.

189

As pointed out in the chapter "Computer Organization I",
a computer system might be thought of as a spectrum of elements
ranging from circuit components such as resistors and transistors on the one hand all the way through logic and computer
organization to computer program instructions on the other end
of the spectrum. The construction of circuits or circuit analysis will not be taken up in this book, for much can be understood about computer hardware and computer operation (the hardware-software totality) knowing the logical operations involved,
and as mentioned any number of means might be used to implement
these logical operations.

One often hears expressions referring to a given manufacturer's digital logic line. This refers to the digital logic
modules produced by the manufacturer. Often these are in the
form of pluggable cards on which the circuit elements have been
mounted. Fig. 1 shows an example of the digital logic cards
produced by one manufacturer. Present day logic cards or as
they are sometimes called, logic modules, typically have transistors or integrated circuits as their primary components.
Those containing transistors with the associated resistors, capacitors and so forth are often referred to as discreet logic,
as opposed to integrated circuit logic.

One logic module may not necessarily have only one logic
circuit on it. There may be a half dozen or more of the same
logical operations represented on the board. That is, there
may be a half dozen or more circuits which perform the same logical operation. These can then be put together in a building
block fashion to make more complex computer circuits.

The modules shown in Fig. 1 are small and a small computer
built from them might contain several hundred such modules.
Some manufacturers prefer to put many more circuits on much
larger logic boards. Small on-line computers built with this
technique may be composed of only two or three such logic boards.

It is possible to take a digital logic line and in a building block fashion construct a complete computer. It is important to note that there are only a very limited number of logical operations that are used in the building of a computer but
the same logical operations are used thousands of times throughout the computer. From this standpoint the computer is really
a rather simple device to understand conceptually. It is built
from a very few simple building blocks and is only complex in
that these building blocks are used thousands of times.

The logic can be used to perform only two functions. One
function is to store binary information and the other is to
perform the basic logical operations.

1.2   The Basic Logical Operations

There are three basic logical operations. They are called
AND, OR, and NOT operations. First look at the AND operation.

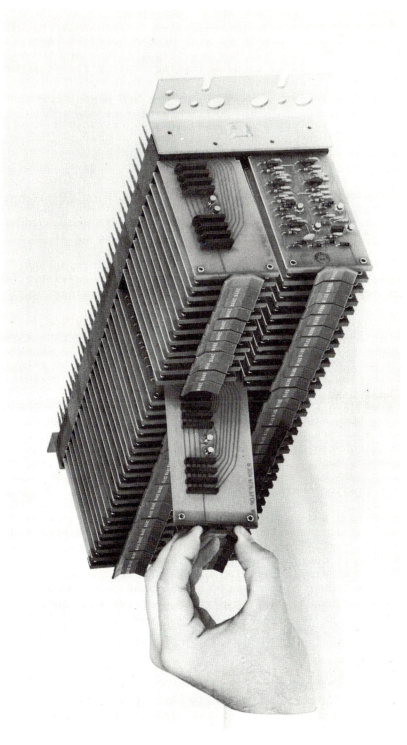

Fig. 1. A photograph showing digital logic cards mounted in a card bin. The photograph is courtesy of Digital Equipment Corporation.

To illustrate that this is truly a logical operation and not
an operation inherent to electronic circuitry look at Fig. 2.
On the left under the column labeled "AND OPERATION" can be
seen a schematic of an elevated water tank with a drain line
that runs through valves A and B. If only valve A is open,
then no water appears at C. Likewise, if only valve B is open,
then no water appears. It is only when A and B are open that
water appears at C. This is an illustration of the logical
AND operation. It literally says that A and B equal C. This
is a binary logic. For example, the logical one can be defined
to correspond to water and a logical zero to correspond to no
water.
        Move down the AND OPERATION column of Fig. 2 to the elec-
trical circuit. The circuit consists of a battery of voltage
V and two electrical switches labeled A and B. The circuit has
two output terminals, one of which is marked C. If we were to
put a voltage measuring device across the output terminals no
voltage would be measured at C if either A or B were open.
Switches A and B must both be closed to complete the circuit.
This too represents the logical AND operation. The logical
one might correspond to voltage and the logical zero to no
voltage. This should indicate that there are many other examples whereby systems perform the logical AND operation.
        It is convenient to have a symbol that represents the AND
operation without having to continually draw the components that
make up the AND operation. The last symbol shown at the bottom
of the AND OPERATION column of Fig. 2 is the military standard
symbol (MIL SPEC) for the AND operation*. This is not the only
symbol that is used to represent the AND operation, e.g., another common one is the NEMA symbol which is often used in industrial applications. In this book the military standard symbols are used. In digital electronics the symbol is normally
referred to as an AND gate. Looking back at the two illustrations above it should be easy to see why these logic circuits
are often referred to as gates.
        Turn now to the column in Fig. 2 labeled OR OPERATION.
At the top, a water tank with drain pipe is again illustrated.
However, this time the drain piping arrangement and the valve
arrangement is different. Examination will show that if valve
A is open, water appears at point C. Likewise, if valve B is
open, water also appears at point C. Thus, water appears at C
if either A or B is open. This is the logical OR operation.
Just as in the first example for the AND operation, water at C
can be defined as the logical one state and no water as the
logical zero state.

---

*The complete set of military standard symbols are given in
 MIL-SPEC 806C.

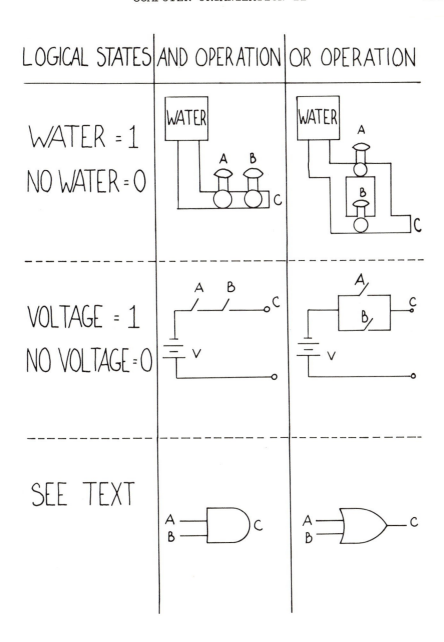

Fig. 2.   The top two diagrams of each column represent examples
          of the logical AND and OR operations respectively. The
          symbols at the bottom of each of the two columns are the
          military (MIL SPEC) symbols for the AND and OR operations
          respectively.

Moving on down the OR operation column the OR operation
is again illustrated with an electrical circuit. There is
still a battery with a voltage V but now the two switches A
and B are arranged in a different manner. Just as in the case
of the water drain, if either A <u>or</u> B is closed, a voltage V
can be measured at the output terminal C.

At the bottom of the OR OPERATION column of Fig. 2 is
shown the military (MIL SPEC) symbol for the OR operation. In
digital electronics this is normally referred to as an OR gate.

It is possible to set down all the outputs associated with
all possible combinations of inputs that may be utilized in
logical operations. These are often referred to as truth tables
or sometimes as tables of combinations. Fig. 3 shows two AND
gates and an OR gate. Under each of the gate symbols is the
corresponding truth table. The first logical operation on the
left is referred to as a two-input AND gate. Looking at the
corresponding truth table, if the logical zero is applied at
the A input and a logical zero is applied at the B input, the
output will be a logical zero. In a similar fashion the truth
table itemizes all possible combinations of the two-input AND
gate and what the resulting outputs C will be for the AND operation. Moving on to the center symbol of Fig. 3 a three-
input AND gate is illustrated. In a similar fashion a truth
table is shown which shows all possible combinations of the
three inputs and the associated output D. Finally, the third
symbol shows a two-input OR gate and the associated truth table.

Descriptively the AND operation is such that if all inputs
correspond to a logical one, the output corresponds to a logical one, otherwise, the logical output is zero. In the case of
the OR operation, if any input is a one, the output is a one.

The final basic logical operation is the NOT operation.
The NOT operation complements the logical state of its input.
This is equivalent to a one's complement. The military symbol
for a NOT operation and its truth table is shown in Fig. 4.
This circuit is often referred to as an inverter in digital
electronics.

The NOT operation is indicated notationally by putting a
bar over the symbol or quantity that has been operated upon by
a NOT operator. For example,

$\overline{\text{water}}$ = no water

$\overline{\text{no water}}$ = water

$\overline{\text{switch open}}$ = switch closed

$\overline{\text{switch closed}}$ = switch open

$\overline{\text{logical one}}$ = logical zero

$\overline{\text{logical zero}}$ = logical one

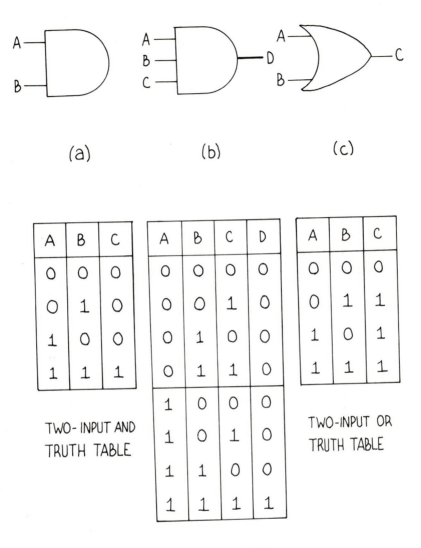

Fig. 3. Examples of truth tables, or as they are sometimes known, tables of combinations. From left to right the truth tables are for a two-input AND gate, a three-input AND gate, and a two-input OR gate.

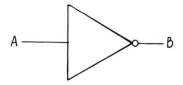

A	B
0	1
1	0

NOT
TRUTH TABLE

Fig. 4. The military standard symbol and truth table for the
NOT operation. This symbol is also often referred
to as an inverter.

Although it is not one of the three basic logical operations, there is another operation that should be mentioned because it is often encountered. This is the EXCLUSIVE OR operation. In contrast, the OR operation that has been defined
above is the INCLUSIVE OR operation. Verbally the EXCLUSIVE
OR operation can be defined by saying that if the inputs are
different, then the output is a logical one, and if the inputs
are the same, the output is a logical zero. This is illustrated
in the truth table of Fig. 5. It is shown later in this chapter
that the EXCLUSIVE OR operation can be implemented using the
three basic logical operations AND, OR, and NOT. Thus, the
EXCLUSIVE OR is not classified as one of the basic logic operations.

     For digital computer logic the quantities that are nor-
mally of interest are either voltage pulses or current flows.
What then would be the logical operations in terms of these
voltage pulses or voltage levels? Suppose that a digital
logic is being used where plus 5 volts corresponds to a logical one, and 0 volts corresponds to logical zero. Some resulting logical operations are illustrated in Fig. 6 which consists
of an AND gate followed by a NOT operation (an inverter). This
truth table is identical to the one that is usually shown except
the voltage levels have been substituted for the logical 0's
and 1's. These voltages are those that would actually be found
within the circuit itself.

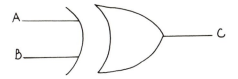

A	B	C
0	0	0
0	1	1
1	0	1
1	1	0

EXCLUSIVE OR
TRUTH TABLE

Fig. 5.   The military standard symbol and truth table for
          the EXCLUSIVE OR operation.

        Similar truth tables could be drawn up with other digital
logic systems which might, for example use a plus 3 volts to
correspond to a logical one and 0 volts to correspond to a
logical zero, or 0 volts to correspond to a logical one and
minus 5 volts to correspond to a logical zero, etc.

        1.3   Boolean Algebra

        Boolean algebra is an algebra developed by the mathema-
tician Bool to serve as a mathematics for logical determinations.   The algebra permits variables to take on only two values;
0 and 1.   Many years ago it was discovered that Boolean algebra
serves as a perfect vehicle to describe digital logic.   The
application of Boolean algebra to digital logic permits it to
be treated in an abstract way and, as we shall see, also allows
checks and eliminations for redundancy in digital circuitry.

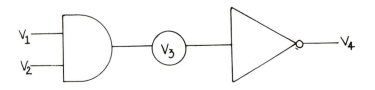

V_1	V_2	V_3	V_4
0	0	0	5
0	5	0	5
5	0	0	5
5	5	5	0

Fig. 6.   A small logical circuit consisting of an AND gate and
a NOT gate. A truth table is shown for a circuit, but
the entries are voltages rather than the binary state
assuming a logic where 5 volts corresponds to logical
one and 0 volts corresponds to logical zero.

Look at the expression A + B = C.   Remember that A, B
and C can all only take on the values 0 and 1.   The + is not
to be taken as addition in the usual sense.   The operation
designated by the + can be defined by the following results
for the equation above.

$$0 + 0 = 0$$
$$0 + 1 = 1$$
$$1 + 0 = 1$$
$$1 + 1 = 1$$

Looking at these results and comparing them with those shown
in Fig. 3c, it follows that the operation described by the +
defines the OR operation.   Thus, the equation is read A OR B
= C.

Now turn to a new equation, A $\cdot$ B = C.   Define this new operation by the following consequences:

$$0 \cdot 0 = 0$$
$$0 \cdot 1 = 0$$
$$1 \cdot 0 = 0$$
$$1 \cdot 1 = 1$$

Comparing this with the truth table of Fig. 3a, it can be seen that this equation does not represent the usual multiplication but the logical AND operation.

The symbolism for the NOT operation has already been defined. From previous discussion A NOT is represented by $\bar{A}$.

As with any mathematics it is necessary to know what the characteristics of Boolean mathematics are. These can be discovered by looking at several theorems that apply to Boolean algebra.

Commutation theorems

$$A + B = B + A$$
$$AB = BA$$

The commutation theorems shows that the order in which the AND or the OR operation is performed does not matter. It should also be noted that like normal multiplication, the dot for the AND operation is often assumes.

Absorption theorems

$$A + BA = A$$
$$A(A + B) = A$$

The first line is deducable from the second.

$$AA + AB = A$$
$$\text{but } AA = A$$
$$\text{Therefore } A + AB = A$$

Associative Theorems

$$A + (B + C) = (A + B) + C$$
$$A(BC) = (AB)C$$

The associative theorem tells us that multiple operations may be performed in any order with the same result.

Distribution theorems

$$A + BC = (A + B)(A + C)$$
$$A(B + C) = AB + AC$$

DeMorgan's theorems

$$\overline{A + B} = \bar{A}\,\bar{B}$$

$$\overline{AB} = \bar{A} + \bar{B}$$

The general conclusion to be drawn from DeMorgan's Theorems is that by the use of the NOT operation, it is possible to invert an AND operation into an OR operation and vice versa. Thus, of the three basic logical operations, AND, OR and NOT, the NOT operation plus one of the other two is enough to perform all three logical operations. It is possible to build a computer in which only the AND and the NOT operations are used, or in a similar manner, only the OR operation and the NOT operation.

The theorems can be demonstrated with the use of truth tables. For example, Table I shows the proof of the first DeMorgan's Theorem.

The theorems may also be vividly demonstrated by the use of the symbols for the logical operations. Fig. 7 shows two logic circuits. Each of the logic circuits represents one side of the equation for the first of the distribution theorems. Fig. 7 also illustrates the practical nature of Boolean algebra. From the first distribution theorem the two logic circuits shown in Fig. 7 perform in exactly the same manner, i.e., if the same inputs A, B and C are applied to the two circuits, they will have the same logical outputs. Yet, the bottom circuit requires one less gate than the top circuit. Thus, it is more efficient in both space and cost.

The reader can now refer back to Fig. 5 and see that the EXCLUSIVE OR operation is given by the Boolean expression

$$A \bar{B} + B \bar{A}$$

This expression is often written with the notation

$$A \oplus B = A \bar{B} + B \bar{A}$$

The + circumscribed with a circle is the symbol used for the EXCLUSIVE OR operator.

It will not be explored here, but there is a parallel digital logic that may be developed around a slightly different viewpoint of the basic logical operations. The two operations involved are often referred to as the NAND and the NOR operations. Schematically the NAND operation is simply the AND operation followed by an inverter. Thus, the basis for the acronym; it stands for negative AND. Likewise, the NOR is the negative OR and schematically is an OR gate followed by an inverter. All the illustrations that have been given using AND or OR gates may also be implemented in a parallel fashion with NAND and NOR gates. The author feels that no further basic information can be derived from pursuing the NAND and NOR operations, and that enough information has been provided here for the reader to understand a presentation of these operations.

1.4   The Flip-Flop

The three basic logical operations have now been covered. There are many functions that could be explored such as producing continuous signal trains and the shaping of signal pulses. Space does not permit the coverage of these topics, nor is there such need for what follows. However, it was

Table I. A truth table which demonstrates the proof of the
          first of DeMorgan's Theorems.

A	B	A + B	$\overline{A + B}$	$\overline{A}$	$\overline{B}$	$\overline{A} \cdot \overline{B}$
0	0	0	1	1	1	1
0	1	1	0	1	0	0
1	0	1	0	0	1	0
1	1	1	0	0	0	0

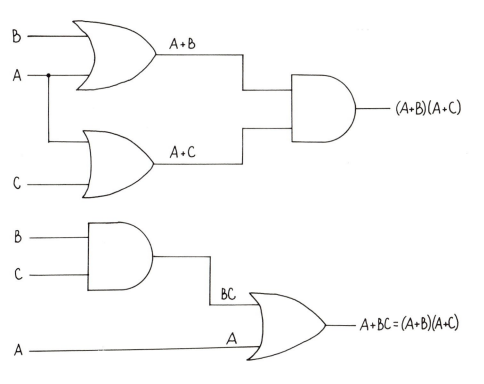

Fig. 7. Two logic circuits that represent the two sides of the
         equation expressing the first distribution theorem.
         Both circuits perform the same logical operation but
         the lower circuit accomplishes the operation with one
         less gate.

mentioned earlier that two functions are performed with logic. One was the logical operations and the other was storage. It is to this latter subject, that of storage, which we are going to now turn our attentions.

Many actions within a computer are one-shot in nature. For example, many signals consist of pulses or pulse trains. Therefore, it is necessary to have some form of storage function within the computer logic so that one-shot events may be remembered. One of the most common storage elements in a computer is a circuit referred to as a flip-flop. Analogous to other computer logic the flip-flop circuit can be built from any number of different components such as transistors, integrated circuits and vacuum tubes. Again, it is not necessary to go into this kind of detail to know how a flip-flop circuit performs and to understand the operation of a computer to the desired depth. Therefore, the flip-flop is explained entirely using logical operations. Fig. 8a shows the logical operations and the inter connections that constitute a flip-flop circuit. The basic flip-flop circuit shown is composed of two OR gates and two inverters*.

The two terminals labeled A and B are the inputs to the flip-flop, and the two terminals labeled b and b̄ are the outputs. The name that has been given to this circuit is quite descriptive. The two output terminals b and b̄ always reside either with b as a logical one and b̄ as a logical zero or vice versa; hence the circuit has two stable states. If the circuit is flipped into one of these states, it will remain there until another input causes it to flop back to the original status of the two outputs. Fig. 8b shows a more schematic presentation of the flip-flop circuit. The little arrowheads on the inputs indicate that the inputs are pulse inputs. The fact that there are no arrows on the outputs indicates that these are levels rather than pulses.

Suppose that the output b is setting at a logical one and the output b̄ is setting at a logical zero. Further suppose that a logical one is applied at the A input and a logical zero at the B input. Starting at the A input, the OR gate there now has a logical one on one input and a logical zero on the other input. This means that the output of this OR gate will change to a logical one, which is then passed through the inverter and becomes a logical zero. Therefore, the b output is changed from the logical one state to the logical zero state. Note that the inverter that feeds the b output is also connected back to the input of the OR gate at the B terminal. Therefore, this OR gate now has logical zeros on both inputs which will result in a logical zero at its output. This becomes a logical one upon passing through the inverter. Therefore, the state

---

*A basic flip-flop may also be constructed using AND gates and inverters.

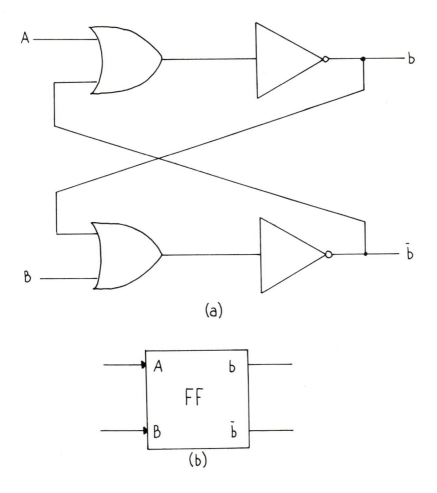

(a)

(b)

Fig. 8.   The basic flip-flop circuit. As the inputs A and B
are changed the outputs b and b̄ flip back and forth
between two stable states.

of the b̄ terminal is now a logical one. Now it can be seen
that placing the logical one at the A terminal and the logical zero at the B terminal has flipped the state of the flip-
flop circuit, and the b and b̄ outputs are the inverse of the
beginning situation.

By trying other combinations of inputs the truth table
can be developed for the flip-flop circuit as shown in Table II.
Notice that the last two sets of conditions in the truth table
have been set off with a dotted line. These conditions represent logical zeros at both the inputs. There are two possibilities depending on which state the flip-flop was in last. For

Table II.   The truth table for the flip-flop circuit.

A	B	b	$\bar{b}$
1	1	0	0
0	0	0	1
0	1	1	0
0	0 (last 1)	1	0
0 (last 1)	0	0	1

example, the first of these entries shows the case when two
zeros are placed on the inputs where the B input was last a
one. This leads to the b output being a logical one and the
$\bar{b}$ output being a logical zero. Likewise, the last line shown
is for the application of logical zeros at the inputs when the
last condition of the flip-flop was with a logical one at the
A input. These last two states lead to an indeterminate output, i.e., if logical zeros are placed on both inputs, it is
impossible to know what the outputs of the flip-flop circuit
will be unless the last state of the flip-flop is known. For
the normal mode of operation it is not permissible to apply
zeros to both inputs simultaneously.

A terminology will now be adopted that is normally used
in conjunction with flip-flops and is somewhat more meaningful in terms of their actual use. Suppose that the A input
is relabeled as the RESET input and the B input is relabeled
as the SET input. Further, suppose that the b output is to
be referred to as the ONE output and the $\bar{b}$ as the ZERO output.
Finally, assume that the b output is the point which is checke
for information stored in the flip-flop. The flip-flop will
indeed store information if one of its outputs is thought of
as being a storage element. Since the output can only be a
logical one or a logical zero, only one binary bit of information can be stored per flip-flop. Using these new definitions of the inputs and the outputs, refer now to Fig. 9 which
shows a typical diagram for flip-flop circuits. Note that
there is a third input indicated on the diagram. This T input
is known as the TRIGGER or complement input. With slight modification a flip-flop circuit can be given the capability to
flip its state whenever a pulse is applied at the added TRIGGE
input. With the conventions just established flipping the sta
of the flip-flop is equivalent to complementing the bit of information that it holds. This is a one's complement. Of cour
the flip-flop inputs labeled R and S are the RESET and SET inputs respectively.

The terminology should now be more meaningful. If a puls
is applied at the RESET input, the output considered the stora
element is set to a logical zero. Likewise, a pulse applied a
the SET input automatically forces the storage element to a

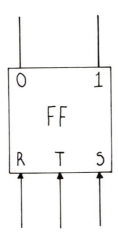

Fig. 9. A more schematic diagram of the basic flip-flop
         circuit. The b and b̄ states are now represented
         by 0 and 1, and the A and B inputs are represented
         by R and S standing for RESET and SET respectively.
         T stands for the TRIGGER input.

logical one. Thus, it is possible to set a zero or a one into
a flip-flop by using the appropriate input. Table III gives
the truth table for a flip-flop using the new terminology.
Note that the condition where both the RESET and SET inputs
are a zero is not listed because this situation should never
be permitted to occur.

1.5 Computer Registers

     In the chapter "Computer Instructions" some attention has
already been given to the intimate relationship between computer
registers and computer instructions. Also characteristics of
computer registers and what might be called a chronological
description of their operation was given. Conceptually a computer register was thought of as a series of related bits as
shown in Fig. 10. Figure 10 is a four bit register with the
bits arbitrarily numbered starting at zero from the left going
toward the right. Sometimes the right most bit is thought of
as bit zero, but that is merely a matter of convention. The
previous discussion also mentioned that there are two major
types of registers; hardware and magnetic core memory registers.
     We are now in a position to look at hardware registers in
more detail. Remember that flip-flops can be thought of as
storage devices with a one binary bit capacity. Therefore, it
is easy to see that a computer hardware register may be constructed from several flip-flop circuits. Fig. 11 shows an

Table III.   The truth table for a flip-flop using normal
terminology and conventions.

RESET	SET	0 Output	1 Output
0	1	0	1
1	0	1	0
1	1	0	0

bit 0 | bit 1 | bit 2 | bit 3

Fig. 10.   An abstract way of representing a four bit register.

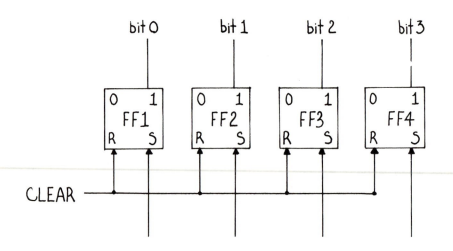

Fig. 11.   A hardware register constructed from an array of
flip-flop circuits. A logical one on the CLEAR
line causes all bits of the four bit register to
be set to a logical zero, i.e., the register is
zeroed.

array of four flip-flop circuits which represent a four bit
binary register. The original convention of using the one
output as the information storage element is being used. Thus
bit zero corresponds to the logical state of the one output of
flip-flop one, bit one to the one state of flip-flop two, and
so forth, across the register. Also note that all the RESET
inputs of the flip-flops have been connected to a common line

labeled CLEAR. A pulse applied at the terminal marked CLEAR
causes all bits of the four bit register to be simultaneously
cleared to the logical zero state. In terms of the PDP-8 instruction set this is exactly the operation that the CLA instruction performs on the accumulator register.
The register of Fig. 11 may be loaded by applying pulses
to those S inputs corresponding to the bits that are to be set
to a logical one state. It is possible to also interconnect
all the S inputs and make provisions for a SET pulse that will
set all bits in the register to a one. In a similar manner,
if the trigger inputs of the individual flip-flops are tied to
a single line, it is possible to complement the contents of
the register with one pulse. This latter is the operation performed by the CMA instruction* of the PDP-8 on the accumulator
register. If now the CLA and the CMA instructions are given
in sequence, the accumulator register is set so that all bits
equal one.
Suppose that it is now desired to transfer the contents
of one computer hardware register into another hardware register. This can be accomplished with the logic shown in Fig. 12.
The contents of the register which is composed of flip-flops
5 through 8 are to be loaded into the register composed of the
flip-flops 1 through 4. AND gates have been inserted between
the one outputs of the lower register and the SET inputs of
the upper register. The remaining inputs of the two-input
AND gates are tied together and run to an input terminal labeled STROBE. A CLEAR line is shown for the upper flip-flop register. If a logical one is applied to the STROBE line, logical
ones will appear at the outputs of those AND gates attached to
the flip-flops in the lower register which have a logical one
at the one output. The logical ones at the AND gate outputs
set corresponding flip-flops in the upper register to a logical one. It is important to note that those flip-flops in the
bottom register which are in the logical zero state at their
one outputs do not instigate any action at the corresponding
SET input of the flip-flops in the upper register. These upper
register flip-flops are left in their original state, and the
data transfer may not be carried out correctly. This is easily
solved by adding one more operation. With the logic shown in
Fig. 12 it is necessary to put a logical one on the CLEAR line
to set all the flip-flops of the upper register to zero. When
this is done, a pulse may be applied on the STROBE line and the
contents of the lower register will be correctly transferred
to the upper register.
Considering the details of transferring data from one
flip-flop register to another flip-flop register, it is easy

---

*The CMA and other PDP-8 instructions are defined in Appendix
 IV.

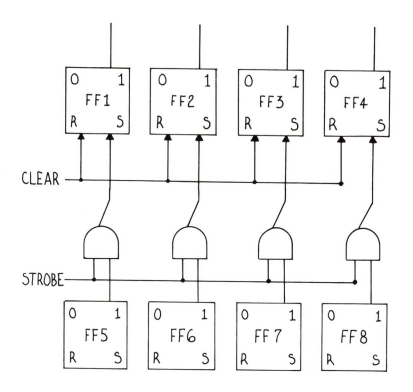

Fig. 12. A logic diagram illustrating how the contents of
one register may be transferred to another register
In this case a logical one is placed on the CLEAR
line followed by a logical one on the STROBE line.
This results in the contents of the register composed of flip-flops 5 through 8 to be transferred
to the register composed of flip-flops 1 through 4.

to understand how the term "strobing data into a register" ha
come into usage.

If it is desired to transfer data from one register to
another with only the STROBE operation, it can be accomplishe
by a slight modification of the logic as shown in Fig. 13.
Only one bit of each of the two flip-flop registers has been
shown for brevity. In Fig. 13 AND gates have been interposed
between both outputs of the lower register flip-flop and the
RESET and the SET inputs of the upper register. A little
thought and the construction of a truth table for this logic
circuit will show that when a logical one is applied to the
STROBE line the exact state of the lower flip-flop is transferred to the upper flip-flop.

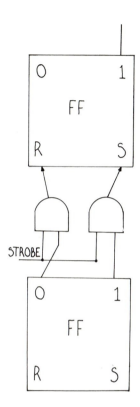

Fig. 13. A logic diagram showing one bit from each of two
          registers that illustrates how a means may be im-
          plemented to transfer data from one register to
          another with only a STROBE pulse.

1.6 Adders

Enough background has been developed now to permit a
brief look at how mathematical operations can be performed
with computer logic. Turn back to the EXCLUSIVE OR logic
shown in Fig. 5 and its associated truth table. A little
study of the truth table will show that it represents the addition of two binary bits, that is A + B = C, in binary arithmetic. There is one exception; 1 + 1 = 0 with the carry of
a 1. Thus, the EXCLUSIVE OR logic operation does not take
account of a carry bit.

Remember that in Boolean notation the EXCLUSIVE OR operation is given by the following:

$$A \oplus B = A\bar{B} + B\bar{A} = SUM$$

Turn now to Fig. 14. The two inverters, the two AND gates, and the OR gate of the upper portion of the picture represent the EXCLUSIVE OR operation. Thus, their output may be referre to as the SUM which is shown at the right hand terminal. Now by adding the third AND gate of the lower portion of the figu it is possible to know if the carry is a 0 or a 1.

The logic circuit shown in Fig. 14 is referred to as a ha adder. Although it does find the value of the carry bit, no provision is made to add the carry to the next column of bina bits which would occur to the left in the natural order of add two binary numbers.

To add two binary bits together and take proper account of the carry and the carry operation it is necessary to construct what is called a full-adder which is shown in Fig. 15*. A full-adder can add one column consisting of two binary bits. Looking at Fig. 15 it can be seen that the full-adder has thre inputs. The A and B inputs represent the binary bits of one column. The CARRY IN input represents the carry bit that results from the addition of the column of binary bits to the right of the one presently being summed. Following the operation of the logic circuit in Fig. 15 and seeing the results as denoted there in Boolean algebra, it can be seen that the appropriate sum is presented at the output labeled SUM and that the carry for the next right most column of binary bits is presented at the CARRY OUT terminal. One method of adding several columns of binary bits is to take the SUM output and set a bit in a register corresponding to the column that has just been totaled, and to take the CARRY OUT output and run it to the CARRY IN input of the adder for the next column to the left.

There are two ways of adding binary numbers from the har ware standpoint. One can add binary numbers together with on full-adder as shown in Fig. 15 by operating on each column of the binary numbers in a serial fashion. On the other hand, it can be arranged that there be a full-adder for each binary column in the numbers to be added so that the addition of all columns takes place simultaneously. The first type of additic logic is referred to as a serial adder and the latter is referred to as a parallel adder. The major considerations are that the serial adder is more economical, but is much slower than the parallel adder.

In an earlier chapter it has been shown that it is possible to build a computer which performs nothing but the addition operation. By using the addition operation, subtraction can be performed with two's complement arithmetic, and the necessary logic to complement the contents of a register has

---

*It can be seen that a full-adder is composed of two half-adders and an OR gate.

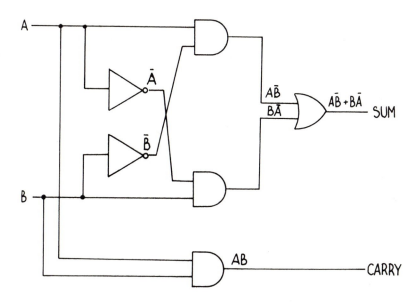

Fig. 14. A half-adder circuit. This is an EXCLUSIVE OR
circuit plus an AND gate for the carry bit.

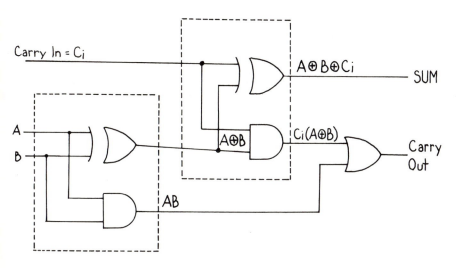

Fig. 15. A full-adder circuit. This circuit is composed of
two half-adder circuits plus an OR gate.

been discussed. Furthermore, multiplication can be done by
repeated additions, and division may be done with repeated
subtractions. Therefore, enough is now know to understand a
computer and its hardware in a rather fundamental way.

2.0 CENTRAL PROCESSING UNIT REGISTERS

At this point there is one major aspect of computer hardware that has not been taken into account; timing. Some of the
logic operations that have been given as examples have left
this only as an inference. For example, the clear and transfer
operation that was shown in the illustration of information
transfer from one register to another. Later in this chapter
another example appears in the discussion of I/0 channels. It
is shown there that timing, as related to magnetic core memories, is particularly important.

In most of the present computers the CPU acts as a controller over the timing in relation to the step sequences,
timed durations, etc. of the events that are taking place within the computer. However, to delve into the subject of the
timing of logic operations is beyond the scope of this book.
What will be discussed here are the registers represented in
the CPU. Most of the major registers in a computer are associated with the CPU. All of those mentioned in the following
are not necessarily found in any given computer. Similarly,
there might be a few that are found in some computers but are
not mentioned here.

The naming of registers is not universal, i.e., one manufacturer may label the registers within his computer with
names different than another manufacturer, although they may
perform exactly the same functions. Register names that are
found fairly frequently are simply letters. For example, A,
B, P and X, which often represent the accumulator register,
the extension register, the program counter, and the index
register(s) respectively.

It should also be noted that it is not always possible to
uniquely identify a register. For example, several registers
within a given computer might be usable as index registers; or
they might also be used as several accumulators. Thus, the
registers described are more important for the function they
perform than what name might be attached to them. Registers
have been broken into three major categories: the arithmetic
group of registers, the program control registers, and the
group of memory related registers.

2.1 Arithmetic Registers

Accumulator. The accumulator is usually the most complex
and versatile register in a computer. It is not totally relat

to the arithmetic operation, e.g., it is often heavily used
for Input/Output operations and logical operations.
Typically, the contents of the accumulator can be complemented, incremented by one, decremented by one, shifted
left or right, added to, and subtracted from, and often can
have both the INCLUSIVE and EXCLUSIVE OR performed between its
contents and the contents of other registers (including memory
registers).

As just noted, the accumulator register may also be used
as an Input/Output register. Normally, the sequence that takes
place in using the accumulator register as an output register
is to transfer the contents of the accumulator to some peripheral. At least one computer program instruction is required
to extract the data from the computer memory and place it in
the accumulator. At least one more instruction is required
to transfer it from the accumulator to the peripheral. Of
course, the accumulator can also be used as an input register.
That is, to bring data in from some peripheral device and deposit it in memory. The sequence of events for incoming data
is just the reverse of those for outgoing data. Some computers
have several registers which may be used as accumulators at
the choosing of the programmer. On the other hand, some computers have several registers all of which are accumulators
and may not be used for any other purpose.

Accumulators are always directly addressable from the
computer program. That is, instructions in the computer repertoire can always deposit information into the accumulator
register and read information directly from the accumulator
register. Thus, to say that a register is directly addressable, or as the term is sometimes used--accessible to the programmer, simply means that there are instructions in the computer repertoire which permit the direct accessing of that
particular register.

Normally the length of the accumulator register in bits
equals the word-length of the computer, e.g., a sixteen bit
computer will have a sixteen bit accumulator register.

Extension Register. This register is so named because
it can be used as an extension of the accumulator register;
primarily for performing double precision arithmetic. In using
the extension register in this way one can conceptually think
of the extension register as being positioned to the left of
the accumulator register. This combined register would have
the least significant bits of a double precision number in the
accumulator register and the most significant bits in the extension register. Other functions that often may be performed
with these two registers linked are to rotate the contents of
both registers simultaneously (left or right), or the ability
to transfer the contents of the accumulator register into the
extension register, or the extension register into the accumulator register. On some computers the extension register can
be used as an independent accumulator.

The extension register is normally directly addressable.
Usually the length of the extension register is equal to
the word length of the computer.

2.2 Program Control Registers

Program Counter. The basic function of the program counter
register is to keep track of the address containing the next instruction. In other words, if this register is examined at any
time, its contents will be the memory location where the next
computer instruction to be executed is stored.
     The program counter register is not always addressable.
It is a strong feature of a computer to be able to address the
program counter, but it also calls for more care on the part
of the programmer. Obviously, if the program itself can modify
the contents of the program counter, inadvertent modifications
can cause the program to go amuck.
     There is not usually any direct relation between the length
of the program counter and the word length of the computer. However, it is true that the length of the program counter has to
be at least equal to the largest portion of memory that the
computer can address directly. For example, suppose that a
computer is delivered with 4096 words of memory, then this computer has, by one means or another, the ability to address 4096
memory locations. This means that the program counter must be
at least twelve bits in length. Likewise, if the computer is
later expanded with another 4096 word module, then it must be
possible to expand the length of the program counter so that
it can now have at least thirteen bits to indicate all 8,192
words of memory.
     Index Registers. The index register is not universally
found in computers. A computer may have none, one, or several.
Index registers are usually very versatile. At a minimum they
may be incremented and decremented. Often this increment and
decrement function is combined as a part of the instruction
format for the computer so that the increments or decrements
may be done before, after, or before and after executing an
instruction. As a simple example, suppose that a program has
a list of data somewhere in its memory and each piece of data
is to be extracted one at a time and operated upon. Then a
pointer may be set up which is the memory address of the first
element of the list, and this can be placed in an index register. Then as a part of the instruction to extract data from
the list, the index register containing the pointer can be incremented after the withdrawal of each piece of data.
     Index registers are also often used in relation to ad-
dressing within the computer. The index register, for example,
may contain what is called a base address. The purpose of the
base address is to combine it in some prescribed manner with
the address field of a memory reference instruction to get the

absolute address that is to be referenced. In this type of
operation it is desirable to combine both the base addressing
and the increment and decrement feature of index registers.
The instruction that combines its address field with the base
address contained in the index register might also instruct
that the index register be incremented before or after the memory reference has been performed.

Index registers are usually directly addressable.

Index registers are usually equal to one word length of
the computer.

2.3 Memory Related Registers

Memory Buffer Register. Suppose that a word of data is
to be transferred to the computer memory. The word of data
is transferred from its original location to the memory buffer
register and is then transferred to the specified location in
the computer memory. Likewise, if data is to be extracted
from the computer memory, it is first placed in the memory buffer register and then finally transferred on to its eventual
destination. All data that passes to or from the computer
memory must momentarily reside in the memory buffer register,
hence the word buffer.

The memory buffer register is not directly addressable.

The memory buffer register is equal in length to a memory
word. In almost all cases, the memory words are equal to the
word length of the computer.

Memory Address Register. The memory address register
performs a function that is directly related to the memory
buffer register. As indicated, the data going to and from the
memory must always pass through the memory buffer register.
It is the memory address register which specifies the memory
location to or from which the data is to be transferred. Thus,
there is always an action on the part of both the memory buffer
and the memory address register whenever a memory word is to
be transferred.

The memory address register is not directly addressable.

The memory address register must be of sufficient length
to permit it to contain the address of the largest addressable
word in the memory of the computer.

3.0 MEMORY MODULES

The memory discussed here is specifically that found on
the basic computer and does not include the many other on-line
and off-line methods of storage such as disk, paper tape and
magnetic tape. These other means of storage are covered in
the chapter "Computer Peripherals". In the chapter "Computer
Instructions" the manner in which the binary bits of a memory

are grouped into words has been discussed.   In this chapter,
the discussion delves a little further into the manner in which
magnetic core memories operate.

It should be mentioned that the memories now used in the
basic on-line computers are almost universally magnetic core
memory. Magnetic core memories are constructed from small
ferromagnetic, donut-shaped objects which are referred to as
magnetic cores. Each donut can store one binary bit because
it can be magnetized in one of two different directions. Therefore, each of the two directions correspond to either a logical zero or a logical one. These magnetic donuts permit construction of memories that are relatively small in size.
Typically, the donuts are only a few thousands of an inch in
diameter, e.g., twenty thousandths of an inch.

3.1   Read/Write

The term read/write in relation to magnetic core memories
is used to describe the typical memory in which information can
both be read and written. A binary bit is stored in a core
(magnetic donut) by passing current through that particular
core and setting its state of magnetization. A current in one
direction will set the core to the state that corresponds to
a logical one, and a current in the opposite direction will
place the core in the opposite state of magnetization corresponding to a logical zero. To read the information that is
contained in the core, it is necessary to pass a sense current
through the core. This causes the core to change status which
induces a current in sensing wires. This current pulse can be
detected, and the binary core has now been "read". Unfortunately, as we have just seen, the sensing current also changes
the state of magnetization, thereby destroying the information
contained in the magnetic core. For this reason magnetic core
memories are referred to as destructive read-out memories. The
act of reading information from the memory destroys its contents.
However, magnetic core memories are used as permanent storage
devices. Each time information is read from magnetic cores the
next operation must be to write the same information back into
the same cores. Therefore, it is necessary to have two cycles.
One is referred to as a read cycle which reads the information
from the memory, and the second is the write cycle which writes
the information back into the memory.

When data is being written into the memory for the first
time, the read cycle effects the clearing of the memory. That
is, the read cycle sets all the cores that have been selected
to a logical zero. Then, the write cycle sets the cores with
the information being placed in the memory.

The total time that is required for the read cycle plus the
write cycle is referred to as the memory cycle time. When one
breaks the memory cycle time into the individual read and write

cycles, it is usually found that the read cycle is shorter than the write cycle. In present-day on-line computers the memory cycle time is the order of one to two microseconds.

Because of the small size of the magnetic cores and the small wires that are threaded through them to read, write and sense, memory stacks tend to be small. Most of those found in on-line computers are only a few inches in each dimension.

Magnetic core memories are randomly accessible. This means that any address, i.e., location in the memory, may be selected for either reading or writing information by loading the appropriate number into the memory address register.

3.2 Read-Only

Read-only memories are special purpose memories that are coming into widespread use. One often sees the term read-only memory shortened to the letters ROM. Just as the term implies, read-only memories can only be read and hence, contain permanent information. Normally the desired information is placed in the read-only memory by the manufacturer. Because the data is written there permanently, the read operation is nondestructive. Thus, the time to extract information from a read-only memory is shortened considerably because there is no longer need for a write cycle. Read times on some of the present memories are the order of a hundred nanoseconds.

At present read-only memories are being used in two major ways. One is to use a read-only memory as a part of the central processing unit of the basic computer. For example, the read-only memory can be used to accomplish very fast internal operations such as instruction decoding.

Another use for read-only memory is to store programs that are used frequently or those programs that it may be desirable to execute very fast. An example of the latter category might be a program to perform the Fast Fourier Transform. This is a mathematical operation that requires extremely large numbers of computations to be performed and, therefore, must be executed as fast as possible. Read-only memories, used for this purpose of storing programs, are now being provided in some computers and in such a manner that they may be plugged directly into the CPU. This then permits the user to have on hand several read-only memories containing different programs. If this pluggable capability is available, then one of the read-only memories can contain what are normally referred to as maintenance programs. Maintenance programs are those that are used to exercise the computer to see if it is in good operating condition. Thus, to run a routine maintenance check on the computer, the read-only memory containing the maintenance programs are plugged in, and these programs are executed to put the computer through its paces.

3.3   Memory Protection and Parity

There are many occasions when it is desirable to have a
means of protecting memory so that data may not be written
into it. For example, if a computer system is being run with
an elaborate monitor system, or other important programs or
data, these important portions of memory can be protected.
Memory protection is available either as standard equipment or
options on almost all on-line computer systems.

Memory protection can be implemented in at least two ways.
One is to add an extra bit to each memory word and designate
that bit as the memory protection bit. The computer is then
constructed in such a way that if a word is addressed and the
memory protect bit is set to a one, it is impossible to write
into that memory word. Of course, this approach increases the
size of the memory in terms of the total number of bits. For
example, a computer that is referred to as a sixteen bit computer and which has such a memory protection option actually
has seventeen bits in each of its memory words. In some computers enough capability is provided to make it possible under
program control to set the memory protect bit of any arbitrary
word in the memory. This allows the maximum possible amount of
flexibility in protecting memory, but may be rather demanding
on the programmer if the addresses to be protected are scattered
haphazardly throughout the memory.

Another method is to arrange in the design of the computer
for the facility to protect whole blocks of memory at once. In
this approach the programmer only has to designate a given block
of memory and then issue a command or commands which causes that
whole block to become a protected portion of memory. Hardware-
wise this type of protection can still be implemented by setting
a bit in each memory word, or it can be accomplished by using
registers within the computer which, on each memory access, look
at the contents of the memory address register and determine
if the address being accessed is within a protected block.

Another method may be used for memory protection, and that
is to have monitor programs written in such a manner that the
programmer can designate to the monitor areas of memory that
he wishes to be protected. This is protection by software.
Although this is considerably more economical than hardware
protection, it is not nearly as infallible.

Another feature that is frequently found in computer systems
is memory parity. If a computer memory has the parity feature,
a bit is added to each word in the memory which is called the
memory parity bit*. Each time a word is written into the memory,
the memory parity bit is set or not set according to the bit

---

*A computer with both memory protection and memory parity may
  have two extra bits per word for these features.

combination of the word being stored. Likewise, when the word
is again read from the memory, the condition of the memory
parity bit is checked to see if an error has occurred in either
the reading or writing of the word into memory. Assume a memory in which the convention of odd parity has been chosen.
What does this mean? Suppose that the computer is a sixteen
bit computer. Then when a word is about to be stored into the
computer's memory, hardware within the CPU will, in effect,
count the number of bits in the sixteen bit word that are set
equal to a one. If the number of bits is odd, then the parity
bit in the memory will be set to zero. However, if the number
of one bits in the word is even, the parity bit will be set
equal to a one. Thus, to say that the memory has odd parity
is to say that each time a word is stored the number of bits
that are set to one are always odd, if the parity bit is included along with the bits of the normal word. If the word
is extracted from the memory and it is found that the number
of bits including the parity bit are not odd, then an error
has obviously occurred. This does not indicate where the error
occurred, but only that an error has occurred. Another short-
coming of this approach is as follows: if the error is such
that two bits* are in error, then the total number of one bits
remains odd and the error is not detected.

     Typically, the programmer does not have to be concerned
with the memory parity bits. The parity bits do not appear
in registers such as the accumulator, index registers, etc.
If a memory parity error is detected, most computers set a
flag which notifies the programmer that an error condition
has occurred. It is then up to the programmer to decide what
action the program shall take upon the detection of the error.

     As an aside, it is interesting to note that the type of
flags just mentioned are normally flip-flop circuits. A flip-
flop circuit with its one output sitting on a logical one is
normally referred to as a "raised flag".

4.0   INPUT/OUTPUT CHANNELS

     The input/output (I/O) channels are a very important part
of an on-line computer because they normally determine many of
the important characteristics of the computer. For example,
the I/O channels determine how fast data can be transferred
to and from the computer memory, how easy it is to attach peripherals to the computer, and how fast the computer can respond to peripheral devices.

     The electrical path that the data actually travels over
is normally referred to as the I/O bus. The I/O bus, in the

---

*Or any even number of bits.

usual electrical sense of the word bus, is a path with several
entry and exit points. A computer may actually have two I/0
buses; one for incoming data and one for outgoing data. On the
other hand, it may only be one I/0 bus which is bi-directional,
i.e., data may pass in both directions on the bus.

4.1 Program Controlled Transfers

There are three major methods of moving data in and out
of an on-line computer; the program controlled transfer is the
simplest.* The term program controlled comes from the fact
that the program being executed in the computer actually controls the data that is transferred. In this method the accumulator usually acts as an I/0 register. The normal sequential
order is to load a data word into the accumulator, give an I/0
instruction, and then wait for notification from the peripheral
that the transfer has taken place.

A program controlled transfer can be illustrated with the
PDP-8 instruction set and the teleprinter by the following program:

```
LØØP,   CLA             /CLEAR THE ACCUMULATØR
        TAD  I  DATA    /LØAD AC WITH DATA WØRD
        TLS             /PRINT DATA WØRD
        TSF             /PRINT CØMPLETE?
        JMP     .-1     /NØ, CHECK AGAIN
        ISZ     DATA    /YES, ADVANCE TØ NEXT DATA WØRD
        JMP     LOOP    /REPEAT PRINT ØPERATIØN
```

Going through the instruction sequence, the accumulator is
first cleared and then loaded with one data word. The TLS
command causes this data word (character) to be printed on the
teleprinter. The next instruction, the TSF instruction, then
checks to see if the print operation has been completed. The
TSF instruction is to be interpreted as "skip on the teleprinter
flag". In other words, a flip-flop register, which is the teleprinter flag, is being repeatedly checked to see if it is in
the one state which indicates flag up. It is necessary to check
this flag because the computer operates so much faster than the
printer that the computer would very soon be far ahead of the
printer and most of the information to be printed would be lost.
Since the computer operates on time scales the order of a microsecond, the print command, TLS, is given in a few microseconds
at the most. However, the teleprinter requires approximately
one hundred milliseconds to perform the print operation. Thus,
the computer can easily load a new word and instruct the printer

---

*The other two are the data channel transfer and the direct
memory access. Both will be taken up shortly.

to print this new word long before the previous character has
been printed. In fact, looking back at the program, it can be
seen that if the teleprinter flag is not up, then the next instruction executed is the jump command (JMP .-1) which will
cause the program to again loop back and execute the TSF instruction to see if the flag has yet been raised. These two
instructions are executed many thousands of times before the
print operation is complete. Once the flag raises, notifying
the computer that the transfer is complete, the next TSF instruction executed by the program executes a skip to the instruction ISZ DATA. This instruction advances the pointer
DATA to the next piece of data in the memory, and then the program jumps back to the tag LØØP and repeats the sequence for
the next character.

For program controlled transfers into the computer the
sequence of the example above is essentially reversed. The
peripheral device must notify the computer that it has data
to transfer, and then the appropriate action takes place. This
is illustrated by the following small program which shows how
data can be brought in from the Teletype keyboard and stored
in the computer memory.

```
LØØP,  KSF              /HAS A KEY BEEN DEPRESSED?
       JMP    .-1       /NØ, CHECK AGAIN
       KRB              /YES, READ THE DATA WØRD
       DCA I  DATA      /STØRE AC
       ISZ    DATA      /ADVANCE TØ NEXT DATA LØCATIØN
       JMP    LØØP      /CHECK KEYBØARD
```

The first instruction of the program checks the keyboard flag.
This is again a flip-flop, and the KSF instruction checks to
see if the one output is in the logical one state. The KSF
command can be interpreted to mean "skip on the keyboard flag".
If the flag is not up, the next instruction executed is the
JMP instruction which loops the computer back to again check
the flag. When the user strikes a key, the keyboard flag is
raised and the next time the KSF instruction is executed, the
program skips to the instruction KRB. The KRB instruction
reads the character from the keyboard and places it in the
accumulator. The DCA instruction then deposits the character
in the address designated by the pointer DATA. Finally, the
program increments the pointer DATA to prepare for the next
character and jumps back to the tag LØØP which starts the computer checking the keyboard flag again. The computer will be
back-checking the flag long before the user has lifted his
finger from the key.

Note the different sense of the keyboard flag and the
printer flag. In the case of the printer the raising of the
flag essentially says, "I am through", i.e., a character has
been printed. In the case of the keyboard the raising of the
flag indicates that the teleprinter has data for the computer.

Therefore, the teleprinter flag indicates the completion of an action whereas the keyboard flag indicates the beginning of an action.

4.2   Interrupt Structures

The program controlled transfers which have just been illustrated are somewhat inefficient in the utilization of the computer CPU because of the time spent checking the individual flags. If a means can be devised whereby the computer does not have to repeatedly check the keyboard or some other flag, then a good deal of computer time can be made available for other purposes. A means must be found to get the attention of the computer whenever a flag is raised. This is accomplished with an interrupt structure in the computer.

The action of an interrupt may be taken literally. The raising of a flag causes the operation that is currently in progress in the computer to be interrupted so that attention may be given to the peripheral device which raised the flag. There is more than one way to implement an interrupt structure. The simplest method is to construct a one-level interrupt structure. To implement a one-level interrupt structure the on-line computer is provided with an interrupt bus. A level is put on the interrupt bus whenever any device raises a flag. Normally the computer finishes the execution of the current instruction and then acknowledges the interrupt, i.e., recognizes that the level of the bus has been raised. The next action depends on the specific computer being used. Some computing systems save the condition of the computer at this point. By saving the condition of the computer, it is meant that all the major registers must be stored in memory. This might include the accumulator register, the extension register and the index registers. In some computers the condition is not automatically saved, and the programmer has to make provisions in his interrupt handling programs to save the condition of the computer.

After the condition of the computer has been saved, with the one-level interrupt system, it is then necessary to identify the source of the interrupt. It is important to note that in raising the level of the bus, the peripheral device has, in no way, been identified.* The identification of the device can be illustrated with a small PDP-8 program as shown below.

```
        .
        .
        TSF              /PRINTER INTERRUPT?
        SKP              /NØ, TRY ANØTHER DEVICE
```

---

*Assuming there is more than one device connected to the interrupt bus.

```
JMP   PRINT    /YES, SERVICE PRINTER
KSF            /KEYBØARD INTERRUPT?
SKP            /NØ, TRY ANOTHER DEVICE
JMP   KEYBD    /YES, SERVICE KEYBØARD
  .
  .
```

The identification of the interrupting device is accomplished in this case by using what is called a skip chain. This a- rises from the fact that the PDP-8 device testing instructions are in the form of skips. The sample program above tests the printer and keyboard flags to see if either raised the inter- rupt bus. Looking at the program in more detail, the first skip is for the printer. If the printer flag is up, then the program skips to the JMP PRINT instruction. Presumably PRINT is a routine which services the printer. If the printer is not the device that raised the level of the interrupt bus, then the SKP instruction is executed, taking the program to the KSF instruction which then checks the keyboard flag. A similar sequence is followed here, and the program jumps to the routine called KEYBD to service the keyboard, if it was indeed the key- board that raised the interrupt bus.

The service routines for each device should restore the condition of the computer when service has been completed. This means taking the initial contents of all the registers before the interrupt and reloading them into the registers.

When using a chain of test commands as has been done a- bove, the order of the chain gives one device priority over another. If a device is to be given a higher priority, its skip instruction is placed higher in the skip chain. This does not permit equal priorities to be given to devices.

The one-level interrupt structure has partially accompli- shed the original goal. Namely, the computer no longer has to repeatedly check each device to see if it is active, and hence can continue operation until a device gets attention via the interrupt bus. However, with the one-level interrupt it is still necessary to use programming to identify which device interrupted the computer and little sophistication may be used in assigning priorities to one device over another. ·As an ex- ample of the need for priority assignment, consider a device attached to a computer which is of such a nature that the com- puter must respond to any interrupt request within a set period of time. Further suppose that another device, such as a tele- printer, is attached to the computer which has no such time re- quirement. Then, it is desirable to give the device, which has a time requirement, priority over the teleprinter, i.e., if these two devices interrupt the computer simultaneously, the device with the time requirement is served first (given pri- ority).

To overcome the disadvantages of having to identify the device that has caused the interrupt with software, and the

problems of assigning priorities to various devices, computer
systems are often provided with a multilevel interrupt structure. This is also referred to as a hardware priority interrupt structure. The usual approach to implementing a priority
interrupt structure is to permanently assign one or more memory
locations to each level of interrupt. This concept can be
better explained by referring to Fig. 16. Suppose the system
is such that priority zero is the highest priority, priority
one is the next higher priority, and so forth through M levels
of priority. In this example the priority zero device is
associated with memory address N and memory address N + 1.
Likewise the priority one device is associated with memory
addresses N + 2 and N + 3 and so forth. To illustrate how
such an interrupt structure might work, suppose that the device
at priority M - 1 becomes active and sends an interrupt signal
to the computer. As in the case of the one-level interrupt the
computer discontinues execution of the program that is in process. Also, as in the case of the one-level interrupt structure,
the condition of the computer may automatically be saved, or
the program may have to save the condition of the computer.
In the present example, it is assumed that the computer will
at least save some information about the condition of the CPU.
This might be the program counter plus some status bits. These
are stored in the memory address N + 2M - 2. Then the computer
automatically executes the instruction contained in memory
address N + 2M - 1. Normally the instruction located in this
last address is a jump to a service routine for the device
having priority M - 1. Often there is only one memory address
associated with each device on the interrupt bus. In this instance the instruction in that single memory address is the
jump instruction to the service routine.

Now, while the service routine for the device at the priority level M - 1 is being executed, suppose the device at
priority level one generates an interrupt. Because this device has a higher priority, the service routine for the device
at the level M - 1 will be interrupted. This interrupt takes
place in exactly the same manner that the original main program
was interrupted by the device at priority level M - 1. That
is, the condition of the computer must again be saved. Once
the interrupt from the priority one level has been acknowledged,
the computer deposits the necessary information in memory
address N + 2, proceeds to the memory address N + 3, and jumps
to the service routine for the priority one device.

This process can continue all the way up the priority
scale. If the device on priority level zero became active
while the priority one device is being serviced, the service
routine for the priority one device is interrupted, and the
computer turns its attention to the priority zero device. It
is important to note that if the sequence of events just described takes place, there are several different conditions
of the computer that have been saved. The interrupt structure

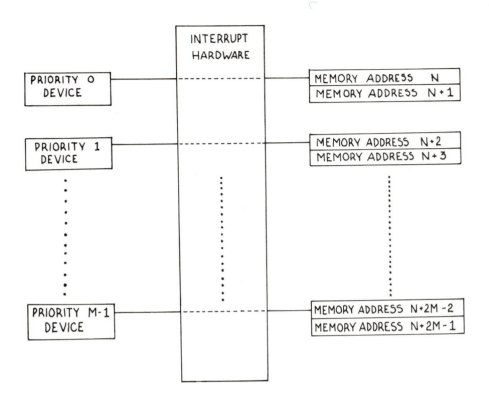

Fig. 16. An example of how a priority interrupt structure might be implemented. In this example each device is connected directly to two memory locations via the interrupt hardware.

sees that this string of events is properly unwound. When the service routine for the priority zero device is completed, its return causes the computer to be restored to the condition it was in when the priority one level device was being serviced. That service routine is completed and its return in turn causes the computer to be restored to the condition when the priority M - 1 level was being serviced and finally, this return restores the computer to its original condition when the first interrupt occurred.

Some of the advantages of a hardware priority interrupt structure can now be seen. Because each device is associated with a specific memory address, or group of addresses, identification of the device that caused the interrupt is automatic. Furthermore, the priority of the device in relationship to other devices is determined by the level to which it is attached.

The priority level interrupt structure on some computer systems has many program controls to go with the interrupt structure. For example, it is often possible to arm or disarm any individual level of interrupt. Suppose that for some reason during the operation the priority one level device is to be ignored. Then a command is given which disarms that particular device level so that it cannot interrupt the computer. The arming and disarming of priority levels may take two forms: the disarming might literally shut off the device attached to that level, i.e., not permit it to interrupt the computer at all, or the disarm might be of the nature of putting that particular level of interrupt in a wait state. This means that if an interrupt request occurs while that level is in a wait state, no interrupt occurs, but the fact that an interrupt request occurred is remembered, and as soon as that priority level is again armed, an interrupt would immediately occur.

Interrupts may not always be associated with devices external to the computer. It is quite common to have such functions as power-failsafe, parity, internal clocks, and other CPU hardware attached to the interrupt bus. In the case of the power-failsafe, any loss of power to the computer immediately establishes an interrupt state which typically is very high in priority and automatically saves the condition of the computer. This implies that a power-fail feature has been attached to the computer which keeps the power at high enough levels to allow these steps to be executed before the computer ceases operation.

It is quite convenient to have clocks attached to the interrupt system to utilize them as a means of keeping time. For example, if a clock emits a pulse every one sixtieth of a second, and it is desired to interrupt the computer every second, then a negative sixty is placed in some memory address. On each clock pulse the hardware increments the negative number. After the sixtieth increment the location goes to zero and the hardware senses this and notifies the program that one second has elapsed.

Priority interrupt programs can give rise to some special programming problems. One that is particularly complex is associated with what is referred to as reentrant coding. Suppose that the programmer has written a utility subroutine; for example, a routine to print characters. Call this print routine UTIL. Suppose that UTIL can be called by several interrupt service routines which accommodate different levels of priority.

With this set of conditions it is inevitable that at some time the following events will occur. A low level priority interrupt occurs and execution of the subroutine UTIL will be in progress when a higher level interrupt occurs. After the higher level interrupt the computer goes to the appropriate service subroutine which again calls the subroutine UTIL. Once UTIL has been executed the interrupt structure causes the

computer to return to the service of the lower priority interrupt which means returning to the execution of UTIL. However,
at this point there has been an execution of UTIL in the inter-
im which means any constants that are computed during the execution of UTIL have been lost and the completion of this subroutine will now, in all probability, give wrong answers.

The subroutine UTIL is reentrant, if in the situation just
described, it has provisions to keep track of its own constants
in such a manner that the correct answers are found when the
computer returns from the higher level interrupt. It is easy
to see that the writing of reentrant coding is considerably
more complex than normal service subroutine coding.* However,
the only alternative is to waste computer memory by writing the
same subroutine several times and using some guise such as
giving each of these subroutines, that are actually identical,
different names so that they may be called by only one service
routine.

4.3   Data Channel Transfers

Program controlled data transfers are time consuming because several instructions are typically executed for each word
that is transferred. This leads to lower data transfer rates
and requires complete control of the transfer by the program.
Data channel transfers on the other hand, are designed to operate with minimal interaction from the program and to provide
for rather high speed block transfers.

Normally each device on the data channel is assigned two
memory locations. These memory locations are not to be con-
fused with those of a priority interrupt structure that might
also exist in the computer. One of the addresses might contain
the first memory address to which the data is to be transferred
and the second memory location might be the number of words that
are to be transferred. In any event, the two memory addresses
must be a combination of any two of the following three variables: the first address in the computer's memory to or from
which the data is to be transferred, the last address in the
computer's memory to or from which data is to be transferred,
and the number of words to be transferred.

In a data channel transfer of a block of data** the computer program typically loads the appropriate numbers in the

---

* There are exceptions. A few on-line computers have hardware
  features which make reentrant programming rather easy.
**By block of data here we mean one or more data words are
  being transferred to consecutive locations in the memory,
  or from consecutive locations in the memory.

two addresses associated with the device in question. After
loading these two memory locations the program, in effect,
says, "go". At this point the sequence proceeds something
like the following for the transfer of each data word to or
from the memory of the computer: the first memory cycle increments one of the two registers in the memory associated
with that data channel device; the second memory cycle increments the second register in memory associated with that data
channel device; and the third, and possibly a fourth, memory
cycle actually transfers the data to or from the memory of the
computer. Thus, three or four memory cycles are typically required for the transfer of each data word. However, this sequence takes place completely automatically, and no program
interference or control is required. The first two memory
cycles perform the functions of the programs that were given
earlier to illustrate program controlled data transfers, i.e.,
they update the pointers that indicate where the data is to
go and keep track of the number of words transferred.

A device on a data channel is normally attached to the
interrupt structure of the computer also, and the interface
to the device, is built in a manner such that when the complete block transfer has taken place, an interrupt is generated to notify the computer program that the transfer has been
completed.

4.4   Direct Memory Access Transfers

In principal the direct memory access transfers of data
are not materially different from data channel transfers.
Direct memory access (DMA) transfers are designed to transfer
blocks of data to or from consecutive memory locations in the
computer memory at higher speeds. Two registers are again required for the same information, i.e., the place in memory to
or from which the data is to be transferred and the number of
data words to be transferred.

The primary difference between the DMA transfer and the
data channel transfer is that in the DMA transfer the two
registers, which keep track of the memory locations and the
number of words transferred, are no longer permanently assigned registers in the computer magnetic core memory, but are
hardware registers. Usually these hardware registers are located in the peripheral interface. By utilizing hardware
registers rather than memory registers, the contents of the
registers may be incremented in less than one memory cycle
time. Therefore, in the DMA transfer of one memory word only
one memory cycle is required rather than the three or four
memory cycles of the data channel transfer.

One might ask why all transfers are not DMA transfers
since they are three to four times faster than data channel
transfers. The answer is two-fold. First, many devices are

not fast enough to utilize the speeds that can be obtained in
a DMA transfer. Secondly, the building of the hardware registers makes the interfacing of a device to the DMA ports more
expensive than to a data channel because the amortized cost
of a memory location is less than the cost of a hardware register. It must be noted that with the advent of integrated
circuitry, this cost difference is not nearly so great as it
has been in the past.

With the DMA transfer, as with the data channel transfers,
devices are again attached to the computer interrupt structure
so that a program may be notified of the completion of a data
transfer. If a computer program is in execution, program instructions may continually be executed interspersed with the
DMA transfers. Whether or not any program instructions are
executed during the transfer depends upon the speed and priority of the peripheral device. If the peripheral device is
inherently as fast as, or faster than the computer memory cycle
time, and the priority is higher, then the transfer blocks out
all other operations.

4.5 Synchronous and Asynchronous Computers

Synchronous computers operate on a time base which is
centered around a clock in the computer whose frequency is
directly related to the memory cycle time; hence, the frequency of the clock is normally some submultiple of the computer memory cycle time. All operations that take place in
the computer are synchronized on this clock frequency and are
themselves directly related to the computer's memory cycle
time.

In the synchronous computer the CPU might be said to act
as the keeper of the time. Also as an interrelated fact the
CPU determines the utilization of the I/0 bus. If data is
flowing on the I/0 bus to or from memory, the CPU must be
actively involved even though it may not be actually controlling the transfer of the data in the sense of the program controlled transfer.

In the synchronous computer the computer might be characterized as being CPU oriented. In the asynchronous computer
a different tact is taken. It is no longer necessary to have
all events within the basic computer taking place in lock step
with a frequency related to the memory cycle. Perhaps the
asynchronous computer might be characterized by saying that
it is I/0 bus oriented.

The CPU, the memory, and the peripheral devices all use
the I/0 bus. In the asynchronous computer, i.e., one with an
asynchronous bus, the CPU no longer strictly controls the flow
of data on the I/0 bus. In fact, in the asynchronous computer
the CPU, the memory, and the peripheral devices must all request use of the I/0 bus. The CPU is no longer the controlling
element of the situation.

This newer approach to computer organization is very significant for it now means that the CPU can be performing independent operations, such as program instruction executions,
while for example, data is flowing through the I/0 bus to or
from peripherals and memory. Also, since the computer does no
operate in lock step with the memory, it is possible to place
several different magnetic core memories on the I/0 bus with
each memory having a different memory cycle time. This, obviously, has considerable economic advantage. Programs and
data transfers that need to be executed in the fastest time
possible are placed in the fastest memory on the I/0 bus. How
ever, large quantities of data and program storage are placed
in slower memories on the same I/0 bus. Of course, the advantage acrues from the fact that the slower memories are considerably lower in cost than the faster memories.

When extremely high data transfer rates are required, the
asynchronous computer makes it possible to transfer data faster than the basic memory cycle time. To illustrate this, imagine a computer with an asynchronous I/0 bus on which four
memories with equal memory cycle times are attached. Then it
is possible to transfer data at rates which are approximately
one fourth the memory cycle time of the individual memories.
This is done in the following manner: the first data word is
transferred to memory number one. After this transfer has
been initiated, the transfer of the second data word is initiated to memory number two. With this transfer in progress
the transfer of word number three is started to memory three
and finally, the initiation of the transfer of the fourth memory word to the fourth memory. The fifth word goes into memory number one, the six into memory number two, etc.* Thus,
by what is called memory interleaving it is possible to transfer data to these four memory banks faster than to an individual memory bank. The technique of memory interleaving has
come into rather wide acceptance in large scale computing systems. This leads to what is sometimes described as an apparent memory cycle time or sub-cycle time.

4.6   Input/Output Processors

On some computers, particularly very large computer systems, the I/0 channels have become very sophisticated; in some
instances they can execute instruction sets. Sophisticated

---

*If the first word was placed in location N of memory one,
then the fifth word would be placed in location N + 1 of
memory one, the ninth word in N + 2, etc.

I/0 processors often have a considerable formatting capability.
That is, if formatting of data words is required as they are
transferred to or from peripheral devices, the formatting is
done by the I/0 processor rather than by the CPU of the computer system.

It can be seen that the sophisticated I/0 processors begin to take on many of the features of small computers. In a
few instances computer manufacturers have actually used small
computers to act as the I/0 processors for larger computer
systems.

PART III

ON-LINE COMPUTER UTILIZATION

CHAPTER 8

COMPUTER PERIPHERALS

1.0 INTRODUCTION

The input or output of information to computer peripherals is one of the first realities the beginning programmer must face. Usually, he has read the programming manual for the computer and has come to at least partially understand the significance of the computer's instructions. All will seem straightforward until that time he sets down to write his first program and approaches the point in the program where information must be read from a peripheral device or written into a peripheral device. It is at this point that the programmer realizes he does not understand the instruction set for input/output instructions as well as he thought, and also finds that he does not know enough about the computer peripheral he is attempting to use.

In assembly language programming it is necessary to have a fairly intimate knowledge of each of the peripherals that are to be used and how they work. In writing input/output instructions for various computer peripherals, the programmer will find certain flags are involved, time sequences are involved, and certain registers must be used for input or output transfer.

If the instance is one which involves an engineer, only a matter of degree differs from the instance of the programmer. The engineer still needs to know the flags, the timing sequences and the registers involved. Of course, the engineer has to know the electronic circuitry of these devices in order that he may build or repair computer interfaces. Nevertheless, the engineer still needs to know how to program input/output devices to see that they work correctly.

Computers may be interfaced to almost an infinity of devices. It is impossible to proceed in this chapter with such depth. However, an attempt has been made to cover the more common peripherals that are attached to computers and a few others that have been chosen because it is felt that they will be of significance in the near future. An attempt has

been made to cover each peripheral with enough depth to provide the reader with the knowledge that will enable him to
read the manufacturer's specifications for these peripherals
with enough comprehension to understand how each device might
be used in his own personal application.

2.0 THE TELETYPE TERMINAL

2.1 Role of the Teletype Terminal

The Teletype terminal plays a rather unique role with
present-day on-line computers because of its general availability and economic considerations. In one piece of equipment it combines a keyboard entry device, a printing device
and in many instances a paper tape punch and a paper tape
reader. In addition, it can contain a telecommunications link
in the form of a data modem or an accoustic coupler.
On-line computer systems are almost universally delivered
with a Teletype unit, and in fact, many systems are delivered
with no other peripheral device. Thus, the Teletype unit
plays a very important and unique role in on-line computer
systems.
A photograph of a Teletype unit has already been shown in
the chapter "Editing, Assembling, and Debugging".

2.2 Standard Configurations

Until recently, two basic Teletype models were commonly
used with on-line computers. These are the models 33 and 35
each of which comes in different configurations. The units
found with most on-line computers have the prefix ASR or KSR
standing for automatic send/receive and keyboard send/receive
respectively. The basic difference between these two prefixes
is that the units having the prefix ASR have paper tape reader
and punch equipment on them. The KSR models have no paper tape
equipment. The model 35 has the same alphanumerics available
as those on the model 33. It is primarily a heavier duty version of the 33 for use in those instances where the Teletype
terminal will find constant use (which is almost always true
of on-line computer systems).
Recently a new Teletype model has been marketed which is
called the Inktronic, and which uses a new printing technique.
Whereas the model 33 and model 35 teletypes are mechanical im-
pact printers the Inktronic prints by squirting small ink
droplets onto the page. These ink droplets form a pattern of
dots which makes up the characters. The dot patterns are obtained by controlling the flight of the ink droplets with an
electricstatic field device. The Inktronic model has the

advantages of faster speed (120 characters per second, versus
10 characters per second), and more reliability because there
are far fewer moving parts, and it is silent.

2.3   Important Features

The Teletype terminal is a bit serial device. Associated
with each character there is an 11 bit binary code. If a key
is struck, the 11 bits are sent serially to the computer; that
is, one at a time. Likewise, to initiate printing of a character the computer must send 11 bits in serial fashion to the
Teletype unit. The same comments hold for the punching and
the reading of paper tape.

To be specific the 11 bit code that is generated and received by the Teletype terminal is the ASCII code.* This is
an acronym for USA Standard Code for Information Interchange.
The ASCII code is becoming one of the more widely used codes.

The question often arises as to whether a Teletype unit
may be used with other than the ASCII code. The answer is
"no" because the Teletype unit is primarily a mechanical device which means the code is obtained by mechanical linkages
in the terminal itself. Therefore, modification of the code
is not an easy task.

With respect to mechanical linkages, it is important to
note that the printer and the paper tape punch are directly
linked. If the punch is turned on, any external input is both
typed by the teletypewriter and punched by the paper tape punch.
Therefore, it is impossible to prevent the printing of characters while punching paper tape. However, there is a switch
on the punch unit and it is possible to print but not punch
paper tape. In a similar manner the paper tape reader and the
keyboard of the Teletype unit are linked through common hardware. When the computer receives a character from the unit
it cannot distinguish as to whether the character originated
from the paper tape reader or the keyboard. This makes it
possible to provide input to a program by paper tape that normally has its input derived from the keyboard.

There are a myriad of options available for Teletype units.
A few are the ability to turn the paper tape equipment on and
off manually or automatically, different character sets and
keyboards, units with and without parity on the paper tape
equipment, and different paperfeed mechanisms.

---

*Remember that the ASCII code is normally a 7 or 8 bit code.
 The extra bits here are control bits used in the transmission
 of characters.

2.4   Programming Considerations

During the course of this chapter several sections such
as this are inserted to describe some of the special programming considerations that are related to the device being
described. These considerations are usually not so specific
as to require examples of programming but to point out some
of the aspects of each device that are unique.

2.4.1   Keyboard

As already mentioned, when a key is struck on the Teletype keyboard a series of 11 bits corresponding to an ASCII
character are transmitted to the computer. A flag is also
set indicating that the key has been struck, and until this
flag is lowered no more characters may be sent. This flag
can be utilized in two different ways. The primary purpose
of the flag is to notify the computer that a character has
been sent. Therefore, one way that the computer can determine that a character has been sent is to repeatedly check to
see if the flag has been raised. Once the flag has been detected, the computer can transfer the character into its own
registers and the computer program can manipulate it as desire
The flag may also be used to generate an interrupt to the computer. Since an interrupt breaks into the current program, th
method does not require frequent and periodic checking by the
computer. The computer only need respond when a character has
actually been sent.

In stating that the character is read from the Teletype
unit into the computer register it has been implied that a
certain operation has occurred. Because the bits have arrivec
in a serial fashion, it is necessary that hardware associated
with the computer or within the computer itself collect these
serial bits into one computer word or a portion of a word.
This is known as a serial-to-parallel conversion. Once the
character has been transferred, the computer clears the flag
to permit another character to be received from either the key
board or the paper tape reader.

After a character has been transferred to the computer it
might be directly stored in the computer memory or further decoding might be performed. A frequent need for further decoding follows from the striking of several keys sequentially
to enter decimal digits. It is often necessary to take these
decimal digits and convert them to a binary number. The chapter "Programming Examples" has a program to illustrate decimal
to-binary conversion.

2.4.2 Teleprinter

In analogy to the keyboard the computer sends an 11 bit serial code to the teleprinter. In so doing it is necessary to have hardware that performs a parallel-to-serial conversion. That is, to take the 11 bit characters as they exist in the computer's memory and send them to the Teletype unit one binary bit at a time.

A flag is associated with the teleprinter. However, in this case the flag has the reverse sense. It raises after a character is printed indicating availability of the teleprinter for printing another character.

A typical programming example for the printing operation is taking binary numbers from the computer core and converting them to decimal digits, i.e., a binary-to-decimal conversion. Again, there is an example in the chapter "Programming Examples".

2.4.3 Paper Tape Reader and Punch

The next section takes up codes and formats that are associated with the paper tape medium, therefore, these are not covered here.

Both the paper tape reader and punch of the Teletype terminal are mechanical devices. In the case of the paper tape reader one inch wide paper tape is pulled through the reader unit. This pulling action is facilitated by a sprocket that meshes with a strip of holes that run the length of the paper tape. As the paper tape moves it passes over a set of eight pins which are in a line at right angles to the direction of the tape motion. As each frame or line of holes on the paper tape passes over the eight pins they rise toward the paper tape. Where holes occur in the paper tape the pins momentarily pass through and the holes are sensed as logical ones. Where holes do not occur in the paper tape the pins strike the tape and rise no further. In this manner a character is read as eight binary bits where a hole in the paper tape corresponds to a logical one and no hole corresponds to logical zero.

It is important to note that this method of reading the paper tape permits any paper tape code to be read. The code need not specifically be ASCII as in the case of the keyboard and the printer.

The paper tape punch operates in a manner quite similar to the paper tape reader. In this case the blank paper tape is pulled over the punch head. There are eight punch pins in the head that are driven by solenoides. When an eight bit character is sent to the paper tape punch, each punch pin corresponding to a one is driven up through the paper. The punch pins that correspond to a zero in the character are not actuated. Again, the paper tape punch is completely code

independent.   Any combination of the eight pins may be
punched.
    Because of the independence of the paper tape equipment
from codes it is possible to devise any code that one desires
punch it on the paper tape and read it on the paper tape read
Of course, this requires the user to do the appropriate programming.

3.0   PAPER TAPE

3.1   General Comments

    The paper tape that is commonly used for computer oper-
ations is one inch wide and somewhat heavier than ordinary
notebook paper.   It usually comes in one of two forms.   One
form is to have the one inch strip rolled in a reel.   The
second form is referred to as fan-fold.   In this case the
paper is creased and folded back and forth in a zig-zag fashion much in the manner a roadmap is folded.
    The design of the actual paper tape reader and punch de-
termines whether paper tape in the form of rolls or in the
fan-fold form is to be used.   Equipment that uses rolls of
paper tapes requires reels upon which the paper tape may be
wound or unwound.   Equipment using fan-fold paper tape has
box-like structures for input and the output of the paper tap
so that it can be lifted off and stacked back in the fan-fold
pattern.
    Paper tape is available in different colors.   Therefore,
some color coding may be used.   Some paper tapes are impregnated with oil.   This is actually a lubrication feature for
some types of paper tape equipment.
    A modest investment in accessories greatly facilitates
the handling of paper tape.   A motor driven reel for winding
and rewinding large lengths of paper tape is a necessity.   It
is convenient to have small boxes or wall racks with slots ir
them for storage of the paper tape.   It is also very convenie
to have a splicer available to rejoin pieces of paper tape th
have been torn apart.
    Paper tape suffers from wear.   Tape that has been read r
peatedly will come to have elongated holes and eventually is
not read correctly.   Mechanical readers are particularly harc
on paper tape.   Wear can be reduced by using aluminized mylar
tape for those tapes that need to be read frequently.
    Paper tape is an inexpensive medium that has several ad-
vantages.   One of the major advantages is that the code that
is punched into the paper tape can be read visually.   This oi
ten is a convenient feature in identifying tapes and in also
checking for possible malfunctions or programming errors.

Paper tape is a permanent storage medium with rather low
density of information. Normally ten lines of holes are punched
per linear inch of the paper tape. To modify a paper tape, in
reality, means repunching the tape completely.

3.2 Formats

Formats for paper tape are to be distinguished from paper
tape character codes. Formats are the general layout of information on the paper tape itself.

3.2.1 Leader/Trailer

It is necessary in some way to indicate where the information on a paper tape begins and where the information ends.
This is normally accomplished by what is referred to as leader/
trailer. Typically for leader/trailer a special code is chosen.
Leader/trailer is illustrated in Fig. 1. The leader code
is punched in the front or beginning portion of the paper tape.
The end of the leader code marks the beginning of the information on the tape. Likewise, the ending of the information is
marked by the beginning of the trailer code. Usually the code
used for the leader and the trailer are identical. Thus, the
only differentiation between leader and trailer is the relative
positions they occupy on the paper tape. Fig. 1a shows a
common leader/trailer code; blank tape. That is, no characters
are punched in any of the eight levels of the tape. Fig. 1b
also shows another typical leader/trailer code. In this case
all eight levels of the paper tape are punched. It is necessary that the leader/trailer code be different from other
characters in the body of the information.
There is no specified length for leader or trailer code,
but both the leader and trailer is normally several inches in
length. This is primarily for ease of mounting the paper tape
in the reading equipment.
The leader/trailer concept permits more than one block of
information to be put on a continuous tape. That is leader/
trailer code can appear between blocks of information. In this
case the trailer for one piece of information becomes the
leader for the next piece of information.
Fig. 1 shows the usual format for a paper tape. The lower
portion of the paper tape is the leader code. Above this is
the information that has been punched into the tape. Finally,
at the top of the paper tape occurs the trailer code. As
can be seen a row of small holes go the length of the paper
tape. These are the sprocket holes by which the paper tape
is driven through the readers and punches. The sprocket holes
do not occur in the center of the paper tape; they occur between the third and fourth level of the eight levels on the
paper tape.

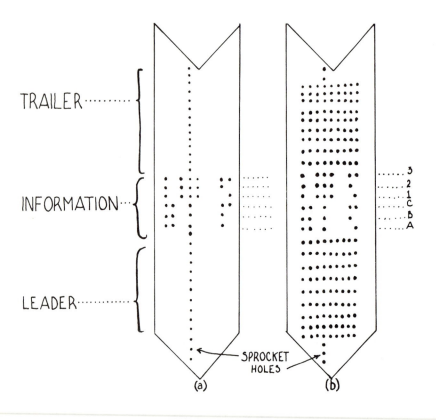

Fig. 1.   Examples of punched paper tape format.

3.2.2   The ASCII Code

Because the Teletype terminal uses the ASCII code and because the Federal Government now has, in principle, adopted ASCII as its standard code, particular attention is given to the ASCII code. One format used for ASCII on paper tape is shown in Fig. 1. Starting at the front of the tape, the first frame of information (character) is an A followed by B, C, 1, 2, 3, respectively. In ASCII an A is 301 on the base eight or 11 000 001 in binary.* Thus, it is possible to read directly from the tape shown in Fig. 1 remembering that a hole corresponds to a one, and no hole corresponds to a zero. It can be seen that B, C, 1, 2, 3 are 302, 303, 261, 262, and 263

---

*An A might also be 101 depending upon which form of the ASCII code is being used. See Appendix V.

respectively. Thus, the eight levels, when interpreted in
this way, are eight bit binary numbers. By referring to the
complete ASCII code given in Appendix V, it is possible to
determine which ASCII characters appear on a paper tape.

3.2.3 Other Codes

There are almost an infinite number of paper tape codes
that could be constructed. One which is often used for numerical data is shown in Fig. 2. This is sometimes referred
to as an eight-four-two-one code. It is also referred to as
binary-coded-decimal or BCD for short.
This code is read in the same manner as the visual method
that was presented in the chapter "Number Systems" for converting binary to hexadecimal numbers. A weight or value is
given to each level of the tape; in this case the weights 8,
4, 2, 1. Adding the levels punched in a frame according to
the weights gives the value of the number. The sprocket holes
again serve to give the orientation of the tape. Therefore,
looking at Fig. 2 it can be seen that 9 is a combination of an
eight level and a one level punch and 7 is a combination of the
4, 2, 1 level punches.
It should be apparent that up to eight bits of binary
information can be included in one frame of the tape. These
eight bits can be used in many combinations to design many
paper tape codes.

3.2.4 Parity

To assist in the detection of punch and reading errors
parity may be incorporated into a paper tape code. Fig. 3
shows an example of the BCD code of Fig. 2 with parity added.
Here the seventh level of the paper tape has been chosen for
parity. Parity has been defined to be odd. That is the
parity level is either punched or not punched in order to make
the number of punches in a given frame odd. If a frame is read
that does not have an odd number of punches then a read error
has occurred or the paper tape was punched improperly at the
time it was generated. Looking at Fig. 3 it can be seen that
there is an odd number of punches in all frames of the paper
tape. For example, there is only one punch for the character
one while there are three for the frames containing the seven
and the nine.

3.3 Associated Equipment

Paper tape as a medium requires two different pieces of
associated equipment; paper tape readers and paper tape punches.

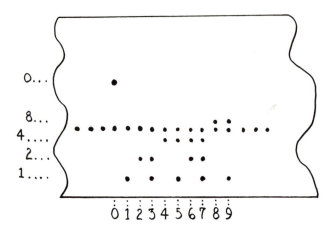

Fig. 2.   An example of a Binary-coded-decimal (BCD) format.
This particular code is sometimes referred to as
an 8-4-2-1 code.

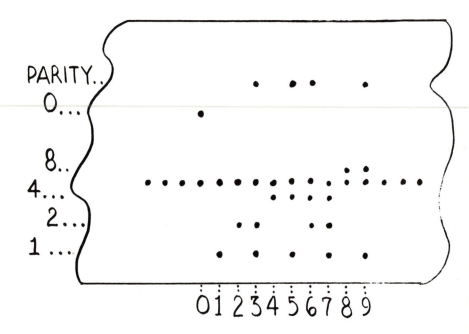

Fig. 3.   An 8-4-2-1 code with parity added.
This example illustrates odd parity.

Although these are two distinct devices, they may be packaged in one box.

3.3.1 Punches

The paper tape punches used on computers are mechanical. Small cylindrical steel pins (punches) are driven up through the paper tape to form the hole. Usually, eight pins are ganged so that all eight levels of one frame may be punched simultaneously. In a few punches only five pins are available permitting only five bits to be punched to a frame.

Because punches are mechanical their speed is severely limited in relation to computer speeds. One frame and one character are interchangeable; therefore to say that a Teletype unit punches ten frames per second is synonomous to ten characters per second. Other speeds that are commonly available are sixty characters per second and one hundred and twenty characters per second.

3.3.2 Readers

There are two varieties of paper tape readers available. One is a mechanical device and the other uses photoelectrical techniques to detect the holes in the paper tape.

3.3.2.1 Mechanical

Mechanical paper tape readers operate in a manner quite similar to mechanical paper tape punches. Eight pins (sensors) are simultaneously driven toward the paper tape; where no holes are punched the pins stop at the tape signifying a zero, where holes are punched the pins momentarily pass through the tape sensing the binary one. Because the mechanical paper tape reader is quite similar to the mechanical paper tape punch, it operates at much the same speeds as the punch.

3.3.2.2 Photoelectric

The photoelectric paper tape readers detect holes in the paper tape by light sensors, e.g., photocells, photodiodes, and phototransistors. A light source shines on the paper tape as it is passed over the reading head. Where a hole occurs the light passes through and is detected by one of the eight photoelectric sensors thus registering a binary one.

Photoelectric readers are desirable in that they can operate at greatly increased speeds compared to the mechanical readers. Three hundred characters per second is typical.

Also less tape wear is experienced and the need for mechanical adjustment is eliminated. They do present some operating problems that are not found in the mechanical reader. For example, more care must be taken in choosing the paper that is to be used. Some paper tape readers do not work well with lightly colored paper tape; in fact, some require that black paper tape be used. Also some photoelectric readers do not perform properly with oil impregnated paper tape.

3.4 Programming Considerations

As with all programming, and particularly with the case of input/output programming, it is important to write the code for paper tape programs in a modular form. With paper tape there are really two categories of modularity. One is writing the program in reusable portions, and the other is making it as easy as possible to switch from one paper tape code to another. The latter is particularly important because there are so many paper tape codes, and it is frequently found that codes which differ only slightly need to be read by the same computer system.

It is desirable to write the program in such a manner that leader/trailer will be automatically punched on the paper tape without any operator intervention. If this is not done the operator often forgets to punch either the leader or the trailer code making it difficult to read the paper tape.

4.0 MAGNETIC TAPE

4.1 General Comments

Recording on magnetic tape and reading magnetic tape is conceptually very simple. The process is illustrated in Fig. 4. A horseshoe-shaped object is portrayed in Fig. 4 which is constructed of a magnetizable material. This horseshoe in turn has a length of wire coiled around it. If a current is passed through the wire, a magnetic field is generated at the open end of the horseshoe. If, as in Fig. 4, a material that can be permanently magnetized is placed under the horseshoe, the spot directly below the horseshoe is magnetized. This is a writing head for it gives a means of writing magnetic spots on the tape.

Inversely, if the magnetic spot is passed below the horseshoe a current is generated in the coil by the magnetic field induced in the horseshoe. This is a reading head. Using this approach it is possible to record on magnetic tape in a binary manner. A magnetized spot now corresponds to a logical one and a non-magnetized spot corresponds to a logical zero.

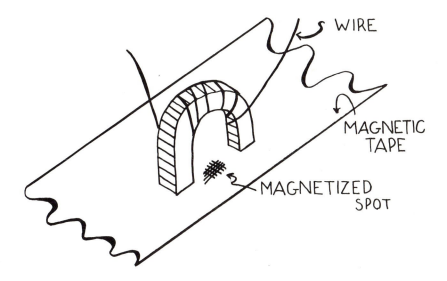

Fig. 4. A schematic presentation of magnetic tape recording.
Spots on the tape are magnetized when a current is
passed through the wire. Inversely, a current passes
through the wire when a magnetized spot on the tape
is passed below the horseshoe-shaped magnet providing
a means of reading magnetic tape.

In the normal case reading and writing heads are composed
of a series of horseshoe-shaped magnets. These are placed in
a line perpendicular to the direction of travel of the tape in
a manner quite similar to the pins in the punch head of a paper
tape punch. The magnetic tape itself is usually an acetate or
mylar base with an oxide coating which is the magnetizable
material.
     Magnetic tape recordings can be divided into two general
categories; discreet (digital) and analog. To record in a
digital fashion the current in the recording head is pulsed
(alternately turned off and on). As the magnetic tape is
passed by the head, these pulse currents result in a series
of magnetized spots on the tape corresponding to those points
under the head when the current was on. If one sprinkles iron
filings on the tape the spots become visible and the tape may
be read in a manner similar to the paper tape examples shown
in Figs. 2 and 3.
     To record an analog signal a current which varies with
time is continuously passing through the heads as the tape
moves by. A continuous representation of the current wave
forms passing through the writing heads is thus recorded on
the magnetic tape. This is the technique by which stereo tapes
are recorded.

Magnetic tape must be kept dustfree and handled with
reasonable care. Particles on the tape will cause errors in
reading the tape. Also particles on the tape may damage the
tape if they become lodged between the reading or writing heads
and the tape.

Magnetic tape is a very widely used storage medium because
it can be stored off-line from the computer, can be read rather
fast, and has a rather high density of storage.

Four different type of magnetic tape are widely used:

I.B.M. compatible. This particular type is referred to
as I.B.M. compatible because the I.B.M. corporation instigated
it many years ago. It has become the most widely used digital
tape in the computer industry. Physically the tape is one-half
inch wide.

DECtape. This type of magnetic tape was introduced by
Digital Equipment Corporation. It represents a different recording approach and permits rather inexpensive recording and
reading equipment for the magnetic tape.

Cassettes. This type of magnetic tape is also referred
to as cartridges. It is a rather recent innovation in the computer field and utilizes tape cassettes, which are exactly the
same in physical dimension as those now in popular use in
home stereoes and car stereo systems. This particular type
of tape also has the characteristic of inexpensive reading and
recording equipment.

Analog. This is a type of tape that is often used to continuously record the waveforms of various kinds of instrumentation. Our discussion here does not include the analog tapes
used for stereo and video purposes because they are not commonly connected to on-line computer systems. In order to be used
with computers, analog tape must be digitized before it is
entered into the computer. This means that the continuous wave
forms that have been written on the tape must be digitized with
the appropriate devices before the information is entered into
the computer. The device that is required is an analog-to-
digital converter which is discussed later in this chapter.

In all the four types of magnetic tape enumerated above
the read and write head, and the associated electronics are
mounted in one physical package commonly referred to as a magnetic tape transport.

4.2 Formats

In the following the formats are the patterns with which
data are recorded on the various types of magnetic tapes.

4.2.1 I.B.M. Compatible

There are two major recording formats that are used with
the I.B.M. compatible magnetic tape. One is referred to as

seven-track tape. Seven-track tape is illustrated in Fig. 5 which shows a portion of tape and one way that the numbers one through ten might be recorded. Of course, some liberties have been taken in Fig. 5 in that the dots shown there represent the magnetized spots which are not visible in the actual case. In the seven-track format the lower six tracks are the data tracks. The seventh track is the parity track, or more properly speaking, the vertical parity track.* It is typical to also record a longitudinal parity frame which is recorded at the end of a block of data. Thus, in this recording format there are both vertical and horizontal (longitudinal) parity checks to detect any errors that occur in the reading or writing of the magnetic tape.

The other type of I.B.M. compatible format is the nine-track tape. Nine-track tape is quite similar to the seven-track except that there are now eight data tracks and the ninth track is the vertical parity track. The longitudinal parity is more sophisticated in that a cyclic redundancy code is used for error detection.

The density with which information may be written on an I.B.M. compatible tape varies. The density is defined to be the number of frames per inch that are recorded on the tape. This, unfortunately, is erroneously referred to as the number of bits per inch (bpi). Frames per inch would be a much more appropriate unit. Each frame represents either seven or nine bits of information. Thus, when one is reading magnetic tape specifications and sees the number two hundred bits per inch, it really means that the tape is being recorded at two hundred frames per inch. The common recording densities are 200 bits per inch, 556 bits per inch and 800 bits per inch. Sixteen hundred bits per inch is now coming into use, and experiments with higher bit densities are being made.

Other descriptive conventions are commonly used. For example, one continuous block of data is often referred to as a record. Records are usually separated by what are called end-of record (EOR) gaps.** Which are 3/4 inches of blank tape, i.e. tape which has no recorded spots on it. The terminology refers to one or several records as a file. The file has a special record as the last information recorded on the tape which is referred to as the end-of-file (EOF) mark.

Physically the I.B.M. compatible tape is one half inch wide and is wound on reels that are a maximum of ten inches in diameter. Reels of smaller diameter may be obtained. The ten inch diameter reel contains 2400 feet of magnetic tape. A quick computation shows that if one record were recorded on a 2400 foot tape at 800 bits per inch and six data bits per

---

* Note, that a track on magnetic tape is the direct analog of a level on paper tape.
**These are also referred to as inter-record gaps.

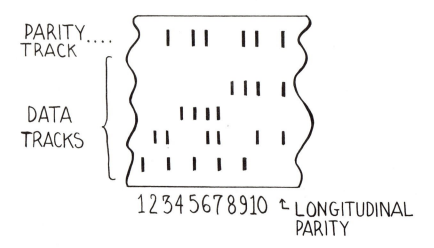

Fig. 5.   The format of an I.B.M. compatible, seven channel
           magnetic tape. The dark areas represent magnetized
           spots which would not normally be visable to the
           naked eye.

frame, then slightly less than 140 million bits of information
are contained on the tape.

4.2.2 DECtape

     This is pronounced deck-tape. DECtape is a ten track tape.
Unlike the I.B.M. compatible tape DECtape is not composed of a
parity track and nine tracks of information. One half of the
tape is composed of a timing track, a mark track, and three
information or data tracks, summing to five tracks of information. These five tracks are recorded redundantly, in a mirror
image form, on the other five tracks of the tape. The timing
track establishes the timing relationship between the magnetic
tape and the magnetic tape controller; it announces the arrival
of a frame position under the read/write heads. The mark track
is used to format the tape. In this case consecutive information on the tape is referred to as a block and these are not
separated by EOR gaps. They are separated by information that
is written in the mark track. The information in the mark
track not only separates the blocks but identifies the blocks
by numbering them in a sequential order from one end of the
tape to the other. With this technique of formatting the tape,
it now becomes possible to go to any specified block on the
tape and to read or write information on that block.
     Under normal operation it is not possible to write on the
timing or mark tracks, but there is a prescribed procedure for

recording information into these tracks before a tape is u-
tilized. The recording density on DECtape is nominally 355
bits per inch. By the nature of the way the recording is
accomplished, utilizing the timing track, a constant speed of
the tape is not particularly necessary. Physically the tape
is three fourths of an inch wide and the reels are three and
one half inches in diameter.

4.2.3 Cassettes

The formats of recording on cassettes have not yet become
widely standardized, and one must look at each individual unit
to find what formats are being used. Recording densities are
on the order of six hundred bits per inch. Some of the tape
is one fourth of an inch wide and the length is variable all
the way up to at least 300 feet.

4.2.4 Analog

In relation to analog tape remarks are confined to those
applications where continuous signals have been recorded on the
tape. The terminology for what has been called a track in our
previous examples of magnetic tape is referred to as a channel
on an analog tape. Each channel may have one continuous signal
recorded on it. Fourteen channel tapes are common. There is
no individual standard format. In many cases a signal of a
known frequency may be recorded on one channel as a comparison
for later analysis of the data in the other channels.
Often the signals are filtered before they are played onto
the magnetic tape. This is to remove unwanted frequency components from the signal.
When individual signals are recorded on different channels
the relationship of one signal to another on a time basis can
be obtained. Often the data is recorded in a frequency modu-
lated manner.

4.3 Associated Equipment

4.3.1 I.B.M. Compatible

There are two types of I.B.M. compatible magnetic tape
transports. One will be referred to as a continuous transport
and one will be referred to as an incremental transport. In
the case of the continuous transport the magnetic tape must
first be brought up to speed before a reading or writing operation can occur. Once this speed is reached the tape motion
is held very constant and considerable effort is put into the

design to prevent the tape from moving across the heads in a diagonal fashion or in a fluttering motion.

The incremental transport works in an entirely different fashion than the continuous magnetic tape transport. The data is written on the magnetic tape one frame at a time. The tape is moved over the reading and recording head in an incremental manner by stepping motors. The sequence of action is to write one frame of data, then instruct the motor to step ahead. Then a new frame is recorded and a new step is given, etc. Of course the length of the step is one frame separation which depends upon the density with which the tape is being recorded.

Fig. 6 shows a picture of a continuous magnetic tape transport. The tape is spun from one reel to another and in the meantime passes over the read and write heads. The tape movement is often accomplished by a small roller mechanism called a capstan. In Fig. 6, the tape drops into two vertical channels. These are evacuated and are referred to as vacuum columns. By letting tape loops form in these vacuum channels it is possible to obtain a smoother motion of the tape over the recording and writing heads.

The movement of the tape over the heads is done at high speeds; movements of 75 inches of tape per second (ips) across the heads is not uncommon and considerably higher speeds are available. In addition to the normal recording and reading speeds there is a slew mode of operation which moves the tape at very high speeds. The slew mode of operation is normally used to rewind the tape when no reading or writing operations are in progress. For this type of magnetic tape transport to perform properly it is necessary to be able to start and stop the tape motion very quickly.

In the write-step write-step operation of incremental recording typical speeds are 200 to 400 steps per second. The incremental tapes also often have a slew mode which in this case permits more or less continuous writing on the tape. This is often accomplished by simply performing the steps continuously at a rapid rate. The appearance of this type of magnetic tape transport is somewhat similar to that of Fig. 6 although it is usually smaller and vacuum columns are not provided. An incremental transport is shown in Fig. 2 of the chapter "Introduction".

4.3.2 DECtape

A dual DECtape transport is shown in Fig. 7. The transport fits into a relay rack nineteen inches wide. There are no capstans to move the magnetic tape; it is pulled directly from one reel to the other reel over the read/write heads. Both reels are provided with driving motors. Thus, to move the tape one motor pulls the tape while the other maintains the tension on the tape. The speed of movement of the tape

Fig. 6.   An I.B.M. compatible transport courtesy
          of Ampex Corporation.

is nominally 80 inches per second.   It is not necessary to
bring the tape up to speed for reading or writing because of
the timing tracks that have already been described.
    The advantages of this type of transport are that it can
be produced rather economically, the associated tape can be
very easily stored, and because of a coating on the tape itself,
is not as subject to the effects of dirt and other foreign materials.
    The major disadvantage of this type of transport is its
incompatibility with the I.B.M. compatible magnetic tapes.
This arises from the fact that central computing facilities
almost universally use the I.B.M. compatible tape.   Thus, if
data or other information is recorded on DECtape a means must
be found to rewrite the information on to an I.B.M. compatible
transport before it may be utilized at a central computing
facility.

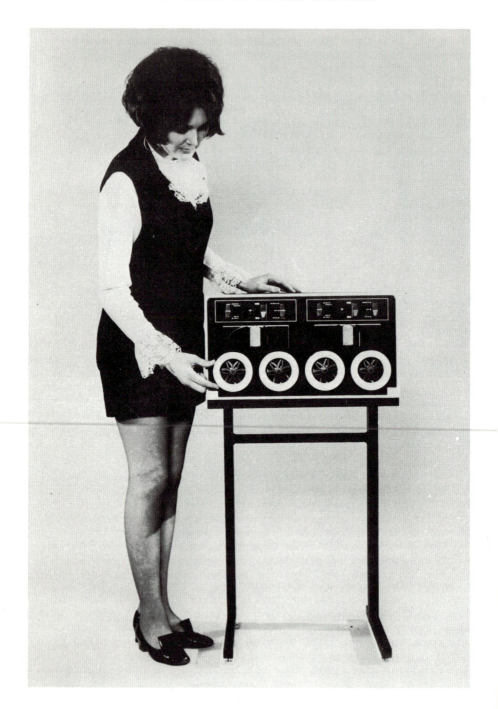

Fig. 7.   A DECtape transport courtesy of Digital
Equipment Corporation.

4.3.3 Cassettes

A cassette transport unit is shown in Fig. 8. The cassette
units, like the cassette tapes, have not yet become standardized.
Many are using the widely distributed four track stereo tape
configurations. This is the type shown in Fig. 8; it is often
referred to as a Philip's Cassette.

The advantages of the cassette units are similar to those
of DECtape; they are economic and easily stored. Also in this
case the magnetic tape is almost completely protected from the
surrounding environment.

Cassettes suffer from the same disadvantages as DECtape.
They are not compatible with the magnetic tape used in a
central facility.

4.3.4 Analog

The appearance of an analog tape transport is somewhat
similar to that of an I.B.M. compatible transport. However,
in this case associated equipment is required for calibration
of the unit prior to each utilization. Because the signals
are analog and are, therefore, not of standard amplitudes it
is necessary that care be taken before recording to see that
the amplitudes of the input signals do not exceed those that
can be accommodated by the transport. This is taken care of
by the appropriate adjustment of amplification.

Often analog transports have a choice of several speeds
with which data may be recorded and played back. This makes
it possible to play back the tape faster or slower than the
real time in which it was recorded, which can have considerable
advantage in digitizing the data. For example, a signal with
rather high frequency components might be recorded at some
given speed. If this is played back and digitized at a considerably slower speed, the requirements that must be made of
the analog-to-digital converters are reduced considerably. As
already mentioned, the only feasible way of using an analog
tape transport with a digital computer is to digitize the tape
output. The output signal of the tape transport may be filtered before the signal is digitized.

There are also rather special units built which do not
have the tape wound on a reel but instead stack the tape in a
random manner in an enclosure. The tape is a loop which permits data to be recorded continuously. If the recording goes
on for a time in excess of the length of the tape new data is
recorded over the old. Tape can be moved over the recording
heads in this manner at very high speeds.

4.4 Programming Considerations

Fig. 8. A cassette transport courtesy of Ampex Corporation.

4.4.1 I.B.M. Compatible

As always the programming for magnetic tape must be modular in nature. Also, when storing programs in similar files,
it may be desirable to standardize on file lengths. In the
case of on-line computers, situations are often found where
magnetic tapes are recorded on other devices that may be experimental or data logging in nature. These tapes are then
read by the on-line computer for reformatting, or for reduction of the data contained on them. It is important in writing
the on-line computer programs to provide for the arbitrary
length of files that are generated by such off-line devices.
It should also be kept in mind that the length of the records
may be very long and thus relate directly to the amount of computer storage that must be available to store them. An incremental transport can be of value in this case, since it can
read less than one record.

A point that is often overlooked is in the handling of
errors that occur in reading magnetic tape. Too often the

programming is written in such a way that the computer automatically dumps the job when an error is encountered. This is
not the appropriate approach. Arrangements should be such that
a parity error is noted but reading continues. The loss of one
bit in a piece of data is often not a very serious problem and
may only result in a very small fractional loss of information.
Thus, it is more important to read the valid data than abort
reading the magnetic tape because of a parity error(s).

One difficulty that is often encountered is the lack of
labeling on the tape itself. Appropriate conventions should
be set up for putting labeling information directly on the
tape before data is recorded.

Another important consideration is that data taken with
an on-line computer and recorded on magnetic tape often is an
unattended operation. This means that the program should be
able to detect when a reel of tape is full and notify an operator to take appropriate action. Also in a data collecting
operation there are trade offs between the buffer lengths that
are required to store the data and wasted tape for end-of-record
gap recording. In other words, one does not want to use any
more memory than is required for the buffering of data to be
written on a magnetic tape. However, a buffer length usually
corresponds to one record on tape. With the high recording
densities that are presently used one may literally have a tape
that on a per centage basis is largely end-of-record gaps resulting in a great waste of tape.

4.4.2 DECtape

Because it is possible to specify the block lengths on a
given tape, data storage can often be optimized by making the
length of the blocks correspond to the lengths of the data that
is typically recorded. Also DECtape reels are relatively small
making it especially important to sense the end of the tape
with the programming so that the programming may automatically
switch to another DECtape transport to continue recording data.

5.0 DISKS AND DRUMS

Disks and drums are discussed jointly because there are
many similarities between these two devices. They are similar
both from the standpoint of how they operate and in the manner
in which data is written and read from them. Both disks and
drums use magnetic techniques for recording data. From the
standpoint of the actual magnetization of disk and drum surfaces the explanations that were given for the magnetic tape
recording apply. Read and write heads somewhat similar to those
on magnetic tape transports are used and operate in an analogous
manner.

5.1   Drums

Drum is a very descriptive name for this device because
it resembles an ordinary right angle cylinder. This can be
seen from the illustration of Fig. 9. Physically the drum is
a metal cylinder with a magnetic coating on the surface. Information is written upon this magnetic surface with writing
heads that are quite similar to those used on magnetic tape
transports. The drum spins around the long axis as shown in
Fig. 9. Thus, the recording of the write head results in a
strip of magnetized surface that runs around the drum in a
small band. These bands upon which the recording actually
takes place are referred to as tracks. Many read/write heads
are located along the long length of the drum to record and
read each track of information. These are known as fixed position heads because they remain over one track. The information on the track is written in a binary format, i.e. magnetized spots correspond to one and non-magnetized portions correspond to zeros. There are timing tracks quite similar to
those discussed in the case of DECtapes. These timing tracks
indicate when a read or write operation should take place as
the drum spins by the read/write heads. Because each track
does represent a linear series of binary bits, there are two
methods of recording complete computer words. One approach
is to record a word as a linear series of bits in one track.
A computer with a sixteen bit word length would require sixteen bits in a line along the track. Another approach is to
write the bits of one word on parallel tracks. In the case of
the 16 bit word the bits are simultaneously applied to sixteen
adjoining write heads. Thus, the adjoining positions on sixteen different tracks contain the bits of one word.

Because there is a point on each track that is thought of
as the starting point for that track, it is possible to access
any word on the drum. If a bit serial type recording is being
used and there are, say, 256 words per track then the first
position on the first track is the first bit of the first word
on the drum. Likewise, the first bit in the second track is
the first bit of the 257th word on the drum. Thus, the information on a drum can be formatted in what might be called a
matrix where one dimension is the tracks and the other dimension is the words within a track.

An important timing consideration associated with drums
is the access time. The access time is that time which it takes
to bring a word into the computer from the drum, measured from
the time that the computer requested the word. Because the drum
is constantly spinning, the time to retrieve a word from the
drum is not constant; it depends on the relationship of the
position which the word occupies on the drum to the current position of the head. Thus, the maximum time to find a word on
the drum is the time that it takes the drum to make one revolution.

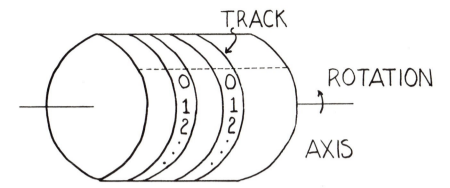

Fig. 9.   A schematic representation of a magnetic
          drum showing the spin axis and the recording
          tracks.

5.2 Disks

Whereas drums are right cylinders, disks are more appropriately described as platters. This can be seen from Fig. 10a.
In this platter configuration the magnetic coating is on the
flat surface and the reading and recording take place on this
surface. As indicated in Fig. 10 linear binary series are recorded on the disk surface and are still referred to as tracks.
However, in this case the tracks become concentric circles.
Unlike the drum, the diameters of the tracks are no longer constant. The read/write heads are directly over the platter surface. In some instances the magnetic coating is put on both
sides of the platter and there are read/write heads for each
surface.
     Disks are classified according to read/write heads. One
classification is referred to as a fixed head disk and one is
referred to as a movable head disk. In the case of the fixed
head disk there is a read/write head over each track. On the
other hand, the movable head disk can have as few as one set of
read and write heads for each platter surface. This makes it
necessary to mechanically position the heads over the track on
which the recording or reading is to take place.
     In the case of the fixed head disk the access time is com-
pletely analogous to that for a drum. The maximum time to access
a piece of data on the disk is one revolution time. The movable
head disk has another time factor to be added; the time to position the heads over the desired track plus the rotation time
of the disk. The track positioning is much the slower of the
two times, and, as a result the access time of movable head
disks are usually an order of magnitude slower than those for
fixed head disks.
     The idea of a single disk platter as shown in Fig. 10a
can be expanded to much higher storage capacities by stacking

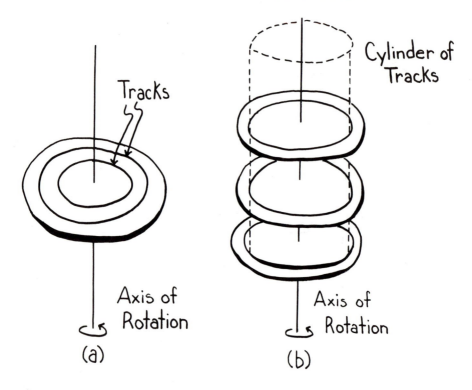

Fig. 10.   Figure (a) is a schematic representation of a
            disk showing the recording tracks. Figure (b)
            is a schematic representation of a disk pack
            showing the concept of a disk cylinder.

platters in the manner shown in Fig. 10b. This type of configuration is normally referred to as a disk pack. Disk packs
are typically for movable head disks. Primarily they are used
as an off-line storage medium. Packs are much like magnetic
tapes in that data can be written on them and then the disk
pack removed from the disk drive and stored off-line.* At a
later time the disk may again be mounted on the drive.
     Another term is used in relation to disk packs; "cylinders"
on a pack. Cylinders can be thought of conceptually as shown
in Fig. 10b. If one remembers that each platter on the disk
pack is made up of a series of concentric tracks, then it can
be seen that a series of tracks of equal diameter exist on
succeeding platters. All tracks of the same diameter on the
platters of a pack constitute a cylinder.

_____

*As long as it is removable a disk pack could be as little
 as one platter.

5.3 Common Considerations

The rate that information may be transferred to or from a disk or drum is directly related to the number of bits that pass under a read/write head per unit time. This rate is derived from the rate of rotation of the drum (disk) and the density with which the data has been recorded. The density is defined as the number of bits per inch recorded on the disk or drum tracks.

For the drum this concept should be straightforward because the recording density on the surface is the same everywhere. Therefore, given the density, the diameter and the rate of rotation of the drum one can calculate directly what the maximum transfer rate to and from the drum is.

In the case of the disk it may at first appear somewhat more complicated. The platter is still rotated at a constant speed but the tracks vary in diameter and therefore the linear velocity of the tracks under the read/write head varies from track to track. However, a little thought will show that the difference in track diameter and therefore the linear velocity under the read/write head is compensated for by a change in density in going from track to track. This can be put another way. If the data is originally written on the disk at a constant clock rate, then the density on the different diameter tracks must vary in a manner that exactly compensates for the different linear velocities. Therefore, transfer rates to and from a disk are constant regardless of the tracks being utilized.

It has already been pointed out that the time to find data on a drum or disk varies from access to access. Another term that is often used in this regard is latency time. The latency time is that time that elapses from the time a piece of information is requested from a drum or disk until it arrives at the computer. Thus, the latency time varies from access to access. In looking at the literature for disks and drums usually either a maximum access time is quoted or an average access time. Of course the maximum access time is just the time that it takes the disk or drum to make one revolution.* A little thought will show that the average access time is just one half the maximum access time. In other words, if the drum or disk is accessed many times, the access time will vary from essentially zero to the full revolution time with an average being one-half of the revolution time.

Many disks are rotated at 1800 revolutions per minute. Therefore, a maximum excess time is about 32 milliseconds and the average access time is about 16 milliseconds. On the other

---

*Plus the positioning time in the case of the movable head--which is also variable depending on the number of tracks the head has to be moved.

hand drums are typically rotated on the order of 3600 revolutions per minute giving a maximum access time of 16 millisecon
and an average access time of 8 milliseconds.

It should be clearly understood that although the access
time for a word may seem high, this does not mean that the tra
fer rate is the order of one half revolution time per word.
Data is usually written on a drum or disk in a continuous manner so that blocks of data adjoin each other on the recording
surface. Therefore, the average time to access the first word
is one half of the revolution time. However, the following
word in the block can be transferred at the maximum transfer
rate of the disk or drum, which can be the order of 10 to 50
microseconds per word.

The capacity of disks and drums that are currently being
manufactured vary rather widely with the range spanning from
a few tens of thousands of words to tens of millions of words.
Those with a capacity of tens of millions of words are physically quite large. These large devices are usually drums and
are fixed head with no physical removable capability.

Usually, disk and drum units have a lockout feature consisting of switches on the disk or drum cabinet, which when
thrown, lockout specific tracks. Once the switches have been
thrown it is impossible to write on those tracks. This makes
it possible to put systems programming and other important pro
grams or data on protected tracks to insure that they will not
be inadvertently destroyed by other programming, or data colle
tion in the computer.

Another feature that is commonly incorporated is to add
a parity bit to each word as it is recorded. This is done by
the control hardware for the disk or drum which also checks
this parity bit when the data is read back from the drum or
disk and notifies the program of errors via flags.

5.4 Programming Considerations

When a device has a transfer rate of the order of a disk
or drum it becomes advantageous to use double buffers. Disks
and drums typically transfer blocks of words rather than singl
words at any given command to read or write via data channel
or DMA transfers. Suppose that one has a drum or disk that
transfers data to or from the computer in blocks of 256 computer words. Further suppose that several thousand words are
to be transferred. Then two 256 word buffers are created.
Designate one buffer as number one and the other as number two
Let the first transfer of 256 words be into buffer one. Then
the computer program indicates to the disk or drum that the
second block of 256 words goes into buffer two. While the
second block of words are streaming into buffer two, the computer can return to buffer one and manipulate the words there
in any way desired. When the manipulation is complete,

presumably before buffer two is filled, the computer program, upon the filling of buffer two commands the transfer of the next 256 word block into buffer one. Thus a flip-flop action is set up between these two buffers that permits the computer to operate on the data block transferred while the drum or disk continues to transfer the next block.

If a computer is to be used in a data acquisition mode and the data is to be stored on a disk or drum, it is very important to ascertain that the latency times of the disk or drum involved permits the transfer of the data as it is acquired. In other words, if the arrival rate of the data is faster on the average than the transfer rate plus the consideration for latency factors of the disk or drum, it is impossible to use the disk or drum as the direct storage device. In the case of data that arrives randomly this can sometimes be a fairly difficult chore. However, random data will, over any given interval of time that is long in proportion to the arrival times of individual events, have an average data arrival rate which has little variance. In this case a buffer can be created in the computer memory to in effect derandomize the date by being large enough to have a sizeable number of events accumulated before it is transferred to the disk or drum. This is a natural state of affairs from the standpoint of the disk or drum where block transfers are the normal mode of operation.

6.0   THE OSCILLOSCOPE DISPLAY

A great deal has been said about the man-computer interface. This is a term that refers to methods of the computer user communicating with the computer. Some input/output media are not very desirable for communication with a computer. Therefore, there is a continuing effort to make the computer more accessible to the user in a manner that is both fast and meaningful. The oscilloscope display is rapidly becoming one of the most important means of communication with the computer user. As an output device it can display large amounts of complex information very rapidly.

The basic element in an oscilloscope display is the cathode-ray tube, of which, a schematic drawing is shown in Fig. 11. A stream of electrons (commonly referred to as an electron beam) is generated at the cathode of the tube. The electron beam is then accellerated by a potential on the plate in front of the cathode. Once the electrons have been accellerated, they pass through two sets of parallel deflection plates. The two sets of deflection plates are at right angles to each other and are used to divert the electron beam in the desired direction. If no potential is applied to the deflection plates, then the

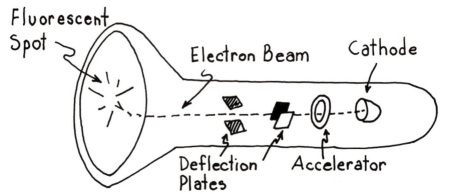

Fluorescent Spot

Electron Beam

Cathode

Deflection Plates

Accelerator

Fig. 11. A drawing to illustrate the operation of a cathrode-
ray tube. A beam of electrons is generated at the
cathode, accelerated, and then directed to the CRT
face by deflection plates. A fluorescent spot
occurs where the electron beam strikes the phosphor
on the CRT face.

electron beam strikes the center of the cathode-ray-tube face.
The cathode-ray-tube face is covered with a fluorscent material. Thus, wherever the electron beam strikes the face with
sufficient energy, a spot of light momentarily appears.

Now, it is possible to see how a picture is constructed
on the oscilloscope screen. The beam is moved to various portions of the face causing light spots to appear wherever the
beam strikes, and in this way an image is built up over the
surface of the cathode-ray-tube face.

The deflection of the electron beam may be done in two
different ways. An electrostatic field may be utilized between deflection plates to give electrostatic deflection of
the electron beam or a magnetic field may be utilized to give
magnetic deflection of the electron beam. Therefore, one finds
oscilloscopes characterized in the literature as having either
electrostatic or magnetic deflection systems. There are advantages for both deflection techniques that space does not
permit us to introduce here.

6.1 Oscilloscope Phosphors

This is not a detailed discussion of the phosphors that
may be put on a cathode-ray-tube for the fluorscence of the

---

*In tubes used for computer peripherals it is often arranged
that no potential on the deflection plates results in the
beam striking the lower left-hand corner of the tube face.

electron beam. It is meant to be a review of the characteristics of phosphors that explains the effects observed visually on the face of a cathode-ray-tube display. If the descriptions succeed from this point of view then there should
be sufficient knowledge to understand the control of an oscilloscope display through computer instructions.

6.1.1 Short Persistence

When the cathode-ray-tube surface is coated with a short
persistence phosphor a light spot fades away rather quickly
after the electron beam leaves that point on the face. Typical times for a spot to fade away vary from a fraction of a
second to no more than a few seconds. Because the persistence
of the fluorscent spot is so short this means that the picture
on the cathode-ray-tube face can be changed very rapidly with
no after effects from the previously displayed picture. Inversely, this also means that if a picture is to persist, the
same picture must be "painted" on the cathode-ray-tube face
repeatedly. These characteristics have made it possible to
make computer movies. A camera is pointed at the face of an
oscilloscope display driven by a computer and the end result
is a true movie.
The intensity of the fluorscence on a short persistence
oscilloscope can often be changed under computer control.
There are two ways of doing this. One is to simply accelerate
the electrons in the electron beam to a higher energy. The
second method is to leave the electron beam energy constant
but allow the beam to reside on the chosen spot for a longer
period of time. In some instances several levels of intensity
are provided and it is possible in theory to make half-tone
pictures on a cathode tube ray face. This has not yet been
accomplished in a completely general way because of the mass
of information that must be displayed.

6.1.2 Long Persistence

The long persistence oscilloscope displays to be described
here are often referred to as storage oscilloscopes. The persistence of the fluorescence after the electron beam strikes the
face can be hours or longer. It is only necessary to paint the
picture on the oscilloscope face once and the picture will remain. However this also suggests that there now must be an
erase action and this erase action takes a finite amount of
time. Therefore, an oscilloscope display that uses a long
persistence phosphor is not applicable to the moving picture
concept. However, on the advantageous side of the trade-off
large amounts of time are no longer required to repeatedly
paint the same picture on the cathode-ray-tube face.

Some storage oscilloscopes also have what might be described as a live or short persistence display feature. It
is possible to have a cursor that moves about the screen but
does not leave a persistent image on the screen as it moves
about. By cursor it is meant that there is a single spot of
light or a small geometric pattern that is moving about the
oscilloscope face.

The storage oscilloscope can often be used as a short
persistence scope also. This arises from the fact that the
picture is maintained on the tube face by bathing it with a
low energy electron beam. If the bathing beam is turned off
the oscilloscope reverts to being a short persistence scope.

6.1.3 Color

The phosphors to be considered here are of a short persistence type; however, the result is a colored picture. One
approach uses three electron guns all of which contribute an
electron beam. Each electron gun corresponds to a different
color. Turning on a single gun results in a pure color spot.
If two or more of the guns are directed at closely adjacent
spots on the oscilloscope screen a shading of color is achieve
This gives a completely new dimension to what can be done with
oscilloscope displays. Colored oscilloscope displays are only
becoming available at this point in time and a good deal remai
to be done.

6.2 Picture Generation

There are at least three different approaches to the manner in which the electron beam can be moved about the cathode-
ray-tube face to construct a picture. These three approaches
are discussed in a phenomenological manner.

6.2.1 Point-Plot

It is necessary to imagine the cathode-ray-tube face as
a rectangle divided into a grid that is 1,024 points by 1,024
points. In a few instances this grid may be as high as 4,096
by 4,096 points. These are referred to as ten or twelve bit
displays respectively. In other words 2^{10} or 2^{12} points a-
chievable along the X and Y axes of the rectangle on the
cathode-ray-tube face. In the ten bit display there are appro
imately one million points (1024 x 1024) on the grid.

The typical sequence in a point-plot approach is for the
computer to give the oscilloscope control hardware an XY coordinate pair. This is usually followed by an intensify command. The oscilloscope control hardware moves the beam to the

position specified by the coordinate pair and then intensifies, with a fluorescent spot resulting at the specified XY position on the grid. Hence, the term point-plot.

In order that the coordinate pair, which is in a digital form within the computer, be converted to a space or physical location on the cathode-ray-tube face, it is necessary to perform a digital-to-analog conversion. That is, take the digital values (the X and Y values of the coordinate pair) and convert these to analog voltages on the deflection plates of the cathode-ray tube, which then results in the beam being positioned at the desired point on the oscilloscope face. Digital-to-analog converters are discussed in more detail in a later section of this chapter.

It should be apparent now why this is called the point-plot mode of picture generation. The picture is literally constructed a point at a time on a grid of at least one million positions. Although the picture is constructed from points the visual image does not necessarily appear to be an array of points. For example, if the picture screen is ten inches on a side and divided into one thousand positions, adjoining points on the grid are only ten thousandths of an inch apart. Therefore, if adjoining spots are intensified, for all practical purposes, a solid line will result. This brings up another topic which is the generation of vectors i.e. straight lines. Vectors are constructed by intensifying adjoining points in the grid to construct the straight line.

Occasionally, with some point-plot oscilloscope systems difficulty is experienced in intensifying certain coordinate pair combinations. Suppose that it is desired to intensify the coordinate pair (0,0) which is the lower left-hand corner of the oscilloscope screen, and this is to be followed by the intensification of the point corresponding to the coordinate pair (1,023, 1023), which is the upper right hand corner of the screen. With some systems the oscilloscope controller gives the intensify command for the second coordinate pair before the electron beam has time to move diagonally across the screen. This will either result in no intensified dot at (1023, 1023) or a visible streak of light along the diagonal starting at the point where the intensify command was given. This type of problem can be solved in the computer program by building in short delays, if such long beam movements are to be made. It can also be solved in the hardware itself.

Figure 12 shows a photograph of an oscilloscope display generated with the point-plot approach.

6.2.2 Stroke

Visualize now, instead of a system where the beam is moved and then the intensification takes place as in the point-plot mode, an intensification as the beam is being moved. In other

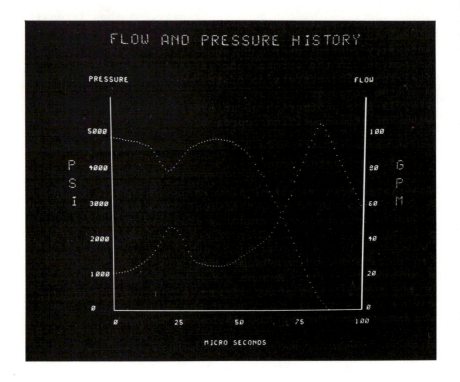

Fig. 12.   An oscilloscope display created using the
           point-plot approach.

words a sweeping of the electron beam across the cathode-ray
tube slowly enough, and with the intensity on, to cause a stroke
or line of fluorescence across the tube face. This is stroke
writing.

     It is still appropriate to think of the oscilloscope face
as being made up of a matrix as in the point-plot example. How
ever, to draw a straight line or a vector it is necessary to
specify only the beginning and the ending XY coordinate pairs
to the oscilloscope controller. The beam is then moved to the
first XY coordinate pair, the intensity turned on, and the beam
swept to the second XY coordinate pair. In this type of pictur
generation the picture is now actually composed of many straigh
lines or strokes. However, these strokes may be so short as to
be nearly visually indistinguishable; thus, even circular curve
may be drawn of a very good visual quality.

     Unlike the point-plot method of picture generation, the
stroke method does not readily permit closely adjoining points
to be of markedly different intensity. In theory the point

lot mode permits the generation of two closely adjoining
oints with greatly different intensity. In practice the two
oints tend to visually diffuse into each other. In the stroke
ode intensity control over such short intervals is difficult.

Of course, in the stroke mode it is still necessary to have
digital-to-analog conversion of the coordinate pairs that are
tored in the computer.

Fig. 13 is a photograph of an oscilloscope display gener-
ted with the stroke writing approach.

6.2.3 Raster Scan

The raster scan method of picture generation is similar
o the point-plot method of generation. However, in the point-
lot mode the beam is moved randomly from one XY position on
ne oscilloscope screen to other XY positions where points are
o be written. In the raster scan method the electron beam is
oved in a quite methodical manner over all points on the face
f the cathode-ray-tube. Assume a ten bit by ten bit matrix
nd for the sake of simplicity designate the coordinate pair
),1023) as the starting position of the raster scan. The
lectron beam moves through the following sequence:

$$y=1023; \quad x=0,1,2, \quad \ldots\ldots, \quad 1023$$
$$y=1022; \quad x=0,1,2, \quad \ldots\ldots, \quad 1023$$
$$\cdot$$
$$\cdot$$
$$y=1 \quad ; \quad x=0,1,2, \quad \ldots\ldots, \quad 1023$$
$$y=0 \quad ; \quad x=0,1,2, \quad \ldots\ldots, \quad 1023$$
$$y=1023; \quad x=0,1,2, \quad \ldots\ldots, \quad 1023$$

Thus, the beam is moved in this left-to-right sequence
ross the matrix of the cathode-ray tube and the intensify
mmand is given at those XY coordinates which are to be in-
nsified.

The raster scan method of picture generation just de-
ribed is similar to the way a picture is constructed on the
thode-ray-tube face of a television set. The scan starts at
e upper left hand corner and proceeds from left to right
ross the screen of the television face. In this case the
trix on the tube face is not a ten bit matrix. Also, tele-
sion sets use another principal which is called interlace,
ereby every other line of the scan is traced in one frame
d then in the next frame the alternate lines are scanned.

It is possible to build a computer controller with the
propriate scan mechanism to feed an unmodified television
t with a signal that appears as if it came from an ordinary
levision antenna. Fig. 14 is a photograph of an oscilloscope
splay generated with the raster scan approach. The display
s generated by a computer linked to a commercial television
t.

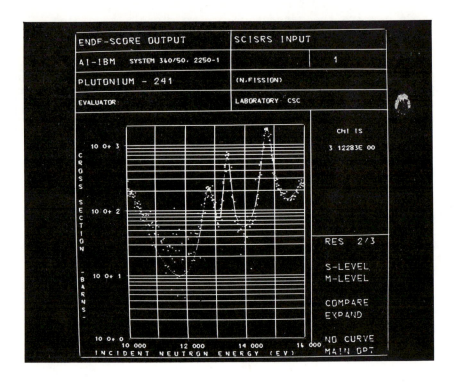

Fig. 13. An oscilloscope display created using the stroke method.

6.3 Methods of Driving Oscilloscopes

Once information is to be displayed there are several ha.
ware approaches to getting it into final form and onto the oscilloscope face. This section reviews some of the more commo:
techniques that are used to accomplish this.

6.3.1 Computer Memory

This approach is the simplest of all the approaches in
terms of the complexity and amount of hardware required in
addition to the basic computer. The piece of information to
be displayed is taken from the computer memory. This informa
tion may already be in a suitable XY coordinate pair format o
it may have to be manipulated into an appropriate format. On
the proper format is obtained it is passed on to the digital-
to-analog converters which generate the analog outputs to mov

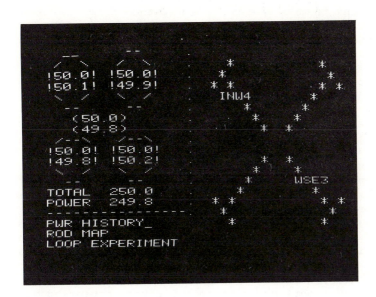

Fig. 14.   An oscilloscope display created using the raster
            scan approach. This picture was generated on an
            unmodified commercial television set linked to a
            computer.

the beam to the desired position on the cathode-ray-tube face.
At this point the computer gives the intensify command. As
mentioned earlier, if the display is of the short persistence
type then it is necessary to constantly refresh the picture on
the oscilloscope face. Such methods can use large amounts of
computer time. In fact if the picture being displayed is complex enough, the computer may not be able to replenish the display rapidly enough to keep the picture visually present, i.e.
the picture flickers.

6.3.2 Disk or Drum

     This approach to driving oscilloscope displays is partic-
ularly amenable to short persistence displays which need constant refresh. The idea is easily visualized. Suppose that
the XY coordinate pairs that are to make up the oscilloscope
display are written in a string on a track of a disk or a

drum. Now, assume that reading heads have been attached to
read these XY coordinate pairs from the disk or drum surface,
and present them to the cathode-ray-tube display. Because
these XY pairs are on a track, and the disk or drum is rotati
they automatically pass under the reading heads again and aga
which gives an automatic means of refreshing the display.

This approach cuts the demand for computer time drastica
The computer needs only to paint any given picture once, i.e.
write the display commands on the tracks of the disk or drum.
It is then no longer necessary for the computer to be concerr
with the oscilloscope display until that time when the pictur
is to be changed; then a new string of XY coordinates are wri
on the disk or drum.

Although the concept above is somewhat simplistic in tha
the display is visualized as being written on one track it do
not substantially change in the practical cases where more th
one track is used. Tracks can in turn be bundled into groups
each of which contain one display picture. If the heads atta
to these different groups of tracks are run to different osci
scopes it is then possible to drive several different oscillo
displays from one disk or drum. Because the computer can wri
any picture that it desires in the groups of tracks, it is po
sible to have entirely different pictures appearing on each o
scilloscope display. This approach gives a very powerful mea
of generating many oscilloscope displays simultaneously with
low computer overhead.

6.3.3 Display Processor

The display processor represents one of the cycles seen
occur in the computer peripherals industry. The cycle goes s
thing like this: originally one attaches an oscilloscope dis
play to a computer using the memory method of driving. Then
is desired to take less computer time to drive the display an
some special hardware is attached to take over some of the fu
tions of the computer. At this point the obvious thing to do
is to give the display controller the ability to interpret a
few instructions specifically for its own use. The next step
is to add a few instructions to permit the display controller
to execute its own subroutines. This process continues a lit
further and it is suddenly realized that one has built a spec
purpose computer to use as a display controller.

A display processor is really an oscilloscope display co
troller that is a special purpose computer. Often the memory
that is used for this special purpose computer is the memory
of the main computer to which the oscilloscope is attached.
already mentioned, the display processor can execute an instr
tion set of its own, and often can execute subroutines.

Because the display processor often "steals" time from t
main memory it can still use considerable portions of the tim

f the main computer. This time in some instances may be hard-
are limited. For example, it might be arranged that the display
rocessor can only take every other memory cycle of the main
omputer.

Fig. 15 shows an on-line computer which includes a dis-
lay using the display processor approach.

6.3.4 Intermediate Memory

This method is really a simple version of the display
rocessor. A small memory is placed in the oscilloscope dis-
lay controller and then the hardware of the controller takes
he information from this small memory and displays it on the
creen. There is no computer instruction capability. The mem-
ry must contain information in a format that is acceptable to
he display controller. A good example of this type of oscillo-
cope display driver is a system whereby a television display
s attached to the computer via an intermediate memory. In-
ormation in the intermediate memory is in a raster scan format.

The important distinctions of this approach are that the
isplay has its own memory and can extract information from
his memory and display it without any action on the part of
he computer. The disk and drum driven memories are really
laborations of this approach.

The memory can take many different forms. Among those
hat have been used are: magnetic core, delay line, disk,
rum, and more recently electronic disks. The electronic disks
re large shift registers. The shift register has a feature
hich permits all bits in the register to be shifted right or
eft one bit at a time. (See the descriptions of the RAL and
AR instructions in Appendix IV). The bits appear in a serial
tring at the end of shift register in exactly the same manner
hat they would from a disk or drum read head. After a bit is
hifted out of one end of the register it is shifted into the
pposite end making the shift register a "rotating" memory.

6.4 Associated Devices

The associated devices or accessories that are used with
scilloscope displays may be broken into three broad categories:
) Those that permit the user to identify a position on the
athode-ray-tube face, 2) those that permit the user to control
he picture that is being displayed, and 3) those devices which
llow special subunits to be displayed on the screen. In this
atter category the subunits are actually small portions of
he picture. Examples are vector generators and character
enerators. Another device that should perhaps be included in
his section is the XY tablet. However, it is felt that this
evice is sufficiently important to merit a separate section.

Fig. 15.   An on-line computer system which includes an
           oscilloscope display. The unit on the left
           is the display and display processor.

6.4.1   Light Pens

     Physically a light pen is similar to an ordinary ball-
point pen. In fact, it is often referred to as a light pencil
or a light stylus. The function of the light pen is to permit
the user to identify a position on a cathode-ray-tube face.
     Refer to Fig. 16 for the schematic presentation of how a
light pen operates. For the moment consider the light pen
simply as a photosensitive device which is sensitive only to
a light spot on the cathode-ray tube at that instant when the
beam strikes the tube phosphor. The light pen is not sensitive
to a spot that is decaying away after the electron beam has
left a position on the cathode-ray-tube face. In Fig. 16 the
dashed line represents the path of the electron beam at the
time of interest. Because the electron beam is striking the
cathode-ray-tube face at that point where the light pen is
pointed, the light pen detects the resulting light from the

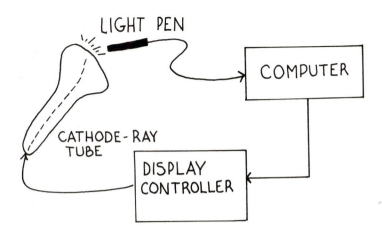

LIGHT PEN

COMPUTER

CATHODE-RAY
TUBE

DISPLAY
CONTROLLER

Fig. 16.   A schematic presentation of how a light pen
           operates. The computer directs the electron
           beam of the cathode-ray tube via the display
           controller. The beam results in a flash of
           fluorescent light which is detected by the
           light pen. The light pen in turn notifies the
           computer.

oscilloscope face and transmits a signal to the computer.*
However, just prior to the instant of detection, the computer
has specified the position of the electron beam via the display
controller; therefore, somewhere in the computer memory or hardware registers resides the XY coordinate which the electron beam
is striking. Upon notification of the light pen detection, it is
possible to read from these registers the XY position of the e-
lectron beam, and for the computer program to take any action desired by the user.

     There are two general types of light pens used. One uses
a photodiode or phototransistor to detect the light on the oscilloscope screen. The other uses a photomultiplier tube. In
the case of the photomultiplier tube, the connection from the
light pen to the computer can be a bundle of optical fibers
which pipe the light from the light pen to the face of the photomultiplier tube. The photodiode and the phototransistor are
light sensitive devices which are placed directly in the pen

---

*The detection of the light spot is often referred to as a
 light pen hit. Also, the light pen signal may actually be
 transmitted to the display controller which then transmits
 a signal to the computer.

itself and the detection of a light pulse results in an electrical pulse.

The identification of the XY coordinate at which the light pen is pointed has been somewhat simplified. The description given is actually for an oscilloscope display that is driven by the computer memory method. With some of the other methods of driving oscilloscope displays other means are required to identify XY coordinate pairs selected by the light pen. For example, in the case of displays driven by disks or drums, the XY coordinate information must be derived from relative positions on the disk or drum tracks. Thus, it is necessary to provide some intermediate level of determination. Similarly, in the case of raster scan displays it is necessary to provide an intermediate level of determination to get the XY position from the raster scan in some intermediate memory.

It should now be obvious that the only function a light pen can perform is to identify an _intensified_ position on the cathode-ray-tube face. Any other action that follows the detection is predetermined in the program residing in the computer. The light pen does permit follow-on action or mode selection. For example, a strip across the bottom of the oscilloscope display might be displayed as shown in Fig. 17. Each rectangle corresponds to some action. For example, pointing the light pen at any part of the labeling in the left-most rectangle is to initiate the printing of information, specified by the program, on the teleprinter. Likewise, if a light pen hit is recorded within the confines of the middle rectangle data specified by the program is displayed on the oscilloscope screen. A hit in the third rectangle might cause the program to jump to a subroutine which requests information to be entered by the Teletype keyboard. Areas on the oscilloscope screen used for purposes of this nature are often referred to as light buttons.

Referring back to Fig. 13, the lower right-hand corner contains a series of light buttons labeled S-LEVEL, M-LEVEL, COMPARE, etc. These buttons are used to modify the way the data is displayed. For example, if the light pen is pointed at NO-CURVE the solid line through the data will be removed and only the data points remain.

An over-touted use of light pens is to "draw" on the CRT face. There are two typical methods of drawing on the oscilloscope face with the light pen. The first is by far the easiest. In this method the whole grid of the oscilloscope is intensified. Then, as the light pen is passed over the oscilloscope face points are detected, and whenever detected no longer intensified. Thus, one might think of this method as drawing by erasing. There are severe disadvantages to this approach. Many display systems are not capable of intensifying all the points on the oscilloscope face without a severe flicker. In addition, the drawing that is created is somewhat akin to looking at a photographic negative, and is therefore not always considered comfortable for viewing.

OUTPUT TO TTY	DISPLAY DATA	INPUT CONTROL PARAMETERS

Fig. 17. An example of light buttons that might be displayed on the face of the cathode-ray tube.
The buttons are identified with a light pen to
indicate actions that are to take place.

The second and probably most commonly used means of drawing on an oscilloscope face is by using a tracking cross or a
cursor. The tracking cross or cursor is simply a pattern that
is intensified on the oscilloscope face. The light pen is
pointed at this pattern and then the pattern is moved about
the screen with the light pen leaving behind the lines that
have been drawn. It is necessary to use a mechanism such as
the tracking cross because it is not possible to know the position of the light pen when it is pointed at some portion of
the screen which is not intensified.

Fig. 18 shows a frequently used method of implementing a
tracking cross. The solid area represents the tracking cross
pattern. The nine dots are on the coordinate matrix of the
screen face and are intensified. The center dot in the square
represents the last point at which the light pen was known to
be. Suppose now that the light pen is moved. The desired
action is to have the tracking cross follow the light pen. In
order to follow the light pen, it is necessary to identify
which direction the light pen is being moved. This is determined by the position of the next light pen hit. Suppose that
the next light pen hit occurs at the dot in the upper right
hand corner of the tracking cross as illustrated in Fig. 18.
This identifies the direction of the light pen movement and an
instant later the tracking cross pattern will be displayed with
the point of this light pen hit as its new center, as indicated
by the dashed lines. Thus as sequential light pen hits are received, the cross follows the light pen about the screen and
those points where the light pen hits occurred are continually
intensified constituting the drawn line.

The tracking cross method is not without problems. For
example, if the user moves the light pen too fast none of the
points in the tracking cross may result in hits and no intensified points are left to be identified. When this happens the
cross ceases to move and no longer follows the light pen. The
user must move the light pen back into the area of the tracking
cross and pick it up again.

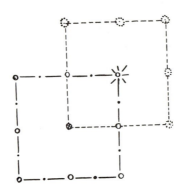

⊗ matrix position of last light pen hit

⊰⊱ matrix position of current light pen hit

—·— last position of tracking cross

---- current position of tracking cross

Fig. 18.   An illustration of how a tracking cross is used
to detect the position of a light pen as it is
moved about the oscilloscope screen.

This method also suffers from the disadvantage that the
amount of programming required to support the tracking cross
is fairly large.* Another related problem is that it is not
always possible to point the light pen at a desired point and
get that point as a hit. Because of the problems of parallelax
and the finite time for the user to depress the light pen switch
mechanism, adjoining points are sometimes picked up as hits
rather than the desired point.

When drawing pictures on an oscilloscope display with a
light pen it is possible to add other programming features that
result in cleaner drawings. It is possible to use buttons,
light pen or otherwise, to select constraints on the lines that
might be drawn. For example, the computer might be instructed
that the next line drawn is to be a straight horizontal line.
Then when the user draws the line, the line that appears on the
oscilloscope is the closest horizontal line that approximates
the one actually drawn. Similar constraints can be enforced

---

*This problem can be greatly alleviated by performing most of
the tracking chores with hardware.

with vertical and other lines at arbitrary angles. Also circles
can be forced on curves that are drawn and one can specify
other niceties like dashed lines.

A little reflection on the manner in which a light pen
functions and the examples given here, should lead to the conclusion that drawing with a light pen in a manner that in any
way approaches the use of a normal pencil requires a large
programming effort.

6.4.2 Mechanical Tracking Devices

Mechanical tracking devices are commonly used to move a
cursor about the oscilloscope screen. The cursor is just an
intensified spot, or perhaps a pattern such as a cross. The
tracking device is used to specify the position of the cursor
on the screen face. As the tracking device is operated a series
of XY coordinate pairs is generated. The cursor moves about
the screen in the positions specified by the coordinate pairs
as they are generated.

There are several mechanical tracking devices presently
available. One is called a track ball. The track ball is a
sphere that is mounted in a box in such a manner that the user
can place the palm of his hand or his fingertips on the track
ball and rotate it in any direction. These rotations are picked
up and decoded into a series of XY positions which instructs
the computer where to place the cursor on the oscilloscope screen.

A second mechanical device for positioning cursors is called
a joy stick. If the reader is familiar with the joy stick in
an airplane he probably immediately sees the analogy. The joy
stick can be moved in any angular direction. That is, forward,
backward, left and right and at angles intermediate to these.
Again, these movements result in a series of XY coordinate pairs
being sent to the computer for positioning the cursor on the
oscilloscope screen.

A third tracking device is known as a mouse. The mouse
is a small box-like structure with wheels on its underneath
surface. As the mouse is rolled about any flat surface the
wheels decode the actions into XY coordinate pairs specifying
the placement of the cursor.

When a decision must be made about which of these devices
is to be used for a given application the choice probably rests
largely with personal preference.

6.4.3 Function Boxes

Physically the function box is just a rectangular box with
an array of push buttons on its furface. These buttons are not
unlike the array of buttons on a typewriter keyboard or an adding machine keyboard. However, in this case the buttons are

rarely labeled permanently. The number of buttons on a typical function box might vary all the way from four or five to perhaps fifty buttons. A function box may be seen on the table in front of the oscilloscope screen in Fig. 15.

From the operational standpoint, the function box is a very simple device and like the light pen can perform only one action. However, this action may again instigate many different actions on the part of the computer program, giving the function box more apparent power than it really has. When the user of the computer system decides to take an action he depresses the appropriate button on the box. The depression of the button sets a flag which causes an interrupt to the computer. After the interrupt has occurred, hardware is available to permit the computer to identify which button has been depressed. The identification of the button is often accomplished by simply using a flip-flop register. Flip-flop 1 can be associated with a button designated number one. Flip-flop 2 can be associated with button number two and so forth. When a button is depressed the computer reads the contents of the flip-flop register and determines which button or buttons had been depressed.

On some occasions it is advantageous to build a slightly more sophisticated function box which generates two interrupts on each button action. When the button is first depressed an interrupt is sent to the computer, then when the finger is taken away and the button released a second interrupt is generated. Thus, there is an interrupt indicating the button is going down and an interrupt indicating that the button is coming up. This type of action is needed where the user wants to employ a function box to start an action which is to continue as long as the button is depressed and stop when the button is released.

As already pointed out the action which results from the depression of a button depends entirely upon which program has been loaded into the computer, and in fact, the action taken may vary widely from program to program. For this reason the buttons are not normally labeled permanently. Since several programs may use the function box it is necessary to find some means of labeling the buttons in a manner that corresponds with the program that is loaded into the computer's memory. This is often done with small sheets of paper or plastic used as overlays. The overlays have holes punched in them so that they slip down over the buttons on the function box and rest on top of the box itself. The overlays have labeling that designates the function of each of the buttons on the box. With this approach there is an overlay which corresponds to each computer program that utilizes the function box.

6.4.4   Character and Vector Generators

As mentioned earlier, there are devices for displaying
subunits of pictures on the oscilloscope screen. Two of the
most frequently used are units to generate characters (alphanumerics) and units to draw straight lines (vectors).
Although the generation of characters and vectors using
computer programming is straightforward it does have disadvantages. First, the programs to generate these patterns require computer memory space, and two, these programs are fairly
time consuming to execute. Therefore, in some applications it
is desirable to have hardware that generates characters and
vectors. Hardware character and vector generators have the
advantages of convenience, considerable less computer overhead,
a guaranteed compatibility, and modularity from program to program.
Several features are found in character generators. They
often have the complete alphabet, the digits 0 to 9, and several of the special characters found on a typewriter keyboard
such as the plus sign and the minus sign. Often one has a
choice of character size and in some of the more sophisticated
units of character font.
Some character generators have been marketed which have
features that are intermediate between software generation and
hardware generation. In this case software is used to construct
the characters that can be displayed on the oscilloscope screen.
However, the hardware actually executes the displaying of these
figures. The displaying of the figures is faster than those
generators which are strictly programming but are slower than
the completely hardware oriented character generators. The advantage is that the user can design characters (by programming)
of any type that he desires; for example, the Greek alphabet
and special mathematical symbols.
To use a character generator for a given display on the
oscilloscope screen, the character generator is initialized
telling it the character size, font and other variables that
might be associated with it, and the screen position at which
the characters are to be placed. Following this the programmer
gives a series of codes which identify those characters that
are to be displayed on the screen. In some cases this is the
ASCII code. The ASCII code has some advantage in that the displaying of characters on the oscilloscope screen then becomes
quite similar to outputing characters to the teleprinter.
Ideally, one would like this to be true to the extent that output can be displayed on either the oscilloscope display or the
teleprinter by one simple command from the user.
In the case of a hardware vector generator there are really
only two basic pieces of information required. The beginning
and termination points of the vector. However, there is more
than one way to specify this. One can actually specify the
beginning and ending coordinate pairs, or one might specify

the beginning coordinate pair and the angle at which the vector
departs from the beginning point. Often hardware vector generators have what are called long and short vector modes. The
term long and short vectors can be taken somewhat literally.
Usually the crux of the situation is that if one is to draw a
long vector, the number of bits of information required for the
beginning and ending points will exceed one computer word length.
Then it is necessary to have a mode of operation in which more
than one computer word is considered by the vector generator to
specify the vector to be drawn. Thus, saying that a generator
has a long and short vector mode is usually analogous to saying
that vectors which require more than one word length fall in
the class of the long vector mode and those that can be specified
by one word length are the short vector mode.

6.5 Programming Considerations

The foregoing material shows that the producing of a CRT
display is not difficult to understand. However, reasonably
complex oscilloscope displays will benefit from programming
skill.

6.5.1 Flicker

On all but the storage oscilloscopes the picture on the
oscilloscope screen will visibly flicker if the picture is not
"painted" on the CRT face frequently enough. This is due to
the fact that the fluorescent spot on the screen is dying away
below visual limits before the beam returns to that point and
causes it to fluoresce again. Because of this, the number of
times that the picture must be painted on the CRT screen is
directly related to the decay times of the phosphor used.
Those phosphors having longer decay times do not have to be
struck so often by the electron beam to maintain a visible
image. As a rule of thumb it is desirable to display at
least 30 frames per second. That is the complete picture should
be painted on the oscilloscope screen 30 times every second.
In conjunction with flicker and the number of frames per
second displayed it is interesting to note a curious phenomenon.
If, a picture is displayed on the order of 20 frames per second,
then the flicker is very disconcerting, resulting in a considerable discomfort in trying to view the display. However, if
the flicker rate is the order of 5 frames per second, the flicker is rather slow and pecularily enough, is not really uncomfortable to view.
What actions can be taken in the computer programming to
eliminate or reduce the amount of flicker on an oscilloscope
display? The five steps shown below are those that are normally used in the simplest of memory driven displays:

1. Extract data point from list in memory.
2. Manipulate data point.
3. Send XY coordinate pair and intensify command to CRT.
4. Advance to next position of data list.
5. Return to step 1.

If the oscilloscope display flickers using this approach, then the flicker can only be eliminated or reduced by modifying these five steps. Some gain may be had by the ordering of the list of display points in a more optimum fashion. This can speed up the execution of steps 1, 4 and 5.

If optimum ordering of the list does not eliminate or reduce the flicker to a satisfactory point, the only remaining avenue is to eliminate step 2. This can be accomplished by setting aside a portion of computer memory for a display buffer. Then the data is manipulated only once and placed in its manipulated form in this display buffer. From that point on the data is displayed directly from the display buffer eliminating step 2. The display buffer has the added advantage that it provides program modularity, for if a buffer is used, many programs can use the same display routine and buffer.

The five steps outlined above represent a computer program that uses the minimal amount of memory to display data that is already resident in the memory of the computer. However, this is one of the slowest means of displaying data on an oscilloscope screen. Thus, one has two diametrically opposing goals: speed and minimal usage of memory. In general, the faster the speed of display the more memory required and vice versa.

6.5.2 Scaling

It has already been pointed out that for programming purposes the oscilloscope is often thought of as a matrix that is typically 1,024 integer units along the X axis and 1,024 integer units along the Y axis. In this scheme the lower left hand corner of the screen is typically thought of as the X=0 Y=0 position, the upper left hand corner is the (0,1023) position, the upper right hand corner is (1023, 1023) and the lower right hand corner is the (1023,0) position.

Now suppose that a set of data which is made up of 256 individual points, the amplitudes of which range in value from 0 to 4095 is to be displayed on the oscilloscope screen. This might be a curve displaying voltage along the Y axis and time along the X axis. Because the vertical range of the data is larger than the maximum value that may be accommodated, by the oscilloscope via its digital-to-analog converters, it is necessary to scale the Y values of all the XY coordinate pairs of this 256 point data set. In this somewhat simplified example, it is easy to see that maximum utilization will be made

of the display area, if all the Y values are divided by four.
This makes the maximum amplitude of any data point 1023 which
exactly corresponds with the largest Y value that may be displayed.

The data can now be displayed as a series of Y values
that range between 0 and 1023 with X values corresponding exactly to those on the oscilloscope. However, if the data is
displayed this way, all 256 points are shown in the left most
fourth of the oscilloscope screen. The picture would be more
pleasing if the points were spread completely across the oscilloscope screen, i.e. across all possible X values of the
digital-to-analog converters. This is easily attained by
displaying X values on the scope of 0,4,8,...,1016,1020.

What has been discussed in this simple example is a process that almost always takes place whenever any data is to
be displayed on an oscilloscope screen. A choice of scales
must be made and then the individual display points scaled to
make optimum use of the full area of the display.

6.5.3 Memory Requirements

When applications of computer displays require complex
pictures to be shown, very large amounts of memory may be
necessary. To give a feeling for the order of magnitude, suppose that a raster scan display is to be used on a 10 bit matrix (1024 by 1024 points). Assume the picture is to be stored
as a long sequence of bits. If a bit is zero the corresponding
point on the oscilloscope screen will not be intensified; if
the bit is a one the corresponding point will be intensified.
This means that a minimum of one million bits is required
which is approximately 60,000 words in a 16 bit computer. Although this example is somewhat extreme it is not at all unrealistic. Because magnetic core memory is the most expensive
part of the basic computer it is a quantity that must be con-
served. Unfortunately, we have already seen that the optimi-
zation of memory and the speed of display are conflicting
goals.

In terms of these conflicting goals, turn to the example
of 256 data points to be displayed using the five step method
mentioned earlier. The memory needs are optimized by getting
the data directly each time and then performing the manipulation (divide by 4) before displaying the data. But, on the
other hand, the flicker is reduced by dividing all the numbers
by four and placing them in a 256 word display buffer. Thus,
to optimize the speed of the display it has been necessary to
increase the amount of memory used by 256 words.

6.5.4   Character Generation

Both vectors and characters can be generated via program
controls in the computer. For example, if one wants to write
an alphanumeric character on the oscilloscope screen it can be
done by having a pattern of dots generated on the screen that
resemble the character. Normally this is written as a character generation subroutine which contains within it the patterns of each of the characters that are to be drawn.
Each character is thought of as occupying a small rectangular array of dots on the screen. These arrays are usually
at least five by seven dot rectangles. If much smaller rectangles are used, there may be difficulty in distinguishing
certain characters. Fig. 19 shows a five by seven dot rectangle. The black points represent those points in the rectangle
which are intensified to resemble the character C. In the character generator subroutine certain conventions are chosen. In
the present case the conventions would probably be to think of
the rectangular array as being swept by a raster scan and some
corner of the array chosen as the position from which the scan
starts. In this case there are a total of 35 binary bits in
the character rectangle. Suppose that the upper left hand
corner of the array is chosen as bit 1, the position to the
right of that as 2, the next position as 3, and so forth, and
the first position in the second line of the scan, number 6,
and so forth. Then, it is possible to specify each character
by putting in the memory of the computer a series of 35 bit
groupings where a zero corresponds to no intensity and a one
corresponds to an intensified point.
Once these conventions have been established then any
character may be generated on the screen by specifying what
position on the screen the character is to be placed and using
some algorithm to select the appropriate array of binary bits.
It is almost always desirable to be able to have at least
two different sizes of characters available. Rather than store
two complete sets of characters with dot matrices representing
the different sizes, it is much more desirable to have a program that can take one size of dot matrix and scale it to a
different character size.
It is often desirable to be able to rotate characters 90
degrees, to permit labeling axes and other graphical information that gives a preference to writing characters vertically
on the screen.
Finally, intensity is a variable that is often very useful
in composing a display with the maximum amount of information.
Therefore, it is desirable to be able to specify to the character generator program that characters be displayed with different intensities.
Although the above description is for a point-plot display it is easy to extrapolate these same techniques for a
stroke writer display. The stroke writer display has some

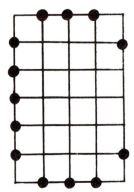

Fig. 19. An example of how the letter C can be con-
          structed on an oscilloscope display grid using
          a 5x7 dot matrix. The black spots represent
          those points on the grid that are intensified.

advantages when scaling characters over fairly large ranges.
In the dot matrix approach if a character is increased by say
a factor of 4 in size the dots may spread apart to the extent
that the character is not nearly as pleasing to look at.

      Raster scan displays are not amenable to character gener-
ation by software. It should be obvious how difficult it is
to program character generators where a portion of each character is to be included in each line of scan. This becomes
doubly complex if one insists upon the ability to scale and
rotate the characters.

                6.5.5 Three Dimensional Displays

      There are many applications where it is desirable to create
drawings on an oscilloscope face that have a three dimensional
aspect. Of course, this really means executing the drawings in
perspective. This is too lengthy a discussion to enter into here.
Suffice it to say that there are two major problems in executing
three dimensional displays. One is that three dimensional displays tend to be very complex, and therefore the amount of information to give a feeling of three dimensions to a picture on
an oscilloscope screen results in serious problems with flicker.
An irregular surface can only be given the proper illusion of
shape by drawing several vectors that convey this feeling for
shape. The generation of hundreds and thousands of vectors
places very severe limitations on most display equipment.

      The other major problem is the so-called hidden-line prob-
lem. If one looks at an object in three dimensions, it is impossible to see those surfaces that face away from the viewer.
The hidden line problem is to find a way that the computer can

determine which surfaces are hidden from the viewer and therefore should not be drawn on the oscilloscope screen.

6.5.6 Display Motion

Another desirable feature is that of motion, i.e. to give
a motion picture aspect to whatever is being displayed on the
oscilloscope screen. To give a simple example of this in a two
dimensional case refer to Fig. 20. Suppose that all the points
shown in Fig. 20 are a data set that is to be viewed on the
oscilloscope screen. Further suppose that there are enough
data points that the visual quality of the display would be
very poor if all the points were crowded on to the oscilloscope
screen at the same time. One would like to have some means of
displaying a portion of the data points, but with the ability
to move on to other portions of the data whenever desired. One
way is to traverse (pan) the data set from left to right displaying some constant number of points at all times. The effect
is analogous to having the data on a long banner with the viewer
looking through a window at the banner as it is pulled by the
window. How this is accomplished is illustrated in Fig. 20 by
use of the rectangle. Suppose at some instant those points
within the rectangle are being shown on the oscilloscope screen,
and that in the next instant those points with the circles about
them are shown on the oscilloscope screen. A little thought
should show that this gives the same effect as the banner being
pulled by the window. The mechanism is to display some portion
of the data for an instant then to subtract a point from the
left hand side of the screen and add a point to the right hand
side of the screen to give the illusion of the data moving across
the oscilloscope face from right to left. From a programming
standpoint adding and subtracting the points is quite easy.
The more complex case is to create motion with a three dimensional picture. This also greatly aggravates the hidden
line problem.
From the practical standpoint creating motion on the display face tends to add a heavy computational load to the computer. This is true even if a buffer is being used because the
buffer is also constantly being changed.
Another approach which partially solves the problem of the
heavy computational load associated with moving displays is to
add analog controls to the display hardware. This then permits
some display motion to be accomplished by the simple turning of
knobs and similar analog control devices.

7.0 THE PLOTTER

The material here will be concerned with what will be
referred to as XY plotters; also called incremental plotters.

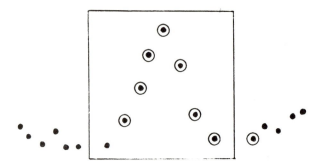

Fig. 20. A method for creating transverse motion on an
          oscilloscope display. The points within the
          rectangle represent the points displayed at some
          given instant. In the next instant those points
          within the circles are displayed. Repeatedly
          displaying points one position to the right in
          this manner will give the illusion that the data
          points are moving from right to left across the
          oscilloscope screen.

These plotters are two dimensional* in that they draw upon a
surface. Some XY plotters take paper from a continuous roll
and pass it over a drum. When the paper is on the drum an
inking mechanism is used to draw on the paper. The direction
of the paper motion is typically considered to be the X direction and the plotter head moves perpendicularly to this direction to obtain the necessary Y values. The drum direction is
reversible permitting the drum to be moved backwards to X
values that have already been passed over. The drawings may
be continuous or point plot. Because of the manner in which
these plotters operate the X axis can be essentially infinite
in length whereas the maximum Y amplitudes are determined by
the width of paper that is used.

     Stepping motors advance the paper in the X direction and
the plot head in the Y direction. Thus, the plotting pen is
moved to any desired position by moving a series of X and Y
steps. The precision of the drawings therefore depends on the
smallness of the steps and the precision with which the pen may
be stepped back to an original position. Plotters currently
available can move in steps as small as 0.005 inches. As a

---

*It might be noted in passing that three dimensional plotters
are now available. These accomplish a three dimensional
effect by poking wires through a board at XY positions specified by the computer. The length of the wire constitutes
the Z value in three dimensional space.

point of reference, this is approximately the diameter of a
human hair, therefore, drawings of great precision can be
executed with this type of plotter. It must be realized that
there is an inverse relationship between the step size and the
speed with which a plot may be drawn; the smaller the step
size the slower the execution of the drawing and vice versa.

Another type of XY plotter is known as a flat-bed plotter.
In this case the paper is placed over a flat surface and the
plotting head is moved about over the surface as the paper remains stationary. Probably the major physical distinction between the two types of XY plotters is physical size. Whereas
the larger drum plotters use 30 inch wide roles of paper, the
larger flat-bed plotters reach very large dimensions, sometimes
on the order of five by ten feet. One of the major applications
for flat-bed plotters is the precision drawing of masks for the
production of large scale integrated circuits.

From the programming standpoint there are essentially four
commands that may be given to the XY (incremental) plotter.
They are move one step in the X direction, move one step in the
Y direction, pen up, and pen down. It should be noted that
these are similar to CRT commands, if one equates intensity on
with pen down, and intensity off with pen up. In fact, at some
computing centers the plot and CRT display programs can be used
interchangeably.

8.0   THE XY TABLET

The oscilloscope display and the incremental plotter permit a computer system to output sophisticated graphic material.
The light pen permits reasonably sophisticated input. The XY
tablet is the most sophisticated input device for many applications.

The XY tablet satisfies a need that has existed for some
time in the utilization of computers. That is to find some
means by which a free hand drawing can be literally digitized
and placed in a computer memory as the user executes the drawing. The original tablet was developed at the RAND Corporation.
In terms of construction the RAND tablet can be thought of as
lengths of wire that are laid out in a pattern which creates
a rectangular mesh. When in use, a stylus or pencil-like device is passed over the mesh which is imbedded in a translucent surface. The wire mesh is pulsed with a gray code.
Through capacitive coupling with the stylus it is possible to
determine at which point on the rectangular mesh the stylus is
residing. The result is that as the pencil moves about the
translucent surface a series of XY coordinate positions are
fed from the tablet to the computer. The capacitive coupling
can take place through reasonable thicknesses of paper, permitting the user to lay a piece of paper on the translucent
surface and make a drawing upon it if the stylus has an inking

tip. The whole operation culminates in the direct digitization of any picture which is being drawn. Some of the uses for such tablets have been the analysis of handwriting, use of the computer to recognize characters and other symbols and to directly digitize pieces of data printed on strip chart paper.

Another approach to the XY tablet is called the sonic tablet In this approach two strip microphones are laid at right angles t each other on a plane. A stylus is used but this time the stylus has a spark generating mechanism within it. Therefore, as the user writes with the stylus, sparks are generated and the position of the stylus is determined from the time of flight of the sound to the two microphones. The stylus can again contain a ballpoint pen and a drawing can again be executed on a piece of paper while simultaneously being digitized and stored in the computer memory. In this case there is no problem with capacitive coupling through the paper, because the sound travels from the stylus through the air to the microphone. In fact, in this case no particular surface is required for the tablet. The microphones can be set up on a desk, on a wall or any place that it is desired to execute a drawing.

Recently a third approach to the XY tablet has been developed. In this approach electronic sensors are placed below the drawing surface which can detect a ring that generates a magnetic field and is passed over the surface by the user. The ring may be mounted in a stylus with a ballpoint tip or the ring may be similar to a small magnifying glass. In the latter case the device is primarily used as a digitizing device, whereas in the former case it is primarily a drawing device.

It is usually desirable to show the drawing as it is digitized; one of the more popular outputs from the tablets is an oscilloscope display. The display is generated from the digitized data stored within the computer memory.

Probably the major programming problem with tablets as input devices is the large number of XY coordinates that are generated in even the most minimal drawings. Therefore, the optimuzation of storage must be strenuously pursued in order to store drawings in a reasonable amount of computer memory.

9.0   ANALOG-TO-DIGITAL CONVERTERS

It should be apparent by this time that devices coupled to on-line computers fall into distinct categories; digital devices and analog devices. A digital device is one that presents its output to the computer in the form of a digital number; as a series of binary bits in a register. On the other hand, the analog device presents an output to the computer in the form of a voltage or some other continuous signal. Analog signals are not directly compatible with the digital computer. Therefore, whenever an analog device is to be interfaced to a digital computer it is necessary that its output be converted to a digital form. This conversion of an analog signal to a digital signal is the purpose of an analog-to-digital converter.

There are two major types of signals that are digitized. These are illustrated in Fig. 21. In Fig. 21a the signal is a function of time. The amplitude (Y axis) might be a voltage or a current. This is the type of signal that is produced by thermocouples, strain gauges and similar devices.

The other type of signal is shown in Fig. 21b and will be described as a pulse signal. This type of signal, rather than being continuous in nature, occurs at discreet times, and is often found in association with random phenomenon, e.g. radioactivity.

As would be suspected, two different types of analog-to-digital converters are required for the two kinds of signals. In both cases there are three major characteristics of the analog-to-digital converters (ADC's) that are of interest: resolution, speed and linearity. The resolution of an analog-to-digital converter is the smallest difference in amplitudes that it can detect. The linearity of an ADC is defined by how closely its output is directly proportional to its input.

9.1 Successive Approximation ADC'S

The successive approximation, or as it is sometimes known the binary approximation ADC, is used to digitize continuous signals.* Typically the sequence of events that occur when a point is digitized is as follows: sample, hold, and digitize. The continuous line of Fig. 21a represents the signal as it actually occurs as a function of time. The dots along this continuous line represent those points at which the amplitude has been sampled and digitized. The time (delta T) between samples is usually constant but need not necessarily be. When the amplitude is measured at one of these discreet points, the sample portion of the measurement might be thought of as a snapshot action. The amplitude is sampled and then circuitry is provided during the hold portion of the sequence to keep this amplitude constant within the ADC.** Finally, this "held" amplitude is digitized. The amplitude is digitized by comparing it against amplitudes within the ADC that are known. This is the reason for the name successive approximation. Through a series of incremented steps the amplitude is successively compared to other amplitudes until a final result is obtained.

---

* Other ADC's are available for digitizing continuous signals but the successive approximation is probably the most common.
**In some applications ADC's are fast enough to preclude the need for a hold operation.

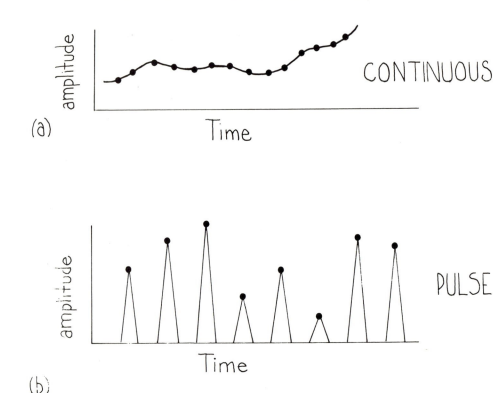

Fig. 21. The two types of signals most frequently digitized
by analog-to-digital converters are shown. Figure
a) is a signal whose amplitude varies with time
and typically is digitized by sampling the amplitudes
as indicated by the dots. Figure b) represents a
series of pulses which occur randomly in time and
amplitude. The object in this case is to detect the
presence of a pulse and then to measure its maximum
amplitude as indicated by the dots.

9.2   Ramp ADC

This type of ADC is variously referred to as a rundown
ADC, a ramp ADC, or a Wilkinson ADC. Whereas the successive
approximation ADC is normally used to digitize samples of continuous signals, the ramp ADC is more often used to measure the
amplitude of pulses such as those shown in Fig. 21b. In order
to accomplish this it is necessary that the ADC be able to perform two specific tasks. The first is to detect the presence
of a pulse and the second is to measure the amplitude of the
pulse.

Ramp ADC's are often used in applications where radio-activity is involved. This means that the pulses arrive at random time intervals with no particular amplitude sequence. Because of this randomicity of both the amplitude and the time intervals it is important that the ADC be able to accurately detect the presence of pulses. These pulses have been ampli-fied in amplitude and their shapes have been optimized for the operation of the ADC.*

Most ADC's that are used to detect and measure pulse am-plitudes utilize a capacitance and scaler to measure amplitude. When a pulse arrives at the input of the ADC a gate is opened, and the pulse is permitted to charge a capacitance in the ADC. When the peak detecting circuitry finds the top of the pulse the charging action is stopped. At this point a scaler (counter register), which has been set equal to zero, is gated open and allowed to count pulses from an oscillator. Simul-taneously with the gating of the scaler the capacitance is allowed to start a linear discharge. At the end of the dis-charge the scaler is stopped. Because the amount of charge is proportional to the pulse amplitude and because the dis-charge time is proportional to the charge stored, the number in the scaler at the end of the discharge is proportional to the original pulse amplitude. It can be seen that two conver-sions have actually occurred. The pulse amplitude has first been converted to time units which then are converted to a digital number by the scaling action. If the ADC is attached to an on-line computer, the number in the scaler is transferred to the computer memory. After the transfer and storage of the digitized pulse the computer usually resets the ADC so that it may detect another pulse.

9.3 Programming Considerations

Two entirely different programming approaches are required for the two types of ADC's that have been described. In the case of the successive approximation ADC the computer provides a command to the ADC which causes it to sample and digitize the signal amplitude. Once the sample has been taken and digitized the ADC usually sends a signal to the computer announcing that it has a digitized number. At this point the computer reads the digitized value into its memory. The command to the ADC to

---

*The shape of the pulse is the characteristics that describe the time that it takes the pulse to rise to its full amplitude and the time that it takes to fall back to zero plus the width of the pulse in units of time. The units of time typically involved are the order of a microsecond for the pulse width. Typical amplitudes are in the range of zero to ten volts.

digitize, and the transfer of the digitized number is performed
under computer control. Thus, it is the computer which determines, by one of several different means, the time difference
between successive samples of signal amplitude. Because the
time difference is under computer control, it is possible to
have the samples taken at equal time intervals or to take them
at any arbitrary time designated by the user.

The time for a successive approximation ADC to digitize
a number is independent of the amplitude of the signal digitize
Thus, the programmer in writing the program can determine exactly the rate his program can take data.

The class of measurements that utilize successive approximation ADC's normally store the data in the form of amplitude
versus time. Referring to Fig. 21b imagine that the continuous
line is not present and only the dots representing the times at
which the signal was sampled are plotted. This is the form of
the data when it is stored and plotted after the series of meas
urements have been performed.

The events are handled quite differently in the ramp ADC.
In this instance the ADC detects the event, performs the rundow
and then notifies the computer. Unlike the case of the success
approximation ADC the computer program has no control over when
a digitization will take place. Once the rundown is complete
and an interrupt signal has been sent to the computer, the program transfers the digitized number to its memory. Often this
action is followed by a control signal, issued under program
control, which resets the ADC in preparation for the detection
and measurement of another event.

In the case of the ramp ADC the data is no longer stored
as a series of measurements versus time. The measurement is to
determine the number of pulses as a function of amplitude. The
fore, in this type of data the digitized numbers are stored in
form of a histogram. The X axis units of the histogram are oft
referred to as channel numbers and represent values that are pr
portional to the original amplitudes of the pulses. As each e-
vent is brought into the computer the content of the correspond
channel number is incremented by one.

Because the rundown time is proportional to the pulse amplitude, the time to digitize an event is directly related to
the amplitude of the event. Thus, the times to digitize different signals can vary dramatically. This coupled with the
randomicity of the pulse amplitudes permits the programmer to
determine the rate at which his programs can handle events only
in an average way. Often rather than store each event as it
arrives at the computer in its appropriate channel, the events
are allowed to accumulate in a few consecutive memory locations
By doing this very little time elapses before the computer resets the ADC after transferring the digitized number. This is
often referred to as buffering or derandomizing the data. Derandomizing takes advantage of the fact that although the pulse
arrive at random time intervals they will, over a period of tir

arrive at an average rate. Therefore, by storing several amplitudes in a buffer, before performing the computations required to determine which channel number they correspond to has
a derandomizing effect.

10.0   DIGITAL-TO-ANALOG CONVERTERS

The previous section has shown that it is often necessary
to couple devices with analog outputs to computers. This gives
rise to the need for analog-to-digital converters. In the inverse direction it is often necessary to control a device which
requires analog inputs. Therefore, it is necessary to develop
digital-to-analog converters which, as might be expected, takes
a digital number and converts it to an analog signal.

There will be no attempt here to summarize the various
methods of accomplishing a digital-to-analog conversion. Instead, one example is concentrated on to give a feeling for
what is to be accomplished in a digital-to-analog conversion
(DAC).

The diagram of Fig. 22 shows a considerably simplified
digital-to-analog converter. The four resistors shown form a
resistance chain (ladder), and have been given arbitrary values
from one to eight, forming a binary progression, i.e. powers
of two. Note that each resistor is paralleled with a switch.
If the switch is closed the contribution of that resistor is
removed from the resistance chain. A voltage $V_1 - V_2$ is being
applied across the resistance chain from a constant current
source. If all the switches are open, then the voltage measured across the output is

$$V = V_m = V_1 - V_2 \quad .$$

conversely, if all switches are closed then the voltage across
the output is zero.

Now, suppose that this resistance chain is coupled to a
four-bit output register in an on-line computer in such a manner
that a bit in the register set to one leaves the corresponding
switch open, and a bit equal to zero closes the corresponding
switch. For convention's sake, suppose that the most significant bit in the register corresponds to switch S1 and the least
significant bit corresponds to the switch S4.

Now if the register is loaded with the binary number 1011,
the voltage measured across the output is given by,

$$V = \frac{8+2+1}{15} V_m = \frac{11}{15} V_m .$$

Likewise, if the number in the register is 0101 then the output
voltage is given by

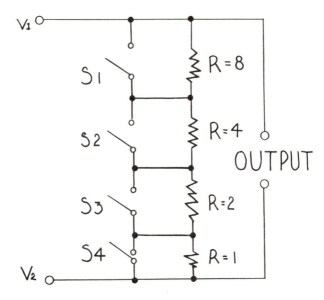

Fig. 22.   A simplified diagram of one type of digital-to-
analog converter. The output voltage is proportional to the digital input represented by the
pattern of the switch settings.

$$V = \frac{4+1}{15} V_m = \frac{1}{3} V_m$$

        Thus, it can be seen that the voltage measured at the out
put of this simplified DAC can be varied by the computer via
the four bit output register anywhere from zero volts to the
maximum V_m. It is necessary to consider three primary parameters when specifying DAC's; resolution, speed and linearity.
The resolution is the fineness with which an output voltage ca
be generated. In the example of Fig. 22 the smallest increment of voltage is 1/16 of the largest output voltage. In mol
typical DAC's the resolution might be the order of one part il
a thousand. It is possible to build DAC's with resolutions of
one part in one hundred thousand and better. In general, the
better the resolution the lower the speed. Hence, higher resolutions and higher speeds mean increased costs.
        The other parameter, linearity, is a measure of how nearl
the output voltage is proportional to the binary number in the
register.
        The binary scale that has been given in the example of Fi
22 is not necessarily the best scale. Suppose that the regist
contains the binary number 0111. The error in the output volt
corresponding to this number is the sum of the errors in the
values of the resistors that equal one, two, and four. Howeve

if the output is now stepped one resolution increment, i.e.
the contents of the register is changed to 1000, then the error
in the output voltage depends only on the error of the resistance with the value eight. Thus, as the DAC is stepped by
resolution increments through the possible output voltages the
magnitude of the error associated with various steps can vary
rather dramatically. It is desirable to arrange that the error
in consecutive output steps remain almost constant. This can
be accomplished by using a gray scale rather than the binary
scale of Fig. 22. Referring to Table I a voltage V in arbitrary
units is shown with a corresponding binary scale and a gray
scale. Looking at the gray scale column it can be seen that in
progressing through the scale by consecutive steps, only one
binary bit changes value on each successive step.

11.0 SCALERS

Basically a scaler is a pulse counting device, i.e. a pulse
detected at its input causes the contents of the scaler to be
incremented by one. From the logic standpoint it is simply a
counter register. The individual flip-flops of the register
are connected together in such a way that a series of events
cause the flip-flops to be set in a binary progression; i.e. to
count the events and have the total number of events stored in
the flip-flops at any given time.

Two of the more common uses for scalers are to count events
and to use them as timers. The counting application has already
been described above. In using scalers as timers a clock is
connected to the input of the scaler. A clock in this sense is
any electronic device that emits pulses at periodic intervals
in time. Thus, the number of events in the scaler does not represent absolute time, as presented by a wrist watch, but rather
represents an elapsed time. There are many important uses in
on-line computers for such clocks and elapsed time scalers.

There are at least two common ways of implementing scalers
in on-line computers. In the first, the scaler is built as a
flip-flop register just as described above. In this case the
computer can zero the scaler, i.e. set all the flip-flops to
the logical zero state, it can open a gate so that the scaler
can start counting, and it can close the same gate to stop e-
vents from reaching the scaler. The computer can also read the
contents of the scaler and transfer them to its own memory. Often
the scaler is built so that an overflow of the scaler results
in an interrupt which notifies the computer of the overflow. The
overflow of a scaler takes place when more total events have been
detected at its input than it is capable of counting. For example,
in a twelve bit scaler, i.e. 12 flip-flops in the register, it
is only possible to count 4,095 events. On the 4,096th event
the scaler flips to zero. It is this 4,096th event that causes
the interrupt to the computer. All the functions that have been

Table I.   Comparison of a binary scale and a gray scale. V
           is the DAC output voltage in arbitrary units, and
           the two remaining columns represent the digital
           inputs for both a binary and a gray scale.

V	Binary Scale	Gray Scale
0	000	000
1	001	001
2	010	011
3	011	010
4	100	110
5	101	111
6	110	101
7	111	100

mentioned (reset, start, stop) can be implemented so that they
can be performed manually as well as by the computer.
     The other major method of implementing scalers with on-li
computers is to use memory locations in the computer magnetic
core memory as scalers. These obviously can be read by the co
puter and can be set to zero. Thus, it is only necessary to
add a rather minute amount of electronic logic to provide gate
which can start and stop the entry of pulses (events) into the
particular memory locations. In addition it is necessary to
supply the logic to permit these memory locations to be incremented by one. This latter method of implementing scalers may
be more economic than building external flip-flop registers.

12.0   CONTROL PANELS

     Whenever a device is attached to an on-line computer de-
cisions must be made about the manual operations that are to
be implemented in connection with the control of that device.
Often with small on-line computer systems the only device avai
able is the Teletype unit. Thus, the only means of controllin
a peripheral on the computer via the program in the computer
memory is to type commands on the Teletype keyboard. In many
cases this is a quite satisfactory means of control. However,
in many others it leaves something to be desired. There are
many control actions that are inherently better performed by
using rotary switches with many positions or push-button switc
     The use of rotary switches and push button switches can b
implemented via control panels. The control panel can be some
what fixed i.e. it may be constructed in such a way that it ca
only be used with one peripheral on the computer. It is the
author's feeling that this is often not the most satisfactory
way to proceed. In keeping with this the author and collabora

---

*Mr. G. B. Morgan and Mr. C.W. Richardson.

have developed a digital control panel which is flexible in
nature because it can be used with many different peripheral
devices that are attached to the on-line computer. The panel
can accommodate both inputs and outputs. For example, the inputs can include rotary knobs, push buttons, thumb wheels, and
toggle switches. The outputs might include strip recorders and
digital strips of lights. The important point is that both the
input and output controls are not permanently tied to any function or any peripheral. That is, the action that results from
the depression of any button or the turning of any switch is
entirely dependent on the program resident in the computer.
Whenever any switch is activated on the panel, the computer is
interrupted and the program must determine which switch has been
activated and what its current position is. At this point the
computer program determines what action is to take place as a
result of that switch setting. Fig. 23 shows a typical digital control panel.

    Because the action carried out by the various switches is
determined by the program a non-permanent method must be found
to label both the switches and indicators. This has been accomplished by constructing a plastic overlay with holes punched in
it which fit over the switches. It is on this overlay that the
functions of the indicators and switches are labeled. There is
an overlay which corresponds with each program that utilizes the
digital control panel. Fig. 24 shows the panel of Fig. 23 with
an overlay mounted. Also Fig. 2 of the chapter "Introduction"
shows such a panel attached to an on-line computer system.

13.0 LINE PRINTERS

    This type of printer is characterized by the fact that it
usually prints a whole line of alphameric characters simultaneously, or at least subunits of the line which are longer
than one character. Line printers are rather fast with speeds
that vary from the order of one hundred lines per minute to the
order of twelve hundred lines per minute. There are usually
the order of one hundred and thirty characters per line.

    The paper used in line printers is a continuous, fan-fold
strip. The paper is perforated at the folds so that it may be
torn into individual sheets. It is available in many different
varieties. For example, it may be packaged several layers thick
so that carbon copies can be printed. Almost any type of form
may be printed on suitable paper. As an example many companies
presently print their payroll checks utilizing such line printers
with continuous strips of blank check forms.

    Fig. 25 shows a line printer suitable for a small on-line
computer system.

    Line printers have either one or two buffers that hold one
line of print each. Therefore, the action taken by a computer
program is to load a line of characters into the buffer and then

Fig. 23. A typical digital control panel. The row of
          lights beside each rotary switch indicates the
          switch position. The row of lights across the
          top are used by the program as status lights.
          This panel also has several push-button switches.

issue a print command. The printer responds with a signal
when the line has been printed.

14.0 PUNCHED CARDS

     Punched cards are undoubtedly the most popular I/O medium
at large computer facilities. This is not the case with on-
line computer systems. Cards do not serve in the same capacit
on on-line computer systems because of the entirely different
utilization of on-line computers as compared with central computing facilities. Also, punched card equipment often exceeds
the price of the on-line computer.
     Physically a punched card appears as shown in Fig. 26.
One corner of the card is beveled. When looking at the printe

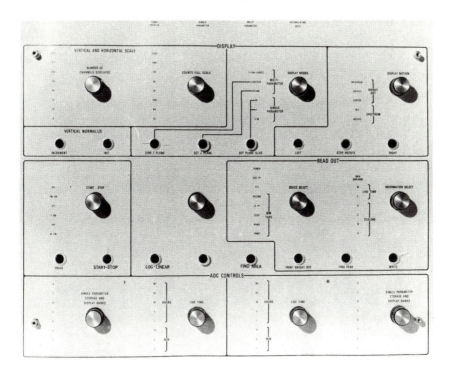

Fig. 24. The control panel of Fig. 23 with an overlay
mounted. The overlay in this case is for use
in gamma-ray spectrometry experiments using
ramp analog-to-digital converters. The overlay
is translucent so that indicator lights on the
panel may still be seen.

side of the card the bevel is to be at the upper left hand
corner. Across the card from left to right are eighty columns
which may contain "punches". Punches meaning holes through the
card made by punching devices which are discussed below. The
punching of cards is quite similar to the punching of paper tape
which has already been discussed previously.

Fig. 25. A photograph of a line printer courtesy of Potter Instrument Company, Inc.

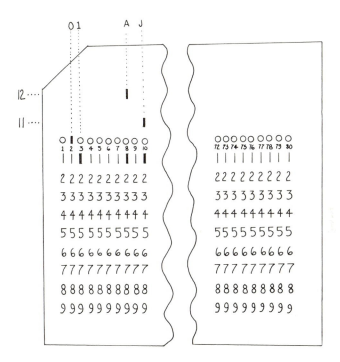

Fig. 26.   An example of a punch card.   The dark rectangles
           represent holes that have been punched in the card.

14.1   Format

Referring to Fig. 26* it can be seen that from top to
bottom there are 12 horizontal rows which may be punched on a
card. Ten of these rows, the lowest 10, are numbered 0 through
9. The topmost rows are not labeled. There are 80 columns as
one proceeds from the left going to the right of the card.
The dark squares of Fig. 26 represent holes that have been
punched in the card. The pattern of the holes gives some idea
about the code shown. For example, a punch in the first column

---

*The card shown in Fig. 26 is typical, however, it should be
 noted that it is possible to print any information desired on
 the face of a card. The information that is printed on the
 card shown in Fig. 26 is common and also advantageous for the
 present explanation.

only indicates a zero. A punch in the second column represent
a one and so forth. For the alphabet and other alphameric
characters multiple punches are used. For example, the A is
a punch in the 12 position and the 1 position. The B is a pun
in the 12 position and in the two position, and so forth. The
code represented in Fig. 26, and given in its entirety in
Appendix VI, is referred to as a Hollerith Code.* Recently
I.B.M. has switched to a different code for its series 360 com
puters. The new code is primarily different in that the speci
characters are represented by different punching combinations.
This new code is called the Extended Binary-Coded-Decimal Inte
change Code (EBCDIC), and is also given in Appendix VI.

Most manufacturers also have a code that corresponds to
the binary code on paper tape which has been discussed previou
The binary code compacts much more information into each verti
column on the card. Typically, the object versions of program
that have been assembled are punched in the manufacturer's respective binary code.

14.2 Associated Equipment

Although the equipment to be described here for punching
cards and for reading cards is referred to as two separate phy
cal units both operations are sometimes combined into one unit

14.2.1 Punches

There are two types of punches available for punching car
One is attached directly to a computer and the other provides
manual means of punching cards and is commonly referred to as
keypunch. The keypunch is usually equipped with a keyboard wh
is very similar to the keyboards found on typewriters. Information is punched into the card by depressing various keys on
the keyboard. Often keypunches are equipped to print each cha
acter directly above the column in which the character is punc
There are usually two hoppers for cards; one for unpunched car
coming into the keypunch and one to gather those cards that ha
been punched.

In addition to the more sophisticated punch which has bee
described and which is mounted on a desk-like piece of furnitu
there are also very small card punches that are eight or ten
inches in length which hold only one card and are operated by
a small set of buttons. These, of course, are not to punch
large volumes of cards but to be used in those cases where it
is desired to quickly punch one or two cards.

---

*After Herman Hollerith who developed this type of code.

In addition to the manual keypunch there are also punches which are designed to be connected directly to computers. Speeds of this type of punch typically range from the order of one hundred cards per minute to the order of a thousand cards per minute. Depending on the sophistication, speed and cost of such punches, they may punch only one column on the card at a time or all 80 columns simultaneously.

14.2.2 Readers

Card readers usually have in/out hoppers also to hold the cards that are to be read and those that have already been read. There are also small models that only accept one card at a time. Quite similar to paper tape readers, there are two methods used to read cards. The first one is to read them by mechanical means. One way of accomplishing this is to arrange for the card to pass under a row of small brushes. Where holes are punched the brushes pass through and indication is registered that a logical one has been detected. Mechanical reading of cards may also be implemented by a star wheel. The star wheel is simply a round wheel with small spokes protruding from it which also penetrate the holes. In both the case of the star wheel and the brush, the detection mechanism is the closing of an electrical circuit when the reading mechanism penetrates the hole in the card.

The other method of reading cards is through photoelectrical schemes. Light is shone upon the cards and wherever a hole occurs the light passes through and is detected by a photoelectrical sensor.

Cards can be read from the order of a hundred cards per minute to a thousand cards per minute.

14.2.3 Others

There are several other devices that are used in connection with the handling of punched cards. Although these are not normally used or interfaced directly with a computer, it is of interest to know of their availability and their functions. One such device is called a card verifier. The verifier looks very much like a keypunch. Cards that have already been punched are placed in the input hopper and the operator types on the keyboard exactly the same material that was typed earlier by the keypunch operator. However, in this case instead of holes being punched in the card, the holes that were punched earlier are sensed and compared with those keys that are being struck. If the holes in the card do not match the character struck an error signal is given.

Another device that is used in connection with punched cards is a duplicator. Just as the name implies the purpose of this

device is to take a deck of punched cards, read them one at a
time, and punch an identical deck of cards.

The final device to be mentioned is the interpreter.
Most card duplicators do not print across the top of the new
card the characters punched in the columns. The interpreter
reads the new deck and prints the characters across the top of
the cards.

15.0 COMMUNICATIONS EQUIPMENT

Although very little space is devoted here to communications equipment, it is becoming a very important field in the
utilization of on-line computers. It is becoming quite common
to link ordinary phone lines to computers. One way of implementing this link is to connect data modems to the computer.
Data modems are quite similar to the ordinary telephone sets
used in the home and office, however they are specifically designed to transmit data over telephone lines. Data is transmitted by converting binary numbers to tones, i.e. to audio
frequencies.* Once the modem is connected directly to the computer it is possible for one computer to communicate with another computer over the phone line or to any other device that
can be connected via phone. Some modems have what is called a
self-answering option, and if the option is incorporated, it
is possible to build into the interface between the modem and
the computer the necessary logic to enable the computer to answer the telephone. Thus, each time the number of that partic
ular phone is dialed the computer detects the ringing signal
and answers so that data may be transmitted. Typical speeds
for modems are 100, 200, and 300 characters per second. In
telecommunications parlence the number of pulses per second
transmitted is referred to as bauds. Until recently bits per
second and bauds were synonomous, but present techniques permit transmitting more than one bit per pulse.

Another device that is becoming quite popular is the acou
tic coupler. The acoustic coupler converts any ordinary hand
telephone set into a data modem. This is done by dropping the
telephone receiver into the coupler which does the necessary
conversion of binary numbers to frequency and frequency back
to binary numbers.

Several ordinary telephone lines can be grouped together
to give what is often referred to as broad band service. This
allows more data to be transmitted per unit of time by transmitting it in parallel over many lines. This type of service
is referred to as Telpack A,B,C, or D. These are groupings of

---

*Large efforts are now being made by the telephone companies t
 provide facilities that transmit digital data as pulses rathe
 than frequencies.

12, 24, 60, and 240 ordinary voice circuits respectively.
Telpack lines make it possible to transmit data at high rates.

16.0 MULTIPLEXERS

Strictly speaking a multiplexer is not a computer peripheral. It might, in fact, often be considered as a part of
some interfaces between the computer and other peripherals.
However, it is of such importance that a few words are going
to be spent on the subject. As intimated a multiplexer plays
a very close relationship with computer peripherals. This
role can perhaps best be illustrated with an example. Suppose
that it is desired to sample and digitize several different
continuous signals and that only one ADC is to be used to digitize all these signals. This can be accomplished by inserting
an analog multiplexer in front of the ADC. It is the task of
the multiplexer to connect each of the individual signals to
the ADC in a prescribed manner. For example, a typical means
of implementing a multiplexer in this situation is for the
multiplexer to connect each of the signals to the ADC on a
round-robin basis. That is, the multiplexer goes from signal
to signal in a sequential pattern. This round-robin technique
satisfies many needs. However, it is sometimes desirable to
look at certain of the signals more frequently than others.
In this particular situation enough control is provided between the computer and the multiplexer to allow the program
to specify which signal the multiplexer is to connect to the
ADC at any given time. This permits the signals to be selected
in a random manner or some signals may be selected more frequently than others.
The purpose of a multiplexer is to fan several different
Another important function of multiplexers within computer
systems is to allow several different devices to be attached to
a single direct memory access channel on the computer (this is
a digital multiplexer). Here again, the program specifies which
device the multiplexer is to connect to the data channel. A
method akin to the round-robin approach may be established
according to the physical positions each individual computer
peripheral is given on the multiplexer. This automatically
gives priority to those computer peripherals which are hooked
to the first positions of the multiplexer.
The purpose of a multiplexer is to fan several different
devices, signals, etc. into one port whether it be an ADC or a
computer data channel. Multiplexers often are found in several
different parts of an on-line computer system and can play a
very key role in the performance of the total system.

CHAPTER 9

COMPUTER INTERFACES

1.0 WHAT CAN BE INTERFACED TO A COMPUTER?

Perhaps this question is best answered in a somewhat ob-
lique manner. When one examines the design criteria of on-
line computers the primary criterion is probably ease of connection of the computer to other devices. With this as the
basic design criterion, it should therefore not be surprising
that there are an extraordinary number of devices that can be
connected to on-line computers. In fact, it is probably well
to differentiate at this point between connecting devices to
a computer and connecting the computer to devices. There is
no strict definition but in general it relates to size. One
normally thinks of coupling devices to the computer where the
devices are in some sense smaller than the computer. On the
other hand, if the computer becomes a small part of the total
system, then it is probably better to think of the computer as
being coupled to the system. This latter category includes
many of the applications that are normally referred to as process control. Examples might be using computers in large power
plants, steel mills, and other facilities of this type.
     In the more strictly technical sense, what can be con-
nected to a computer is almost entirely limited by the current
state of the electronics art and the economics of building interfaces. Two types of problems where computers are still sometimes limited, and may not be used in a satisfactory manner,
are those where extremely high data rates are involved, and
those where very large volumes of data are to be collected.
In the first case the computer is usually the limiting factor
in that it simply may not have a fast enough memory cycle time
and memory transfer capabilities to accommodate the data rate.
In the second case the problem resides more with peripherals
than with the computer itself. It is not customary to store
large volumes of data in magnetic core memory because of the
high cost. Large volumes of data are usually stored on peripheral devices such as magnetic tape, disk, or drum. Thus,

when one speaks of volumes that are too large for the computer
system, it is an indirect way of saying that the mass storage
devices on the computer do not have sufficient capacity for the
data.

There are still instances where economics preclude the use
of a computer system, because another equipmental approach is
more attractive economically. However, the drastic reduction
of cost that has taken place with on-line computers in the last
few years has made the on-line computer competitive in many
cases that it hasn't been before.

Perhaps it is well to define at this point the terms process
and device as they will be used in this chapter. The usage of
these terms is along the lines implied above. The process will
be the instance where the computer is a small element of a much
larger system. The computer may be controlling the system, but
its cost and its size are small compared to the total system.
In this type of system the process is not readily thought of
as being peripheral to the computer. On the other hand when
speaking of devices, elements in the system, which are completely
controlled by the computer and essentially serve the computer
only, are under consideration. Included in this category are
magnetic disks, drums, magnetic tapes, printers, keyboard, and
some analog-to-digital converters.

What can be interfaced to a computer can be further explored
by looking at the primary purposes for providing a process with
an on-line computer capability. Applications may be broadly
broken into two different areas. The first area is datalogging,
and the other area is control.

1.1 Data Logging

There are many processes which, for different reasons, require large blocks of information to be collected and saved,
either permanently or temporarily. Among the reasons for collecting such large volumes of data are: to later examine and
analyze the data, to provide operating information, and to provide histories of the operation.

The utilization of computers for the data logging application represents a change that has taken place in the operation
of many processes. In the past the data logging operation would
probably have been served with recording devices such as the
strip charge recorder. (The strip chart recorder is simply a
roll of plotting paper that is pulled from one roller to another
and is written upon by one or several ink-filled pens. Thus,
a continuous record can be kept of any parameter being fed to
a pen). As processes have become much larger and more complex,
better means are required to record the larger and larger volumes of data that occur. Computers have entered the picture
primarily for two reasons: (1) the capability to handle very
large volumes of data, and (2) to interact with the data via

computer peripherals such as keyboards, printers and oscilloscope displays.

Data logging operations where many hundreds, and sometimes
thousands, of signals must be monitored are now common. Good
examples of processes which require very large data logging operations are modern power plants, steel mills, nuclear reactors,
and multi-parameter nuclear physics experiments.

It is only natural that one would turn to computers to monitor such a large number of inputs. The major interface question is how fast can the data be digitized and transmitted to
some other location? This question really subdivides into two
considerations. The first is: how fast can the data be digitized and transferred to the computer? The second is: once
the data has been transferred to the computer, is it feasible
to perform manipulations on the data before transferring it to
a permanent storage medium or the computer memory? Thus, time
is required to bring the data into the computer, and time is
required to store it. It is the sum of these two times that
determines the rate at which the data can be handled by the computer system. Generally, the time required to get the information to the computer is completely hardware dependent, and primarily the interface hardware. The second time, may be partially
hardware dependent, for example, in the access time of a disk
or a drum, but it is heavily dependent on the computer program,
and therefore, depends on the computer instruction times and the
efficiency with which the manipulation and storage tasks are programmed. In large data logging operations this consideration becomes more complex. Because of the many signals arriving at
the computer, some are sampled and stored on a rather infrequent
basis, while others must be attended to very rapidly.

Having decided that it is possible to interface a process
to the computer, and to handle the resulting data rates, it is
then necessary to determine if enough storage capacity is on
hand. This question cannot be discussed in detail without pick-
ing a specific application. However, it is unusual to find on-
line computer systems with more than say 32,000 to 64,000 words
of core memory. In the case of magnetic disks and magnetic drums
typical sizes for small on-line computers are now on the order
of one half million to one million 16 bit words. Finally, up-
wards of 150 million bits of information can be stored on a standard size reel of I.B.M. compatible tape. These, in most instances, represent the three types and speeds of storage medium
that are readily available.

In conclusion, I think that it is fair to say that the processes that cannot be interfaced to on-line computers because
of data detection, transmission, and storage factors are certainly the exception rather than the rule.

1.2   Control

In many applications it is necessary for the on-line computer to control the process. The control of the process can
be of two different types; one is referred to as open-loop control, and the other is referred to as closed-loop control.

1.2.1   Open-Loop

Open-loop control is illustrated diagramatically by Fig. 1,
if one removes the arrow labeled "feedback". In this type of
control the computer simply instructs the process, i.e., it
gives the process a series of commands such as start, stop, and
transfer data. The computer has little or no knowledge of the
state of the process. The state of the process is known by
those variables that describe the process and its condition.
Example variables might be speed of the process and temperature
of the process.
Most standard computer peripherals are controlled on an
open-loop basis. All of those discussed in the chapter "Computer Peripherals" are normally controlled on an open-loop
basis. What we have described, for the purposes of this chapter, as devices are typically open-looped controlled.

1.2.2   Closed-Loop

The diagram of Fig. 1 demonstrates closed-loop control
when the feedback arrow is included. In this case the computer
still sends control signals to the process but their nature depends upon the state of the process itself. Information from
the sensing of the condition of the process is passed back in
the feedback portion of the loop. A normal sequence of events
goes something like the following: the computer sends a controlling signal to the process. Measuring equipment determines
what the result of this control signal has been on the state
of the process by measuring the parameters of the process.
These measurements are then fed back to the computer which compares them with the desired results. If the comparison of the
state of the process with the desired state of the process does
not match within some specified tolerance, the computer again
sends a control signal to the process and the sequence of events
is repeated. Thus, closed-loop control is usually an iterative
procedure with the computer constantly comparing the state of
the process with the desired state of the process, and sending
compensating control signals.
A simple example of closed-loop control is a computer controlling an engine which is turning a variable load. Suppose
that the computer controls the throttle of the engine and has
the necessary facilities to measure the amount of load. This

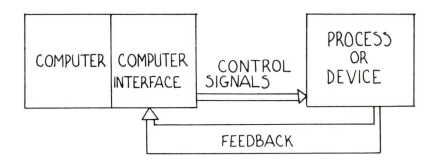

Fig. 1.   A schematic representation of a closed-loop control
system.

measurement of the load provides the feedback information.   If
the load increases, this information is fed back to the computer which then opens the throttle.   This will probably be
done in several steps, i.e. the load increase is observed, the
computer opens the throttle of the engine; the feedback loop
indicates that the engine still requires more throttle, the
computer applies more throttle, and so forth.   Eventually, this
progression either opens the throttle too much for the load,
or the load decreases and the computer begins to iteratively
reduce the throttle on the engine.

Return again to the central question of what can be interfaced to a computer.   Whether an on-line computer can be used
to control some process on a closed-loop basis may center a-
round the ability of the user to model the process that is to
be controlled.   The model is usually mathematical and describes
the inputs and the outputs of the process.   One is in effect
asking the question; what do the outputs in the process do when
the inputs are changed in a prescribed way?   If such a model
can be developed then the model can probably be implemented on
a computer.   The model may not be of a closed form.   That is,
the process may not be describable by an exact mathematical
formulation.   However, it is often possible to construct a
model on an emperical basis.   The process might actually be
run in a manner to allow data to be collected which will give
tables of numbers or other emperical information which describes
what the outputs do when the inputs are changed.   In a very
simple case it might be enough to know that the output goes up
as the input goes down.

If enough is not known about the inputs and outputs of the
process, any attempt to control the process may lead to insta-
bility.   The inputs may continually overcompensate for the feedback information and the process may go into oscillation, or in
fact, progressively go in one direction until some equipment is
out of limit or some destructive process sets in.

It may be entirely possible to build an electronic interface which provides and receives the appropriate information
for closed-loop control of a process. However, it may not be
possible to control the process with an on-line computer because a satisfactory model cannot be constructed, and hence,
a proper program can not be written for the computer to successfully control the process.

2.0   WHO SHOULD DESIGN AND CONSTRUCT INTERFACES?

The design and construction of interfaces often becomes
very important in putting together an on-line computer system.
In some respects this results from the fact that so many devices and processes may be interfaced to computers. This means
that there are really very few standard systems, and that a
very large diversity of systems are in existence.
In many, if not most, instances the eventual user has to
be involved in at least the conceptual design of on-line computer interfaces. This is because the chances are very good
that he is the only one who understands in depth the process
for which the computer is to be used. This is particularly
significant because the interface represents an area where entirely different talents and backgrounds meet. The user, particularly the new user, very often does not know very much
about computers, and on the other hand, it is a good bet that
the computer manufacturer knows very little about the process
to which the computer is to be applied. Thus, these widely
diverse backgrounds meet and, in the hardware sense, they meet
at the interface. It is for this reason that it is almost a
necessity that the user of a computer system be involved in the
conceptual and later design of the computer interface to insure
that it will properly perform its assigned task.

2.1   Alternatives

There are at least three different approaches to designing
and constructing interfaces. One approach is for the user to do
it himself. Of course, this assumes that sufficient engineering
and programming capability is available to carry out the design,
construction, and implementation of the interface.
A second approach is to arrange for the manufacturer of
the computer to design and build the interface.
A third choice has become available in recent years.
There are now firms that specialize in doing this type of work,
which is often referred to as "systems work".
A major influence in considering which approach or combination of approaches is to be used depends upon the nature of
the interface. If the interface is common, e.g., a magnetic
tape transport, then it is probably already offered by most

computer manufacturers. This is often referred to as a "standard interface". In other words, it is offered as a part of
a product line by the computer manufacturer. If the interface is available as part of a product line, this normally
represents the most economical source because of mass production.

On the other hand, the interface may not be common, and
in fact, it may have never been done before. Also there are
instances where the interface may be provided by some manufacturer and not others. One may have chosen the computer of
one manufacturer who does not make the desired interface, but
the interface is available as a standard product of another
manufacturer. Because there is very little compatibility from
computer manufacturer to computer manufacturer, the fact that
it is offered as a standard device in some other manufacturer's
line is of little importance. The user in this situation will
have to have the interface built by one of the three alternate
approaches just mentioned.

If the user decides not to design and construct a non-
standard interface on his own, then a serious problem can arise.
The problem might be referred to as the communications triangle.
First, suppose that the computer manufacturer is to build the
interface from his computer to the device or process. At this
point, there are at least three groups of individuals involved
in the design building and implementation of the interface.
The manufacturer of the process equipment, the computer manufacturer, and the user. The communication problems that can
arise within this triangle are not to be taken lightly. The
manufacturer of the process equipment, in all probability, does
not know much about the computer. He also may know very little
about the application to which the user is going to put his
equipment. Likewise, the computer manufacturer may know very
little about the process and next to nothing about the user's
application, and finally, the user may not know a great deal
about either the process equipment or the computer. With this
in mind, it is easy to see that one has to be extremely careful
to see that all parties of the triangle are communicating in
the same language and understand what the interface is to do
and how it is to perform. In larger systems this situation
can become even more complex because there can be several sub-
contractors, and in some cases one might even have difficulties
with various company proprietory items.

2.2 User Built Interfaces

As anybody who has worked in large organizations knows,
it is difficult to determine exactly the economics of building
something within the organization. It is often candidly ad-
mitted that a device built in-house might cost twice that of
one built out-of-house, but the people working on the project

are already on the payroll and paid out of other budgets. Thus, the cost of building the device in-house appears as the cost of the components. Because of this, and many other budgeting and accounting vagaries, it is very difficult to give a general dis- cussion of the economics of building interfaces in the user organization as opposed to having them built outside the user's organization.

To undertake interfaces in the user organization program- ming and engineering personnel should be available and have had considerable experience and capability in the art of electronic design and programming of computers. Emphasis is being put on capability; for although these personnel may have a rather good understanding of the process and its application, they must also have a very good understanding of the computer and its concept of design. Thus, they must cover a large spectrum of equipment and applications.

One of the greatest advantages of performing the design and construction of interfaces in the user organization is the ease and quickness of communication. In other words, almost complete elimination of the communications triangle that was spoken of earlier. I am excluding those cases where the or- ganization is very large and the interface is built by another group in the user's organization. In this case the triangle will probably reappear.

To build interfaces in the user's organization several ser- vices should either be available or accessible in the immediate geographic area. These include the drafting of prints, the re- production of prints, and all the other associated paperwork that goes with electronic hardware. Various services, such as construction of printed circuit boards, may also be needed.

One of the most difficult tasks is the documentation of interfaces that have been built within the user's organization. In fact, they often don't get documented at all; or documenta- tion is done very poorly. Needless to say, poor documentation leads to expense, loss of time, and not unoccassionally em- barrassement.

2.3   Interfaces Built By Computer Manufacturers

Many manufacturers of on-line computers provide a service for building non-standard interfaces. This activity serves several purposes for the computer manufacturer. It keeps him abreast of process applications in the areas where he is selling computers; it provides challenging problems to his engineers; and it helps sell computers. Unless the computer firm is ex- tremely small, or new, it is usually admirably equipped with manpower and equipment to design interfaces. Personnel that work on the interface know the computer well, and often have access to the people that originally designed the computer. However, they may not know the process or device that is to

be interfaced to the computer. This is part of the communications problem that was discussed earlier.

   If it is at all possible, the equipment which is to be
interfaced to the computer should be drop-shipped* to the
computer manufacturer. No matter how good the communications
between the user, the manufacturer of the process equipment,
and the computer manufacturer are; and no matter how good the
documentation is in terms of specifications and hardware prints,
nothing can replace the advantages of having the actual device
at the location where the interface is being constructed and
checked out.

   If it is a process that is being interfaced to the computer, the user should write and supply the best specifications
and information on the process that he possibly can. This
again returns to the communications problem and the fairly
certain fact that the computer manufacturer will know little
about the process. On a project of any size the computer
manufacturer will probably have engineers on the user's site
for at least installation and checkout, and perhaps, even
during portions of the design and construction phase.

   One still has to be aware of documentation difficulties
in this approach to interface design. These difficulties arise
from at least two different sources and therefore don't necessarily mesh. First, the computer manufacturer sometimes does
a poor job of documenting such interfaces. This is probably
attributable to human nature, and the fact that with special
interfaces only a few individuals in the computer manufacturer's
organization are knowledgeable about the project. Second, the
prints of the interface electronics are particularly bother-
some. One difficulty that often arises in this respect is that
the interface may actually be a modified version of a standard
product. This probably means that it was built from marked-up
prints of the standard product and final prints are never made
of the resulting hybrid interface.

2.4 Custom-Built Interfaces

   The type of firm which is involved in this kind of activity is often referred to as a systems house. They may or
may not specialize solely in building systems around on-line
computers. In many instances they also build systems of a
more conventional nature.

   If this service is sought, the user should determine the
capabilities of the firm that he is considering doing business
with. This survey should cover the complete spectrum from the
equipment the firm has available, to its engineering depth.

---

*Shipped to other than its final destination.

This is necessary because of the great variations that may be
found in such firms. They can vary in experience from being
quite reliable to being completely uninitiated. They can vary
in size from the very large to garage operations. It, therefore, behooves the user to know exactly what kind of firm he
is dealing with and the nature of the risks, if any, involved.

The communications problem still exists in this instance
and, in fact, is now expanded to include one more party. The
systems house may not know anything of the process involved.
It may not be particularly knowledgeable of the computer, and
it may know nothing of the user's application. On the other
hand, the investigation of the firm may indicate that it has
had considerable experience in all areas.

In summary, it might be said that custom-built interfaces
have the same disadvantages as those built by computer manufacturers. However, there is probably more incentive for them
to do a proper job than in the case of the computer manufacturer.
The user does not have to be concerned about the systems house
worrying over the maintenance and efficient operation of an
assembly line. Also, the systems house is not so likely to
patch and modify an existing interface to obtain the new interface specified by the user.

3.0   THE ROLE OF PROGRAMMING IN INTERFACE DESIGN

Unfortunately, interface design is often thought of as
only an engineering task. Nothing could be further from the
truth, and nothing could be a worse error. There are several
major advantages to having interface design teams composed of
both programmers and engineers. The terms engineer and programmer are being used in a very generic way here. Specifically,
programmer is to mean anybody that has a good programming knowledge of the computer. This might be another engineer. On the
other hand, the engineer is that person who actually designs the
hardware for the interface, and is the one who implements and
supervises the checking of the device.

One of the advantages of composing such teams to design
and build interfaces is self-obvious; two heads are still better
than one. Particularly, if the persons involved have different
but related backgrounds. Secondly, even though the programmer
may have little knowledge of engineering, he can suggest many
desirable features in interfaces. For example--
   a)   The programmer can often cut costs by eliminating
        options that are not really desirable or useful.
   b)   The programmer can suggest options that are useful
        and add greatly to the flexibility of the interface.
   c)   The programmer can participate in the design and im-
        plementation by trying to write programs from the
        conceptual design specifications and suggest modifi-
        cations that are needed in the interface to make it
        more programmable.

Finally, the programmer-engineer team is the only approach that makes sense when it comes time to make a new interface operate properly. The engineer has the knowledge and know-how to understand the hardware aspects of the interface and what is happening on an electronic basis. On the other hand, the programmer usually has at his fingertips a bank of programs that are useful to exercise the interface via the computer. The programmer can also sit with the engineer and quickly write small programs that make the interface execute in some fashion which tends to accentuate and display difficulties.

4.0   THE CAMAC CONCEPT

The CAMAC concept of computer interfacing represents a philosophy that is long overdue. The concept originated from the European Standard of Nucleonic Equipment (ESONE) which is a committee of Euratom Ispra. Originally the concept was denoted by a different acronym IANUS.*

Historically computer interfaces have been built with very little standardization. This has lead to a rather large waste of money and manpower because of a large duplicity of efforts and interfaces. For example, it is not difficult to see that the interface which connects one manufacturer's computer to a magnetic tape transport does not differ marketedly from the interface that connects another manufacturer's computer to his tape transport. Interfaces to many of the standard peripherals have been separately designed by all manufacturers, and by many large laboratories and other organizations with electronic capability. This past approach to computer interfacing also leads to an added disadvantage in that a peripheral, such as a magnetic tape transport, cannot be moved from one computer manufacturer's computer to another. The CAMAC concept strives to make computer interfaces as independent as possible from a specific model of computer. This is accomplished in two ways. First, the physical packaging of the interfaces themselves are standardized. The interfaces are constructed as modules which plug into a standard crate. This crate is visually similar to the NIM bins that have been used in the nuclear industry in the United States for several years.**

---

* Proceedings of the Fall Joint Computer Conference, I.N. Hooton and R.C.M. Barnes, Volume 33, Part 2, 1077 (1968), Thompson Book Co., Washington, D.C.
**The NIM concept provided primarily for a standardization of packaging with little electrical standardization other than power supply voltages. It was primarily for nuclear modules such as scalers, analog-to-digital converters, etc. NIM modules may be plugged into CAMAC crates by the use of an adaptor.

The CAMAC philosophy provides computer independence in a second way by standardizing the paths or busses that the signals travel over. These are called data highways or dataways. The connectors on the back of the modules plug into this highway and each wire in the highway is reserved for a specific signal type. The signal characteristics and functions are also specified. That is rise time, pulse durations, and so forth of signals are specified by the CAMAC standard. The construction of the dataways has been done in such a way that there is considerable flexibility in using the modules.

The modules themselves are oriented toward construction with integrated circuitry. The standard module width is 3/4 of an inch wide. However, it is possible to build modules that are as many multiples of 3/4 of an inch as desired. Each crate has slots for twenty five 3/4 inch modules. In addition to what might be referred to as the interface modules each crate can also have a control module. This serves as an interface between the computer and the controller module, which as we have seen, are completely standardized as to size and signal characteristics. In addition the capability has been provided through a different bussing system to attach several different CAMAC crates to the same computer.

Using the CAMAC concept of computer interfacing, the only difference that one encounters is going from computer to computer is the small interface that is needed between the computer and the CAMAC crate. This interface can be as simple as a plug on the computer cabinet which supplies the appropriate signals to the appropriate points in the dataway or it may take the form of a control module, as described above, in the dataway.

The CAMAC philosophy makes possible a flexibility that has not been available previously. Suppose that two computer systems are available and each has a CAMAC crate attached to it. Further, suppose that a tape transport is attached to one of the computers, but a need arises for a tape transport on the second computer. Then it is only necessary to unplug the tape transport with its CAMAC module and to move the transport to the second computer system and plug in the CAMAC module. The tape transport is then ready to operate on the second computer--if the appropriate programs have been written. It is difficult to stress enough the advantages of being able to perform such a switch of peripherals from one computer system to another. Also, one can think of this flexibility in reverse. If the user decides to replace the computer within a system, then it is only necessary to install a CAMAC crate on the new computer and all of the peripherals may still be utilized.

The CAMAC concept also has very important implications in terms of the maintenance of computer peripherals. Suppose that one has a system to which several printers have been attached, each via a CAMAC module. In the event that any printer fails, it may be replaced by simply plugging in a new printer with its CAMAC module. The inoperable printer can then be repaired off-line. In fact, it is conceivable to have a small computer system with a CAMAC crate attached on which the printer is checked and maintained. Thus, the small computer system becomes a maintenance device for many kinds of peripherals.

At this writing, it is not yet clear that the CAMAC concept is going to be embraced in the United States. It has been given the blessing of the Atomic Energy Commission NIM committee. This bodes well for the concept. Apparently CAMAC is coming into rather wide acceptance in the European countries and England. It is the author's opinion that this concept of interfacing is badly needed to advance the utilization of on-line computers.

5.0 INTERFACE SPECIFICATIONS

In this particular section interface specifications are not entered into in detail. So doing would only draw us into individual computers and their associated digital logic and philosophy of construction. Instead general areas that should be considered when specifying an interface are examined. The emphasis is on non-standard computer interfaces.

If the interface to be built is sizable a specification should be written, even if the user organization is designing and constructing the interface. ·Conversely on many occasions it is desirable for the user to do a conceptual design even if an outside organization is designing and building the interface.

5.1 Maintenance and Packaging

Maintenance is usually thought of as two separate activities. One is often referred to as preventive maintenance and the other as repair maintenance. Preventative maintenance can be anything from periodic replacement of mechanical components to the exercising of the equipment on a regular basis. Repair maintenance should be self-explanatory.

Because many computer peripherals are periodically checked by exercising them under program control, the specifications for the interface should say something about the checkout programs that are envisioned. In most instances, it may be desirable to specify to the manufacturer of the interface that he write programs to accomplish certain functions along this line.

Although it has not been common in the past to build check points on the external panels of interfaces, it is the author's opinion that this is an extremely useful feature. Specifications should call out test points that can be accessed from the front or back panel with oscilloscopes, volt meters and other devices.

Specifications for an interface should also call out any display devices such as lights or cold cathode display tubes. Also any mode switching that is to be controlled by rotary switches or push buttons should be specified.

Specifications should ask that a spare parts list be made available with the computer interface. In this regard, it is often common to specify the mounting of electronic components. For example, with integrated circuit chips one may want to specify that they be soldered into printed circuit cards, or on the other hand, that they should be plugged into sockets.

From the standpoint of repair maintenance it is highly desirable to be able to remove an interface from the computer system. Too often interfaces are built in such a manner that when any given interface is removed the remainder of the system becomes inoperable. In fact, two sins that have often been committed in the past are; 1) the interfaces are wired and packaged in such a way that individual interfaces literally can't be removed from the computer system, and 2) if interfaces are disconnected the rest of the computer system becomes inoperable.

Such practices can lead to very expensive consequences. If a system has been constructed with either of these two very poor practices and attached to some large process, it is possible to have a million dollar process idled by a peripheral worth a few thousand dollars. It has happened!

Finally, the specifications should call out packaging details. These include dimensions, types of cable connectors, front panel arrangements, access panels, and so forth. In the CAMAC philosophy many of these details are automatically taken care of.

5.2 Command Implementation

It is important to specify the commands associated with a computer interface. This does not mean that the manufacturer of the interface must be directed in great detail about individual commands, but that they be specified in manner. For example, it is possible, as many interfaces are added to an on-line computer system, to exhaust the available commands, i.e. the input/output instructions of the computer no longer permit commands to be added.* It is therefore advantageous to conserve commands. As an example, instead of using up several I/O commands, for one interface, it may be possible to construct the interface in such a manner that bits are set in a register, such as the accumulator, before issuing a single I/O command. When this command is issued, the specific actions taken by the interface depends on which bits in the accumulator are set.

The specifications should demand that documentation be supplied with any interface which states very clearly what each

---

*This was discussed in detail in the chapter "Computer Instructions" under Input/Output Instructions.

command does. It is not uncommon that a programmer and an engineer must get together over the electrical diagrams of an interface to determine exactly what action(s) are associated with a given command. Or even worse, the user might have to determine what the commands do on a trial and error basis through programming. Vagueness in the details of what commands do is often a result of the communications triangle discussed earlier.

5.3 Transfer Rates

In order that an interface be built properly it is necessary to specify in some detail the data transfer rates. To specify the transfer rates is more than just quoting the number of bits per second that the interface must be capable of transferring. For example, there is a large difference between handling a data rate in bursts and handling that same data rate on a continuous basis.

Consideration must also be given to the data rates of the devices that are already attached to the computer. The builder of the interface might look at the computer and decide that it can easily handle the data rates that his interface is capable of providing. On the other hand, it may turn out that there are already several devices attached to the computer with high data rates which directly affect the real transfer rate of any new interface. Also, if a priority interrupt structure is being used it may turn out that there are many other devices on the system of a higher priority than the new interface and that this prevents attainment of the desired data rate.

The user, in specifying an interface, must also give careful attention to the amount of program manipulation that must be performed on data arriving from the interface before it is stored in the computer memory or some peripheral device. If it turns out that a large amount of computation must be done on an event-by-event basis as data arrives from the interface, then the limit on the transfer rate may be largely program execution time and not the interface hardware.

Although one should be careful to specify that the interface be capable of handling the data transfer rates that will occur, care should also be taken not to specify unduly high data rates.

In those instances where an interface uses the direct memory access of the computer, the scheme for utilizing memory should be well thought out. Often the addition of a register or two to assist in the determination of the final storage location of data may make an immense difference in the time required to transfer and store data. For example, it may be wise to place a base register* in the interface which can be set

---

*The contents of the base register are added to any memory address originating in the interface to determine the final storage address.

under program control. Although a direct memory access method
is being used, the program then has some control relating to
where in memory the data eventually resides.

5.4 Other Considerations

What logic is to be used in the computer interface? Often
the user does himself a disservice if he does not specify the
same digital logic for the interface as that used in the computer
It should be obvious that the computer manufacturer's own logic
is more compatible with his computer than any other logic line.
Similar considerations come into play if the computer is being
attached to a process. Then, it may be desirable to specify
that the interface logic be that of the process rather than the
computer. In any event, decisions upon what logic to use reflect
upon everything from the electronic technicians that will maintain the system to the spare parts inventory that must be kept
on hand for the maintenance of the total system.

If the interface is packaged as a separate module, there
may be advantages to specifying logic separate from the others
that occur in the system. This could be the case with CAMAC
modules.

Finally, it cannot be overemphasized that the specifications
for an interface to be built by somebody other than the user
must include a great amount of detailed information about the device or the process being linked to the computer. This includes
timing, logic levels, and significance of signals.

6.0 COMPUTERS AS INTERFACES

Fig. 2 indicates diagramatically the concept of using a
computer as an interface. As shown there, a small interface
computer stands between the main computer and the peripherals
and/or processes.

There are a number of reasons why small on-line computers
should be considered for use as interfaces. One example has
already been given in a previous chapter of using small computers
as input/output controllers in large computer systems. Other
reasons are as follows:

1) Small computers as interfaces have a great deal of
    flexibility due to the ability to program them. This,
    for example, can be extremely helpful in formatting.
    Suppose that the computer is acting as an interface
    to a magnetic tape transport; the interface computer
    can decode all information into the form desired by
    the main computer as input or vice versa format all
    data coming from the main computer before writing it
    on the magnetic tape.

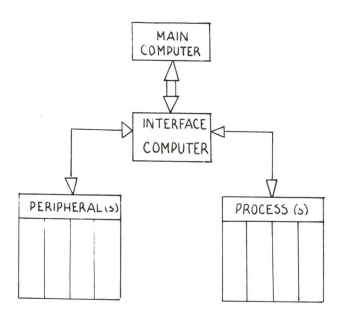

Fig. 2.   Illustration of how a computer can be utilized as
an interface between another computer and its
peripherals.

2)   A small computer acting as an interface can greatly
reduce the load on the main computer. In fact, this
is one of the primary reasons for utilizing a computer
as an input/output controller on a larger computing
system. The larger system is released from doing
tasks that can be easily accomplished by the smaller
computer.

3)   Interestingly enough, a major advantage of using small
computers as interfaces is cost. Now that computers
may be purchased for $5,000 and less, they can easily
compete with the design, construction, and engineering
of complicated interfaces. The economic advantages
become great particularly in those instances where
more than one peripheral is attached to the interface
computer; for then, the cost of the interface computer
is ammoritized over several devices and actually acts
as several different interfaces.

4)   Interface computers can have an added advantage in
maintenance of peripherals. Since they can be programmed, they have flexibility in exercising peripherals for maintenance purposes and they can also
perform these activities without involving the main
computer.

Programming of the small interface computer need not be a problem when forethought is given to the system. If the small computer must be programmed through its own peripherals, then a good deal of difficulty can arise. However, if the small computer is programmed by using the peripherals on the main computer, then programming should present no real difficulty. In fact, off-line assemblers can be written for the interface computer which runs in the main computer and are immediately loaded after assembly into the interface computer for checking. Since the interface computer is directly linked to the main computer, it essentially has all the peripheral devices, such as printers, on the main computer at its disposal.

Enough thought must be given to an interface computer to make sure that one is not exchanging the hardware difficulties of conventional interfaces for software difficulties in the interface computer. The programming of very small computers is certainly more tedious and difficult than even the intermediate size computers, and therefore, one would not like to undertake large and continuing programming efforts.

CHAPTER 10

PROGRAMMING EXAMPLES

1.0 INTRODUCTORY REMARKS

When the novice first begins to learn computer programming
a certain amount of reading is profitable. He certainly should
look at the programming manuals supplied by the manufacturer
of the computer, and manuals about the computer itself. Although this background reading gives a certain confidence,
there is usually something of a shock the first time the new
user attempts to write a program and execute it on the computer. He will find that no matter how confident he was in
the beginning there are usually numerous errors committed in
writing the first program. At this point it is often useful
to look at programs that have already been written by somebody
with programming experience. Probably the most useful information that is derived from looking at completed programs is
the insight that is provided into how instructions work in detail and how they are grouped. The studying of existing programs is particularly helpful in programming peripherals. In
this chapter the only peripheral dealt with is the Teletype
terminal. This is almost universally available on on-line computers and represents a good starting point for the novice programmer.

The programming examples presented in this chapter have
been chosen on the basis that they are usually among the first
a beginning programmer writes. They are often incorporated into larger programs.

The programs presented here do not represent the only way
of accomplishing the goal in each case. Given a specific programming application for a computer and given a number of individuals to write it, each will write a program that is different. This is not to say that only one will work; all of the
programs can accomplish the computations and come up with the
right solutions. Perhaps this should not be too surprising
because a computer programming language is similar to a very
restricted spoken language. A story told by two different
individuals can have the same end results but each chooses

327

entirely different words from his respective vocabulary. Like
wise, in computer programming, programmers develop a style tha
is not unlike a writer's style. In fact, it is rather easy to
identify who wrote a program when one has had experience working with that person. This diversity of style in writing programs for the same application is the major reason why it is
often difficult for a programmer to understand the programs
of another programmer in detail. It is also the reason for
the oft quoted claim that it is easier to rewrite a program
than to try and understand one written by someone else.

As has been the case throughout this book, all the example programs are written in the PDP-8 assembly language.
The reasons for this have been covered in detail in the introductory chapter.

The format for each program discussion is the same. Fir:
general comments are made about the purpose of the program and
its application, plus remarks about conventions for using the
program. These general comments are followed by a flow diagr
which, in turn, is followed by a listing of the program. The
listings appear as they would normally be written for the PDP
with one exception; each line of the program, including the
comments, is given a number. These line numbers provide a co
venient means of identifying portions of the program for discussion. Finally, specific comments are made about each program on a line basis.

All the examples of this chapter are written as subroutines. The reader that wishes to refresh himself on the conventions for entering and exiting from subroutines in the PDP
assembly language should return to the subroutine section of
the chapter "Programming".

2.0   ASCII-TO-BINARY CONVERSION

2.1   General Comments

This first program is concerned with the converting of
numbers in the ASCII code* to the equivalent binary represent
tions. It should be kept clearly in mind that when one speak
of an ASCII number, a loose nomenclature is being used in tha
one is specifically talking about a single integer represente
in the ASCII code. There is no convenient way to combine integers into multi-integer numbers and represent them with one
ASCII character. The problem then, is to take an ASCII integer into the computer and convert it to its equivalent bina
representation. A program of this sort is needed for enterin

---

*See Appendix V.

numbers into the computer from keyboards. Suppose that one
wants to enter the number 123 then this would mean that the
usser depresses the keys for 1, 2, and 3 in that order. These
three integers arrive at the computer at three different times.
Normally it is necessary to not only convert each integer to
binary, but to combine these integers in such a way that the
binary equivalent of the number 123 is stored in the computer
memory. The subroutine DECBIN, which combines the digits, is
presented later. The specific task for this first programming
example is to convert ASCII integers to binary numbers.

Turn now to the program itself. As always, one must check
the keyboard input for any possible errors. The present program checks each character as it arrives to see that it is an
integer and not, for example, a letter of the alphabet. In
the ASCII code this is easily accomplished by checking to see
if the ASCII character has any value from 260_8 through 271_8.

If an improper character has been entered, then an error
message should be printed to warn the user. In this example
program the error message is extremely simple, whenever an improper character is entered the program prints a question
mark on the teleprinter. The message could be much more elaborate, and a general method for printing messages is presented
in a later programming example.

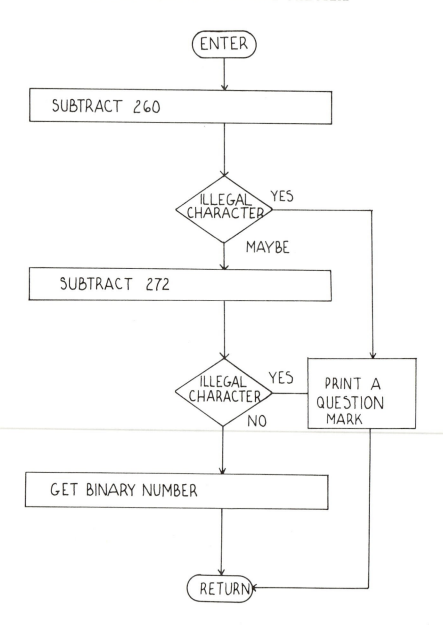

Fig. 1.   Flow diagram for the subroutine ASCBIN.

2.2 Listing

```
1.    /SUBRØUTINE ASCBIN.
2.    /WRITTEN BY WWB APRIL, 1970.
3.    /A SUBRØUTINE TØ TAKE A DECIMAL DIGIT REPRESENTED
4.    /AS AN ASCII CHARACTER AND CØNVERT IT TØ A BINARY
5.    /NUMBER.  IF THE ASCII CHARACTER IS NØT ØNE ØF THE
6.    /DIGITS ZERØ THRØUGH NINE, A QUESTIØN MARK IS PRINTED
7.    /ØN THE TELEPRINTER.
8.    /CØNVENTIØNS:
9.    /            A)   ASCBIN EXPECTS THE ASCII CHARACTER TØ
10.   /                 BE IN THE ACCUMULATØR WHEN ASCBIN IS
11.   /                 ENTERED,
12.   /            B)   THE BINARY NUMBER IS IN THE ACCUMULATØR
13.   /                 WHEN THE PRØGRAM RETURNS FROM ASCBIN
14.   ASCBIN,   0
15.             TAD    M260      /SUBTRACT 260 BASE EIGHT
16.             SPA              /ILLEGAL CHARACTER?
17.             JMP    ASC1      /YES, PRINT ERRØR MESSAGE
18.             DCA    NUM       /MAYBE, SAVE AS PØSSIBLE NUMBER
19.             TAD    NUM       /RETRIEVE NUMBER
20.             TAD    M12       /SUBTRACT 272 BASE EIGHT
21.             SMA CLA          /ILLEGAL CHARACTER?
22.             JMP    ASC1      /YES, PRINT ERRØR MESSAGE
23.             TAD    NUM       /NØ, GET BINARY NUMBER
24.             JMP I  ASCBIN    /RETURN
25.   ASC1,     CLA
26.             TAD    QUES      /GET ASCII QUESTIØN MARK
27.             TSF              /TELEPRINTER BUSY?
28.             JMP    .-1       /YES, TRY AGAIN
29.             TLS              /NØ, PRINT QUESTIØN MARK
30.             CLA
31.             JMP I  ASCBIN    /RETURN
32.   M260,     -260
33.   M12 ,     -12
34.   QUES,     277              /ASCII QUESTIØN MARK
35.   NUM ,     0                /BINARY NUMBER
```

2.3 Specific Comments

Line 15. Remember that the ASCII character is placed in the accumulator before jumping to the subroutine ASCBIN. Therefore, it is still in the accumulator at this point and the octal number 260 is being subtracted from it.

Line 16. It should be noted that the SPA command of the PDP-8 includes all of the numbers that are conventionally thought of as positive including zero. Recall the discussions of the chapter "Number Systems" where it is shown that zero may be considered to be positive or negative depending on the number system used. The PDP-8 is a two's complement computer, and therefore, zero is always a positive number.

Line 20. This program could just as easily have been
written to accept octal rather than digital numbers. If this
were the case, then at this point a negative 10, base 8, would
be subtracted instead of a negative 12, base 8.

Line 24. As this return is being made remember that the
binary number is in the accumulator having been placed there
by the instruction in line 23.

Line 31. The convention has been taken here that if an
error has occurred, a question mark will be printed on the
Teletype, and then the subroutine returns in the normal manner
There are many other choices. For example, a special error
return could be set up so that a specific word in the memory
or a special number in the accumulator on the return from the
subroutine indicates that an error has occurred.

Line 34. Note that octal 277 is the ASCII character for
a question mark.*

3.0 PRINTING MESSAGES ON A TELETYPE

3.1 General Comments

There are many occasions in the programming of on-line
computers to print messages. Among the types of messages are;
instructions about the setting of equipment, instructions abou
numbers that should be entered into the computer, and the an-
nouncement of events of interest. Specifically, the printing
of a message is taken as the printing of any group of characters on the teleprinter for some reason detected by computer
programming.

It is extremely useful to have a general routine for
printing messages. Such a routine serves the following purpos
1. It saves memory space in a program that prints
    many messages.
2. Its very nature forces the programmer to establish
    a convention for printing messages. Establishing
    such a convention avoids confusion.
3. Time is saved because it is not necessary to write
    new and slightly different message routines for
    each new program that is written.
Since the ASCII characters here consist of eight bits it
is extremely wasteful to store only one ASCII character per
word in any computer with a word length greater than eight bit
In the present program example a scheme is used which permits

---

*In the examples of this chapter the 8-bit ASCII (8th level)
 form of the ASCII code is used. See Appendix V.

two characters to be packed in one twelve bit PDP-8 word. Because 16 bits are required to store two full ASCII characters, it has been necessary to establish a convention for compacting two characters into one 12-bit PDP-8 word. The method used removes the most significant octal integer from each ASCII character. A close examination of the ASCII code will show that the removal of the most significant integer creates an ambiguity between certain characters. The ambiguity relates to 18 characters, which can be paired into two groups of nine which can not be distinguished without the most significant integer. One solution is to abandon the use of one group of nine characters. This choice is easy to make on the basis of frequency of use. In the present program the following ASCII characters may not be used ALT MODE, RUB OUT, EOT, WRU, RU, BELL, RETURN, and LINE FEED. Of these, the only characters required in routine usage are the LINE FEED and the RETURN. Therefore, it is necessary, with the present conventions, to establish a separate subroutine for printing RETURN and LINE FEED.

Another convention must be established to determine the end of a message. In the current program this is done by making the last location of the message a zero.

It is important to note that only indirect addressing is used to access messages. This permits messages to be scattered throughout the program at any place the user finds convenient. Although the messages themselves may be scattered, it is important to remember that an individual message must occupy consecutive locations in memory.

The sample program has been written with two messages following it. The first message starts with line 86 and reads THIS IS MESSAGE 1". The second message starts with line 97 and reads "ENTER THE AMPLIFIER GAIN".

The subroutine MESS in turn requires three subroutines. They are ASSEM, CRLF, and PRINT. The first subroutine, ASSEM, is used to take the stripped ASCII characters and again rebuild them into 'full' ASCII characters for printing. The subroutine CRLF is used whenever it is desired to print a RETURN and LINE FEED. The RETURN and LINE FEED characters, when combined on the Teletype terminal, are the equivalent of the carriage return on a standard typewriter. Finally, the subroutine PRINT is called each time an ASCII character is assembled, and is the programming that transfers the ASCII character to the Teletype terminal to be printed.

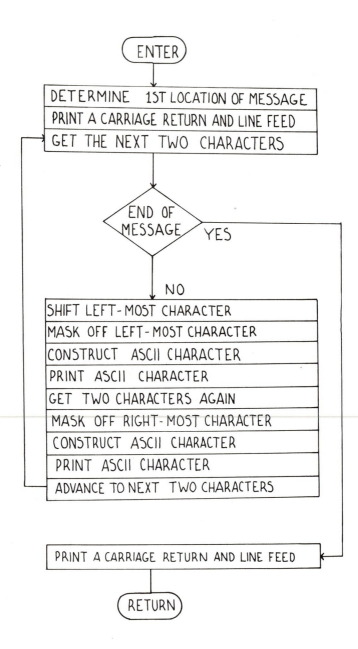

Fig. 2. Flow diagram for the message printing subroutine MESS

3.2 Listing

```
1.    /SUBRØUTINE MESS
2.    /WRITTEN BY WWB 1966
3.    /THIS SUBRØUTINE HAS THE FØLLØWING CØNVENTIØNS:
4.    / 1.   MESSAGES ARE DESIGNATED BY NUMBER.  MESSAGE ØNE
5.    /      IS TAGGED MES1, MESSAGE TWØ MES2, ETC.
6.    / 2.   IF THE NTH MESSAGE IS TØ BE PRINTED, JUMP TØ
7.    /      SUBRØUTINE MESS WITH N IN THE ACCUMULATØR
8.    / 3.   MESSAGES ARE ASSEMBLED BY PACKING TWØ ASCII
9.    /      CHARACTERS PER 12 BIT PDP-8 WØRD.  THIS IS
10.   /      ACCØMPLISHED BY ØNLY RETAINING THE SIX LEAST
11.   /      SIGNIFICANT BITS ØF EACH ASCII CHARACTER.
12.   / 4.   THE PACKING SCHEME USED DØES NØT PERMIT THE
13.   /      USE ØF THE FØLLØWING ASCII CHARACTERS:  ALT MØDE,
14.   /      RUB ØUT, EØT, W RU, RU, BELL, LINE FEED, RETURN.
15.   / 5.   THE END ØF A MESSAGE IS DESIGNATED BY A
16.   /      MEMØRY LØCATIØN CØNTAINING ZERØ.
17.   MESS,     0
18.             TAD      FING      /ADD CØNSTANT TØ MESSAGE #
19.             DCA      FINGER
20.             TAD I    FINGER    /GET 1ST LØCATIØN ØF MESSAGE
21.             DCA      FINGER    /SAVE
22.             JMS I    CRL       /PRINT A CR AND LINE FEED
23.   MESS1,    TAD I    FINGER    /GET NEXT TWØ CHARACTERS
24.             SNA                /END ØF MESSAGE?
25.             JMP      MESS2     /YES
26.             CLL RTR            /NØ, SHIFT 1ST CHARACTER
27.             RTR                /TØ THE RIGHT ØF
28.             RTR                /THE ACCUMULATØR
29.             AND      M77       /MASK ØFF 6 BITS
30.             JMS      ASSEM     /CØNSTRUCT ASCII CHARACTER
31.             JMS I    PRIN      /PRINT ASCII CHARACTER
32.             TAD I    FINGER    /GET CHARACTERS AGAIN
33.             AND      M77       /MASK ØFF 2ND CHARACTER
34.             JMS      ASSEM     /CØNSTRUCT ASCII CHARACTER
35.             JMS I    PRIN      /PRINT ASCII CHARACTER
36.             ISZ      FINGER    /ADVANCE TØ NEXT CHARACTERS
37.             JMP      MESS1
38.   MESS2,    JMS I    CRL       /PRINT A CR AND LINE FEED
39.             JMP I    MESS      /RETURN
40.   /SUBRØUTINE ASSEM
41.   /A RØUTINE TØ RECØNSTRUCT ASCII CHARACTERS FRØM THE
42.   /PACKED FØRMAT.
43.   ASSEM,    0
44.             DCA      ACCU      /SAVE THE PACKED CHARACTER
45.             TAD      ACCU
46.             TAD      C40N      /SUBTRACT 40
47.             SPA CLA            /ADD 200 TØ CHARACTER?
48.             TAD      C300      /NØ, ADD 300 INSTEAD
49.             SNA                /HAS 300 BEEN ADDED?
```

```
50.              TAD     C200    /NØ, ADD 200
51.              TAD     ACCU    /ADD PACKED CHARACTER
52.              JMP I   ASSEM   /RETURN WITH ASCII
53.  /SUBRØUTINE PRINT
54.  /A SUBRØUTINE TØ PRINT CHARACTERS.   ENTER WITH ASCII
55.  /CHARACTER TØ BE PRINTED IN ACCUMULATØR.
56.  PRINT,   0
57.              TLS             /PRINT CHARACTER
58.              TSF             /FLAG UP?
59.              JMP     .-1     /NØ
60               CLA             /YES
61.              JMP I   PRINT   /RETURN
62.  /SUBRØUTINE CRLF
63.  /A RØUTINE THAT PRINTS A CARRIAGE RETURN FØLLØWED
64.  /BY A LINE FEED.
65.  CRLF,    0
66.              CLA
67.              TAD     CR      /GET CARRIAGE RETURN CHARACTE
68.              JMS I   PRIN    /PRINT CARRIAGE RETURN
69.              TAD     LF      /GET LINE FEED CHARACTER
70.              JMS I   PRIN    /PRINT LINE FEED
71.              JMP I   CRLF    /RETURN
72.  CR,         215             /ASCII CARRIAGE RETURN
73.  LF,         212             /ASCII LINE FEED
74.  FING,       MS1-1           /LØCATIØN BEFØRE MS1
75.  FINGER,     0
76.  M77,        77
77.  ACCU,       0
78.  C200,       200
79.  C300,       300
80.  CRL,        CRLF            /LØCATIØN ØF SUBRØUTINE CRLF
81.  PRIN,       PRINT           /LØCATIØN ØF SUBRØUTINE PRINT
82.  C40N,       -40
83.  MS1,        MES1            /1ST LØCATIØN ØF MESSAGE 1
84.  MS2,        MES2            /1ST LØCATIØN ØF MESSAGE 2
85.  /MESSAGE ØNE
86.  MES1,       2410            /TH
87.              1123            /IS
88.              4011            /-I
89.              2340            /S-
90.              1505            /ME
91.              2323            /SS
92.              0107            /AG
93.              0540            /E-
94.              6140            /1-
95.              0000            /END ØF MESSAGE
96.  /MESSAGE TWØ
97.  MES2,       0516            /EN
98.              2405            /TE
99.              2240            /R-
100.             2410            /TH
```

01.	0540	/E-
02.	0115	/AM
03.	2014	/PL
04.	1106	/IF
05.	1105	/IE
06.	2240	/R-
07.	0701	/GA
08.	1116	/IN
09.	0000	/END ØF MESSAGE

3.3 Specific Comments

Line 23. This instruction brings in the next two stripped
ASCII characters from the message list.

Line 24. This instruction checks the contents of the memory location just extracted--a zero indicates the complete
message has been printed.

Line 26 through 28. This series of instructions shifts
the contents of the accumulator register six bits to the right.
This positions the left-most character of the two characters
that originally resided in the accumulator in the right-most
portion of the accumulator register. This is often called
right justifying.

Line 29. This instruction performs the logical AND operation that was discussed in the chapter "Computer Organization II". In this case it "ands" on a bit by bit basis, the
contents of the memory location tagged M77 to the bits in the
accumulator. The result is that wherever there are one's in
the "mask" in location M77 the contents of the accumulator
will be preserved, and wherever there are zeros in the "mask"
word the contents of the accumulator will be set to zero. The
result is that the instruction of this line sets the six left-
most bits of the accumulator to zero and leaves the right-most
six bits in their original state. The accumulator now contains
only the left-most character of the original two characters.

Line 33. This is the same mask that was employed in line
29, except now the intervening instructions have positioned the
characters in the accumulator in such a way that the mask now
leaves the six bits of the original right-most character in
the right-most portion of the accumulator.

Line 46. By subtracting octal 40 from the stripped character it is possible to determine whether the most significant
octal integer of the original ASCII character was a 2 or a 3.

Line 47. Because of the conventions that have been adopted,
a packed character less than 40 indicates the octal number 300
should be added, and if the stripped character is greater than
40, then the octal number 200 should be added to reconstruct
the original ASCII character.

Line 86. This location contains the first two characters
of the first message. Note that it contains the stripped characters T and H. This can be seen by noting an ASCII T is 324

and an ASCII H is 310. Therefore, the stripped T gives the
first two octal digits 24 and the stripped H gives a 10, henc
this memory location contains 2410. If the user places a one
in the accumulator and jumps to the subroutine MESS, it will
print the following message: THIS IS MESSAGE 1.

4.0 BINARY-TO-DECIMAL CONVERSIONS

4.1 General Comments

There are several reasons for wanting to write a subroutine which takes a binary number from the memory of the co
puter and converts it to a decimal number. Because the memor
of a computer is almost always a binary format, converting a
number to its decimal format is usually taken to mean that as
the number is converted each decimal digit between zero and 9
is stored in the computer memory in binary. These digits can
then be converted to an ASCII format and printed on a Teletyp
terminal, or converted to some other code for output from the
computer.

This subroutine accommodates integer numbers up through
4095_{10}. This is a direct consequence of the 12 bit word leng
of the PDP-8. If fractional numbers are to be handled, then
it is necessary to write a separate routine for converting fr
binary fractions to decimal fractions.* If a number is great
than one, but fractional, then an integer routine, such as th
example, plus a fractional routine are used to convert the tw
portions of the number. The two resulting decimal numbers ar
then combined to complete the conversion.

The subroutine of this example has been written assuming
that all numbers to be converted are positive. If a negative
number is to be converted to decimal, it is necessary for the
calling routine to complement the negative number to positive
send it to the subroutine for conversion, and then after the
conversion revert the digital number to negative.

With the technique used in this particular binary-to-dec
imal conversion program it is necessary to perform divisions
by powers of ten. In this case the division is accomplished
by repeated subtractions. If the computer has division capability, this can be done with a single instruction.

For the purposes of this subroutine, it has been assumed
that the decimal digits will be printed on a teleprinter; hen
the digits are converted to ASCII before they are stored.

On many occasions it may not be necessary to store the
decimal digits, but only to print them as they are converted.
This is easily done by inserting a jump to a print subroutine
at that point where the decimal digits are stored.

---

*This is discussed in the chapter "Number Systems".

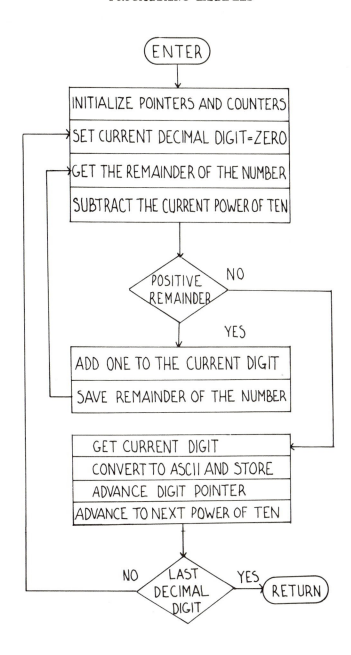

Fig. 3. Flow diagram for the binary-to-decimal conversion subroutine BINDEC.

4.2 Listing

```
1.    /SUBRØUTINE BINDEC.
2.    /WRITTEN BY WWB APRIL, 1970.
3.    /A SUBRØUTINE TØ CØNVERT A NUMBER FROM ITS BINARY
4.    /REPRESENTATIØN TØ ITS DECIMAL REPRESENTATIØN.
5.    /CØNVENTIØNS:
6.    /  A)  THE DECIMAL DIGITS ARE STØRED AS ASCII
7.    /      CHARACTERS IN LØCATIØNS DIGIT1 THROUGH DIGIT1 + 3.
8.    /  B)  THE BINARY NUMBER IS EXPECTED TØ BE IN THE
9.    /      ACCUMULATØR WHEN BINDEC IS ENTERED.
10.  BINDEC,   0
11.            DCA     NUM       /SAVE BINARY NUMBER
12.            TAD     TABLE1    /GET ADDRESS ØF 1ST TABLE ENTF
13.            DCA     TABLPT    /INITIALIZE TABLE PØINTER
14.            TAD     DECML1    /GET ADDRESS ØF 1ST DIGIT
15.            DCA     DIGPT     /INITIALIZE DIGIT PØINTER
16.            TAD     M4        /GET A NEGATIVE 4
17.            DCA     DIGCTR    /INITIALIZE DIGIT CØUNTER
18.  BIN1,     DCA     DIGIT     /INITIALIZE DECIMAL DIGIT
19.  BIN2,     TAD     NUM       /GET REMAINDER
20.            TAD I   TABLPT    /SUBTRACT TABLE VALUE
21.            SPA               /PØSITIVE REMAINDER?
22.            JMP     BIN3      /NØ, SAVE DIGIT
23.            ISZ     DIGIT     /YES, ADD ØNE TØ DIGIT
24.            DCA     NUM       /SAVE REMAINDER
25.            JMP     BIN2
26.  BIN3,     CLA
27.            TAD     DIGIT     /GET DECIMAL DIGIT
28.            TAD     P260      /CØNVERT DIGIT TØ ASCII
29.            DCA I   DIGPT     /STØRE
30.            ISZ     DIGPT     /ADVANCE DIGIT PØINTER
31.            ISZ     TABLPT    /ADVANCE TABLE PØINTER
32.            ISZ     DIGCTR    /LAST DIGIT?
33.            JMP     BIN1      /NØ, DETERMINE NEXT DIGIT
34.            JMP I   BINDEC    /YES, RETURN
35.  TABLE1,   LØCØNE            /LØCATIØN ØF 1ST TABLE VALUE
36.  DECML1,   DIGIT1            /LØCATIØN ØF 1ST DECIMAL DIGI
37.  TABLPT,   0                 /TABLE PØINTER
38.  DIGPT,    0                 /DIGIT PØINTER
39.  NUM,      0                 /REMAINDER
40.  DIGIT,    0                 /TEMPØRARY DIGIT LØCATIØN
41.  P260,     260
42.  DIGCTR,   0                 /DIGIT CØUNTER
43.  M4,       -4
44.  /CØNVERSIØN TABLE
45.  LØCØNE,   -1750             /NEGATIVE 1000
46.            -144              /NEGATIVE 100
47.            -12               /NEGATIVE 10
48.            -1                /NEGATIVE 1
49.  /STØRAGE LØCATIØNS FØR DECIMAL DIGITS
```

```
50.   DIGIT1,    0            /THE THØUSANDTHS DIGIT
51.              0            /THE HUNDREDTHS DIGIT
52.              0            /THE TENS DIGIT
53.              0            /THE UNITS DIGIT
```

4.3 Specific Comments

Line 11. Remember that the binary number is transferred to the subroutine in the accumulator.

Line 19. The variable NUM, in the first loop of the program, is the original binary number to be converted. After the first loop through the program, the value of NUM is the remainder which results from the repeated subtractions of a power of ten.

Line 23. Each time that a power of ten is subtracted from NUM, and a positive remainder is found, this instruction increments the location called DIGIT. After a subtraction in which the remainder goes negative this variable contains the value of the current decimal digit.

Line 24. Because the variable NUM will eventually go negative, after successive subtractions, it is necessary to save it here on each pass through the loop.

Line 28. This line converts the decimal digit to ASCII. If the decimal digit were to be saved in its binary form, it is only necessary to delete this line.

Line 29. If there is no need to store the decimal digit, but only to print it, then at this point a jump to a print routine can be effected and no storage of the decimal digits would occur.

5.0   DECIMAL-TO-BINARY CONVERSION

5.1 General Comments

This subroutine is the inverse of the previous programming example. It is often used in conjunction with a program like that of the first example, ASCBIN, because there is frequent need to enter decimal numbers at a Teletype keyboard, and then assemble and store them in a binary representation. The sequence is as follows: A decimal digit is entered at the keyboard and the subroutine ASCBIN converts the digit to its binary representation. The digit, in its binary form, is then transmitted to the current subroutine, DECBIN, to be assembled into the binary representation of the complete decimal number. Note, that DECBIN is entered each time a decimal digit is transmitted from the keyboard. Upon each return DECBIN will have in the accumulator the current binary representation of the decimal number up to that point.

Before the conversion of a decimal number it is necessary for the calling routine to set the flag DECFLG equal to zero. When a digit arrives this flag tells the subroutine whether this is the first digit of a series, or whether previous digits have already been converted.

Any digit or series of digits up to 4095_{10} may be entered. After the last digit is entered the binary version of the number is in the location tagged BINNUM. If a number larger than 4095 is entered, it is treated modulo 4096. This simply means that the number is converted to the nearest value above the last integer multiple of 4096_{10}, e.g., 4097_{10} or 8193_{10} will be returned as 1.

The technique used in this subroutine is somewhat similar to that used in the previous programming example, except it is now necessary to perform multiplications by ten. In this particular example the PDP-8 multiply instruction has been used to accomplish this. It could have also been accomplished by repeated additions.

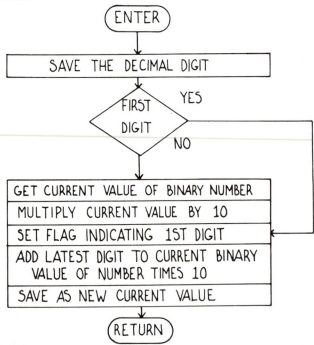

Fig. 4.   Flow diagram for the decimal-to-binary conversion subroutine DECBIN.

5.2 Listing

```
1.   /SUBRØUTINE DECBIN
2.   /WRITTEN BY WWB APRIL, 1970
3.   /A SUBRØUTINE THAT TAKES A DECIMAL NUMBER, A DIGIT
4.   /AT A TIME, AND CØNVERTS IT TØ A BINARY NUMBER.
5.   /CØNVENTIØNS:
6.   / A)  DECBIN EXPECTS THE DIGIT TØ BE IN THE
7.   /     ACCUMULATØR WHEN DECBIN IS ENTERED.
8.   / B)  BEFØRE THE FIRST DIGIT ØF THE DECIMAL
9.   /     NUMBER IS ENTERED, THE FLAG CALLED DECFLG
10.  /     MUST BE SET TØ ZERØ.
11.  / C)  RETURNS WITH BINARY NUMBER IN ACCUMULATØR.
12.  DECBIN,  0
13.           DCA      DIGIT    /SAVE DECIMAL DIGIT
14.           TAD      DECFLG
15.           SNA CLA           /FIRST DIGIT?
16.           JMP      DEC1     /YES
17.           TAD      BINNUM   /NØ
18.           MUY               /MULTIPLY BINNUM TIMES TEN
19.           12                /DECIMAL TEN
20.           MQA               /LØAD PRØDUCT INTØ AC FRØM MQ
21.           SKP               /UNCØNDITIØNAL SKIP
22.  DEC1,    ISZ      DECFLG   /SET FLAG INDICATING FIRST DIGIT
23.           TAD      DIGIT    /ADD LATEST DIGIT
24.           DCA      BINNUM   /SAVE AS CURRENT BINARY NUMBER
25.           TAD      BINNUM   /LØAD BINARY NUMBER BACK IN AC
26.           JMP I    DECBIN   /RETURN
27.  DIGIT,   0                 /CURRENT DECIMAL DIGIT
28.  DECFLG,  0                 /FLAG INDICATING ARRIVAL ØF 1ST DIGIT
29.  BINNUM,  0                 /CURRENT VALUE ØF BINARY NUMBER
```

5.3 Specific Comments

Line 13. Again remember that the binary argument is transferred to the subroutine from the calling routine via the accumulator.
     Line 15. As mentioned earlier if DECFLG equals zero, the
digit just transferred is the first of a series of digits. If
this flag is not equal to zero then at least one digit has preceded the current one.
     Lines 18 and 19. The multiply instruction in the PDP-8
requires the following convention. The multiplicand, BINNUM,
is placed in the accumulator. The multiplier is placed in the
location immediately following the multiply instruction, MUY.
In the present case the multiplier is in Line 19. Line 20 is
the next instruction executed after line 18.
     Line 20. The product of a multiplication contains twice
as many bits as the two original numbers. Therefore, a product
is 24 bits, and the 12 most significant bits are in the accumulator

and the 12 least significant bits in the multiplier-quotient (MQ) register. In this particular program only single precision is required; hence, we are only interested in the least significant bits. That is, the most significant bits are known to be zero.

Line 22. This instruction increments the flag from its zero value so that subsequent decimal digits will be handled properly when they enter the subroutine.

6.0 PRINTING DOUBLE PRECISION DECIMAL NUMBERS

6.1 General Comments

There are often cases where it is necessary to perform double precision integer arithmetic. This particular example converts a 24 bit integer number (two PDP-8 word lengths) to 8 decimal digits, and prints these decimal digits on the teleprinter, if the user so specifies.

This routine must accomplish one of the functions of an earlier programming example. It is necessary to convert binary numbers to decimal numbers for printing. The subtraction technique used here is quite similar to that of the previous programming example, except now, all mathematical computation must be done in double precision. This double precision subtraction is accomplished by the subroutine TWØADD, which is really a double precision addition routine. Of course, this only means that of the two numbers that are transferred to the addition routine, one is negative and one is positive. As in the previous example, it is necessary after each subtraction of a power of 10 to determine if the remainder is negative. The check for this negative value is most easily done in the subroutine TWØADD.

The double precision binary number to be converted, stored, and perhaps, printed is transferred to PRTTWØ via the following format (This type of argument transfer to a subroutine was discussed under the section on subroutines in the chapter "Programming"):

```
            JMS        PRTTWØ
HIBITS,    XXXX                    /MØST SIGNIFICANT 12 BITS
LØBITS,    XXXX                    /LEAST SIGNIFICANT 12 BITS
```

PRTTWØ stores the 8 decimal digits in consecutive memory locations starting at the location tagged DIGSTØ.

The subroutine PRTTWØ contains a flag called PRIPT. If this flag is zero when the subroutine is called, the decimal digits are both stored and printed. If this flag is positive and greater than zero, then the digits are only stored. The value of this flag is transferred by placing it in the accumulator before entering PRTTWØ.

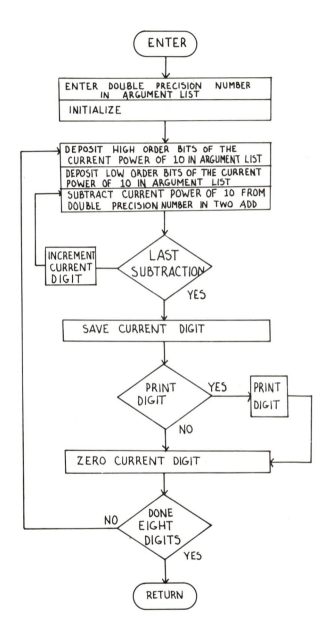

Fig. 5. Flow diagram of the subroutine PRTTWØ.

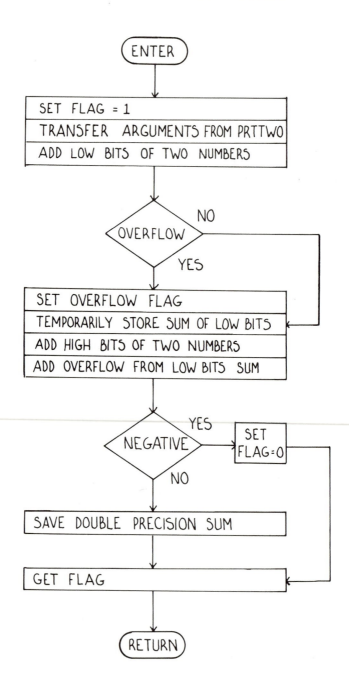

Fig. 6.   Flow diagram of the subroutine TWØADD.

6.2 Listing

```
1.   *40
2.   PRIN,      PRINT
3.   ADDLØC,    TWØADD
4.   PRTLØC,    PRTTWØ
5.   *200
6.              /PRTTWØ  WWB        PDP-8
7.              /A RØUTINE TØ CØNVERT A 24 BIT NUMBER TØ
8.              /DECIMAL, ENTERED IN FØLLØWING WAY
9.              /LØCATIØN        CØNTENTS
10.             /N              JMS PRTTWØ
11.             /N+1            HIGH ØRDER BITS ØF NUMBER
12.             /N+2            LØW ØRDER BITS ØF NUMBER
13.             /ENTER WITH VALUE ØF PRIPT IN AC.
14.             /DECIMAL DIGITS ARE STØRED IN DIGSTØ TØ DIGSTØ
15.             /+7.
16.             /IF DECIMAL NUMBER IS TØ BE PRINTED AND STØRED
17.             /    PRIPT=0
18.             /IF DECIMAL NUMBER IS TØ BE STØRED ØNLY
19.             /    PRIPT=1
20.             /REQUIRES SUBRØUTINES PRINT AND TWØADD
21.  PRTTWØ,    0
22.             DCA     PRIPT   /SAVE PRIPT
23.             TAD I   PRTTWØ  /GET HIGH BITS
24.             DCA     ARG3
25.             ISZ     PRTTWØ
26.             TAD I   PRTTWØ  /GET LØW BITS
27.             DCA     ARG4
28.             ISZ     PRTTWØ  /SET UP RETURN LØCATIØN
29.             TAD     DEPR1   /INITIALIZE DIGIT LIST
30.             DCA     DPTEM
31.             DCA     DIGIT
32.             TAD     CNTRZA
33.             DCA     CNTRZB  /INITIALIZE TØ -8
34.             TAD     ADDRZA
35.             DCA     ARRØW   /INITIALIZE INSTRUCTIØN
36.             TAD     ADDRZA
37.             IAC
38.             DCA     ARRØW1  /INITIALIZE INSTRUCTIØN
39.  ARRØW,     TAD     TENPWR
40.             DCA     ARG1
41.             ISZ     ARRØW   /SET UP NEXT LIST ELEMENT
42.             ISZ     ARRØW
43.  ARRØW1,    0               /INSTRUCTIØN TAD (TENPWR+1)
44.             DCA     ARG2
45.             ISZ     ARRØW1  /SET UP NEXT LIST ELEMENT
46.             ISZ     ARRØW1
47.  ARRØW2,    JMS I   ADDLØC
48.  ARG1,      0
49.  ARG2,      0
```

```
 50.  ARG3,      0
 51.  ARG4,      0
 52.             SZA              /LAST SUBTRACTIØN
 53.             ISZ     DIGIT    /NØ
 54.             SZA CLA          /LAST SUBTRACTIØN
 55.             JMP     ARRØW2   /NØ
 56.             TAD     DIGIT    /YES
 57.             DCA I   DPTEM    /SAVE DIGIT IN LIST
 58.             ISZ     DPTEM    /ADVANCE DIGIT LIST
 59.             TAD     PRIPT
 60.             SZA CLA          /PRINT DIGIT
 61.             JMP     DEPR2    /NØ
 62.             TAD     DIGIT    /YES, GET DIGIT
 63.             TAD     K260     /MAKE ASCII
 64.             JMS I   PRIN     /PRINT DIGIT
 65.  DEPR2,     DCA     DIGIT    /ZERØ DIGIT LØCATIØN
 66.             ISZ     CNTRZB   /DØNE EIGHT DIGITS
 67.             JMP     ARRØW    /NØ, DØ MØRE
 68.             JMP I   PRTTWØ   /YES RETURN
 69.  ADDRZA,    TAD     TENPWR
 70.  CNTRZA,    -10
 71.  TENPWR,    3166             /HIGH BITS NEGATIVE 10 MILLIØN
 72.             4600             /LØW BITS NEGATIVE 10 MILLIØN
 73.             7413             /HIGH BITS NEGATIVE 1 MILLIØN
 74.             6700             /LØW BITS NEGATIVE 1 MILLIØN
 75.             7747             /HIGH BITS NEGATIVE 100 THØUSAND
 76.             4540             /LØW BITS NEGATIVE 100 THØUSAND
 77.             7775             /HIGH BITS NEGATIVE 10 THØUSAND
 78.             4360             /LØW BITS NEGATIVE 10 THØUSAND
 79.             7777             /HIGH BITS NEGATIVE 1 THØUSAND
 80.             6030             /LØW BITS NEGATIVE 1 THØUSAND
 81.             7777             /HIGH BITS NEGATIVE 100
 82.             7634             /LØW BITS NEGATIVE 100
 83.             7777             /HIGH BITS NEGATIVE 10
 84.             7766             /LØW BITS NEGATIVE 10
 85.             7777             /HIGH BITS NEGATIVE 1
 86.             7777             /LØW BITS NEGATIVE 1
 87.  K260,      260
 88.  DIGIT,     0
 89.  CNTRZB,    0
 90.  DEPR1,     DIGSTØ           /1ST ADDRESS ØF DIGIT LIST
 91.  DIGSTØ,    0                /1ST DECIMAL DIGIT
 92.             0
 93.             0
 94.             0
 95.             0
 96.             0
 97.             0
 98.             0                /8TH DECIMAL DIGIT
 99.  DPTEM,     0
100.  PRIPT,     0
```

```
101.              /TWØADD
103.              /RØUTINE TØ DØ DØUBLE PRECISIØN ADDS FØR
104.              /IF AC=1, DIFFERENCE ØF TWØ NUMBERS IS
105.              /PØSITIVE.  IF AC=0 DIFFERENCE IS NEGATIVE.
106.              /ENTER IN FØLLØWING WAY.
107.              /
108.              /LØCATIØN        CØNTENTS
109.              /N                  JMS TWØADD
110.              /N+1       HI ØRDER BITS NEGATIVE NUMBER
111.              /N+2       LØ ØRDER BITS NEGATIVE NUMBER
112.              /N+3       HI ØRDER BITS PØSITIVE NUMBER
113.              /N+4       LØ ØRDER BITS PØSITIVE NUMBER
114.              /N+5       TWØADD RETURNS HERE
115.              /
116.              /IF THE ANSWER IS PØSITIVE, ANSWER IS RETURNED
117.              /IN   N+3 and N+4.   IF ANSWER NEGATIVE.
118.              /CØMPUTATIØN NØT PERFØRMED AND ØRIGINAL VALUES
119.              /REMAIN IN N+3 and N+4.
120.  TWØADD,     0
121.              DCA       LINKCK
122.              ISZ       LINKCK
123.              TAD       TWØADD   /GET HI BITS ØNE ADDRESS
124.              DCA       TWØHI1
125.              ISZ       TWØADD
126.              TAD       TWØADD   /GET LØ BITS ØNE ADDRESS
127.              DCA       TWØLØ1
128.              ISZ       TWØADD
129.              TAD       TWØADD   /GET HI BITS TWØ ADDRESS
130.              DCA       TWØHI2
131.              ISZ       TWØADD
132.              DCA       ØVFLØW
133.              TAD I     TWØLØ1   /GET LØW BITS ØNE
134.              CLL
135.              TAD I     TWØADD   /ADD LØW BITS TWØ
136.              SZL
137.              ISZ       ØVFLØW   /YES
138.              DCA       TWØTEM   /NØ, SAVE TEMPØRARILY
139.              TAD I     TWØHI1   /GET HIGH BITS ØNE
140.              CLL
141.              TAD I     TWØHI2   /ADD HIGH BITS TWØ
142.              TAD       ØVFLØW   /ADD 12 BIT ØVERFLØW
143.              SZL                /ANSWER NEGATIVE
144.              DCA I     TWØHI2   /NØ
145.              SNL CLA            /ANSWER NEGATIVE
146.              JMP       TWØA1    /YES
147.              TAD       TWØTEM   /NØ
148.              DCA I     TWØADD
149.              SKP
150.  TWØA1,      DCA       LINKCK
151.              ISZ       TWØADD
152.              TAD       LINKCK   /GET FLAG
```

```
153.                JMP  I    TWØADD
154.   TWØHI1,      0
155.   TWØH12,      0
156.   TWØLØ1,      0
157.   LINKCK,      0
158.   TWØTEM,      0
159.   ØVFLØW,      0
160.   *400
161.   PRINT,       0
162.                TLS
163.                TSF
164.                JMP       .-1
165.                CLA
166.                JMP  I    PRINT
```

6.3 Specific Comments

Lines 23 through 27. The instructions in these memory locations take the double precision number and deposit it in the argument positions ARG3 and ARG4.

Lines 34 and 35. This is an initialization procedure which takes a computer instruction from the constants list and deposits it in the location at line 39. The instruction is TAD TENPWR.

Line 36. This instruction also retrieves the instruction TAD TENPWR, and the instruction in line 37 adds one, which means that the instruction is modified to be TAD TENPWR + 1. The instruction of line 38 deposits this modified instruction in line 43.

Lines 39 and 40. On the first pass through the program these two instructions take the 12 most significant bits of -10^7 and deposit them in the location ARG1.

Lines 41 and 42. On the first pass through the program these two instructions modify the instruction of line 39 to become TAD TENPWR + 2.

Lines 43 and 44. On the first pass these two instructions take the 12 least significant bits of -10^7 and deposit them in the location ARG2.

Lines 45 and 46. These are similar to the instructions in lines 41 and 42 in that they modify the instruction of line 43 to be TAD TENPWR + 3.

Line 47. This jumps to the double precision ADD subroutine, TWØADD.

Lines 50 and 51. Originally these two locations contain the 24 bits of the binary number that is to be converted to decimal. However, on successive passes through the program this number gets smaller and smaller as successive powers of ten are subtracted by the subroutine TWØADD.

Line 52. As mentioned earlier TWØADD checks after each subtraction to see if the remainder is negative. This instruction checks that possibility. If the remainder is negative, then the instruction of this line skips to line 54, which in turn skips to line 56.

Lines 56 and 57. These instructions pick up the current decimal digit and store it in the appropriate location in the list starting at DIGSTØ.

Lines 121 and 122. These two locations set the flag LINKCK to one. It is this flag that indicates whether the remainder is negative after the subtraction of a power of ten.

Lines 123 and 124. These instructions take the address of the high order bits of the negative number and deposit it in line 154.

Line 125. This instruction advances the location of the return address contained in line 120.

Lines 126 and 127. These two instructions take the address of the low order bits of the negative number and deposit it in line 156.

Lines 129 and 130. These instructions take the address of the high order bits of the positive number and deposit it in line 155.

Line 132. This instruction sets ØVFLØW equal to zero. This flag indicates whether an overflow has occurred when the low-order bits of the two double precision numbers are summed.

Line 133. This instruction gets the low-order bits of the negative number.

Line 134. This instruction clears the link bit which can be conceptually thought of as a 13th bit of the accumulator for present purposes.

Line 135. This instruction adds the low-order bits of the first number to the low-order bits of the second number.

Line 136. If the addition results in an overflow the link will automatically be set equal to one. This instruction SZL, skips on zero link.

Line 137. If the link is set, i.e. an overflow has occurred, then this is remembered by setting the flag ØVFLØW equal to one.

Line 138. This instruction saves the sum of the low order bits of the two numbers.

Line 139. Get the high order bits of the negative number.

Line 141. Add the high order bits of the positive number.

Line 142. Add the overflow from the previous additions of the low order bits.

Line 143. This again checks the link. If the link is equal to one, the subtraction of the power of ten has left a positive remainder. If the link is equal to zero the remainder is negative.

Line 144. If the remainder has been positive, save the sum of the high order bits in the location TWØH12, which through the indirect addressing reaches back to the location ARG3.

Lines 147 and 148. If the remainder was positive, save
the sum of the low order bits indirectly in the location TWØADD,
which couples back to the location tagged ARG4.

Line 150. If the remainder was negative the program jumps
to here from line 146. This line sets the flag LINKCK equal
to zero indicating that a negative remainder was found.

Line 151. This sets up the final return address.

Line 153. This returns from the subroutine TWØADD to
line 52 of the program PRTTWØ.

PART IV

OTHER CONSIDERATIONS

CHAPTER 11

CHOOSING A COMPUTER SYSTEM

1.0 GENERAL CONSIDERATIONS

Some of the discussion of this chapter does not apply to
the specific acquisition of every computer system. However, if
an organization ever purchases more than one computer, it is
almost certain that all the considerations discussed here will
have to be given some thought.

1.1 Keeping Abreast of the State-of-the-Art

Because on-line computers and computer peripherals are
part of a fast changing art it is difficult to keep abreast
of the current developments, but for the same reason, also,
very important. As long as the current rate of change continues, a sustained effort will be required on the part of any on-
line computer user to keep abreast of the state-of-the-art.
Keeping abreast of the state-of-the-art has two aspects.
For example, in the basic research laboratory it is natural to
be always actively seeking state-of-the-art equipment in order
to push the experiments to further frontiers. This is an environment in which change is standard. However, on the other
side of the coin there are those who are seeking stability.
An extreme example of this is an electrical utility. The average power utility is buying equipment on a 30-40 year basis.
Thus, the concern is not with the latest state-of-the-art, but
the manufacturer's ability to provide spare parts, warranties,
and maintenance services on a long-term basis.
In the past, computer manufacturers have tended to cater
to that group seeking the state-of-the-art. However, there is
a real need to be filled in the other area. It is to be hoped
that the future will see stabilization of at least some of the
computer models to fill these latter needs. The current situation is really akin to what happened in the field of automobiles several years ago. At one time there was the so-called
horsepower race where each manufacturer tried every year to

announce automobiles with horsepowers greater than his compet-
itors. At the present time, there is a similar horsepower race
in the computer industry, particularly in memory cycle times.
     The question at hand, is how does the typical on-line com-
puter user go about keeping abreast of the state-of-the-art.
There are at least five different ways to pursue this knowledge,
all of which, contribute to one extent or another. These are:
literature, personal contact, conferences, sales representatives
of the computer and peripheral manufacturers, and the user societies established by the various computer manufacturers.

Literature

     There are at least three types of literature which are
profitable to peruse. The first of these are the journals
published by the professional societies. Some of the better
known are those journals published by the Association for
Computing Machinery (ACM). On a scale where very applied problems are discussed on one extreme and very theoretic problems
are discussed on the other extreme, the ACM journals tend towards the theory portion of the spectrum. Trade journals and
papers are a second source of computer literature. There are
numerous trade journals which publish papers tending toward
the applied end of the spectrum, and are heavily advertised in
by both the computer manufacturers and the peripheral manufacturers. Subscriptions to many of these are free to qualified
persons. A third source is the product literature and manuals
that are provided by computer and peripheral manufacturers.
These can be obtained directly from the manufacturer and can
also be obtained by mailing cards which are inserted in many
of the trade journals. Anyone active in the field would do
well to create a file of product literature to be perused on
its arrival and to be used when any new system is being considered.
     A partial list of periodic publications and the addresses
of the editorial offices are given in Table I.

Personal Contact

     Many of us make contact with people in our own fields and
other fields that use on-line computers.

Conferences

     This is another time-honored method of gathering informa-
tion in any field. There are at least three types of conferences that can be of value for keeping abreast of the state-of-
the-computer art. These are: conferences sponsored by the
professional societies, topical conferences in which specific
subject matter is discussed, and seminars.
     Probably the largest conferences sponsored by professional
computer societies at present are the Spring Joint Computer
Conferences (SJCC) and the Fall Joint Computer Conferences (FJCC)
which are sponsored by the American Federation of Information
Processing Societies (AFIPS), of which, the ACM is one member.
These conferences combine convention exhibits with the presentation of technical papers. The proceedings are published

Table I.   A partial list of periodic publications and the
           addresses of the editorial offices.

SOFTWARE AGE   ELECTRONIC NEWS
2211 Fordem Ave.   7 East 12th St.
Madison, Wisconsin   53701   New York
                                     New York   10003
COMPUTER DESIGN
Professional Building   DATA PROCESSING MAGAZINE
Baker Ave.   134 North 13th Street
West Concord, Massachusetts   Philadelphia
                      01781   Pennsylvania   19107

DATAMATION   COMPUTERWORLD
94 South Los Robles Ave.   60 Austin St.
Pasadena   Newton
California   91101   Massachusetts   02160

COMPUTER DECISIONS   COMPUTER GROUP NEWS
850 Third Ave.   Suite 321
New York   16400 Ventura Blvd.
New York   10022   Encino, California   91316

          Journals of the Association for Computing Machinery
                 1133 Avenue of the Americas
                 New York
                 New York   10036

          JOURNAL OF THE ASSOCIATION FOR COMPUTING MACHINERY
                 COMMUNICATIONS OF THE ACM
                    COMPUTING SURVEYS
                    COMPUTING REVIEWS

at the time of the meeting and contain all of those technical
papers formally presented at the meeting. The equipment exhibits at the SJCC and FJCC are certainly the largest in the
computer equipment and computer peripheral industries. Tra-
ditionally, the Spring Joint Computer Conference is held on
the East Coast of the United States and the Fall Joint Computer
Conference is held on the West Coast.
     Sales Representatives
     Sales representatives encountered in the area of on-line
computers and computer peripherals usually represent two types
of firms. In one case the sales representative is a direct
employee of the computer manufacturer and only represents that
one computer manufacturer. The other sales representative is
employed by firms which represent many manufacturers of

electronics equipment. Normally such a firm represents only
one computer manufacturer, but it may also represent several
computer peripheral manufacturers and market electronic equipment outside of the computer field.

It behooves anybody that is actively involved in the on-
line computer field to become acquainted with as many of the
representatives in his geographic area as possible. This is,
without a doubt, one of the best ways to keep abreast of the
state-of-the-computer art and represents the quickest and
easiest avenue to specific information.

Representatives of computer manufacturers often serve
many different roles. They may deliver or assist in deliverin
any equipment that is purchased. They often are the ones tha
prepare bids in response to requests for quotation from customers. They may also serve in any warranty difficulties that
arise.

If these representatives know the user's organization and
they know the applications for which he is using on-line computers, they can give much more precise and qualified response
on any bids or requests for proposal that are put out by the
user's organization. This particular topic will be pursued
further later.

Table II is a partial list of manufacturers who make computers suitable for on-line applications. This is neither mea
to be exhaustive or current. Needless to say, in such an act
field many manufacturers are constantly joining the fraternity
and on occasion some are leaving.

User Societies

In many instances computer manufacturers form user societies which are made up of individuals who have acquired that
particular manufacturer's computers. These societies provide
a means of interacting with people who have similar equipment.
Some of the user societies organize technical conferences at
which papers are presented by society members. It is becoming
increasingly popular to hold user society meetings just prior
to, or just following the Spring Joint and Fall Joint Compute
Conferences, and in the same city.

1.2 Long-Term Philosophy

This discussion is not applicable to one computer system,
or computer systems that are immersed in a much larger proces
Instead, we are speaking of an orderly plan within an organization for the acquisition of several on-line computer system
If there is any possibility that a given organization will ac-
quire several on-line computer systems, economies and efficien
cies can be effected if a long-range plan is developed. If
possible, such a plan should begin to evolve even before the
first computer is acquired. There are at least three clearly
identifiable plans or approaches. These are taken up in
section 2.0 of this chapter.

Table II.   A partial list of manufacturers who produce
            computers suitable for on-line applications.

Varian Data Machines
2722 Michelson Drive
Irvine, California   92661

General Automation, Inc.
706 West Katella
Orange, California

Digital Equipment Corp.
146 Main Street
Maynard, Mass.   01754

Micro Systems Inc.
644 East Young Street
Santa Ana, Calif.   92705

Data General Corp.
Southboro, Mass.   01772

Xerox Data Systems
701 South Avaiation Blvd.
El Segundo, Calif.   90245

Raytheon Computer
2700 S. Fairview St.
Santa Ana, Calif.   92704

Monitor Data Corp.
17805 Sky Park Circle
Irvine, Calif.   92664

International Business
   Machines
112 East Post Road
White Plains, N.Y.   10601

Systems Engineering
   Laboratories
6901 West Sunrise Blvd.
Ft. Lauderdale, Fla.   33313

Interdata
2 Crescent Place
Oceanport, N.J.   07757

Business Information
   Technology
5 Strathmore Road
Natick, Mass.   01760

UniComp Inc.
Northridge, Calif.

Control Data Corp.
P. O. Box 1980
Minneapolis, Minn.   55111

Hewlett-Packard
Palo Alto, Calif.   94304

General Electric Co.
1 River Road
Schenectady, N.Y.   12305

Honeywell, Computer Control
   Division
Old Connecticut Path
Framingham, Mass.   01701

Spiras Systems, Inc.
332 Second Avenue
Waltham, Mass.

REDCOR Corp.
7800 Deering Ave.
Canoga Park, Calif.   91304

Datacraft
P. O. Box 23550
Ft. Lauderdale, Fla.   33307

Tempo Computers, Inc.
1550 S. State College Blvd.
Anaheim, Calif.   92806

Cincinnatti Milling Machine
   Company
Lebanon, Ohio   45036

Wilkerson Computer Sciences,
   Inc.
200 Sweetwater Ave.
Bedford, Mass.   01730

Lockheed Electronics
6201 East Randolph St.
Los Angeles, Calif.   90022

Table II.   A partial list of manufacturers who produce
            computers suitable for on-line applications.
            (Continued)

Computer Division, EMR   Digital Computer Controls
8001 Bloomington Freeway   Fairfield, N.J.
Minneapolis, Minn.   55420
                                  Computer Automation, Inc.
Westinghouse Electric Corp.   895 West 16th St.
Hagan/Computer Systems Division   Newport Beach, Calif.   92660
Pittsburgh, Pa.   15238
                                  Computer Development Corp.
Compiler Systems Inc.   3001 S. Daimler St.
P. O. Box 366   Santa Ana, Calif.   92705
Ridgefield, Conn.   06877
                                  Digital Systems Division-
Varisystems, Corp   Houston
Plainview, N.Y.   Texas Instruments Inc.
                                  P.O. Box 66027
Multidata   Houston, Texas   77006
7300 Bolsa Ave.
Westminster, Calif.   92683

        Although there are several reasons for considering a long-
range plan for the implementation of on-line computer systems,
one of the most practical reasons is the particular attention
that is being paid to computers at this point in time.   In
most large organizations whether private, governmental or
university, there is a growing concern about, "the proliferation of computers".   Many persons in administrative and legis-
lative positions have become concerned by the almost exponen-
tial growth of computers in the United States.   On one hand,
it is only natural to be concerned that some of these computers
are being bought needlessly, or that some could be shared.   On
the other hand, I seriously doubt that anybody has, for example
worried about the proliferation of oscilloscopes that have take
place in the United States.   The point being that on-line computers like the laboratory oscilloscope, are simply tools.
Therefore, one should not be concerned about the number of tool
but whether they are needed and whether they represent an econo
approach to any given problem.   Unfortunately, such an aura has
been built up around the computer sciences that they have come
into a glaring spotlight which is not wholly deserved.

        1.3   Maintenance

        The type and quality of maintenance service required de-
pends a great deal upon the application for which the on-line

computer system is being used. There are many applications
where the computer system being idle for a few hours does not
present any particular problem. On the other hand, the computer may be attached to a multi-million dollar system which
cannot be allowed to stand idle because of a computer which
represents a small portion of the total system. This kind of
consideration allows one to place a value on the quality and
frequency of maintenance that is required.

The first major decision to be made in connection with the
maintenance of an on-line computer system is: Who? At the
present time there are at least three approaches: (1) The
user may maintain it himself; (2) most computer manufacturers
sell maintenance contracts; and (3) there has been an emergence
of firms that specialize in doing maintenance work on advanced
electronic systems. The purpose of this discussion is to examine some of the considerations that are involved in each case.

Maintenance by the User

The first question is the availability of talent. Does
the user have in his own organization engineers and technicians
with the abilities to maintain a computer and computer peripherals? Computer peripherals are mentioned specifically because they are often electro-mechanical, and are somewhat of
a different maintenance problem than the basic computer. For
this reason, it may be worthwhile to consider a separate person, with mechanical skills, to work on these devices. Not
only do they present a somewhat different maintenance problem
but by their very nature, they tend to require more maintenance
than those components of the system that are strictly electronic
in nature.

If the user organization decides to maintain its own computer systems, then it becomes necessary to stock spare parts.
Most computer manufacturers have a recommended spare parts list
for each product. It then follows, that somebody should be
designated to see that the spare parts are maintained, and if
enough are involved, the distribution of spare parts.

Maintenance by the Computer Manufacturer

One of the first considerations is the quality of service
that can be rendered. This can depend strongly upon the geographic proximity of the user to the nearest office of the
computer manufacturer. This then leads to questions of how
quickly the system must be repaired in case of failure and
whether a 24-hour service is required. Twenty-four hour service is normally offered at a cost above that for the normal
day-time working hours. In some instances a user may have
enough equipment for the manufacturer to warrant the assignment of one man full time.

One advantage of manufacturer maintenance is the elimination of any need for additional staff on the user's part.
Another is the user no longer has to stock spare parts. Maintenance contracts should have guarantees about the availability
of spare parts.

A typical situation is that of peripherals which have been
added to the computer system and were not made by the manufacturer of the computer. The difficulty that often arises in
this situation is the determination of whose equipment is at
fault when a failure occurs.

Speciality Firms

This choice is currently available in some areas of the
United States. The user must first decide what familiarity
the firm has with his equipment. If this question is answered
in the positive, then the speciality firm can often offer the
advantage of more personnel working in a given geographic area.
Care should also be taken to insure that adequate spare parts
are maintained.

2.0 SELECTING A SYSTEM CONFIGURATION

Because there are a large number of on-line computers
available and a vast number of potential peripherals, which
may be attached to these computers, there is usually more than
one combination of peripherals and computer that will satisfy
the requirements in any given application. In the present
sense, configuration will mean one of these combinations. This
is a generic sense because it includes the philosophy of how
the system is used and the way in which it is programmed. In
this section three different configurations are discussed. The
are not entirely unique, for one could imagine configurations
that are combinations between those suggested here. Also, in a
least one instance, it is possible to evolve from one of the co
figurations to another.

Which configuration is the best has often been long and
hotly debated. Therefore, the following must be considered as
the author's own personal observations and biases.

The first approach to be discussed is the one-computer
one-task approach. This has to date been the most successful
of the three approaches. This is probably because it is the
most easily implemented of the three and historically was the
first. This approach is less demanding on both the hardware an
the software.

The second configuration is the time-shared system. Time-
shared systems have been sought for some time. To date they ha
not been spectacularly successful. This probably stems from th
fact that this is the most difficult approach to implement. It
is demanding on both the software and the hardware. The most
successful time-shared systems have been those in what might be
called one-task areas. This is the situation where more than
one device or process is time-shared into one computer, but all
the devices or processes are the same or very similar. On the
other hand, the time-shared systems which have been least
successful to date, are in the multi-task areas where the devices and processes tend to vary substantially.

It is difficult to comment on the successfulness or un-
successfulness of the third configuration to be discussed which
is the hierarchal approach. Only recently have many organizations had a large enough complement of on-line computers to
permit this approach to be tried, or needed.

Like many other considerations relating to on-line computer
systems it is the environment of the organization that counts
heavily in deciding which configuration should be implemented.
With this in mind it is not surprising to see that there are
often identical applications which are attacked in entirely
different ways by different organizations. Thus, the configurations should be compared on the basis of how they best fit
a given organization rather than considering one configuration
to be better than another.

2.1 One-Computer One-Task

For the purposes at hand, the word task is going to be
used in a different way than process has been used in previous
chapters. A task will be the performance of any action or group
of actions that the user sees as one activity. Therefore, the
one-computer one-task concept is very simple; each task has one
computer associated with it.

The task can encompass a wide range of activities. The
task might be anything from a scientific experiment, such as
a computer linked to a multi-channel analyzer, a mass spectra-
graph, a gas chromatograph, or a bubble chamber picture scanner;
to a computer hooked to a typesetting machine, a high school
demonstration, an environmental monitor, or a product checker
on an assembly line.

One of the major advantages of a one-computer one-task
configuration is the lesser demand on both hardware and software. The computer only has to respond to one or a few devices.
The major advantage is simplicity. This simplicity carries
over to the human aspects because it means only one user or
one group of users is involved with the computer. A user or
group of users does not have to wait while others have the
system down for modifications or repairs.

All of these characteristics of the one-computer one-task
configuration tend to lead to smaller on-line computers to fulfill the requirements. They also tend toward systems with a
small complement of peripherals. This tendency toward small
computers and small complements of peripherals in turn leads
to most of the disadvantages of the one-computer one-task
approach. For example, the programming inconvenience from the
lack of fast peripherals and the inability to take advantage
of higher level languages such as FORTRAN or ALGOL. As we
have seen in previous chapters, these disadvantages can be off-
set somewhat, if a central computing facility is available for
the off-line assembly and/or off-line simulation of on-line
computer programs.

2.2 Time-Shared Computer Systems

Basically time sharing a computer is to arrange for the same computer to perform several different tasks. It is often said that the time-shared computer handles all tasks simultaneously. This is not true. It should be obvious by this point, that a computer can only perform one task at any given time.* Thus, the secret of time sharing is for the computer to be enough faster than any of the individual time requirements to be able to respond to any task within some required time interval. The time interval varies according to the task e.g., on the slower end of the spectrum, it may be necessary to only respond fast enough to keep a human user from becoming bored. The computer can easily handle many such tasks. On the other hand, some electronic devices may require fast response times to function properly, and these are the types of devices that strain a time-shared computer system.

As mentioned in previous discussions, the time-sharing approach has been most successful in those applications where all the tasks on the computer are the same or quite similar. The numerous time-sharing services that have sprung up through out the United States are excellent examples of this type of system. Usually these systems are connected to Teletype terminals via telephone lines. The applications are largely program development and computational. Characteristically, terminals are very slow compared to the speeds of the computer. In fact, there are several commercial systems in existence that can serve the order of 100 terminals with a satisfactorally small time lag. Successful laboratory applications of time-sharing computers have also primarily been where the experimen on the computer are the same or of a similar nature.

The primary advantages that stem from the time-sharing con figuration relate to the fact that such systems tend toward larger computers with a large complement of peripherals. Thus there is ample opportunity to program in higher level languages with a diversity of approaches to any given problem.

This largeness of systems also tends to be one of the main sources of difficulties which arise in attempting to implement and use time-shared systems. Much greater demands are made on both the hardware and the programs. In the programming case the demands are particularly high in the supervisory programming i.e., in the programs that control the whole programming system A time-shared system can be extremely difficult to debug from both the hardware and programming standpoint. For these reason it takes a higher level of engineering and programming talent to implement and operate time-shared configurations.

---

*The exceptions are those limited number of cases where basic subunits of the computer are repeated to allow parallel processing.

2.3   A Computer Hierarchy

This approach is partially a combination of the first two configurations already discussed. It is possible to start with a one-computer one-task configuration and evolve to a hierarchical configuration. In the hierarchical approach each task generally has a dedicated computer similar to the one-computer one-task approach. Certainly there will not be more than a very few tasks on a given computer.

These dedicated computers are then in turn connected to an intermediatesize computer. Several such intermediate-size computers might in turn be linked to a larger computer, and so forth. The system assumes as many hierarchical levels as desired.

In the strict sense the intermediate and larger computers are time-shared computers in that they have many different tasks as inputs. However, there is a very important difference from the time-shared configuration as described in the previous section. In the hierarchical approach the dedicated computer services all the fast responses and does much of the detailed chores such as formatting data before passing it on to the next computer in the hierarchy. Although the higher level computers are time shared, they do not have to make fast responses and they are relieved of many small chores. One can think of the dedicated computers acting in a capacity similar to input/output processors.

An important advantage of the hierarchical approach is that the system can evolve in a natural manner from the bottom up. It is a useful system from the day that the first dedicated computer is made operational. No one user has to wait for another. The hierarchical approach also achieves a good balance of peripherals by placing peripherals where they are the most useful. For example, large mass storage peripherals tend to be higher in the structure rather than at the dedicated spots where it is usually only necessary to have buffer memory.

Probably the primary disadvantage of the hierarchical approach is that it works only where a large number of applications exist and assumes a priori that a large equipment investment is going to be made. It is an approach that is definitely not for the small user or the small organization.

3.0   WRITING SPECIFICATIONS

3.1   Guidelines

Writing good specifications for the procurement of equipment is a demanding task. Unfortunately, it is sometimes treated like a war between the eventual user and the equipment supplier. Although penalty clauses and guarantees may serve

some purpose, satisfactory results still eventually rest on
integrity. It isn't much consolation to have been compensate
as a result of a penalty clause, and still have a piece of
equipment that doesn't work.
      Writing a specification greatly challenges the art of co
munication. Emphasis should constantly be placed on being as
exact and as specific as possible. This is not to say that
specifications should be tomes. Emphasis should also be plac
on brevity and conciseness. Remember that the manufacturer
will read many specifications besides yours.
      Do not try to cover ignorance by writing specifications
that are very general and very loose. Specifications are oft
written in this manner in the hope that the manufacturers wil
respond with new or unique solutions to the user's problem.
This rarely happens. First of all, the manufacturer is not a
mind reader. Secondly, a basic fact must be kept in mind; it
costs the manufacturer effort and money to respond to a speci
fication. He obviously must apportion his effort by judging
the likelihood of getting the contract.
      Never ask for more in the way of performance than is nee
ed. The cost is roughly proportionate to the performance required of the unit.
      On every specification give the name and phone number of
a technical contact within the user's organization. Ideally,
this is someone that has written the specification, or helped
to write the specification, or will be an eventual user of th
equipment. In large organizations purchasing agents often st
between the eventual user and the manufacturer. They must nc
be expected to know everything that the user had in mind on
technical matters.

3.2 Contents of the Specification

      <u>General description</u>. There should always be an introduc
tory clause to a specification which gives a general descrip
of what is being specified and what the application of the ec
ment will be. This can offer considerable information by pro
viding a setting which many of the respondees can understand
      <u>Hardware</u>. It is not possible to discuss all the aspects
of hardware that might be specified. Therefore, the remarks
here are confined to essentially the basic computer with general remarks on peripherals. The central processing unit spe
ifications should include at least the following entries.
      1) The number of registers that are to be provided,
          their functions, those accessible to the programmer
          and the word length of the computer.
      2) Details of the actual logic of the machine might
          also be specified. For example, whether the comput
          is to have parallel operation, serial operation, or
          where combinations are permissable.

3) Requirements should be stated on the arithmetic unit of the computer. For example, whether two's complement arithmetic is to be used, and whether floating point operations are available.

4) In many cases it is wise to specify instructions that the computer shall have. This is not to specify the total number of instructions but actual instructions such as jump to subroutine, addition, and complement accumulator.

5) Often it is desirable to specify features that are to be found on the console. These might include the registers that can be displayed, data entry switches, and instruction loads.

6) Attention must be given to the magnetic core memory. This includes the number of words of memory desired, the word length of the memory, the addressing modes of the memory, and the cycle time.

7) Considerable thought should be given to specifying the input/output channels desired. Rather than try to itemize all those things that might be specified, the user is referred to the chapter "Computer Organization II" where detailed discussions are given on input/output channels and their features.

It is impossible to cover here all aspects of specifying computer peripherals. The specification of non-standard peripherals must be done with more detail than the standard peripherals. Enough introductory material must be given about the non-standard peripherals and their application to allow the potential supplier to understand the specifications of the device. This can even go to the lengths of including literature from the manufacturers of the non-standard peripherals.

Software. The amount of detail with which the software is specified relates directly to the application. If the nature of the application is such that the user will do most of the application programming, then it is only necessary to specify what might be called a normal complement of software, such as assemblers, compilers, and loaders. On the other hand, for more exotic applications the user may try to obtain more sophisticated software from the supplier rather than write it himself. Some of the areas that should be covered in the software specifications are as follows:

1) A real time executive system may be required for an application. If so, it is probably desirable to obtain it from the manufacturer of the computer because such software represents a large investment of time and manpower.

2) If the system is of sufficient size to make it advantageous, compilers should be specified. These could include FORTRAN, ALGOL and BASIC compilers. In some instances there are national committees which have

written standards, for example, for FORTRAN. It is
well to reference these if the user desires a standard
compiler. However, it is more often the case that the
user wants an extended compiler, i.e. one with all the
standard features plus more.
3) Specifications should be given for the assembler. The
include what peripherals it will run with, how much me
ory is required and the availability of off-line assem
blers.
4) Specifications should include loader programs. The
loader programs can make a great difference in the eas
of use of the computer system.
5) Editors are one of the programs normally supplied with
the computer but which vary a great deal in their capabilities. It is therefore, wise to specify the edito
features that are desired.
6) Debugging software also varies a great deal from computer manufacturer to computer manufacturer, and even
from model to model with the same manufacturer.
7) Any arithmetic subroutines that are required should be
specified. For example, floating-point operations and
trigonometric functions.
8) Logical conversions might also be included. For examp
the subroutines to do binary-to-decimal and decimal-to
binary conversions.
9) Diagnostic programs should be specified. These are
programs that are loaded in the computer to exercise
various parts of the system for maintenance purposes.

Miscellaneous items. Several miscellaneous items should
be included in a complete specification.
1) The user should include the number and types of manual
that are to be supplied with the equipment. It is als
wise to specify when these shall be delivered. For ex
ample, some should be delivered prior to the delivery
of the equipment, some with the equipment and perhaps
in a few instances after the equipment. Similarly,
it should be specified which circuit diagrams are required. These are particularly important if the user
is to maintain the computer system himself. This material should also include a list of spare parts.
2) It is customary with on-line computers to supply train
ing in both programming and maintenance at offices of
the computer manufacturer. In some instances these ar
free to a certain number of individuals with the user'
organization paying the out-of-pocket expenses. There
fore, it is reasonable to include, in the specificatio
the number of persons to be trained from the user's
organization.
3) There are several miscellaneous and general specifications that might be given about the equipment. Thes
include environmental aspects, for example, the

temperatures and humidities under which the equipment
will operate. In some instances it is necessary to
specify the type of logic used.
4) The specifications should include requirements for
    the acceptance, inspection, and testing of the computer
    system on or before delivery.
5) It is common to give instructions on response to the
    specifications. This can cover a wide variety of con-
    siderations. For example, response to the specifica-
    tions might require that the suppliers itemize
    all those specifications which they do not meet. Also,
    the user may choose to include several different op-
    tions in the specification and ask that separate costs
    be given on each option. As pointed out previously, the
    name and phone number for an individual who is to be
    a technical contact should be given.
As a concluding statement it might be said that a specification should place the heaviest emphasis on those portions of the
on-line computer system which have the most unique and stringent
requirements.

4.0 ACQUIRING A COMPUTER SYSTEM

Often in budgeting for a computer system, the only items
that are included in the budget are the capital (equipment) costs
and perhaps maintenance costs. Unfortunately, the cost of buying
or developing applications software is often overlooked (or in-
tentionally omitted). To give a feeling for the magnitude of
the consequences of not considering software in original budgets,
software costs as a very rough rule of thumb, will equal the
hardware costs.
There are two primary methods of acquiring an on-line computer system; purchase or lease. The purchase method can be
further broken into sole-source procurements and bid procurements. Both methods are discussed below.

4.1 Bid Procurement

Acquiring equipment through the bid procurement process
(which is often referred to as the letting of bids) is meant
to be an open competition between different manufacturers to
supply the equipment specified. Bid procurement is the major
method used by governmental agencies, ostensibly because it increases competition and thereby reduces cost.
The normal procedure is to submit the specifications for
the equipment desired to those manufacturers, who it is felt
will want to bid. In addition to the specifications, standard
purchase agreements are normally included in the bid package.
A deadline date and time is set for the bids to be received

at the user's organization.   In some instances there is a formal
bid opening with bidders attending.
     Several criteria may be applied in awarding the bids. A-
gain, in governmental agencies the procurement ostensibly goes
to the low bidder. However, the low bidder criterion is not
necessarily the best or only criterion. For example, it is
rather rare that nearly identical systems are designed by different manufacturers. Thus, it is not unusual at all to find
cases where a slight increase of expenditure will buy substantially more capability. This is true in some cases where one
manufacturer has a particularly applicable feature on his system
     The past experience and reputation of a manufacturer cannot
be ignored in the evaluating of bids. This is a difficult task
and unfortunately, usually more is known about some firms than
others.
     A particularly difficult situation is that of a small firm
coming in as a very low bidder in an attempt to get established.
Although, at first glance this may seem like a good way for the
user to get a bargain, it often does not turn out that way.
In spite of its best intentions, the small firm tends to over-
extend itself, and may even go bankrupt if the system involved
is a large one. If this happends, everybody looses; the user
has no equipment and the small firm has been eliminated from
the market place. This is not to say in any way that bids
from small firms should not be considered. However, in those
cases where their bids fall far below the competition, an investigation should be made to determine the ability to deliver
the product and to sustain a loss.
     Finally, remember that manufacturers see two types of
specifications. One might be called competitive specifications
and the other is often called restrictive specifications. A
competitive specification is one which can be answered by several different manufacturers. That is, the user has written
in a general way about the requirements of his application. On
the other hand, restrictive specifications are those which do
not permit several manufacturers to respond and are probably
written around the specifications of one manufacturer's product
Restrictive specifications are written for several reasons. In
governmental agencies they are written to obtain one manufacturer's equipment while giving the appearance of meeting the
competitive bidding requirements set down by purchasing regu-
lations. It should be no surprise, if a restrictive specification is offered as a competitive bidding situation, and many
manufacturers respond with no bids.

     4.2   Sole-Source Procurement

     There are many good and valid reasons why the user may
want to negotiate directly with one manufacturer for equipment.
When an application is pushing the state-of-the-art, there are

often cases where only one manufacturer can supply a system which meets the requirements.

Other considerations can enter. For example, if a user already has several computer systems from one manufacturer, and he has a new application which requires computers of a similar nature, then there are a number of reasons for buying from the same manufacturer. Among these are the compatibility of the new equipment with the equipment that is already on hand. This extends to the stocking of spare parts and the elimination of any need for new training of maintenance personnel. Another factor is the investment in programming that the user has made for his present computers.

In these cases, it is a waste of both the user's and the manufacturer's time to go through the motions of a bid procurement. This might seem too obvious to mention, but it often happens and, of course, with restrictive specifications.

Unless the configuration being purchased is a standard item, a specification is still necessary. Writing a specification for a sole-source procurement requires slightly different emphasis. The purpose of the specification in this case is to clarify in the user's mind his own needs and to clearly spell out what is needed to the manufacturer so that there can be no misunderstanding about the equipment to be supplied.

4.3 Leasing

Except for the Federal agencies, leasing has become an increasingly popular means of acquiring computer systems. There are several reasons for this. In the commercial sector there are definite tax advantages, particularly for those firms in high income brackets. Leasing not only gives a tax break but it defers the expenditure of capital money, and therefore, makes it available for investments. In some cases leases are also written to make it easier to replace equipment. If one has an application which is pushing the state-of-the-art, and needs to take advantage of new computer advances as they come along, then a lease permits the replacement of current equipment with the latest equipment on the market. Most lease contracts make it possible to do this by essentially making the necessary adjustments in the lease payments. This is advantageous for the computer manufacturer because in most instances the payments are larger.

Until recently, some leases were being written on the assumption that the equipment could be leased repeatedly. That is, a leasing firm would lease a computer system even though the payments from the original user did not completely pay for the cost of the computer, on the assumption that the computer could be leased a second, and even a third time to recover the original investment. However, this was not the case in many instances; particularly in those instances where on-line computers were

involved. On-line computers have been somewhat volatile, i.e
models have been rapidly replaced by newer, faster, and more
economical models. The second and third lease customers did
not materialize. As a result, most leases are now full payou
leases. This simply means that the contract is written in
such a way that the original lessor pays the total cost of th
equipment plus a satisfactory fee to the party leasing the eq
ment. The switch to full payout leases has increased monthly
payments. Common lease durations are three, four, and five
years for on-line computer systems. This is to be compared
with the non-payout leases which often attempted to amoritize
the cost of the equipment over the order of eight years.

There are at least two avenues by which computer equipme
may be leased. First, the user can lease the equipment direc
from the computer manufacturer, or in some instances a subsid
of the manufacturer. The second approach is the third party
lease. In this case the equipment is leased from a third par
i.e. a firm which purchases the equipment from the original c
puter manufacturer and then leases it to the customer.

Leases obtained from computer manufacturers usually incl
options for a maintenance contract. If a maintenance contrac
is desired, when a third party lease is arranged, the third
party firm usually negotiates with the original equipment man
facturer for the maintenance. As a very rough rule of thumb,
maintenance costs are somewhat less than one per cent of the
new cost of the equipment per month.

4.4   Procurement of Peripherals

There are several complications that can arise in procur
peripherals which do not normally occur in the procurement of
the basic computer. For example, peripherals often lag behin
new computer models. There is a tendency on the part of manu
facturers to develop new computer models and then, after the
fact, develop new peripherals to go with them. Particularly
with on-line computers, it is fairly normal to find that many
peripherals can not be purchased immediately after the announ
ment of a new computer model. This means that a late deliver
of the whole system must be anticipated, or that the user tak
delivery on the basic computer and await later delivery of pe
ipherals.

By the very nature of on-line computer systems, peripher
are often purchased from manufacturers other than the compute
manufacturer. This leads to the difficulties of the communic
tions triangle that have often been mentioned, and to the dif
culties of marrying two pieces of equipment that were never o
iginally intended to be linked.

CHAPTER 12

CONVERSATIONAL LANGUAGES

1.0   WHAT, WHERE, AND WHY?

   The conversational language represents a major advance in
both computer programming and the ease of use of computers.
These languages provide a means of programming computers which
eliminates much of the detail of more typical programming languages.   The instructions of conversational languages tend to
be quite English-like in nature--so much so, that they are to
a large extent self-teaching.
   Some of the conversational languages presently available
are AID, BASIC, CAL,ESI, FOCAL, JOSS, and TELCOMP.   Of these
BASIC is probably the most widely used at the present time.
The first two languages were JOSS and BASIC.   JOSS was developed at the RAND corporation and BASIC was developed at Dart-
mouth College.
   Where and when are conversational languages used?   Conversational languages are designed to fill a void that has existed
for some time in the spectrum of computations.   There are a
large class of problems which are too time consumming or too
tedious to perform on a desk calculator or slide rule.   However,
the answers sought are needed on a one-time basis, or it is felt
that they are not important enough to merit the time and expense
of having them programmed and run on a larger computer system.
Another class of problems are those solved often enough to
justify the expense of programming them on a larger computer
system, but of such a nature that there is little value in
performing a computation if the answers cannot be obtained on
a very short time basis.   To fill requirements of this type,
the user needs a terminal to a computer that is in his immediate
work area, and which is so easy to program that one can use it
effectively even after months of disuse.
   Some example applications of conversational languages are:
an engineer evaluating complicated formulas from engineering
handbooks, a scientist performing simple model calculations or
data reduction, and a businessman working up some numbers for
the preparation of a proposal.

This brings us to the why. What are the advantages and disadvantages of using conversational languages and terminals? There are a number of advantages. First, conversational languages are easy to learn. This is primarily because they have English-like instructions, and there is not a wealth of procedural details to be memorized. This latter makes it possible to use programs very infrequently and still use them efficiently. Furthermore, one does not need a long and cumbersome manual because the quick interaction time of a conversational language permits operational questions to be answered by simple trial and error. If a question arises about the legality of an operation the user simply tries it and the computer either performs his request or gives him an error message.

Typically conversational languages are operated from Teletype terminals. As this discussion progresses it will be seen that a user can, in one setting, write the program, debug it and obtain his answers. Also it is important to note that the settings are not hours in length but often are only tens of minutes. A final important point is the ease of installing the Teletype terminals. In the case of the on-line computer, the terminal already exists and in the case of purchasing computer time elsewhere they are easy to install. This is covered in more detail below.

Now what about the disadvantages of conversational languages? The disadvantages are mostly equipmental in nature. The most fundamental one is the limited input/output capability of the typical terminal. One cannot easily run problems that require a large amount of input data and/or print a large amount of output data. Limited output capability will probably not persist much longer. Equipment is now coming on the market with cathode-ray-tube displays which provide a very fast output capability. If one needs a printed copy, devices are also coming on the market which print a copy of anything on the cathode-ray-tube screen.

2.0 AVAILABILITY

There are two entirely different situations. First, if the user has access to an on-line computer system, then there is a good chance that he has the wherewithal to use conversational languages. In the second case the user must purchase the use of a computer system from a time-sharing firm.

Several on-line computers are now offered with conversational interpreters. This is an obvious plus factor when one is choosing an on-line computer system. To use a conversational language on an on-line computer is as simple as loading the interpreter, i.e., as simple as loading any other program. Because conversational languages typically operate with Teletype terminals no extra equipment is required. However, some of the conversational interpreters that are now available for

on-line computers do not strictly limit one to using Teletype
terminals. Some allow the user to add functions which access
other equipment attached to the on-line computer--for example,
oscilloscope displays.

The second means of obtaining access to conversational
languages is to purchase time from one of the many time-sharing
systems that are now scattered throughout the United States.
Again, almost all of these commercial services use Teletype
terminals which are connected to the computer from the user's
office by a voice grade telephone line. Many of these systems
can accommodate the order of 100 terminals.

Thus, in addition to the Teletype terminal, one needs a
means of linking to the telephone line. There are two primary
ways of doing this. One is to install a data modem. The data
modem serves the purpose of taking the digital data from the
Teletype terminal and changing it to a form suitable for the
telephone line. In the past, this has been done by converting
the data to a series of tones, i.e., frequencies which are
coded for transmission of the data. However, much of the telephone network is now being converted to transferring data in
digital form. In either event it is the function of the data
modem to transform the data from the Teletype terminal to a
form that is commensurate with the conventions of the telephone
company.

Another method of linking the Teletype terminal to the
telephone line is to use an accoustic coupler. The accoustic
coupler serves the same function as the data modem, i.e. the
transformation of Teletype data to a form suitable for telephone
line transmission. It may be used to, in effect, convert an
ordinary telephone handset to a data modem. The accoustic
coupler has two circular holes which receive the sending and
receiving end of the hand portion of a telephone set. When the
user dials the time-shared computer and receives an answer in
the form of a tone, he simply drops the telephone receiver into the accoustic coupler and the link has been made. The primary advantage of the accoustic coupler is mobility. Since the
coupler can be built directly into the Teletype terminal, the
terminal may be put on a small set of wheels and used anywhere
a telephone is available. A data modem may also be directly
mounted into the Teletype unit but it is permanently attached
to a wall or other fixture. The Teletype terminal can be purchased or leased. The coupler and the data modem can also be
purchased, and in some instances leased.

If a single organization has several terminals operating
to a time-shared, remote computer system, the terminals are
often multiplexed into one telephone line. That is switching
equipment is placed at the user end of the line to multiplex
all Teletype terminals into this single line. In some instances
the user may even choose to lease the telephone line. This is
more economical than paying normal telephone transmission rates
when terminal activity exceeds some threshold usage.

What are the costs of using conversational languages?
In the case of the on-line computer, the cost is negligible,
unless the system has been bought specifically for this type
of use. For the remote system charges are usually based on
the terminal hours with additional charges for using extra
peripherals at the central computer such as line printers,
magnetic tape, and disk. Also extra charges are often made
for magnetic core storage above some minimum amount. Charges
for using a time-shared system range from the order of $5 to
$20 per terminal hour*, and depend upon the expansiveness of
the time-shared computer system and the method of billing for
the extra charges. The extra charges are controllable to some
extent in that they normally represent the use of more than a
basic block of computer peripherals, or more than some basic
unit of computer memory.

3.0   UTILIZATION

In the chapter "Editing, Assembling and Debugging" considerable space was devoted to the edit-assemble-debug cycle.
If one replaces the assemble portion of this cycle with a
compile or interpret operation for the higher level languages,
most of the comments of that chapter are applicable. It is
this cycle that determines some of the most important factors
of any computer language. These include: ease of use of the
language, time required to get programs running, and the effort
required to learn how to use the system. Table I of the chapter
"Assembling, Editing and Debugging" shows a typical edit-assembl
debug cycle for an assembler language. Table I of this chapter
shows the same cycle for a conversational language. The contrast is striking.
Turn now to Table I of this chapter. The user first loads
the interpreter of the conversational language into the computer
He may then load a program previously written in this language,
or he may want to write a new program. At this point the user
enters the cycle. Note that the edit and debug steps are combined. Although these are different activities, one uses exactly the same commands to carry on both activities. Thus, it
is really a matter of viewpoint. The fourth step is the actual
execution of the program itself. At this point, one either receives answers and/or error messages.
Look again at the cycle shown in Table I, but let us describe it in a more narrative manner. First, the user sits
down at the Teletype terminal and calls for the conversational
interpreter to be loaded. If the program has already been

---

*The terminal hours are computed by simply determining the time
 from which the telephone is dialed until the user hangs up the
 telephone receiver.

Table I. Steps in the use of a conversational language.

1. Load Interpreter.
2. Load Source Program.

_____EDIT/DEBUG_____
3. Generate and/or Edit Source Program.

_____EXECUTE_____
4. Receive Answers and/or Error Messages.

written, he reads it into the computer. The user's program
might be stored at the remote computer, if he is using one of
the commercial time-shared systems, or the user may simply
have it punched on a piece of paper tape which is read into
the Teletype terminal.

Assume that the program has not been written; then the
next step is to enter the program into the computer. At any
time mistakes can be corrected by simply retyping any instructions containing errors. Once the program has been entered
to the user's satisfaction, he gives the command for the program to be executed. The program is immediately executed and
if the interpreter finds no errors an answer is printed. The
user receives messages (diagnostics) if errors are detected,
and may get both answers and errors depending upon the conditions. At this point, the user simply finds the source of the
error, retypes the statement or statements containing the errors,
and says, "execute it again".

The important thing to note from this narrative is that
a program (the interpreter) has only been loaded once. Also,
that the user moves back and forth from the edit/debug mode to
the execute mode in a very quick and easy manner. There is no
sharp demarkation between the editing and assembling process
and the execution and debugging process. Since answers and
error messages are essentially instantaneous, most programs are
written at the terminal in one setting and the user leaves with
the answer to his original question.

4.0 EXAMPLE PROGRAMS

The program examples are in the ESI language. This language was chosen because the author has a larger collection of
programs written in this language than other conversational
languages with which he has worked. It was felt that it is
important to give programs which have been debugged and therefore all the programs, with the exception of 4.5, are guaranteed
to the extent that there has been no transcription error from

the original computer printout. Once one of the conversational languages have been mastered, it is not difficult to learn any other.

In the following program examples, it should be noted that slashes are placed through the zeros rather than the 0's. This was the convention on the Teletype terminal used to list the original programs.

4.1 Finding Square Roots

The Newton iteration method for finding roots is used. The program is as follows:

```
9.Ø5   DEMAND A.
9.1    SET O=A/1Ø.
9.2    SET N=(A/O+O)/2.
9.3    IF ABS ((N-O)/N) < 1E-4, TO STEP 9.6.
9.4    SET O=N.
9.5    TO STEP 9.2.
9.6    TYPE A, N.
9.7    END.
```

Note that each line of the program must have a number, and that these numbers are in sequential order. It is important to remember this because the computer automatically arranges the lines in an ascending order regardless of the order they are typed by the user.

A line can be inserted by choosing any intermediate line number. For example, if the user were to enter a line with the number 9.12, it would be placed between lines 9.1 and 9.2. If the user were to continue and enter a new line with the number 9.16, the computer would place it between line 9.12 and 9.2. It should be apparent now why the line numbers are to be in ascending order, and why the computer automatically arranges them in this manner.

Line 9.05. The command DEMAND A in effect says "read the value of A from the keyboard".

Line 9.1. This demonstrates the English-like nature of the conversational languages. This instruction says, "set the variable O equal to the value of the variable A divided by 10".

Line 9.3. Again one can easily determine what this command does. If the absolute value of N-O divided by N is less than 1E-4 (1E-4 = 10^{-4} = 0.0001), go to line 9.6. If this condition is not true, go to line 9.4 (the next line).

Line 9.5. Go back to line 9.2.

Line 9.6. Type the value of A and N. A is the original number and N is its square root.

Line 9.7. The rules of ESI say that all programs must be terminated with this statement.

Suppose the program is yet to be entered into the computer. The user first enters the program, just as it appears here, on the Teletype keyboard. Any editing is done along the lines that have already been indicated for inserting and modifying individual construction. When the user is satisfied he types the command "GO". This instructs the interpreter to execute the program. If any programming errors are detected, error messages are typed on the Teletype terminal. The user then edits out the errors and again gives the command "GO". If no errors are found, the program is executed and the values of A and N are typed.

It should be easy to see that such a program can be written, debugged and running in perhaps ten minutes.

4.2 Determinant and Minors of Matrices

This program is used to find the determinant and the three minors of a 3 x 3 matrix.

```
1.Ø5 TYPE "A ROUTINE TO FIND THE MINORS AND".
1.Ø7 TYPE "DETERMINANTS OF 3 BY 3 MATRICES".
1.1  SET N=3.
1.15 SET M=3.
1.2  SET I=1.
1.22 TYPE "ENTER MATRIX ELEMENTS 11 12 13 21 22 23 31 32 33".
1.25 FOR K=1(1)M, DEMAND A [I,K].
1.3  SET I=I+1.
1.35 IF I>N, TO STEP 1.45.
1.4  TO STEP 1.25.
1.45 SET C=A [1,1]*(A [2,2]*A [3,3]-A [3,2]*A [2,3]).
1.47 SET E=A [1,3]*(A [2,1]*A [3,2]-A [2,2]*A [3,1]).
1.5  SET F=A [1,2]*(A [2,1]*A [3,3]-A [2,3]*A [3,1]).
1.52 SET D=C+E-F.
1.54 TYPE "MINORS ARE "C" "E" "F" ".
1.56 TYPE "DETERMINANT IS "D" ".
1.58 END.
```

Line 1.05. If the type command is followed by an entry enclosed in quotation marks, everything within the quotation marks is typed, including the spaces, when the program is executed. Thus, after the user types GO and line 1.05 is executed, A ROUTINE TO FIND THE MINORS AND is typed on <u>one</u> line.

Line 1.07. This instruction causes another message to be typed on a <u>new</u> line; DETERMINANTS OF 3 BY 3 MATRICES.

Line 1.25. With the programming languages ESI subscripts are indicated with brackets. Thus, A [I,K] is equivalent to A_{IK}. A is the matrix which is to be read into the computer for the computations. The statement FOR K=1(1)M says, "for values of K from one to M in increments of one".

It should be noted that the increment which is the number enclosed in the parentheses can also be fractional and/or negative.

Line 1.45. The * is used to indicate the multiply operation.

Line 1.54. Any quantities contained by quotation marks
within another set of quotation marks are considered to be
variables. Suppose that C equals 1.26, E equals 1.29, and
F equals 2.71. Then, the execution of this line results in
the following being typed on the Teletype terminal:
MINORS ARE 1.26 1.29 2.71.

4.3   Least Squares Fit to a Straight Line

The data is assumed to be estimated by the straight line

$$Y = Z + GX$$

Given a series of measured values X_K, Y_K find the value
for Z and G that best fit the data.

The least square technique is a minimization technique.
If there are N pairs of X_K, Y_K values measured then the "best"
values for Z and G are:

$$Z = \frac{\sum Y_K \sum X_K^2 - \sum X_K Y_K \sum X_K}{N \sum X_K^2 - (\sum X_K)^2}$$

$$G = \frac{N \sum X_K Y_K - \sum Y_K \sum X_K}{N \sum X_K^2 - (\sum X_K)^2}$$

The following program computes Z and G.

```
1.Ø1   TYPE "A ROUTINE TO DO LEAST SQUARES FITS TO A STRAIGHT LINE
1.Ø2   TYPE "N IS THE NUMBER OF DATA POINTS".
1.Ø3   TYPE " ".
1.Ø4   TYPE " ".
1.1    DEMAND N.
1.2    FOR I=1(1)N, DEMAND X [ I ] .
1.3    FOR I=1(1)N, DEMAND Y [ I ] .
1.4    FOR I=1(1)4, SET A [ I ] =Ø.
1.5    FOR K=1(1)N, SET A [ 1 ] =A [ 1 ] +Y [ K ] .
1.52   FOR K=1(1)N, SET A [ 2 ] =A [ 2 ] +X [ K ]↑2.
1.54   FOR K=1(1)N, SET A [ 3 ] =A [ 3 ] +X [ K ] *Y [ K ] .
1.56   FOR K=1(1)N, SET A [ 4 ] =A [ 4 ] +X [ K ] .
1.58   SET D=N*A [ 2 ] -A [ 4 ]↑2.
1.6    SET Z=(A [ 1 ] *A [ 2 ] -A [ 3 ] *A [ 4 ] )/D.
1.62   SET G=(A [ 3 ] *N-A [ 1 ] *A [ 4 ] )/D.
1.64   TYPE " ".
```

```
1.66   TYPE " ".
1.68   TYPE "SLOPE (GAIN)="G" ".
1.7    TYPE " ".
1.72   TYPE "Y INTERCEPT (ZERO) = "Z" ".
1.74   END.
```

Line 1.03. This instruction causes one space to be printed. It actually is a trick to cause the teleprinter to roll the paper up one space.

Line 1.2. The instruction of this line reads in all the values of X_I.

Line 1.5. This line calculates $\sum Y_K$.

4.4   Fourier Transforms of Real Arrays

This program calculates the discreet Fourier transform of real numbers. Both the real and the imaginary parts of the Fourier transform are computed.

```
1.1    DEMAND N.
1.16   SET M=N-1.
1.17   FOR K=Ø(1)M, DEMAND X [K].
1.18   SET P=6.283185.
1.22   SET B=P/N.
1.24   FOR K=Ø(1)M, DO PART 2.
1.26   TO STEP 1.1.
1.28   END.
2.1    SET S=Ø.
2.11   SET I=Ø.
2.12   FOR J=Ø(1)M, DO PART 3.
2.13   SET I=-I.
2.16   TYPE "R("K")="S" I="I" ".
2.18   END.
3.12   SET E=B*J*K.
3.14   SET S=S+X [J] *COS(E).
3.15   SET I=I+X [J] *SIN(E).
3.16   END.
```

First note that there are three separate parts to this program. Each is uniquely identified by the digit to the left of the decimal point. In this particular case part 2 and part 3 may be thought of as subroutines of part 1.

Line 1.18. The variable P is equal to two pi.

Line 1.24. The instruction of this line causes part 2 to be executed M+1 times with values of K ranging from zero through M.

Line 1.26. This instruction returns the program to line 1.1 so that data may be entered for a new transform computation.

Line 2.16. R is the real part of the Kth increment of the Fourier transform. I is the corresponding imaginary part.

Line 3.14. Most conversational languages provide the
ability to evaluate functions. The function used here is for
evaluating cosines. In this case E is the angle in radians.

4.5 An Inventory System

This program is to be used to maintain an inventory. Each
item in the inventory is identified by a part number. Part
numbers run from one through 100. The program has three functions. The user can add or delete items of a given part number, can have the complete inventory printed out, and can ask
for the number of items with any given part number. The user
can specify which function by typing a 1,2, or 3 when the program is first started.

```
1.Ø5   TYPE "CHANGE INVENTORY(1),INTERROGATE(2),PRINT INVENTORY(3)
1.1    DEMAND N.
1.12   IF N=1, TO STEP 2.1.
1.14   IF N=2, TO STEP 3.1.
1.16   IF N=3, TO STEP 4.1.
1.18   TO STEP 1.1.
1.2    END.

2.1    TYPE "PART NUMBER", DEMAND P.
2.12   TYPE "CHANGE OF INVENTORY", DEMAND C.
2.14   SET I [P] =I [P] +C.
2.16   TYPE "CURRENT INVENTORY IS "I [P] " ".
2.18   TO STEP 1.1.
2.2    END.

3.1    TYPE "PART NUMBER", DEMAND P.
3.2    TO STEP 2.16.
3.4    END.

4.1    TYPE "PART NO.  INVENTORY".
4.2    FOR K=1(1)1ØØ, TYPE "K"      "I [K] " ".
4.3    TO STEP 1.1.
4.4    END.
```

Line 1.05. This line tells the user which functions
correspond to the numbers one through three.
Line 1.1. This line reads the number which specifies the
function to be performed.
Line 1.12. If a one was entered in line 1.1 this line sends
the program to part 2 where inventory is changed.
Lines 1.14 and 1.16. Similar to line 1.12 these send the
program to parts 3 and 4 for interrogation and an inventory
listing respectively.
Line 2.1. Tells the user to enter the part number, and
reads the part number.

Line 2.12. Asks for the inventory change. This may be a positive or negative number.

Line 2.14. Adjusts the inventory. Note the inventory is the array I. The subscript P is the part number and the value of I_P is the number of items with the part number P.

Line 2.16. Types the current value of I_P.

Line 4.1. Types two column headings.

Line 4.2. Types a complete list of part numbers and the number of items with each part number.

APPENDIX I

TABLES RELATING TO THE BINARY, OCTAL, DECIMAL AND HEXADECIMAL NUMBER SYSTEMS

	0	1
0	0	1
1	1	10

Binary
Addition
Table

	0	1	2	3	4	5	6	7
0	0	1	2	3	4	5	6	7
1	1	2	3	4	5	6	7	10
2	2	3	4	5	6	7	10	11
3	3	4	5	6	7	10	11	12
4	4	5	6	7	10	11	12	13
5	5	6	7	10	11	12	13	14
6	6	7	10	11	12	13	14	15
7	7	10	11	12	13	14	15	16

Octal Addition Table

	0	1	2	3	4	5	6	7	8	9
0	0	1	2	3	4	5	6	7	8	9
1	1	2	3	4	5	6	7	8	9	10
2	2	3	4	5	6	7	8	9	10	11
3	3	4	5	6	7	8	9	10	11	12
4	4	5	6	7	8	9	10	11	12	13
5	5	6	7	8	9	10	11	12	13	14
6	6	7	8	9	10	11	12	13	14	15
7	7	8	9	10	11	12	13	14	15	16
8	8	9	10	11	12	13	14	15	16	17
9	9	10	11	12	13	14	15	16	17	18

Decimal Addition Table

	0	1	2	3	4	5	6	7	8	9	A	B	C	D	E	F
0	0	1	2	3	4	5	6	7	8	9	A	B	C	D	E	F
1	1	2	3	4	5	6	7	8	9	A	B	C	D	E	F	10
2	2	3	4	5	6	7	8	9	A	B	C	D	E	F	10	11
3	3	4	5	6	7	8	9	A	B	C	D	E	F	10	11	12
4	4	5	6	7	8	9	A	B	C	D	E	F	10	11	12	13
5	5	6	7	8	9	A	B	C	D	E	F	10	11	12	13	14
6	6	7	8	9	A	B	C	D	E	F	10	11	12	13	14	15
7	7	8	9	A	B	C	D	E	F	10	11	12	13	14	15	16
8	8	9	A	B	C	D	E	F	10	11	12	13	14	15	16	17
9	9	A	B	C	D	E	F	10	11	12	13	14	15	16	17	18
A	A	B	C	D	E	F	10	11	12	13	14	15	16	17	18	19
B	B	C	D	E	F	10	11	12	13	14	15	16	17	18	19	1A
C	C	D	E	F	10	11	12	13	14	15	16	17	18	19	1A	1B
D	D	E	F	10	11	12	13	14	15	16	17	18	19	1A	1B	1C
E	E	F	10	11	12	13	14	15	16	17	18	19	1A	1B	1C	1D
F	F	10	11	12	13	14	15	16	17	18	19	1A	1B	1C	1D	1E

Hexadecimal Addition Table

TABLES RELATING TO THE BINARY, OCTAL, DECIMAL
AND HEXADECIMAL NUMBER SYSTEMS (Continued)

One's and Two's Complements

Binary Integer	0	1
One's Complement	1	0
Two's Complement	0	1

Seven's and Eight's Complements

Octal Integer	0	1	2	3	4	5	6	7
Seven's Complement	7	6	5	4	3	2	1	0
Eight's Complement	0	7	6	5	4	3	2	1

Nine's and Ten's Complements

Decimal Integer	0	1	2	3	4	5	6	7	8	9
Nine's Complement	9	8	7	6	5	4	3	2	1	0
Ten's Complement	0	9	8	7	6	5	4	3	2	1

Fifteen's and Sixteen's Complements

Hexadecimal Integer	0	1	2	3	4	5	6	7	8	9	A	B	C	D	E	F
Fifteen's Complement	F	E	D	C	B	A	9	8	7	6	5	4	3	2	1	0
Sixteen's Complement	0	F	E	D	C	B	A	9	8	7	6	5	4	3	2	1

TABLES RELATING TO THE BINARY, OCTAL, DECIMAL
AND HEXADECIMAL NUMBER SYSTEMS (Continued)

	0	1
0	0	0
1	0	1

Binary
Multipli-
cation Table

	0	1	2	3	4	5	6	7
0	0	0	0	0	0	0	0	0
1	0	1	2	3	4	5	6	7
2	0	2	4	6	10	12	14	16
3	0	3	6	11	14	17	22	25
4	0	4	10	14	20	24	30	34
5	0	5	12	17	24	31	36	43
6	0	6	14	22	30	36	44	52
7	0	7	16	25	34	43	52	61

Octal Multiplication Table

	0	1	2	3	4	5	6	7	8	9
0	0	0	0	0	0	0	0	0	0	0
1	0	1	2	3	4	5	6	7	8	9
2	0	2	4	6	8	10	12	14	16	18
3	0	3	6	9	12	15	18	21	24	27
4	0	4	8	12	16	20	24	28	32	36
5	0	5	10	15	20	25	30	35	40	45
6	0	6	12	18	24	30	36	42	48	54
7	0	7	14	21	28	35	42	49	56	63
8	0	8	16	24	32	40	48	56	64	72
9	0	9	18	27	36	45	54	63	72	81

Decimal Multiplication Table

	0	1	2	3	4	5	6	7	8	9	A	B	C	D	E	F
0	0	0	0	0	0	0	0	0	0	0	0	0	0	0	0	0
1	0	1	2	3	4	5	6	7	8	9	A	B	C	D	E	F
2	0	2	4	6	8	A	C	E	10	12	14	16	18	1A	1C	1E
3	0	3	6	9	C	F	12	15	18	1B	1E	21	24	27	2A	20
4	0	4	8	C	10	14	18	1C	20	24	28	2C	30	34	38	3C
5	0	5	A	F	14	19	1E	23	28	2D	32	37	3C	41	46	4B
6	0	6	C	12	18	1E	24	2A	30	36	3C	42	48	4E	54	5A
7	0	7	E	15	1C	23	2A	31	38	3F	46	40	54	5B	62	69
8	0	8	10	18	20	28	30	38	40	48	50	58	60	68	70	78
9	0	9	12	1B	24	2D	36	3F	48	51	5A	63	6C	75	7E	87
A	0	A	14	1E	28	32	3C	46	50	5A	64	6E	78	82	8C	96
B	0	B	16	21	2C	37	42	4D	58	63	6E	79	84	8F	9A	A5
C	0	C	18	24	30	3C	48	54	60	6C	78	84	90	9C	A8	B4
D	0	D	1A	27	34	41	4E	5B	68	75	82	8F	9C	A9	B6	C3
E	0	E	1C	2A	38	46	54	62	70	7E	8C	9A	A8	B6	C4	D2
F	0	F	1E	2D	3C	4B	5A	69	78	87	96	A5	B4	C3	D2	E1

Hexadecimal Multiplication Table

APPENDIX II

DECIMAL-OCTAL-HEXADECIMAL CONVERSION TABLES

These tables give the octal and hexadecimal equivalents
for all the decimal numbers from zero through 8,409. To conserve space only every fifth decimal number is printed. The
top-most column headings allow one to determine the decimal
numbers not listed. For example, the octal and hexadecimal
equivalents of decimal 582 are 1106 and 246 respectively.
Likewise, the equivalents of 587 are 1113 and 24B.

DEC	0/5 OCT	HEX	1/6 OCT	HEX	2/7 OCT	HEX	3/8 OCT	HEX	4/9 OCT	HEX
0	0	0	1	1	2	2	3	3	4	4
5	5	5	6	6	7	7	10	8	11	9
10	12	A	13	B	14	C	15	D	16	E
15	17	F	20	10	21	11	22	12	23	13
20	24	14	25	15	26	16	27	17	30	18
25	31	19	32	1A	33	1B	34	1C	35	1D
30	36	1E	37	1F	40	20	41	21	42	22
35	43	23	44	24	45	25	46	26	47	27
40	50	28	51	29	52	2A	53	2B	54	2C
45	55	2D	56	2E	57	2F	60	30	61	31
50	62	32	63	33	64	34	65	35	66	36
55	67	37	70	38	71	39	72	3A	73	3B
60	74	3C	75	3D	76	3E	77	3F	100	40
65	101	41	102	42	103	43	104	44	105	45
70	106	46	107	47	110	48	111	49	112	4A
75	113	4B	114	4C	115	4D	116	4E	117	4F
80	120	50	121	51	122	52	123	53	124	54
85	125	55	126	56	127	57	130	58	131	59
90	132	5A	133	5B	134	5C	135	5D	136	5E
95	137	5F	140	60	141	61	142	62	143	63
100	144	64	145	65	146	66	147	67	150	68
105	151	69	152	6A	153	6B	154	6C	155	6D
110	156	6E	157	6F	160	70	161	71	162	72
115	163	73	164	74	165	75	166	76	167	77
120	170	78	171	79	172	7A	173	7B	174	7C
125	175	7D	176	7E	177	7F	200	80	201	81
130	202	82	203	83	204	84	205	85	206	86
135	207	87	210	88	211	89	212	8A	213	8B
140	214	8C	215	8D	216	8E	217	8F	220	90
145	221	91	222	92	223	93	224	94	225	95
150	226	96	227	97	230	98	231	99	232	9A
155	233	9B	234	9C	235	9D	236	9E	237	9F
160	240	A0	241	A1	242	A2	243	A3	244	A4
165	245	A5	246	A6	247	A7	250	A8	251	A9
170	252	AA	253	AB	254	AC	255	AD	256	AE
175	257	AF	260	B0	261	B1	262	B2	263	B3
180	264	B4	265	B5	266	B6	267	B7	270	B8
185	271	B9	272	BA	273	BB	274	BC	275	BD
190	276	BE	277	BF	300	C0	301	C1	302	C2
195	303	C3	304	C4	305	C5	306	C6	307	C7
200	310	C8	311	C9	312	CA	313	CB	314	CC
205	315	CD	316	CE	317	CF	320	D0	321	D1
210	322	D2	323	D3	324	D4	325	D5	326	D6
215	327	D7	330	D8	331	D9	332	DA	333	DB
220	334	DC	335	DD	336	DE	337	DF	340	E0
225	341	E1	342	E2	343	E3	344	E4	345	E5
230	346	E6	347	E7	350	E8	351	E9	352	EA
235	353	EB	354	EC	355	ED	356	EE	357	EF
240	360	F0	361	F1	362	F2	363	F3	364	F4
245	365	F5	366	F6	367	F7	370	F8	371	F9
250	372	FA	373	FB	374	FC	375	FD	376	FE
255	377	FF	400	100	401	101	402	102	403	103
260	404	104	405	105	406	106	407	107	410	108
265	411	109	412	10A	413	10B	414	10C	415	10D
270	416	10E	417	10F	420	110	421	111	422	112
275	423	113	424	114	425	115	426	116	427	117
280	430	118	431	119	432	11A	433	11B	434	11C
285	435	11D	436	11E	437	11F	440	120	441	121

	0/5		1/6		2/7		3/8		4/9	
DEC	OCT	HEX	OCT	HEX	OCT	HEX	OCT	HEX	OCT	HEX
290	442	122	443	123	444	124	445	125	446	126
295	447	127	450	128	451	129	452	12A	453	12B
300	454	12C	455	12D	456	12E	457	12F	460	130
305	461	131	462	132	463	133	464	134	465	135
310	466	136	467	137	470	138	471	139	472	13A
315	473	13B	474	13C	475	13D	476	13E	477	13F
320	500	140	501	141	502	142	503	143	504	144
325	505	145	506	146	507	147	510	148	511	149
330	512	14A	513	14B	514	14C	515	14D	516	14E
335	517	14F	520	150	521	151	522	152	523	153
340	524	154	525	155	526	156	527	157	530	158
345	531	159	532	15A	533	15B	534	15C	535	15D
350	536	15E	537	15F	540	160	541	161	542	162
355	543	163	544	164	545	165	546	166	547	167
360	550	168	551	169	552	16A	553	16B	554	16C
365	555	16D	556	16E	557	16F	560	170	561	171
370	562	172	563	173	564	174	565	175	566	176
375	567	177	570	178	571	179	572	17A	573	17B
380	574	17C	575	17D	576	17E	577	17F	600	180
385	601	181	602	182	603	183	604	184	605	185
390	606	186	607	187	610	188	611	189	612	18A
395	613	18B	614	18C	615	18D	616	18E	617	18F
400	620	190	621	191	622	192	623	193	624	194
405	625	195	626	196	627	197	630	198	631	199
410	632	19A	633	19B	634	19C	635	19D	636	19E
415	637	19F	640	1A0	641	1A1	642	1A2	643	1A3
420	644	1A4	645	1A5	646	1A6	647	1A7	650	1A8
425	651	1A9	652	1AA	653	1AB	654	1AC	655	1AD
430	656	1AE	657	1AF	660	1B0	661	1B1	662	1B2
435	663	1B3	664	1B4	665	1B5	666	1B6	667	1B7
440	670	1B8	671	1B9	672	1BA	673	1BB	674	1BC
445	675	1BD	676	1BE	677	1BF	700	1C0	701	1C1
450	702	1C2	703	1C3	704	1C4	705	1C5	706	1C6
455	707	1C7	710	1C8	711	1C9	712	1CA	713	1CB
460	714	1CC	715	1CD	716	1CE	717	1CF	720	1D0
465	721	1D1	722	1D2	723	1D3	724	1D4	725	1D5
470	726	1D6	727	1D7	730	1D8	731	1D9	732	1DA
475	733	1DB	734	1DC	735	1DD	736	1DE	737	1DF
480	740	1E0	741	1E1	742	1E2	743	1E3	744	1E4
485	745	1E5	746	1E6	747	1E7	750	1E8	751	1E9
490	752	1EA	753	1EB	754	1EC	755	1ED	756	1EE
495	757	1EF	760	1F0	761	1F1	762	1F2	763	1F3
500	764	1F4	765	1F5	766	1F6	767	1F7	770	1F8
505	771	1F9	772	1FA	773	1FB	774	1FC	775	1FD
510	776	1FE	777	1FF	1000	200	1001	201	1002	202
515	1003	203	1004	204	1005	205	1006	206	1007	207
520	1010	208	1011	209	1012	20A	1013	20B	1014	20C
525	1015	20D	1016	20E	1017	20F	1020	210	1021	211
530	1022	212	1023	213	1024	214	1025	215	1026	216
535	1027	217	1030	218	1031	219	1032	21A	1033	21B
540	1034	21C	1035	21D	1036	21E	1037	21F	1040	220
545	1041	221	1042	222	1043	223	1044	224	1045	225
550	1046	226	1047	227	1050	228	1051	229	1052	22A
555	1053	22B	1054	22C	1055	22D	1056	22E	1057	22F
560	1060	230	1061	231	1062	232	1063	233	1064	234
565	1065	235	1066	236	1067	237	1070	238	1071	239
570	1072	23A	1073	23B	1074	23C	1075	23D	1076	23E
575	1077	23F	1100	240	1101	241	1102	242	1103	243

DEC	0/5 OCT	HEX	1/6 OCT	HEX	2/7 OCT	HEX	3/8 OCT	HEX	4/9 OCT	HEX
580	1104	244	1105	245	1106	246	1107	247	1110	248
585	1111	249	1112	24A	1113	24B	1114	24C	1115	24D
590	1116	24E	1117	24F	1120	250	1121	251	1122	252
595	1123	253	1124	254	1125	255	1126	256	1127	257
600	1130	258	1131	259	1132	25A	1133	25B	1134	25C
605	1135	25D	1136	25E	1137	25F	1140	260	1141	261
610	1142	262	1143	263	1144	264	1145	265	1146	266
615	1147	267	1150	268	1151	269	1152	26A	1153	26B
620	1154	26C	1155	26D	1156	26E	1157	26F	1160	270
625	1161	271	1162	272	1163	273	1164	274	1165	275
630	1166	276	1167	277	1170	278	1171	279	1172	27A
635	1173	27B	1174	27C	1175	27D	1176	27E	1177	27F
640	1200	280	1201	281	1202	282	1203	283	1204	284
645	1205	285	1206	286	1207	287	1210	288	1211	289
650	1212	28A	1213	28B	1214	28C	1215	28D	1216	28E
655	1217	28F	1220	290	1221	291	1222	292	1223	293
660	1224	294	1225	295	1226	296	1227	297	1230	298
665	1231	299	1232	29A	1233	29B	1234	29C	1235	29D
670	1236	29E	1237	29F	1240	2A0	1241	2A1	1242	2A2
675	1243	2A3	1244	2A4	1245	2A5	1246	2A6	1247	2A7
680	1250	2A8	1251	2A9	1252	2AA	1253	2AB	1254	2AC
685	1255	2AD	1256	2AE	1257	2AF	1260	2B0	1261	2B1
690	1262	2B2	1263	2B3	1264	2B4	1265	2B5	1266	2B6
695	1267	2B7	1270	2B8	1271	2B9	1272	2BA	1273	2BB
700	1274	2BC	1275	2BD	1276	2BE	1277	2BF	1300	2C0
705	1301	2C1	1302	2C2	1303	2C3	1304	2C4	1305	2C5
710	1306	2C6	1307	2C7	1310	2C8	1311	2C9	1312	2CA
715	1313	2CB	1314	2CC	1315	2CD	1316	2CE	1317	2CF
720	1320	2D0	1321	2D1	1322	2D2	1323	2D3	1324	2D4
725	1325	2D5	1326	2D6	1327	2D7	1330	2D8	1331	2D9
730	1332	2DA	1333	2DB	1334	2DC	1335	2DD	1336	2DE
735	1337	2DF	1340	2E0	1341	2E1	1342	2E2	1343	2E3
740	1344	2E4	1345	2E5	1346	2E6	1347	2E7	1350	2E8
745	1351	2E9	1352	2EA	1353	2EB	1354	2EC	1355	2ED
750	1356	2EE	1357	2EF	1360	2F0	1361	2F1	1362	2F2
755	1363	2F3	1364	2F4	1365	2F5	1366	2F6	1367	2F7
760	1370	2F8	1371	2F9	1372	2FA	1373	2FB	1374	2FC
765	1375	2FD	1376	2FE	1377	2FF	1400	300	1401	301
770	1402	302	1403	303	1404	304	1405	305	1406	306
775	1407	307	1410	308	1411	309	1412	30A	1413	30B
780	1414	30C	1415	30D	1416	30E	1417	30F	1420	310
785	1421	311	1422	312	1423	313	1424	314	1425	315
790	1426	316	1427	317	1430	318	1431	319	1432	31A
795	1433	31B	1434	31C	1435	31D	1436	31E	1437	31F
800	1440	320	1441	321	1442	322	1443	323	1444	324
805	1445	325	1446	326	1447	327	1450	328	1451	329
810	1452	32A	1453	32B	1454	32C	1455	32D	1456	32E
815	1457	32F	1460	330	1461	331	1462	332	1463	333
820	1464	334	1465	335	1466	336	1467	337	1470	338
825	1471	339	1472	33A	1473	33B	1474	33C	1475	33D
830	1476	33E	1477	33F	1500	340	1501	341	1502	342
835	1503	343	1504	344	1505	345	1506	346	1507	347
840	1510	348	1511	349	1512	34A	1513	34B	1514	34C
845	1515	34D	1516	34E	1517	34F	1520	350	1521	351
850	1522	352	1523	353	1524	354	1525	355	1526	356
855	1527	357	1530	358	1531	359	1532	35A	1533	35B
860	1534	35C	1535	35D	1536	35E	1537	35F	1540	360
865	1541	361	1542	362	1543	363	1544	364	1545	365

	0/5		1/6		2/7		3/8		4/9	
DEC	OCT	HEX	OCT	HEX	OCT	HEX	OCT	HEX	OCT	HEX
870	1546	366	1547	367	1550	368	1551	369	1552	36A
875	1553	36B	1554	36C	1555	36D	1556	36E	1557	36F
880	1560	370	1561	371	1562	372	1563	373	1564	374
885	1565	375	1566	376	1567	377	1570	378	1571	379
890	1572	37A	1573	37B	1574	37C	1575	37D	1576	37E
895	1577	37F	1600	380	1601	381	1602	382	1603	383
900	1604	384	1605	385	1606	386	1607	387	1610	388
905	1611	389	1612	38A	1613	38B	1614	38C	1615	38D
910	1616	38E	1617	38F	1620	390	1621	391	1622	392
915	1623	393	1624	394	1625	395	1626	396	1627	397
920	1630	398	1631	399	1632	39A	1633	39B	1634	39C
925	1635	39D	1636	39E	1637	39F	1640	3A0	1641	3A1
930	1642	3A2	1643	3A3	1644	3A4	1645	3A5	1646	3A6
935	1647	3A7	1650	3A8	1651	3A9	1652	3AA	1653	3AB
940	1654	3AC	1655	3AD	1656	3AE	1657	3AF	1660	3B0
945	1661	3B1	1662	3B2	1663	3B3	1664	3B4	1665	3B5
950	1666	3B6	1667	3B7	1670	3B8	1671	3B9	1672	3BA
955	1673	3BB	1674	3BC	1675	3BD	1676	3BE	1677	3BF
960	1700	3C0	1701	3C1	1702	3C2	1703	3C3	1704	3C4
965	1705	3C5	1706	3C6	1707	3C7	1710	3C8	1711	3C9
970	1712	3CA	1713	3CB	1714	3CC	1715	3CD	1716	3CE
975	1717	3CF	1720	3D0	1721	3D1	1722	3D2	1723	3D3
980	1724	3D4	1725	3D5	1726	3D6	1727	3D7	1730	3D8
985	1731	3D9	1732	3DA	1733	3DB	1734	3DC	1735	3DD
990	1736	3DE	1737	3DF	1740	3E0	1741	3E1	1742	3E2
995	1743	3E3	1744	3E4	1745	3E5	1746	3E6	1747	3E7
1000	1750	3E8	1751	3E9	1752	3EA	1753	3EB	1754	3EC
1005	1755	3ED	1756	3EE	1757	3EF	1760	3F0	1761	3F1
1010	1762	3F2	1763	3F3	1764	3F4	1765	3F5	1766	3F6
1015	1767	3F7	1770	3F8	1771	3F9	1772	3FA	1773	3FB
1020	1774	3FC	1775	3FD	1776	3FE	1777	3FF	2000	400
1025	2001	401	2002	402	2003	403	2004	404	2005	405
1030	2006	406	2007	407	2010	408	2011	409	2012	40A
1035	2013	40B	2014	40C	2015	40D	2016	40E	2017	40F
1040	2020	410	2021	411	2022	412	2023	413	2024	414
1045	2025	415	2026	416	2027	417	2030	418	2031	419
1050	2032	41A	2033	41B	2034	41C	2035	41D	2036	41E
1055	2037	41F	2040	420	2041	421	2042	422	2043	423
1060	2044	424	2045	425	2046	426	2047	427	2050	428
1065	2051	429	2052	42A	2053	42B	2054	42C	2055	42D
1070	2056	42E	2057	42F	2060	430	2061	431	2062	432
1075	2063	433	2064	434	2065	435	2066	436	2067	437
1080	2070	438	2071	439	2072	43A	2073	43B	2074	43C
1085	2075	43D	2076	43E	2077	43F	2100	440	2101	441
1090	2102	442	2103	443	2104	444	2105	445	2106	446
1095	2107	447	2110	448	2111	449	2112	44A	2113	44B
1100	2114	44C	2115	44D	2116	44E	2117	44F	2120	450
1105	2121	451	2122	452	2123	453	2124	454	2125	455
1110	2126	456	2127	457	2130	458	2131	459	2132	45A
1115	2133	45B	2134	45C	2135	45D	2136	45E	2137	45F
1120	2140	460	2141	461	2142	462	2143	463	2144	464
1125	2145	465	2146	466	2147	467	2150	468	2151	469
1130	2152	46A	2153	46B	2154	46C	2155	46D	2156	46E
1135	2157	46F	2160	470	2161	471	2162	472	2163	473
1140	2164	474	2165	475	2166	476	2167	477	2170	478
1145	2171	479	2172	47A	2173	47B	2174	47C	2175	47D
1150	2176	47E	2177	47F	2200	480	2201	481	2202	482
1155	2203	483	2204	484	2205	485	2206	486	2207	487

EC	0/5 OCT	HEX	1/6 OCT	HEX	2/7 OCT	HEX	3/8 OCT	HEX	4/9 OCT	HEX
160	2210	488	2211	489	2212	48A	2213	48B	2214	48C
165	2215	48D	2216	48E	2217	48F	2220	490	2221	491
170	2222	492	2223	493	2224	494	2225	495	2226	496
175	2227	497	2230	496	2231	499	2232	49A	2233	49B
180	2234	49C	2235	49D	2236	49E	2237	49F	2240	4A0
185	2241	4A1	2242	4A2	2243	4A3	2244	4A4	2245	4A5
190	2246	4A6	2247	4A7	2250	4A8	2251	4A9	2252	4AA
195	2253	4AB	2254	4AC	2255	4AD	2256	4AE	2257	4AF
200	2260	4B0	2261	4B1	2262	4B2	2263	4B3	2264	4B4
205	2265	4B5	2266	4B6	2267	4B7	2270	4B8	2271	4B9
210	2272	4BA	2273	4BB	2274	4BC	2275	4BD	2276	4BE
215	2277	4BF	2300	4C0	2301	4C1	2302	4C2	2303	4C3
220	2304	4C4	2305	4C5	2306	4C6	2307	4C7	2310	4C8
225	2311	4C9	2312	4CA	2313	4CB	2314	4CC	2315	4CD
230	2316	4CE	2317	4CF	2320	4D0	2321	4D1	2322	4D2
235	2323	4D3	2324	4D4	2325	4D5	2326	4D6	2327	4D7
240	2330	4D8	2331	4D9	2332	4DA	2333	4DB	2334	4DC
245	2335	4DD	2336	4DE	2337	4DF	2340	4E0	2341	4E1
250	2342	4E2	2343	4E3	2344	4E4	2345	4E5	2346	4E6
255	2347	4E7	2350	4E8	2351	4E9	2352	4EA	2353	4EB
260	2354	4FC	2355	4ED	2356	4FE	2357	4FF	2360	4F0
265	2361	4F1	2362	4F2	2363	4F3	2364	4F4	2365	4F5
270	2366	4F6	2367	4F7	2370	4F8	2371	4F9	2372	4FA
275	2373	4FB	2374	4FC	2375	4FD	2376	4FE	2377	4FF
280	2400	500	2401	501	2402	502	2403	503	2404	504
285	2405	505	2406	506	2407	507	2410	508	2411	509
290	2412	50A	2413	50B	2414	50C	2415	50D	2416	50E
295	2417	50F	2420	510	2421	511	2422	512	2423	513
300	2424	514	2425	515	2426	516	2427	517	2430	518
305	2431	519	2432	51A	2433	51B	2434	51C	2435	51D
310	2436	51E	2437	51F	2440	520	2441	521	2442	522
315	2443	523	2444	524	2445	525	2446	526	2447	527
320	2450	528	2451	529	2452	52A	2453	52B	2454	52C
325	2455	52D	2456	52E	2457	52F	2460	530	2461	531
330	2462	532	2463	533	2464	534	2465	535	2466	536
335	2467	537	2470	538	2471	539	2472	53A	2473	53B
340	2474	53C	2475	53D	2476	53E	2477	53F	2500	540
345	2501	541	2502	542	2503	543	2504	544	2505	545
350	2506	546	2507	547	2510	548	2511	549	2512	54A
355	2513	54B	2514	54C	2515	54D	2516	54E	2517	54F
360	2520	550	2521	551	2522	552	2523	553	2524	554
365	2525	555	2526	556	2527	557	2530	558	2531	559
370	2532	55A	2533	55B	2534	55C	2535	55D	2536	55E
375	2537	55F	2540	560	2541	561	2542	562	2543	563
380	2544	564	2545	565	2546	566	2547	567	2550	568
385	2551	569	2552	56A	2553	56B	2554	56C	2555	56D
390	2556	56E	2557	56F	2560	570	2561	571	2562	572
395	2563	573	2564	574	2565	575	2566	576	2567	577
400	2570	578	2571	579	2572	57A	2573	57B	2574	57C
405	2575	57D	2576	57E	2577	57F	2600	580	2601	581
410	2602	582	2603	583	2604	584	2605	585	2606	586
415	2607	587	2610	588	2611	589	2612	58A	2613	58B
420	2614	58C	2615	58D	2616	58E	2617	58F	2620	590
425	2621	591	2622	592	2623	593	2624	594	2625	595
430	2626	596	2627	597	2630	598	2631	599	2632	59A
435	2633	59B	2634	59C	2635	59D	2636	59E	2637	59F
440	2640	5A0	2641	5A1	2642	5A2	2643	5A3	2644	5A4
445	2645	5A5	2646	5A6	2647	5A7	2650	5A8	2651	5A9

DEC	OCT (0/5)	HEX	OCT (1/6)	HEX	OCT (2/7)	HEX	OCT (3/8)	HEX	OCT (4/9)	HEX
1450	2652	5AA	2653	5AB	2654	5AC	2655	5AD	2656	5A
1455	2657	5AF	2660	5B0	2661	5B1	2662	5B2	2663	5B
1460	2664	5B4	2665	5B5	2666	5B6	2667	5B7	2670	5B
1465	2671	5B9	2672	5BA	2673	5BB	2674	5BC	2675	5B
1470	2676	5BE	2677	5BF	2700	5C0	2701	5C1	2702	5C
1475	2703	5C3	2704	5C4	2705	5C5	2706	5C6	2707	5C
1480	2710	5C8	2711	5C9	2712	5CA	2713	5CB	2714	5C
1485	2715	5CD	2716	5CE	2717	5CF	2720	5D0	2721	5D
1490	2722	5D2	2723	5D3	2724	5D4	2725	5D5	2726	5D
1495	2727	5D7	2730	5D8	2731	5D9	2732	5DA	2733	5D
1500	2734	5DC	2735	5DD	2736	5DE	2737	5DF	2740	5E
1505	2741	5E1	2742	5E2	2743	5E3	2744	5E4	2745	5E
1510	2746	5E6	2747	5E7	2750	5E8	2751	5E9	2752	5E
1515	2753	5EB	2754	5EC	2755	5ED	2756	5EE	2757	5E
1520	2760	5F0	2761	5F1	2762	5F2	2763	5F3	2764	5F
1525	2765	5F5	2766	5F6	2767	5F7	2770	5F8	2771	5F
1530	2772	5FA	2773	5FB	2774	5FC	2775	5FD	2776	5F
1535	2777	5FF	3000	600	3001	601	3002	602	3003	60
1540	3004	604	3005	605	3006	606	3007	607	3010	60
1545	3011	609	3012	60A	3013	60B	3014	60C	3015	60
1550	3016	60E	3017	60F	3020	610	3021	611	3022	61
1555	3023	613	3024	614	3025	615	3026	616	3027	61
1560	3030	618	3031	619	3032	61A	3033	61B	3034	61
1565	3035	61D	3036	61E	3037	61F	3040	620	3041	62
1570	3042	622	3043	623	3044	624	3045	625	3046	62
1575	3047	627	3050	628	3051	629	3052	62A	3053	62
1580	3054	62C	3055	62D	3056	62E	3057	62F	3060	63
1585	3061	631	3062	632	3063	633	3064	634	3065	63
1590	3066	636	3067	637	3070	638	3071	639	3072	63
1595	3073	63B	3074	63C	3075	63D	3076	63E	3077	63
1600	3100	640	3101	641	3102	642	3103	643	3104	64
1605	3105	645	3106	646	3107	647	3110	648	3111	64
1610	3112	64A	3113	64B	3114	64C	3115	64D	3116	64
1615	3117	64F	3120	650	3121	651	3122	652	3123	65
1620	3124	654	3125	655	3126	656	3127	657	3130	65
1625	3131	659	3132	65A	3133	65B	3134	65C	3135	65
1630	3136	65E	3137	65F	3140	660	3141	661	3142	66
1635	3143	663	3144	664	3145	665	3146	666	3147	66
1640	3150	668	3151	669	3152	66A	3153	66B	3154	66
1645	3155	66D	3156	66E	3157	66F	3160	670	3161	67
1650	3162	672	3163	673	3164	674	3165	675	3166	67
1655	3167	677	3170	678	3171	679	3172	67A	3173	67
1660	3174	67C	3175	67D	3176	67E	3177	67F	3200	68
1665	3201	681	3202	682	3203	683	3204	684	3205	68
1670	3206	686	3207	687	3210	688	3211	689	3212	68
1675	3213	68B	3214	68C	3215	68D	3216	68E	3217	68
1680	3220	690	3221	691	3222	692	3223	693	3224	69
1685	3225	695	3226	696	3227	697	3230	698	3231	69
1690	3232	69A	3233	69B	3234	69C	3235	69D	3236	69
1695	3237	69F	3240	6A0	3241	6A1	3242	6A2	3243	6A
1700	3244	6A4	3245	6A5	3246	6A6	3247	6A7	3250	6A
1705	3251	6A9	3252	6AA	3253	6AB	3254	6AC	3255	6A
1710	3256	6AE	3257	6AF	3260	6B0	3261	6B1	3262	6B
1715	3263	6B3	3264	6B4	3265	6B5	3266	6B6	3267	6B
1720	3270	6B8	3271	6B9	3272	6BA	3273	6BB	3274	6B
1725	3275	6BD	3276	6BE	3277	6BF	3300	6C0	3301	6C
1730	3302	6C2	3303	6C3	3304	6C4	3305	6C5	3306	6C
1735	3307	6C7	3310	6C8	3311	6C9	3312	6CA	3313	6C

C	0/5 OCT	HEX	1/6 OCT	HEX	2/7 OCT	HEX	3/8 OCT	HEX	4/9 OCT	HEX
40	3314	6CC	3315	6CD	3316	6CE	3317	6CF	3320	6D0
45	3321	6D1	3322	6D2	3323	6D3	3324	6D4	3325	6D5
50	3326	6D6	3327	6D7	3330	6D8	3331	6D9	3332	6DA
55	3333	6DB	3334	6DC	3335	6DD	3336	6DE	3337	6DF
60	3340	6E0	3341	6E1	3342	6E2	3343	6E3	3344	6E4
65	3345	6E5	3346	6E6	3347	6E7	3350	6E8	3351	6E9
70	3352	6EA	3353	6EB	3354	6EC	3355	6ED	3356	6EE
75	3357	6EF	3360	6F0	3361	6F1	3362	6F2	3363	6F3
80	3364	6F4	3365	6F5	3366	6F6	3367	6F7	3370	6F8
85	3371	6F9	3372	6FA	3373	6FB	3374	6FC	3375	6FD
90	3376	6FE	3377	6FF	3400	700	3401	701	3402	702
95	3403	703	3404	704	3405	705	3406	706	3407	707
00	3410	708	3411	709	3412	70A	3413	70B	3414	70C
05	3415	70D	3416	70E	3417	70F	3420	710	3421	711
10	3422	712	3423	713	3424	714	3425	715	3426	716
15	3427	717	3430	718	3431	719	3432	71A	3433	71B
20	3434	71C	3435	71D	3436	71E	3437	71F	3440	720
25	3441	721	3442	722	3443	723	3444	724	3445	725
30	3446	726	3447	727	3450	728	3451	729	3452	72A
35	3453	72B	3454	72C	3455	72D	3456	72E	3457	72F
40	3460	730	3461	731	3462	732	3463	733	3464	734
45	3465	735	3466	736	3467	737	3470	738	3471	739
50	3472	73A	3473	73B	3474	73C	3475	73D	3476	73E
55	3477	73F	3500	740	3501	741	3502	742	3503	743
60	3504	744	3505	745	3506	746	3507	747	3510	748
65	3511	749	3512	74A	3513	74B	3514	74C	3515	74D
70	3516	74E	3517	74F	3520	750	3521	751	3522	752
75	3523	753	3524	754	3525	755	3526	756	3527	757
80	3530	758	3531	759	3532	75A	3533	75B	3534	75C
85	3535	75D	3536	75E	3537	75F	3540	760	3541	761
90	3542	762	3543	763	3544	764	3545	765	3546	766
95	3547	767	3550	768	3551	769	3552	76A	3553	76B
00	3554	76C	3555	76D	3556	76E	3557	76F	3560	770
05	3561	771	3562	772	3563	773	3564	774	3565	775
10	3566	776	3567	777	3570	778	3571	779	3572	77A
15	3573	77B	3574	77C	3575	77D	3576	77E	3577	77F
20	3600	780	3601	781	3602	782	3603	783	3604	784
25	3605	785	3606	786	3607	787	3610	788	3611	789
30	3612	78A	3613	78B	3614	78C	3615	78D	3616	78E
35	3617	78F	3620	790	3621	791	3622	792	3623	793
40	3624	794	3625	795	3626	796	3627	797	3630	798
45	3631	799	3632	79A	3633	79B	3634	79C	3635	79D
50	3636	79E	3637	79F	3640	7A0	3641	7A1	3642	7A2
55	3643	7A3	3644	7A4	3645	7A5	3646	7A6	3647	7A7
60	3650	7A8	3651	7A9	3652	7AA	3653	7AB	3654	7AC
65	3655	7AD	3656	7AE	3657	7AF	3660	7B0	3661	7B1
70	3662	7B2	3663	7B3	3664	7B4	3665	7B5	3666	7B6
75	3667	7B7	3670	7B8	3671	7B9	3672	7BA	3673	7BB
80	3674	7BC	3675	7BD	3676	7BE	3677	7BF	3700	7C0
85	3701	7C1	3702	7C2	3703	7C3	3704	7C4	3705	7C5
90	3706	7C6	3707	7C7	3710	7C8	3711	7C9	3712	7CA
95	3713	7CB	3714	7CC	3715	7CD	3716	7CE	3717	7CF
00	3720	7D0	3721	7D1	3722	7D2	3723	7D3	3724	7D4
05	3725	7D5	3726	7D6	3727	7D7	3730	7D8	3731	7D9
10	3732	7DA	3733	7DB	3734	7DC	3735	7DD	3736	7DE
15	3737	7DF	3740	7E0	3741	7E1	3742	7E2	3743	7E3
20	3744	7E4	3745	7E5	3746	7E6	3747	7E7	3750	7E8
25	3751	7E9	3752	7EA	3753	7EB	3754	7EC	3755	7ED

	0/5		1/6		2/7		3/8		4/9	
DEC	OCT	HEX	OCT	HEX	OCT	HEX	OCT	HEX	OCT	HEX
2030	3756	7EE	3757	7EF	3760	7F0	3761	7F1	3762	7F
2035	3763	7F3	3764	7F4	3765	7F5	3766	7F6	3767	7F
2040	3770	7F8	3771	7F9	3772	7FA	3773	7FB	3774	7F
2045	3775	7FD	3776	7FE	3777	7FF	4000	800	4001	80
2050	4002	802	4003	803	4004	804	4005	805	4006	80
2055	4007	807	4010	808	4011	809	4012	80A	4013	80
2060	4014	80C	4015	80D	4016	80E	4017	80F	4020	81
2065	4021	811	4022	812	4023	813	4024	814	4025	81
2070	4026	816	4027	817	4030	818	4031	819	4032	81
2075	4033	81B	4034	81C	4035	81D	4036	81E	4037	81
2080	4040	820	4041	821	4042	822	4043	823	4044	82
2085	4045	825	4046	826	4047	827	4050	828	4051	82
2090	4052	82A	4053	82B	4054	82C	4055	82D	4056	82
2095	4057	82F	4060	830	4061	831	4062	832	4063	83
2100	4064	834	4065	835	4066	836	4067	837	4070	83
2105	4071	839	4072	83A	4073	83B	4074	83C	4075	83
2110	4076	83E	4077	83F	4100	840	4101	841	4102	84
2115	4103	843	4104	844	4105	845	4106	846	4107	84
2120	4110	848	4111	849	4112	84A	4113	84B	4114	84
2125	4115	84D	4116	84E	4117	84F	4120	850	4121	85
2130	4122	852	4123	853	4124	854	4125	855	4126	85
2135	4127	857	4130	858	4131	859	4132	85A	4133	85
2140	4134	85C	4135	85D	4136	85E	4137	85F	4140	86
2145	4141	861	4142	862	4143	863	4144	864	4145	86
2150	4146	866	4147	867	4150	868	4151	869	4152	86
2155	4153	86B	4154	86C	4155	86D	4156	86E	4157	86
2160	4160	870	4161	871	4162	872	4163	873	4164	87
2165	4165	875	4166	876	4167	877	4170	878	4171	87
2170	4172	87A	4173	87B	4174	87C	4175	87D	4176	87
2175	4177	87F	4200	880	4201	881	4202	882	4203	88
2180	4204	884	4205	885	4206	886	4207	887	4210	88
2185	4211	889	4212	88A	4213	88B	4214	88C	4215	88
2190	4216	88E	4217	88F	4220	890	4221	891	4222	89
2195	4223	893	4224	894	4225	895	4226	896	4227	89
2200	4230	898	4231	899	4232	89A	4233	89B	4234	89
2205	4235	89D	4236	89E	4237	89F	4240	8A0	4241	8A
2210	4242	8A2	4243	8A3	4244	8A4	4245	8A5	4246	8A
2215	4247	8A7	4250	8A8	4251	8A9	4252	8AA	4253	8A
2220	4254	8AC	4255	8AD	4256	8AE	4257	8AF	4260	8B
2225	4261	8B1	4262	8B2	4263	8B3	4264	8B4	4265	8B
2230	4266	8B6	4267	8B7	4270	8B8	4271	8B9	4272	8B
2235	4273	8BB	4274	8BC	4275	8BD	4276	8BE	4277	8B
2240	4300	8C0	4301	8C1	4302	8C2	4303	8C3	4304	8C
2245	4305	8C5	4306	8C6	4307	8C7	4310	8C8	4311	8C
2250	4312	8CA	4313	8CB	4314	8CC	4315	8CD	4316	8C
2255	4317	8CF	4320	8D0	4321	8D1	4322	8D2	4323	8D
2260	4324	8D4	4325	8D5	4326	8D6	4327	8D7	4330	8D
2265	4331	8D9	4332	8DA	4333	8DB	4334	8DC	4335	8D
2270	4336	8DE	4337	8DF	4340	8E0	4341	8E1	4342	8E
2275	4343	8E3	4344	8E4	4345	8E5	4346	8E6	4347	8E
2280	4350	8E8	4351	8E9	4352	8EA	4353	8EB	4354	8E
2285	4355	8ED	4356	8EE	4357	8EF	4360	8F0	4361	8F
2290	4362	8F2	4363	8F3	4364	8F4	4365	8F5	4366	8F
2295	4367	8F7	4370	8F8	4371	8F9	4372	8FA	4373	8F
2300	4374	8FC	4375	8FD	4376	8FE	4377	8FF	4400	90
2305	4401	901	4402	902	4403	903	4404	904	4405	90
2310	4406	906	4407	907	4410	908	4411	909	4412	90
2315	4413	90B	4414	90C	4415	90D	4416	90E	4417	90

	0/5		1/6		2/7		3/8		4/9	
	OCT	HEX	OCT	HEX	OCT	HEX	OCT	HEX	OCT	HEX
0	4420	910	4421	911	4422	912	4423	913	4424	914
5	4425	915	4426	916	4427	917	4430	918	4431	919
0	4432	91A	4433	91B	4434	91C	4435	91D	4436	91E
5	4437	91F	4440	920	4441	921	4442	922	4443	923
0	4444	924	4445	925	4446	926	4447	927	4450	928
5	4451	929	4452	92A	4453	92B	4454	92C	4455	92D
0	4456	92E	4457	92F	4460	930	4461	931	4462	932
5	4463	933	4464	934	4465	935	4466	936	4467	937
0	4470	938	4471	939	4472	93A	4473	93B	4474	93C
5	4475	93D	4476	93E	4477	93F	4500	940	4501	941
0	4502	942	4503	943	4504	944	4505	945	4506	946
5	4507	947	4510	948	4511	949	4512	94A	4513	94B
0	4514	94C	4515	94D	4516	94E	4517	94F	4520	950
5	4521	951	4522	952	4523	953	4524	954	4525	955
0	4526	956	4527	957	4530	958	4531	959	4532	95A
5	4533	95B	4534	95C	4535	95D	4536	95E	4537	95F
0	4540	960	4541	961	4542	962	4543	963	4544	964
5	4545	965	4546	966	4547	967	4550	968	4551	969
0	4552	96A	4553	96B	4554	96C	4555	96D	4556	96E
5	4557	96F	4560	970	4561	971	4562	972	4563	973
0	4564	974	4565	975	4566	976	4567	977	4570	978
5	4571	979	4572	97A	4573	97B	4574	97C	4575	97D
0	4576	97E	4577	97F	4600	980	4601	981	4602	982
5	4603	983	4604	984	4605	985	4606	986	4607	987
0	4610	988	4611	989	4612	98A	4613	98B	4614	98C
5	4615	98D	4616	98E	4617	98F	4620	990	4621	991
0	4622	992	4623	993	4624	994	4625	995	4626	996
5	4627	997	4630	998	4631	999	4632	99A	4633	99B
0	4634	99C	4635	99D	4636	99E	4637	99F	4640	9A0
5	4641	9A1	4642	9A2	4643	9A3	4644	9A4	4645	9A5
0	4646	9A6	4647	9A7	4650	9A8	4651	9A9	4652	9AA
5	4653	9AB	4654	9AC	4655	9AD	4656	9AE	4657	9AF
0	4660	9B0	4661	9B1	4662	9B2	4663	9B3	4664	9B4
5	4665	9B5	4666	9B6	4667	9B7	4670	9B8	4671	9B9
0	4672	9BA	4673	9BB	4674	9BC	4675	9BD	4676	9BE
5	4677	9BF	4700	9C0	4701	9C1	4702	9C2	4703	9C3
0	4704	9C4	4705	9C5	4706	9C6	4707	9C7	4710	9C8
5	4711	9C9	4712	9CA	4713	9CB	4714	9CC	4715	9CD
0	4716	9CE	4717	9CF	4720	9D0	4721	9D1	4722	9D2
5	4723	9D3	4724	9D4	4725	9D5	4726	9D6	4727	9D7
0	4730	9D8	4731	9D9	4732	9DA	4733	9DB	4734	9DC
5	4735	9DD	4736	9DE	4737	9DF	4740	9E0	4741	9E1
0	4742	9E2	4743	9E3	4744	9E4	4745	9E5	4746	9E6
5	4747	9E7	4750	9E8	4751	9E9	4752	9EA	4753	9EB
0	4754	9EC	4755	9ED	4756	9EE	4757	9EF	4760	9F0
5	4761	9F1	4762	9F2	4763	9F3	4764	9F4	4765	9F5
0	4766	9F6	4767	9F7	4770	9F8	4771	9F9	4772	9FA
5	4773	9FB	4774	9FC	4775	9FD	4776	9FE	4777	9FF
0	5000	A00	5001	A01	5002	A02	5003	A03	5004	A04
5	5005	A05	5006	A06	5007	A07	5010	A08	5011	A09
0	5012	A0A	5013	A0B	5014	A0C	5015	A0D	5016	A0E
5	5017	A0F	5020	A10	5021	A11	5022	A12	5023	A13
0	5024	A14	5025	A15	5026	A16	5027	A17	5030	A18
5	5031	A19	5032	A1A	5033	A1B	5034	A1C	5035	A1D
0	5036	A1E	5037	A1F	5040	A20	5041	A21	5042	A22
5	5043	A23	5044	A24	5045	A25	5046	A26	5047	A27
0	5050	A28	5051	A29	5052	A2A	5053	A2B	5054	A2C
5	5055	A2D	5056	A2E	5057	A2F	5060	A30	5061	A31

DEC	0/5 OCT	HEX	1/6 OCT	HEX	2/7 OCT	HEX	3/8 OCT	HEX	4/9 OCT	HEX
2610	5062	A32	5063	A33	5064	A34	5065	A35	5066	A
2615	5067	A37	5070	A38	5071	A39	5072	A3A	5073	A
2620	5074	A3C	5075	A3D	5076	A3E	5077	A3F	5100	A
2625	5101	A41	5102	A42	5103	A43	5104	A44	5105	A
2630	5106	A46	5107	A47	5110	A48	5111	A49	5112	A
2635	5113	A4B	5114	A4C	5115	A4D	5116	A4E	5117	A
2640	5120	A50	5121	A51	5122	A52	5123	A53	5124	A
2645	5125	A55	5126	A56	5127	A57	5130	A58	5131	A
2650	5132	A5A	5133	A5B	5134	A5C	5135	A5D	5136	A
2655	5137	A5F	5140	A60	5141	A61	5142	A62	5143	A
2660	5144	A64	5145	A65	5146	A66	5147	A67	5150	A
2665	5151	A69	5152	A6A	5153	A6B	5154	A6C	5155	A
2670	5156	A6E	5157	A6F	5160	A70	5161	A71	5162	A
2675	5163	A73	5164	A74	5165	A75	5166	A76	5167	A
2680	5170	A78	5171	A79	5172	A7A	5173	A7B	5174	A
2685	5175	A7D	5176	A7E	5177	A7F	5200	A80	5201	A
2690	5202	A82	5203	A83	5204	A84	5205	A85	5206	A
2695	5207	A87	5210	A88	5211	A89	5212	A8A	5213	A
2700	5214	A8C	5215	A8D	5216	A8E	5217	A8F	5220	A
2705	5221	A91	5222	A92	5223	A93	5224	A94	5225	A
2710	5226	A96	5227	A97	5230	A98	5231	A99	5232	A
2715	5233	A9B	5234	A9C	5235	A9D	5236	A9E	5237	A
2720	5240	AA0	5241	AA1	5242	AA2	5243	AA3	5244	A
2725	5245	AA5	5246	AA6	5247	AA7	5250	AA8	5251	A
2730	5252	AAA	5253	AAB	5254	AAC	5255	AAD	5256	A
2735	5257	AAF	5260	AB0	5261	AB1	5262	AB2	5263	A
2740	5264	AB4	5265	AB5	5266	AB6	5267	AB7	5270	A
2745	5271	AB9	5272	ABA	5273	ABB	5274	ABC	5275	A
2750	5276	ABE	5277	ABF	5300	AC0	5301	AC1	5302	A
2755	5303	AC3	5304	AC4	5305	AC5	5306	AC6	5307	A
2760	5310	AC8	5311	AC9	5312	ACA	5313	ACB	5314	A
2765	5315	ACD	5316	ACE	5317	ACF	5320	AD0	5321	A
2770	5322	AD2	5323	AD3	5324	AD4	5325	AD5	5326	A
2775	5327	AD7	5330	AD8	5331	AD9	5332	ADA	5333	A
2780	5334	ADC	5335	ADD	5336	ADE	5337	ADF	5340	A
2785	5341	AE1	5342	AE2	5343	AE3	5344	AE4	5345	A
2790	5346	AE6	5347	AE7	5350	AE8	5351	AE9	5352	A
2795	5353	AEB	5354	AEC	5355	AED	5356	AEE	5357	A
2800	5360	AF0	5361	AF1	5362	AF2	5363	AF3	5364	A
2805	5365	AF5	5366	AF6	5367	AF7	5370	AF8	5371	A
2810	5372	AFA	5373	AFB	5374	AFC	5375	AFD	5376	A
2815	5377	AFF	5400	B00	5401	BC1	5402	B02	5403	B
2820	5404	B04	5405	B05	5406	B06	5407	B07	5410	B
2825	5411	B09	5412	B0A	5413	B0B	5414	B0C	5415	B
2830	5416	B0E	5417	B0F	5420	B10	5421	B11	5422	B
2835	5423	B13	5424	B14	5425	B15	5426	B16	5427	B
2840	5430	B18	5431	B19	5432	B1A	5433	B1B	5434	B
2845	5435	B1D	5436	B1E	5437	B1F	5440	B20	5441	B
2850	5442	B22	5443	B23	5444	B24	5445	B25	5446	B
2855	5447	B27	5450	B28	5451	B29	5452	B2A	5453	B
2860	5454	B2C	5455	B2D	5456	B2E	5457	B2F	5460	B
2865	5461	B31	5462	B32	5463	B33	5464	B34	5465	B
2870	5466	B36	5467	B37	5470	B38	5471	B39	5472	B
2875	5473	B3B	5474	B3C	5475	B3D	5476	B3E	5477	B
2880	5500	B40	5501	B41	5502	B42	5503	B43	5504	B
2885	5505	B45	5506	B46	5507	B47	5510	B48	5511	B
2890	5512	B4A	5513	B4B	5514	B4C	5515	B4D	5516	B
2895	5517	B4F	5520	B50	5521	B51	5522	B52	5523	B

	0/5		1/6		2/7		3/8		4/9	
DEC	OCT	HEX	OCT	HEX	OCT	HEX	OCT	HEX	OCT	HEX
900	5524	B54	5525	B55	5526	B56	5527	B57	5530	B58
905	5531	B59	5532	B5A	5533	B5B	5534	B5C	5535	B5D
910	5536	B5E	5537	B5F	5540	B60	5541	B61	5542	B62
915	5543	B63	5544	B64	5545	B65	5546	B66	5547	B67
920	5550	B68	5551	B69	5552	B6A	5553	B6B	5554	B6C
925	5555	B6D	5556	B6E	5557	B6F	5560	B70	5561	B71
930	5562	B72	5563	B73	5564	B74	5565	B75	5566	B76
935	5567	B77	5570	B78	5571	B79	5572	B7A	5573	B7B
940	5574	B7C	5575	B7D	5576	B7E	5577	B7F	5600	B80
945	5601	B81	5602	B82	5603	B83	5604	B84	5605	B85
950	5606	B86	5607	B87	5610	B88	5611	B89	5612	B8A
955	5613	B8B	5614	B8C	5615	B8D	5616	B8E	5617	B8F
960	5620	B90	5621	B91	5622	B92	5623	B93	5624	B94
965	5625	B95	5626	B96	5627	B97	5630	B98	5631	B99
970	5632	B9A	5633	B9B	5634	B9C	5635	B9D	5636	B9E
975	5637	B9F	5640	BA0	5641	BA1	5642	BA2	5643	BA3
980	5644	BA4	5645	BA5	5646	BA6	5647	BA7	5650	BA8
985	5651	BA9	5652	BAA	5653	BAB	5654	BAC	5655	BAD
990	5656	BAE	5657	BAF	5660	BB0	5661	BB1	5662	BB2
995	5663	BB3	5664	BB4	5665	BB5	5666	BB6	5667	BB7
000	5670	BB8	5671	BB9	5672	BBA	5673	BBB	5674	BBC
005	5675	BBD	5676	BBE	5677	BBF	5700	BC0	5701	BC1
010	5702	BC2	5703	BC3	5704	BC4	5705	BC5	5706	BC6
015	5707	BC7	5710	BC8	5711	BC9	5712	BCA	5713	BCB
020	5714	BCC	5715	BCD	5716	BCE	5717	BCF	5720	BD0
025	5721	BD1	5722	BD2	5723	BD3	5724	BD4	5725	BD5
030	5726	BD6	5727	BD7	5730	BD8	5731	BD9	5732	BDA
035	5733	BDB	5734	BDC	5735	BDD	5736	BDE	5737	BDF
040	5740	BE0	5741	BE1	5742	BE2	5743	BE3	5744	BE4
045	5745	BE5	5746	BE6	5747	BE7	5750	BE8	5751	BE9
050	5752	BEA	5753	BEB	5754	BEC	5755	BED	5756	BEE
055	5757	BEF	5760	BF0	5761	BF1	5762	BF2	5763	BF3
060	5764	BF4	5765	BF5	5766	BF6	5767	BF7	5770	BF8
065	5771	BF9	5772	BFA	5773	BFB	5774	BFC	5775	BFD
070	5776	BFE	5777	BFF	6000	C00	6001	C01	6002	C02
075	6003	C03	6004	C04	6005	C05	6006	C06	6007	C07
080	6010	C08	6011	C09	6012	C0A	6013	C0B	6014	C0C
085	6015	C0D	6016	C0E	6017	C0F	6020	C10	6021	C11
090	6022	C12	6023	C13	6024	C14	6025	C15	6026	C16
095	6027	C17	6030	C18	6031	C19	6032	C1A	6033	C1B
100	6034	C1C	6035	C1D	6036	C1E	6037	C1F	6040	C20
105	6041	C21	6042	C22	6043	C23	6044	C24	6045	C25
110	6046	C26	6047	C27	6050	C28	6051	C29	6052	C2A
115	6053	C2B	6054	C2C	6055	C2D	6056	C2E	6057	C2F
120	6060	C30	6061	C31	6062	C32	6063	C33	6064	C34
125	6065	C35	6066	C36	6067	C37	6070	C38	6071	C39
130	6072	C3A	6073	C3B	6074	C3C	6075	C3D	6076	C3E
135	6077	C3F	6100	C40	6101	C41	6102	C42	6103	C43
140	6104	C44	6105	C45	6106	C46	6107	C47	6110	C48
145	6111	C49	6112	C4A	6113	C4B	6114	C4C	6115	C4D
150	6116	C4E	6117	C4F	6120	C50	6121	C51	6122	C52
155	6123	C53	6124	C54	6125	C55	6126	C56	6127	C57
160	6130	C58	6131	C59	6132	C5A	6133	C5B	6134	C5C
165	6135	C5D	6136	C5E	6137	C5F	6140	C60	6141	C61
170	6142	C62	6143	C63	6144	C64	6145	C65	6146	C66
175	6147	C67	6150	C68	6151	C69	6152	C6A	6153	C6B
180	6154	C6C	6155	C6D	6156	C6E	6157	C6F	6160	C70
185	6161	C71	6162	C72	6163	C73	6164	C74	6165	C75

DEC	0/5 OCT	HEX	1/6 OCT	HEX	2/7 OCT	HEX	3/8 OCT	HEX	4/9 OCT	HEX
3190	6166	C76	6167	C77	6170	C78	6171	C79	6172	C7A
3195	6173	C7B	6174	C7C	6175	C7D	6176	C7E	6177	C7F
3200	6200	C80	6201	C81	6202	C82	6203	C83	6204	C84
3205	6205	C85	6206	C86	6207	C87	6210	C88	6211	C89
3210	6212	C8A	6213	C8B	6214	C8C	6215	C8D	6216	C8E
3215	6217	C8F	6220	C90	6221	C91	6222	C92	6223	C93
3220	6224	C94	6225	C95	6226	C96	6227	C97	6230	C98
3225	6231	C99	6232	C9A	6233	C9B	6234	C9C	6235	C9D
3230	6236	C9E	6237	C9F	6240	CA0	6241	CA1	6242	CA2
3235	6243	CA3	6244	CA4	6245	CA5	6246	CA6	6247	CA7
3240	6250	CA8	6251	CA9	6252	CAA	6253	CAB	6254	CAC
3245	6255	CAD	6256	CAE	6257	CAF	6260	CB0	6261	CB1
3250	6262	CB2	6263	CB3	6264	CB4	6265	CB5	6266	CB6
3255	6267	CB7	6270	CB8	6271	CB9	6272	CBA	6273	CBB
3260	6274	CBC	6275	CBD	6276	CBE	6277	CBF	6300	CC0
3265	6301	CC1	6302	CC2	6303	CC3	6304	CC4	6305	CC5
3270	6306	CC6	6307	CC7	6310	CC8	6311	CC9	6312	CCA
3275	6313	CCB	6314	CCC	6315	CCD	6316	CCE	6317	CCF
3280	6320	CD0	6321	CD1	6322	CD2	6323	CD3	6324	CD4
3285	6325	CD5	6326	CD6	6327	CD7	6330	CD8	6331	CD9
3290	6332	CDA	6333	CDB	6334	CDC	6335	CDD	6336	CDE
3295	6337	CDF	6340	CE0	6341	CE1	6342	CE2	6343	CE3
3300	6344	CE4	6345	CF5	6346	CE6	6347	CE7	6350	CF8
3305	6351	CE9	6352	CEA	6353	CFB	6354	CEC	6355	CED
3310	6356	CFE	6357	CEF	6360	CF0	6361	CF1	6362	CF2
3315	6363	CF3	6364	CF4	6365	CF5	6366	CF6	6367	CF7
3320	6370	CF8	6371	CF9	6372	CFA	6373	CFB	6374	CFC
3325	6375	CFD	6376	CFE	6377	CFF	6400	D00	6401	D01
3330	6402	D02	6403	D03	6404	D04	6405	D05	6406	D06
3335	6407	D07	6410	D08	6411	D09	6412	D0A	6413	D0B
3340	6414	D0C	6415	D0D	6416	D0E	6417	D0F	6420	D10
3345	6421	D11	6422	D12	6423	D13	6424	D14	6425	D15
3350	6426	D16	6427	D17	6430	D18	6431	D19	6432	D1A
3355	6433	D1B	6434	D1C	6435	D1D	6436	D1E	6437	D1F
3360	6440	D20	6441	D21	6442	D22	6443	D23	6444	D24
3365	6445	D25	6446	D26	6447	D27	6450	D28	6451	D29
3370	6452	D2A	6453	D2B	6454	D2C	6455	D2D	6456	D2E
3375	6457	D2F	6460	D30	6461	D31	6462	D32	6463	D33
3380	6464	D34	6465	D35	6466	D36	6467	D37	6470	D38
3385	6471	D39	6472	D3A	6473	D3B	6474	D3C	6475	D3D
3390	6476	D3E	6477	D3F	6500	D40	6501	D41	6502	D42
3395	6503	D43	6504	D44	6505	D45	6506	D46	6507	D47
3400	6510	D48	6511	D49	6512	D4A	6513	D4B	6514	D4C
3405	6515	D4D	6516	D4E	6517	D4F	6520	D50	6521	D51
3410	6522	D52	6523	D53	6524	D54	6525	D55	6526	D56
3415	6527	D57	6530	D58	6531	D59	6532	D5A	6533	D5B
3420	6534	D5C	6535	D5D	6536	D5E	6537	D5F	6540	D60
3425	6541	D61	6542	D62	6543	D63	6544	D64	6545	D65
3430	6546	D66	6547	D67	6550	D68	6551	D69	6552	D6A
3435	6553	D6B	6554	D6C	6555	D6D	6556	D6E	6557	D6F
3440	6560	D70	6561	D71	6562	D72	6563	D73	6564	D74
3445	6565	D75	6566	D76	6567	D77	6570	D78	6571	D79
3450	6572	D7A	6573	D7B	6574	D7C	6575	D7D	6576	D7E
3455	6577	D7F	6600	D80	6601	D81	6602	D82	6603	D83
3460	6604	D84	6605	D85	6606	D86	6607	D87	6610	D88
3465	6611	D89	6612	D8A	6613	D8B	6614	D8C	6615	D8D
3470	6616	D8E	6617	D8F	6620	D90	6621	D91	6622	D92
3475	6623	D93	6624	D94	6625	D95	6626	D96	6627	D97

	0/5		1/6		2/7		3/8		4/9	
DEC	OCT	HEX	OCT	HEX	OCT	HEX	OCT	HEX	OCT	HEX
480	6630	D98	6631	D99	6632	D9A	6633	D9B	6634	D9C
485	6635	D9D	6636	D9E	6637	D9F	6640	DA0	6641	DA1
490	6642	DA2	6643	DA3	6644	DA4	6645	DA5	6646	DA6
495	6647	DA7	6650	DA8	6651	DA9	6652	DAA	6653	DAB
500	6654	DAC	6655	DAD	6656	DAE	6657	DAF	6660	DB0
505	6661	DB1	6662	DB2	6663	DB3	6664	DB4	6665	DB5
510	6666	DB6	6667	DB7	6670	DB8	6671	DB9	6672	DBA
515	6673	DBB	6674	DBC	6675	DBD	6676	DBE	6677	DBF
520	6700	DC0	6701	DC1	6702	DC2	6703	DC3	6704	DC4
525	6705	DC5	6706	DC6	6707	DC7	6710	DC8	6711	DC9
530	6712	DCA	6713	DCB	6714	DCC	6715	DCD	6716	DCE
535	6717	DCF	6720	DD0	6721	DD1	6722	DD2	6723	DD3
540	6724	DD4	6725	DD5	6726	DD6	6727	DD7	6730	DD8
545	6731	DD9	6732	DDA	6733	DDB	6734	DDC	6735	DDD
550	6736	DDE	6737	DDF	6740	DE0	6741	DE1	6742	DE2
555	6743	DE3	6744	DE4	6745	DE5	6746	DE6	6747	DE7
560	6750	DE8	6751	DE9	6752	DEA	6753	DEB	6754	DEC
565	6755	DED	6756	DEE	6757	DEF	6760	DF0	6761	DF1
570	6762	DF2	6763	DF3	6764	DF4	6765	DF5	6766	DF6
575	6767	DF7	6770	DF8	6771	DF9	6772	DFA	6773	DFB
580	6774	DFC	6775	DFD	6776	DFE	6777	DFF	7000	E00
585	7001	E01	7002	E02	7003	E03	7004	E04	7005	E05
590	7006	E06	7007	E07	7010	E08	7011	E09	7012	E0A
595	7013	E0B	7014	E0C	7015	E0D	7016	E0E	7017	E0F
600	7020	E10	7021	E11	7022	E12	7023	E13	7024	E14
605	7025	E15	7026	E16	7027	E17	7030	E18	7031	E19
610	7032	E1A	7033	E1B	7034	E1C	7035	E1D	7036	E1E
615	7037	E1F	7040	E20	7041	E21	7042	E22	7043	E23
620	7044	E24	7045	E25	7046	E26	7047	E27	7050	E28
625	7051	E29	7052	E2A	7053	E2B	7054	E2C	7055	E2D
630	7056	E2E	7057	E2F	7060	E30	7061	E31	7062	E32
635	7063	E33	7064	E34	7065	E35	7066	E36	7067	E37
640	7070	E38	7071	E39	7072	E3A	7073	E3B	7074	E3C
645	7075	E3D	7076	E3E	7077	E3F	7100	E40	7101	E41
650	7102	E42	7103	E43	7104	E44	7105	E45	7106	E46
655	7107	E47	7110	E48	7111	E49	7112	E4A	7113	E4B
660	7114	E4C	7115	E4D	7116	E4E	7117	E4F	7120	E50
665	7121	E51	7122	E52	7123	E53	7124	E54	7125	E55
670	7126	E56	7127	E57	7130	E58	7131	E59	7132	E5A
675	7133	E5B	7134	E5C	7135	E5D	7136	E5E	7137	E5F
680	7140	E60	7141	E61	7142	E62	7143	E63	7144	E64
685	7145	E65	7146	E66	7147	E67	7150	E68	7151	E69
690	7152	E6A	7153	E6B	7154	E6C	7155	E6D	7156	E6E
695	7157	E6F	7160	E70	7161	E71	7162	E72	7163	E73
700	7164	E74	7165	E75	7166	E76	7167	E77	7170	E78
705	7171	E79	7172	E7A	7173	E7B	7174	E7C	7175	E7D
710	7176	E7E	7177	E7F	7200	E80	7201	E81	7202	E82
715	7203	E83	7204	E84	7205	E85	7206	E86	7207	E87
720	7210	E88	7211	E89	7212	E8A	7213	E8B	7214	E8C
725	7215	E8D	7216	E8E	7217	E8F	7220	E90	7221	E91
730	7222	E92	7223	E93	7224	E94	7225	E95	7226	E96
735	7227	E97	7230	E98	7231	E99	7232	E9A	7233	E9B
740	7234	E9C	7235	E9D	7236	E9E	7237	E9F	7240	EA0
745	7241	EA1	7242	EA2	7243	EA3	7244	EA4	7245	EA5
750	7246	EA6	7247	EA7	7250	EA8	7251	EA9	7252	EAA
755	7253	EAB	7254	EAC	7255	EAD	7256	EAE	7257	EAF
760	7260	EB0	7261	EB1	7262	EB2	7263	EB3	7264	EB4
765	7265	EB5	7266	EB6	7267	EB7	7270	EB8	7271	EB9

DEC	0/5 OCT	HEX	1/6 OCT	HEX	2/7 OCT	HEX	3/8 OCT	HEX	4/9 OCT	HEX
3770	7272	EBA	7273	EBB	7274	EBC	7275	EBD	7276	EBE
3775	7277	EBF	7300	EC0	7301	EC1	7302	EC2	7303	EC3
3780	7304	EC4	7305	EC5	7306	EC6	7307	EC7	7310	EC8
3785	7311	EC9	7312	ECA	7313	ECB	7314	ECC	7315	ECD
3790	7316	ECE	7317	ECF	7320	ED0	7321	ED1	7322	ED2
3795	7323	ED3	7324	ED4	7325	ED5	7326	ED6	7327	ED7
3800	7330	ED8	7331	ED9	7332	EDA	7333	EDB	7334	EDC
3805	7335	EDD	7336	EDE	7337	EDF	7340	EE0	7341	EE1
3810	7342	EE2	7343	EE3	7344	EE4	7345	EE5	7346	EE6
3815	7347	EE7	7350	EE8	7351	EE9	7352	EEA	7353	EEB
3820	7354	EEC	7355	EED	7356	EEE	7357	EEF	7360	EF0
3825	7361	EF1	7362	EF2	7363	EF3	7364	EF4	7365	EF5
3830	7366	EF6	7367	EF7	7370	EF8	7371	EF9	7372	EFA
3835	7373	EFB	7374	EFC	7375	EFD	7376	EFE	7377	EFF
3840	7400	F00	7401	F01	7402	F02	7403	F03	7404	F04
3845	7405	F05	7406	F06	7407	F07	7410	F08	7411	F09
3850	7412	F0A	7413	F0B	7414	F0C	7415	F0D	7416	F0E
3855	7417	F0F	7420	F10	7421	F11	7422	F12	7423	F13
3860	7424	F14	7425	F15	7426	F16	7427	F17	7430	F18
3865	7431	F19	7432	F1A	7433	F1B	7434	F1C	7435	F1D
3870	7436	F1E	7437	F1F	7440	F20	7441	F21	7442	F22
3875	7443	F23	7444	F24	7445	F25	7446	F26	7447	F27
3880	7450	F28	7451	F29	7452	F2A	7453	F2B	7454	F2C
3885	7455	F2D	7456	F2E	7457	F2F	7460	F30	7461	F31
3890	7462	F32	7463	F33	7464	F34	7465	F35	7466	F36
3895	7467	F37	7470	F38	7471	F39	7472	F3A	7473	F3B
3900	7474	F3C	7475	F3D	7476	F3E	7477	F3F	7500	F40
3905	7501	F41	7502	F42	7503	F43	7504	F44	7505	F45
3910	7506	F46	7507	F47	7510	F48	7511	F49	7512	F4A
3915	7513	F4B	7514	F4C	7515	F4D	7516	F4E	7517	F4F
3920	7520	F50	7521	F51	7522	F52	7523	F53	7524	F54
3925	7525	F55	7526	F56	7527	F57	7530	F58	7531	F59
3930	7532	F5A	7533	F5B	7534	F5C	7535	F5D	7536	F5E
3935	7537	F5F	7540	F60	7541	F61	7542	F62	7543	F63
3940	7544	F64	7545	F65	7546	F66	7547	F67	7550	F68
3945	7551	F69	7552	F6A	7553	F6B	7554	F6C	7555	F6D
3950	7556	F6E	7557	F6F	7560	F70	7561	F71	7562	F72
3955	7563	F73	7564	F74	7565	F75	7566	F76	7567	F77
3960	7570	F78	7571	F79	7572	F7A	7573	F7B	7574	F7C
3965	7575	F7D	7576	F7E	7577	F7F	7600	F80	7601	F81
3970	7602	F82	7603	F83	7604	F84	7605	F85	7606	F86
3975	7607	F87	7610	F88	7611	F89	7612	F8A	7613	F8B
3980	7614	F8C	7615	F8D	7616	F8E	7617	F8F	7620	F90
3985	7621	F91	7622	F92	7623	F93	7624	F94	7625	F95
3990	7626	F96	7627	F97	7630	F98	7631	F99	7632	F9A
3995	7633	F9B	7634	F9C	7635	F9D	7636	F9E	7637	F9F
4000	7640	FA0	7641	FA1	7642	FA2	7643	FA3	7644	FA4
4005	7645	FA5	7646	FA6	7647	FA7	7650	FA8	7651	FA9
4010	7652	FAA	7653	FAB	7654	FAC	7655	FAD	7656	FAE
4015	7657	FAF	7660	FB0	7661	FB1	7662	FB2	7663	FB3
4020	7664	FB4	7665	FB5	7666	FB6	7667	FB7	7670	FB8
4025	7671	FB9	7672	FBA	7673	FBB	7674	FBC	7675	FBD
4030	7676	FBE	7677	FBF	7700	FC0	7701	FC1	7702	FC2
4035	7703	FC3	7704	FC4	7705	FC5	7706	FC6	7707	FC7
4040	7710	FC8	7711	FC9	7712	FCA	7713	FCB	7714	FCC
4045	7715	FCD	7716	FCE	7717	FCF	7720	FD0	7721	FD1
4050	7722	FD2	7723	FD3	7724	FD4	7725	FD5	7726	FD6
4055	7727	FD7	7730	FD8	7731	FD9	7732	FDA	7733	FDB

C	0/5 OCT	HEX	1/6 OCT	HEX	2/7 OCT	HEX	3/8 OCT	HEX	4/9 OCT	HEX
60	7734	FDC	7735	FDD	7736	FDE	7737	FDF	7740	FE0
65	7741	FE1	7742	FE2	7743	FE3	7744	FE4	7745	FE5
70	7746	FE6	7747	FE7	7750	FE8	7751	FE9	7752	FEA
75	7753	FEB	7754	FEC	7755	FED	7756	FEE	7757	FEF
80	7760	FF0	7761	FF1	7762	FF2	7763	FF3	7764	FF4
85	7765	FF5	7766	FF6	7767	FF7	7770	FF8	7771	FF9
90	7772	FFA	7773	FFB	7774	FFC	7775	FFD	7776	FFE
95	7777	FFF	10000	1000	10001	1001	10002	1002	10003	1003
00	10004	1004	10005	1005	10006	1006	10007	1007	10010	1008
05	10011	1009	10012	100A	10013	100B	10014	100C	10015	100D
10	10016	100E	10017	100F	10020	1010	10021	1011	10022	1012
15	10023	1013	10024	1014	10025	1015	10026	1016	10027	1017
20	10030	1018	10031	1019	10032	101A	10033	101B	10034	101C
25	10035	101D	10036	101E	10037	101F	10040	1020	10041	1021
30	10042	1022	10043	1023	10044	1024	10045	1025	10046	1026
35	10047	1027	10050	1028	10051	1029	10052	102A	10053	102B
40	10054	102C	10055	102D	10056	102E	10057	102F	10060	1030
45	10061	1031	10062	1032	10063	1033	10064	1034	10065	1035
50	10066	1036	10067	1037	10070	1038	10071	1039	10072	103A
55	10073	103B	10074	103C	10075	103D	10076	103E	10077	103F
60	10100	1040	10101	1041	10102	1042	10103	1043	10104	1044
65	10105	1045	10106	1046	10107	1047	10110	1048	10111	1049
70	10112	104A	10113	104B	10114	104C	10115	104D	10116	104E
75	10117	104F	10120	1050	10121	1051	10122	1052	10123	1053
80	10124	1054	10125	1055	10126	1056	10127	1057	10130	1058
85	10131	1059	10132	105A	10133	105B	10134	105C	10135	105D
90	10136	105E	10137	105F	10140	1060	10141	1061	10142	1062
95	10143	1063	10144	1064	10145	1065	10146	1066	10147	1067
00	10150	1068	10151	1069	10152	106A	10153	106B	10154	106C
05	10155	106D	10156	106E	10157	106F	10160	1070	10161	1071
10	10162	1072	10163	1073	10164	1074	10165	1075	10166	1076
15	10167	1077	10170	1078	10171	1079	10172	107A	10173	107B
20	10174	107C	10175	107D	10176	107E	10177	107F	10200	1080
25	10201	1081	10202	1082	10203	1083	10204	1084	10205	1085
30	10206	1086	10207	1087	10210	1088	10211	1089	10212	108A
35	10213	108B	10214	108C	10215	108D	10216	108E	10217	108F
40	10220	1090	10221	1091	10222	1092	10223	1093	10224	1094
45	10225	1095	10226	1096	10227	1097	10230	1098	10231	1099
50	10232	109A	10233	109B	10234	109C	10235	109D	10236	109E
55	10237	109F	10240	10A0	10241	10A1	10242	10A2	10243	10A3
60	10244	10A4	10245	10A5	10246	10A6	10247	10A7	10250	10A8
65	10251	10A9	10252	10AA	10253	10AB	10254	10AC	10255	10AD
70	10256	10AE	10257	10AF	10260	10B0	10261	10B1	10262	10B2
75	10263	10B3	10264	10B4	10265	10B5	10266	10B6	10267	10B7
80	10270	10B8	10271	10B9	10272	10BA	10273	10BB	10274	10BC
85	10275	10BD	10276	10BE	10277	10BF	10300	10C0	10301	10C1
90	10302	10C2	10303	10C3	10304	10C4	10305	10C5	10306	10C6
95	10307	10C7	10310	10C8	10311	10C9	10312	10CA	10313	10CB
00	10314	10CC	10315	10CD	10316	10CE	10317	10CF	10320	10D0
05	10321	10D1	10322	10D2	10323	10D3	10324	10D4	10325	10D5
10	10326	10D6	10327	10D7	10330	10D8	10331	10D9	10332	10DA
15	10333	10DB	10334	10DC	10335	10DD	10336	10DE	10337	10DF
20	10340	10E0	10341	10E1	10342	10E2	10343	10E3	10344	10E4
25	10345	10E5	10346	10F6	10347	10F7	10350	10E8	10351	10E9
30	10352	10EA	10353	10EB	10354	10EC	10355	10ED	10356	10EE
35	10357	10EF	10360	10F0	10361	10F1	10362	10F2	10363	10F3
40	10364	10F4	10365	10F5	10366	10F6	10367	10F7	10370	10F8
45	10371	10F9	10372	10FA	10373	10FB	10374	10FC	10375	10FD

	0/5		1/6		2/7		3/8		4/9	
DEC	OCT	HEX	OCT	HEX	OCT	HEX	OCT	HEX	OCT	HEX
4350	10376	1CFE	10377	10FF	10400	1100	10401	1101	10402	110
4355	10403	1103	10404	1104	10405	11C5	10406	1106	10407	110
4360	10410	1108	10411	1109	10412	110A	10413	110B	10414	110
4365	10415	110D	10416	110E	10417	110F	10420	1110	10421	111
4370	10422	1112	10423	1113	10424	1114	10425	1115	10426	111
4375	10427	1117	10430	1118	10431	1119	10432	111A	10433	111
4380	10434	111C	10435	111D	10436	111E	10437	111F	10440	112
4385	10441	1121	10442	1122	10443	1123	10444	1124	10445	112
4390	10446	1126	10447	1127	10450	1128	10451	1129	10452	112
4395	10453	112B	10454	112C	10455	112D	10456	112E	10457	112
4400	10460	1130	10461	1131	10462	1132	10463	1133	10464	113
4405	10465	1135	10466	1136	10467	1137	10470	1138	10471	113
4410	10472	113A	10473	113B	10474	113C	10475	113D	10476	113
4415	10477	113F	10500	1140	10501	1141	10502	1142	10503	114
4420	10504	1144	10505	1145	10506	1146	10507	1147	10510	114
4425	10511	1149	10512	114A	10513	114B	10514	114C	10515	114
4430	10516	114E	10517	114F	10520	1150	10521	1151	10522	115
4435	10523	1153	10524	1154	10525	1155	10526	1156	10527	115
4440	10530	1158	10531	1159	10532	115A	10533	115B	10534	115
4445	10535	115D	10536	115E	10537	115F	10540	1160	10541	116
4450	10542	1162	10543	1163	10544	1164	10545	1165	10546	116
4455	10547	1167	10550	1168	10551	1169	10552	116A	10553	116
4460	10554	116C	10555	116D	10556	116E	10557	116F	10560	117
4465	10561	1171	10562	1172	10563	1173	10564	1174	10565	117
4470	10566	1176	10567	1177	10570	1178	10571	1179	10572	117
4475	10573	117B	10574	117C	10575	117D	10576	117E	10577	117
4480	10600	1180	10601	1181	10602	1182	10603	1183	10604	118
4485	10605	1185	10606	1186	10607	1187	10610	1188	10611	118
4490	10612	118A	10613	118B	10614	118C	10615	118D	10616	118
4495	10617	118F	10620	1190	10621	1191	10622	1192	10623	119
4500	10624	1194	10625	1195	10626	1196	10627	1197	10630	119
4505	10631	1199	10632	119A	10633	119A	10634	119B	10635	119
4510	10636	119E	10637	119F	10640	11A0	10641	11A1	10642	11A
4515	10643	11A3	10644	11A4	10645	11A5	10646	11A6	10647	11A
4520	10650	11A8	10651	11A9	10652	11AA	10653	11AB	10654	11A
4525	10655	11AD	10656	11AE	10657	11AF	10660	11B0	10661	11B
4530	10662	11B2	10663	11B3	10664	11B4	10665	11B5	10666	11B
4535	10667	11B7	10670	11B8	10671	11B9	10672	11BA	10673	11B
4540	10674	11BC	10675	11BD	10676	11BE	10677	11BF	10700	11C
4545	10701	11C1	10702	11C2	10703	11C3	10704	11C4	10705	11C
4550	10706	11C6	10707	11C7	10710	11C8	10711	11C9	10712	11C
4555	10713	11CB	10714	11CC	10715	11CD	10716	11CD	10717	11C
4560	10720	11D0	10721	11D1	10722	11D1	10723	11D2	10724	11D
4565	10725	11D5	10726	11D6	10727	11D7	10730	11D7	10731	11D
4570	10732	11DA	10733	11DB	10734	11DB	10735	11DC	10736	11D
4575	10737	11DF	10740	11E0	10741	11E0	10742	11E2	10743	11E
4580	10744	11E4	10745	11E5	10746	11E6	10747	11E7	10750	11F
4585	10751	11E9	10752	11EA	10753	11EA	10754	11EC	10755	11E
4590	10756	11EE	10757	11EF	10760	11EF	10761	11F0	10762	11F
4595	10763	11F3	10764	11F4	10765	11F5	10766	11F6	10767	11F
4600	10770	11F8	10771	11F9	10772	11FA	10773	11FA	10774	11F
4605	10775	11FD	10776	11FE	10777	11FF	11000	1200	11001	120
4610	11002	1202	11003	1203	11004	1204	11005	1205	11006	120
4615	11007	1207	11010	1208	11011	1209	11012	120A	11013	120
4620	11014	120C	11015	120D	11016	120D	11017	120F	11020	121
4625	11021	1211	11022	1212	11023	1213	11024	1214	11025	121
4630	11026	1216	11027	1217	11030	1218	11031	1219	11032	121
4635	11033	121B	11034	121C	11035	121D	11036	121E	11037	121

DEC	0/5 OCT	HEX	1/6 OCT	HEX	2/7 OCT	HEX	3/8 OCT	HEX	4/9 OCT	HEX
4640	11040	1220	11041	1221	11042	1222	11043	1223	11044	1224
4645	11045	1225	11046	1226	11047	1227	11050	1228	11051	1229
4650	11052	122A	11053	122B	11054	122C	11055	122D	11056	122E
4655	11057	122F	11060	1230	11061	1231	11062	1232	11063	1233
4660	11064	1234	11065	1235	11066	1236	11067	1237	11070	1238
4665	11071	1239	11072	123A	11073	123B	11074	123C	11075	123D
4670	11076	123E	11077	123F	11100	1240	11101	1241	11102	1242
4675	11103	1243	11104	1244	11105	1245	11106	1246	11107	1247
4680	11110	1248	11111	1249	11112	124A	11113	124B	11114	124C
4685	11115	124D	11116	124E	11117	124F	11120	1250	11121	1251
4690	11122	1252	11123	1253	11124	1254	11125	1255	11126	1256
4695	11127	1257	11130	1258	11131	1259	11132	125A	11133	125B
4700	11134	125C	11135	125D	11136	125E	11137	125F	11140	1260
4705	11141	1261	11142	1262	11143	1263	11144	1264	11145	1265
4710	11146	1266	11147	1267	11150	1268	11151	1269	11152	126A
4715	11153	126B	11154	126C	11155	126D	11156	126E	11157	126F
4720	11160	1270	11161	1271	11162	1272	11163	1273	11164	1274
4725	11165	1275	11166	1276	11167	1277	11170	1278	11171	1279
4730	11172	127A	11173	127B	11174	127C	11175	127D	11176	127E
4735	11177	127F	11200	1280	11201	1281	11202	1282	11203	1283
4740	11204	1284	11205	1285	11206	1286	11207	1287	11210	1288
4745	11211	1289	11212	128A	11213	128B	11214	128C	11215	128D
4750	11216	128E	11217	128F	11220	1290	11221	1291	11222	1292
4755	11223	1293	11224	1294	11225	1295	11226	1296	11227	1297
4760	11230	1298	11231	1299	11232	129A	11233	129B	11234	129C
4765	11235	129D	11236	129E	11237	129F	11240	12A0	11241	12A1
4770	11242	12A2	11243	12A3	11244	12A4	11245	12A5	11246	12A6
4775	11247	12A7	11250	12A8	11251	12A9	11252	12AA	11253	12AB
4780	11254	12AC	11255	12AD	11256	12AE	11257	12AF	11260	12B0
4785	11261	12B1	11262	12B2	11263	12B3	11264	12B4	11265	12B5
4790	11266	12B6	11267	12B7	11270	12B8	11271	12B9	11272	12BA
4795	11273	12BB	11274	12BC	11275	12BD	11276	12BE	11277	12BF
4800	11300	12C0	11301	12C1	11302	12C2	11303	12C3	11304	12C4
4805	11305	12C5	11306	12C6	11307	12C7	11310	12C8	11311	12C9
4810	11312	12CA	11313	12CB	11314	12CC	11315	12CD	11316	12CE
4815	11317	12CF	11320	12D0	11321	12D1	11322	12D2	11323	12D3
4820	11324	12D4	11325	12D5	11326	12D6	11327	12D7	11330	12D8
4825	11331	12D9	11332	12DA	11333	12DB	11334	12DC	11335	12DD
4830	11336	12DE	11337	12DF	11340	12E0	11341	12E1	11342	12E2
4835	11343	12E3	11344	12E4	11345	12E5	11346	12E6	11347	12E7
4840	11350	12E8	11351	12E9	11352	12EA	11353	12EB	11354	12EC
4845	11355	12ED	11356	12EE	11357	12EF	11360	12F0	11361	12F1
4850	11362	12F2	11363	12F3	11364	12F4	11365	12F5	11366	12F6
4855	11367	12F7	11370	12F8	11371	12F9	11372	12FA	11373	12FB
4860	11374	12FC	11375	12FD	11376	12FE	11377	12FF	11400	1300
4865	11401	1301	11402	1302	11403	1303	11404	1304	11405	1305
4870	11406	1306	11407	1307	11410	1308	11411	1309	11412	130A
4875	11413	130B	11414	130C	11415	130D	11416	130E	11417	130F
4880	11420	1310	11421	1311	11422	1312	11423	1313	11424	1314
4885	11425	1315	11426	1316	11427	1317	11430	1318	11431	1319
4890	11432	131A	11433	131B	11434	131C	11435	131D	11436	131E
4895	11437	131F	11440	1320	11441	1321	11442	1322	11443	1323
4900	11444	1324	11445	1325	11446	1326	11447	1327	11450	1328
4905	11451	1329	11452	132A	11453	132B	11454	132C	11455	132D
4910	11456	132E	11457	132F	11460	1330	11461	1331	11462	1332
4915	11463	1333	11464	1334	11465	1335	11466	1336	11467	1337
4920	11470	1338	11471	1339	11472	133A	11473	133B	11474	133C
4925	11475	133D	11476	133E	11477	133F	11500	1340	11501	1341

DEC	0/5 OCT	HEX	1/6 OCT	HEX	2/7 OCT	HEX	3/8 OCT	HEX	4/9 OCT	HEX
4930	11502	1342	11503	1343	11504	1344	11505	1345	11506	1346
4935	11507	1347	11510	1348	11511	1349	11512	134A	11513	134B
4940	11514	134C	11515	134D	11516	134E	11517	134F	11520	1350
4945	11521	1351	11522	1352	11523	1353	11524	1354	11525	1355
4950	11526	1356	11527	1357	11530	1358	11531	1359	11532	135A
4955	11533	135B	11534	135C	11535	135D	11536	135E	11537	135F
4960	11540	1360	11541	1361	11542	1362	11543	1363	11544	1364
4965	11545	1365	11546	1366	11547	1367	11550	1368	11551	1369
4970	11552	136A	11553	136B	11554	136C	11555	136D	11556	136E
4975	11557	136F	11560	1370	11561	1371	11562	1372	11563	1373
4980	11564	1374	11565	1375	11566	1376	11567	1377	11570	1378
4985	11571	1379	11572	137A	11573	137B	11574	137C	11575	137D
4990	11576	137E	11577	137F	11600	1380	11601	1381	11602	1382
4995	11603	1383	11604	1384	11605	1385	11606	1386	11607	1387
5000	11610	1388	11611	1389	11612	138A	11613	138B	11614	138C
5005	11615	138D	11616	138E	11617	138F	11620	1390	11621	1391
5010	11622	1392	11623	1393	11624	1394	11625	1395	11626	1396
5015	11627	1397	11630	1398	11631	1399	11632	139A	11633	139B
5020	11634	139C	11635	139D	11636	139E	11637	139F	11640	13A0
5025	11641	13A1	11642	13A2	11643	13A3	11644	13A4	11645	13A5
5030	11646	13A6	11647	13A7	11650	13A8	11651	13A9	11652	13AA
5035	11653	13AB	11654	13AC	11655	13AD	11656	13AE	11657	13AF
5040	11660	13B0	11661	13B1	11662	13B2	11663	13B3	11664	13B4
5045	11665	13B5	11666	13B6	11667	13B7	11670	13B8	11671	13B9
5050	11672	13BA	11673	13BB	11674	13BC	11675	13BD	11676	13BE
5055	11677	13BF	11700	13C0	11701	13C1	11702	13C2	11703	13C3
5060	11704	13C4	11705	13C5	11706	13C6	11707	13C7	11710	13C8
5065	11711	13C9	11712	13CA	11713	13CB	11714	13CC	11715	13CD
5070	11716	13CE	11717	13CF	11720	13D0	11721	13D1	11722	13D2
5075	11723	13D3	11724	13D4	11725	13D5	11726	13D6	11727	13D7
5080	11730	13D8	11731	13D9	11732	13DA	11733	13DB	11734	13DC
5085	11735	13DD	11736	13DE	11737	13DF	11740	13E0	11741	13E1
5090	11742	13E2	11743	13F3	11744	13E4	11745	13E5	11746	13E6
5095	11747	13E7	11750	13E8	11751	13E9	11752	13EA	11753	13EB
5100	11754	13FC	11755	13ED	11756	13EE	11757	13EF	11760	13F0
5105	11761	13F1	11762	13F2	11763	13F3	11764	13F4	11765	13F5
5110	11766	13F6	11767	13F7	11770	13F8	11771	13F9	11772	13FA
5115	11773	13FB	11774	13FC	11775	13FD	11776	13FE	11777	13FF
5120	12000	1400	12001	1401	12002	1402	12003	1403	12004	1404
5125	12005	1405	12006	1406	12007	1407	12010	1408	12011	1409
5130	12012	140A	12013	140B	12014	140C	12015	140D	12016	140E
5135	12017	140F	12020	1410	12021	1411	12022	1412	12023	1413
5140	12024	1414	12025	1415	12026	1416	12027	1417	12030	1418
5145	12031	1419	12032	141A	12033	141B	12034	141C	12035	141D
5150	12036	141E	12037	141F	12040	1420	12041	1421	12042	1422
5155	12043	1423	12044	1424	12045	1425	12046	1426	12047	1427
5160	12050	1428	12051	1429	12052	142A	12053	142B	12054	142C
5165	12055	142D	12056	142E	12057	142F	12060	1430	12061	1431
5170	12062	1432	12063	1433	12064	1434	12065	1435	12066	1436
5175	12067	1437	12070	1438	12071	1439	12072	143A	12073	143B
5180	12074	143C	12075	143D	12076	143E	12077	143F	12100	1440
5185	12101	1441	12102	1442	12103	1443	12104	1444	12105	1445
5190	12106	1446	12107	1447	12110	1448	12111	1449	12112	144A
5195	12113	144B	12114	144C	12115	144D	12116	144E	12117	144F
5200	12120	1450	12121	1451	12122	1452	12123	1453	12124	1454
5205	12125	1455	12126	1456	12127	1457	12130	1458	12131	1459
5210	12132	145A	12133	145B	12134	145C	12135	145D	12136	145E
5215	12137	145F	12140	1460	12141	1461	12142	1462	12143	1463

	0/5		1/6		2/7		3/8		4/9	
DEC	OCT	HEX	OCT	HEX	OCT	HEX	OCT	HEX	OCT	HEX
5220	12144	1464	12145	1465	12146	1466	12147	1467	12150	1468
5225	12151	1469	12152	146A	12153	146B	12154	146C	12155	146D
5230	12156	146E	12157	146F	12160	1470	12161	1471	12162	1472
5235	12163	1473	12164	1474	12165	1475	12166	1476	12167	1477
5240	12170	1478	12171	1479	12172	147A	12173	147B	12174	147C
5245	12175	147D	12176	147E	12177	147F	12200	1480	12201	1481
5250	12202	1482	12203	1483	12204	1484	12205	1485	12206	1486
5255	12207	1487	12210	1488	12211	1489	12212	148A	12213	148B
5260	12214	148C	12215	148D	12216	148E	12217	148F	12220	1490
5265	12221	1491	12222	1492	12223	1493	12224	1494	12225	1495
5270	12226	1496	12227	1497	12230	1498	12231	1499	12232	149A
5275	12233	149B	12234	149C	12235	149D	12236	149E	12237	149F
5280	12240	14A0	12241	14A1	12242	14A2	12243	14A3	12244	14A4
5285	12245	14A5	12246	14A6	12247	14A7	12250	14A8	12251	14A9
5290	12252	14AA	12253	14AB	12254	14AC	12255	14AD	12256	14AE
5295	12257	14AF	12260	14B0	12261	14B1	12262	14B2	12263	14B3
5300	12264	14B4	12265	14B5	12266	14B6	12267	14B7	12270	14B8
5305	12271	14B9	12272	14BA	12273	14BB	12274	14BC	12275	14BD
5310	12276	14BE	12277	14BF	12300	14C0	12301	14C1	12302	14C2
5315	12303	14C3	12304	14C4	12305	14C5	12306	14C6	12307	14C7
5320	12310	14C8	12311	14C9	12312	14CA	12313	14CB	12314	14CC
5325	12315	14CD	12316	14CE	12317	14CF	12320	14D0	12321	14D1
5330	12322	14D2	12323	14D3	12324	14D4	12325	14D5	12326	14D6
5335	12327	14D7	12330	14D8	12331	14D9	12332	14DA	12333	14DB
5340	12334	14DC	12335	14DD	12336	14DE	12337	14DF	12340	14E0
5345	12341	14E1	12342	14E2	12343	14E3	12344	14E4	12345	14E5
5350	12346	14E6	12347	14E7	12350	14E8	12351	14E9	12352	14EA
5355	12353	14EB	12354	14EC	12355	14ED	12356	14EE	12357	14EF
5360	12360	14F0	12361	14F1	12362	14F2	12363	14F3	12364	14F4
5365	12365	14F5	12366	14F6	12367	14F7	12370	14F8	12371	14F9
5370	12372	14FA	12373	14FB	12374	14FC	12375	14FD	12376	14FE
5375	12377	14FF	12400	1500	12401	1501	12402	1502	12403	1503
5380	12404	1504	12405	1505	12406	1506	12407	1507	12410	1508
5385	12411	1509	12412	150A	12413	150B	12414	150C	12415	150D
5390	12416	150E	12417	150F	12420	1510	12421	1511	12422	1512
5395	12423	1513	12424	1514	12425	1515	12426	1516	12427	1517
5400	12430	1518	12431	1519	12432	151A	12433	151B	12434	151C
5405	12435	151D	12436	151E	12437	151F	12440	1520	12441	1521
5410	12442	1522	12443	1523	12444	1524	12445	1525	12446	1526
5415	12447	1527	12450	1528	12451	1529	12452	152A	12453	152B
5420	12454	152C	12455	152D	12456	152E	12457	152F	12460	1530
5425	12461	1531	12462	1532	12463	1533	12464	1534	12465	1535
5430	12466	1536	12467	1537	12470	1538	12471	1539	12472	153A
5435	12473	153B	12474	153C	12475	153D	12476	153E	12477	153F
5440	12500	1540	12501	1541	12502	1542	12503	1543	12504	1544
5445	12505	1545	12506	1546	12507	1547	12510	1548	12511	1549
5450	12512	154A	12513	154B	12514	154C	12515	154D	12516	154E
5455	12517	154F	12520	1550	12521	1551	12522	1552	12523	1553
5460	12524	1554	12525	1555	12526	1556	12527	1557	12530	1558
5465	12531	1559	12532	155A	12533	155B	12534	155C	12535	155D
5470	12536	155E	12537	155F	12540	1560	12541	1561	12542	1562
5475	12543	1563	12544	1564	12545	1565	12546	1566	12547	1567
5480	12550	1568	12551	1569	12552	156A	12553	156B	12554	156C
5485	12555	156D	12556	156E	12557	156F	12560	1570	12561	1571
5490	12562	1572	12563	1573	12564	1574	12565	1575	12566	1576
5495	12567	1577	12570	1578	12571	1579	12572	157A	12573	157B
5500	12574	157C	12575	157D	12576	157E	12577	157F	12600	1580
5505	12601	1581	12602	1582	12603	1583	12604	1584	12605	1585

	0/5		1/6		2/7		3/8		4/9	
DEC	OCT	HEX	OCT	HEX	OCT	HEX	OCT	HEX	OCT	HEX
5510	12606	1586	12607	1587	12610	1588	12611	1589	12612	158A
5515	12613	158B	12614	158C	12615	158D	12616	158E	12617	158F
5520	12620	1590	12621	1591	12622	1592	12623	1593	12624	1594
5525	12625	1595	12626	1596	12627	1597	12630	1598	12631	1599
5530	12632	159A	12633	159B	12634	159C	12635	159D	12636	159E
5535	12637	159F	12640	15A0	12641	15A1	12642	15A2	12643	15A3
5540	12644	15A4	12645	15A5	12646	15A6	12647	15A7	12650	15A8
5545	12651	15A9	12652	15AA	12653	15AB	12654	15AC	12655	15AD
5550	12656	15AE	12657	15AF	12660	15B0	12661	15B1	12662	15B2
5555	12663	15B3	12664	15B4	12665	15B5	12666	15B6	12667	15B7
5560	12670	15B8	12671	15B9	12672	15BA	12673	15BB	12674	15BC
5565	12675	15BD	12676	15BE	12677	15BF	12700	15C0	12701	15C1
5570	12702	15C2	12703	15C3	12704	15C4	12705	15C5	12706	15C6
5575	12707	15C7	12710	15C8	12711	15C9	12712	15CA	12713	15CB
5580	12714	15CC	12715	15CD	12716	15CE	12717	15CF	12720	15D0
5585	12721	15D1	12722	15D2	12723	15D3	12724	15D4	12725	15D5
5590	12726	15D6	12727	15D7	12730	15D8	12731	15D9	12732	15DA
5595	12733	15DB	12734	15DC	12735	15DD	12736	15DE	12737	15DF
5600	12740	15E0	12741	15E1	12742	15E2	12743	15E3	12744	15E4
5605	12745	15E5	12746	15E6	12747	15E7	12750	15E8	12751	15E9
5610	12752	15EA	12753	15EB	12754	15EC	12755	15ED	12756	15EE
5615	12757	15EF	12760	15F0	12761	15F1	12762	15F2	12763	15F3
5620	12764	15F4	12765	15F5	12766	15F6	12767	15F7	12770	15F8
5625	12771	15F9	12772	15FA	12773	15FB	12774	15FC	12775	15FD
5630	12776	15FE	12777	15FF	13000	1600	13001	1601	13002	1602
5635	13003	1603	13004	1604	13005	1605	13006	1606	13007	1607
5640	13010	1608	13011	1609	13012	160A	13013	160B	13014	160C
5645	13015	160D	13016	160E	13017	160F	13020	1610	13021	1611
5650	13022	1612	13023	1613	13024	1614	13025	1615	13026	1616
5655	13027	1617	13030	1618	13031	1619	13032	161A	13033	161B
5660	13034	161C	13035	161D	13036	161E	13037	161F	13040	1620
5665	13041	1621	13042	1622	13043	1623	13044	1624	13045	1625
5670	13046	1626	13047	1627	13050	1628	13051	1629	13052	162A
5675	13053	162B	13054	162C	13055	162D	13056	162E	13057	162F
5680	13060	1630	13061	1631	13062	1632	13063	1633	13064	1634
5685	13065	1635	13066	1636	13067	1637	13070	1638	13071	1639
5690	13072	163A	13073	163B	13074	163C	13075	163D	13076	163E
5695	13077	163F	13100	1640	13101	1641	13102	1642	13103	1643
5700	13104	1644	13105	1645	13106	1646	13107	1647	13110	1648
5705	13111	1649	13112	164A	13113	164B	13114	164C	13115	164D
5710	13116	164E	13117	164F	13120	1650	13121	1651	13122	1652
5715	13123	1653	13124	1654	13125	1655	13126	1656	13127	1657
5720	13130	1658	13131	1659	13132	165A	13133	165B	13134	165C
5725	13135	165D	13136	165E	13137	165F	13140	1660	13141	1661
5730	13142	1662	13143	1663	13144	1664	13145	1665	13146	1666
5735	13147	1667	13150	1668	13151	1669	13152	166A	13153	166B
5740	13154	166C	13155	166D	13156	166E	13157	166F	13160	1670
5745	13161	1671	13162	1672	13163	1673	13164	1674	13165	1675
5750	13166	1676	13167	1677	13170	1678	13171	1679	13172	167A
5755	13173	167B	13174	167C	13175	167D	13176	167E	13177	167F
5760	13200	1680	13201	1681	13202	1682	13203	1683	13204	1684
5765	13205	1685	13206	1686	13207	1687	13210	1688	13211	1689
5770	13212	168A	13213	168B	13214	168C	13215	168D	13216	168E
5775	13217	168F	13220	1690	13221	1691	13222	1692	13223	1693
5780	13224	1694	13225	1695	13226	1696	13227	1697	13230	1698
5785	13231	1699	13232	169A	13233	169B	13234	169C	13235	169D
5790	13236	169E	13237	169F	13240	16A0	13241	16A1	13242	16A2
5795	13243	16A3	13244	16A4	13245	16A5	13246	16A6	13247	16A7

	0/5		1/6		2/7		3/8		4/9	
DEC	OCT	HEX	OCT	HEX	OCT	HEX	OCT	HEX	OCT	HEX
5800	13250	16A8	13251	16A9	13252	16AA	13253	16AB	13254	16AC
5805	13255	16AD	13256	16AE	13257	16AF	13260	16B0	13261	16B1
5810	13262	16B2	13263	16B3	13264	16B4	13265	16B5	13266	16B6
5815	13267	16B7	13270	16B8	13271	16B9	13272	16BA	13273	16BB
5820	13274	16BC	13275	16BD	13276	16BE	13277	16BF	13300	16C0
5825	13301	16C1	13302	16C2	13303	16C3	13304	16C4	13305	16C5
5830	13306	16C6	13307	16C7	13310	16C8	13311	16C9	13312	16CA
5835	13313	16CB	13314	16CC	13315	16CD	13316	16CE	13317	16CF
5840	13320	16D0	13321	16D1	13322	16D2	13323	16D3	13324	16D4
5845	13325	16D5	13326	16D6	13327	16D7	13330	16D8	13331	16D9
5850	13332	16DA	13333	16DB	13334	16DC	13335	16DD	13336	16DE
5855	13337	16DF	13340	16E0	13341	16E1	13342	16E2	13343	16E3
5860	13344	16E4	13345	16E5	13346	16E6	13347	16E7	13350	16E8
5865	13351	16E9	13352	16EA	13353	16EB	13354	16EC	13355	16ED
5870	13356	16EE	13357	16EF	13360	16F0	13361	16F1	13362	16F2
5875	13363	16F3	13364	16F4	13365	16F5	13366	16F6	13367	16F7
5880	13370	16F8	13371	16F9	13372	16FA	13373	16FB	13374	16FC
5885	13375	16FD	13376	16FE	13377	16FF	13400	1700	13401	1701
5890	13402	1702	13403	1703	13404	1704	13405	1705	13406	1706
5895	13407	1707	13410	1708	13411	1709	13412	170A	13413	170B
5900	13414	170C	13415	170D	13416	170E	13417	170F	13420	1710
5905	13421	1711	13422	1712	13423	1713	13424	1714	13425	1715
5910	13426	1716	13427	1717	13430	1718	13431	1719	13432	171A
5915	13433	171B	13434	171C	13435	171D	13436	171E	13437	171F
5920	13440	1720	13441	1721	13442	1722	13443	1723	13444	1724
5925	13445	1725	13446	1726	13447	1727	13450	1728	13451	1729
5930	13452	172A	13453	172B	13454	172C	13455	172D	13456	172E
5935	13457	172F	13460	1730	13461	1731	13462	1732	13463	1733
5940	13464	1734	13465	1735	13466	1736	13467	1737	13470	1738
5945	13471	1739	13472	173A	13473	173B	13474	173C	13475	173D
5950	13476	173E	13477	173F	13500	1740	13501	1741	13502	1742
5955	13503	1743	13504	1744	13505	1745	13506	1746	13507	1747
5960	13510	1748	13511	1749	13512	174A	13513	174B	13514	174C
5965	13515	174D	13516	174E	13517	174F	13520	1750	13521	1751
5970	13522	1752	13523	1753	13524	1754	13525	1755	13526	1756
5975	13527	1757	13530	1758	13531	1759	13532	175A	13533	175B
5980	13534	175C	13535	175D	13536	175E	13537	175F	13540	1760
5985	13541	1761	13542	1762	13543	1763	13544	1764	13545	1765
5990	13546	1766	13547	1767	13550	1768	13551	1769	13552	176A
5995	13553	176B	13554	176C	13555	176D	13556	176E	13557	176F
6000	13560	1770	13561	1771	13562	1772	13563	1773	13564	1774
6005	13565	1775	13566	1776	13567	1777	13570	1778	13571	1779
6010	13572	177A	13573	177B	13574	177C	13575	177D	13576	177E
6015	13577	177F	13600	1780	13601	1781	13602	1782	13603	1783
6020	13604	1784	13605	1785	13606	1786	13607	1787	13610	1788
6025	13611	1789	13612	178A	13613	178B	13614	178C	13615	178D
6030	13616	178E	13617	178F	13620	1790	13621	1791	13622	1792
6035	13623	1793	13624	1794	13625	1795	13626	1796	13627	1797
6040	13630	1798	13631	1799	13632	179A	13633	179B	13634	179C
6045	13635	179D	13636	179E	13637	179F	13640	17A0	13641	17A1
6050	13642	17A2	13643	17A3	13644	17A4	13645	17A5	13646	17A6
6055	13647	17A7	13650	17A8	13651	17A9	13652	17AA	13653	17AB
6060	13654	17AC	13655	17AD	13656	17AE	13657	17AF	13660	17B0
6065	13661	17B1	13662	17B2	13663	17B3	13664	17B4	13665	17B5
6070	13666	17B6	13667	17B7	13670	17B8	13671	17B9	13672	17BA
6075	13673	17BB	13674	17BC	13675	17BD	13676	17BE	13677	17BF
6080	13700	17C0	13701	17C1	13702	17C2	13703	17C3	13704	17C4
6085	13705	17C5	13706	17C6	13707	17C7	13710	17C8	13711	17C9

DEC	0/5 OCT	HEX	1/6 OCT	HEX	2/7 OCT	HEX	3/8 OCT	HEX	4/9 OCT	HEX
6090	13712	17CA	13713	17Cb	13714	17CC	13715	17CD	13716	17CE
6095	13717	17CF	13720	17D0	13721	17D1	13722	17D2	13723	17D3
6100	13724	17D4	13725	17D5	13726	17D6	13727	17D7	13730	17D8
6105	13731	17D9	13732	17DA	13733	17DB	13734	17DC	13735	17DD
6110	13736	17DE	13737	17DF	13740	17F0	13741	17E1	13742	17F2
6115	13743	17E3	13744	17F4	13745	17F5	13746	17E6	13747	17E7
6120	13750	17E8	13751	17E9	13752	17FA	13753	17EB	13754	17EC
6125	13755	17ED	13756	17EE	13757	17EF	13760	17F0	13761	17F1
6130	13762	17F2	13763	17F3	13764	17F4	13765	17F5	13766	17F6
6135	13767	17F7	13770	17F8	13771	17F9	13772	17FA	13773	17FB
6140	13774	17FC	13775	17FD	13776	17FE	13777	17FF	14000	1800
6145	14001	1801	14002	1802	14003	1803	14004	1804	14005	1805
6150	14006	1806	14007	1807	14010	1808	14011	1809	14012	180A
6155	14013	180B	14014	180C	14015	180D	14016	180E	14017	180F
6160	14020	1810	14021	1811	14022	1812	14023	1813	14024	1814
6165	14025	1815	14026	1816	14027	1817	14030	1818	14031	1819
6170	14032	181A	14033	181B	14034	181C	14035	181D	14036	181E
6175	14037	181F	14040	1820	14041	1821	14042	1822	14043	1823
6180	14044	1824	14045	1825	14046	1826	14047	1827	14050	1828
6185	14051	1829	14052	182A	14053	182B	14054	182C	14055	182D
6190	14056	182E	14057	182F	14060	1830	14061	1831	14062	1832
6195	14063	1833	14064	1834	14065	1835	14066	1836	14067	1837
6200	14070	1838	14071	1839	14072	183A	14073	183B	14074	183C
6205	14075	183D	14076	183E	14077	183F	14100	1840	14101	1841
6210	14102	1842	14103	1843	14104	1844	14105	1845	14106	1846
6215	14107	1847	14110	1848	14111	1849	14112	184A	14113	184B
6220	14114	184C	14115	184D	14116	184E	14117	184F	14120	1850
6225	14121	1851	14122	1852	14123	1853	14124	1854	14125	1855
6230	14126	1856	14127	1857	14130	1858	14131	1859	14132	185A
6235	14133	185B	14134	185C	14135	185D	14136	185E	14137	185F
6240	14140	1860	14141	1861	14142	1862	14143	1863	14144	1864
6245	14145	1865	14146	1866	14147	1867	14150	1868	14151	1869
6250	14152	186A	14153	186B	14154	186C	14155	186D	14156	186E
6255	14157	186F	14160	1870	14161	1871	14162	1872	14163	1873
6260	14164	1874	14165	1875	14166	1876	14167	1877	14170	1878
6265	14171	1879	14172	187A	14173	187B	14174	187C	14175	187D
6270	14176	187E	14177	187F	14200	1880	14201	1881	14202	1882
6275	14203	1883	14204	1884	14205	1885	14206	1886	14207	1887
6280	14210	1888	14211	1889	14212	188A	14213	188B	14214	188C
6285	14215	188D	14216	188E	14217	188F	14220	1890	14221	1891
6290	14222	1892	14223	1893	14224	1894	14225	1895	14226	1896
6295	14227	1897	14230	1898	14231	1899	14232	189A	14233	189B
6300	14234	189C	14235	189D	14236	189E	14237	189F	14240	18A0
6305	14241	18A1	14242	18A2	14243	18A3	14244	18A4	14245	18A5
6310	14246	18A6	14247	18A7	14250	18A8	14251	18A9	14252	18AA
6315	14253	18AB	14254	18AC	14255	18AD	14256	18AE	14257	18AF
6320	14260	18B0	14261	18B1	14262	18B2	14263	18B3	14264	18B4
6325	14265	18B5	14266	18B6	14267	18B7	14270	18B8	14271	18B9
6330	14272	18BA	14273	18BB	14274	18BC	14275	18BD	14276	18BE
6335	14277	18BF	14300	18C0	14301	18C1	14302	18C2	14303	18C3
6340	14304	18C4	14305	18C5	14306	18C6	14307	18C7	14310	18C8
6345	14311	18C9	14312	18CA	14313	18CB	14314	18CC	14315	18CD
6350	14316	18CE	14317	18CF	14320	18D0	14321	18D1	14322	18D2
6355	14323	18D3	14324	18D4	14325	18D5	14326	18D6	14327	18D7
6360	14330	18D8	14331	18D9	14332	18DA	14333	18DB	14334	18DC
6365	14335	18DD	14336	18DE	14337	18DF	14340	18E0	14341	18E1
6370	14342	18E2	14343	19E3	14344	18E4	14345	18E5	14346	18E6
6375	14347	18E7	14350	18E8	14351	18F9	14352	18EA	14353	18EB

DEC	0/5		1/6		2/7		3/8		4/9	
	OCT	HEX	OCT	HEX	OCT	HEX	OCT	HEX	OCT	HEX
6380	14354	18EC	14355	18ED	14356	18EE	14357	18EF	14360	18F0
6385	14361	18F1	14362	18F2	14363	18F3	14364	18F4	14365	18F5
6390	14366	18F6	14367	18F7	14370	18F8	14371	18F9	14372	18FA
6395	14373	18FB	14374	18FC	14375	18FD	14376	18FE	14377	18FF
6400	14400	1900	14401	1901	14402	1902	14403	1903	14404	1904
6405	14405	1905	14406	1906	14407	1907	14410	1908	14411	1909
6410	14412	190A	14413	190B	14414	190C	14415	190D	14416	190E
6415	14417	190F	14420	1910	14421	1911	14422	1912	14423	1913
6420	14424	1914	14425	1915	14426	1916	14427	1917	14430	1918
6425	14431	1919	14432	191A	14433	191B	14434	191C	14435	191D
6430	14436	191E	14437	191F	14440	1920	14441	1921	14442	1922
6435	14443	1923	14444	1924	14445	1925	14446	1926	14447	1927
6440	14450	1928	14451	1929	14452	192A	14453	192B	14454	192C
6445	14455	192D	14456	192E	14457	192F	14460	1930	14461	1931
6450	14462	1932	14463	1933	14464	1934	14465	1935	14466	1936
6455	14467	1937	14470	1938	14471	1939	14472	193A	14473	193B
6460	14474	193C	14475	193D	14476	193E	14477	193F	14500	1940
6465	14501	1941	14502	1942	14503	1943	14504	1944	14505	1945
6470	14506	1946	14507	1947	14510	1948	14511	1949	14512	194A
6475	14513	194B	14514	194C	14515	194D	14516	194E	14517	194F
6480	14520	1950	14521	1951	14522	1952	14523	1953	14524	1954
6485	14525	1955	14526	1956	14527	1957	14530	1958	14531	1959
6490	14532	195A	14533	195B	14534	195C	14535	195D	14536	195E
6495	14537	195F	14540	1960	14541	1961	14542	1962	14543	1963
6500	14544	1964	14545	1965	14546	1966	14547	1967	14550	1968
6505	14551	1969	14552	196A	14553	196B	14554	196C	14555	196D
6510	14556	196E	14557	196F	14560	1970	14561	1971	14562	1972
6515	14563	1973	14564	1974	14565	1975	14566	1976	14567	1977
6520	14570	1978	14571	1979	14572	197A	14573	197B	14574	197C
6525	14575	197D	14576	197E	14577	197F	14600	1980	14601	1981
6530	14602	1982	14603	1983	14604	1984	14605	1985	14606	1986
6535	14607	1987	14610	1988	14611	1989	14612	198A	14613	198B
6540	14614	198C	14615	198D	14616	198E	14617	198F	14620	1990
6545	14621	1991	14622	1992	14623	1993	14624	1994	14625	1995
6550	14626	1996	14627	1997	14630	1998	14631	1999	14632	199A
6555	14633	199B	14634	199C	14635	199D	14636	199E	14637	199F
6560	14640	19A0	14641	19A1	14642	19A2	14643	19A3	14644	19A4
6565	14645	19A5	14646	19A6	14647	19A7	14650	19A8	14651	19A9
6570	14652	19AA	14653	19AB	14654	19AC	14655	19AD	14656	19AE
6575	14657	19AF	14660	19B0	14661	19B1	14662	19B2	14663	19B3
6580	14664	19B4	14665	19B5	14666	19B6	14667	19B7	14670	19B8
6585	14671	19B9	14672	19BA	14673	19BB	14674	19BB	14675	19BD
6590	14676	19BE	14677	19BF	14700	19C0	14701	19C1	14702	19C2
6595	14703	19C3	14704	19C4	14705	19C5	14706	19C6	14707	19C7
6600	14710	19C8	14711	19C9	14712	19CA	14713	19CB	14714	19CC
6605	14715	19CD	14716	19CE	14717	19CF	14720	19D0	14721	19D1
6610	14722	19D2	14723	19D3	14724	19D4	14725	19D5	14726	19D6
6615	14727	19D7	14730	19D8	14731	19D9	14732	19DA	14733	19DB
6620	14734	19DC	14735	19DD	14736	19DE	14737	19DF	14740	19E0
6625	14741	19E1	14742	19E2	14743	19E3	14744	19E4	14745	19E5
6630	14746	19E6	14747	19E7	14750	19E8	14751	19E9	14752	19EA
6635	14753	19EB	14754	19EC	14755	19ED	14756	19EE	14757	19EF
6640	14760	19F0	14761	19F1	14762	19F2	14763	19F3	14764	19F4
6645	14765	19F5	14766	19F6	14767	19F7	14770	19F8	14771	19F9
6650	14772	19FA	14773	19FB	14774	19FC	14775	19FD	14776	19FE
6655	14777	19FF	15000	1A00	15001	1A01	15002	1A02	15003	1A03
6660	15004	1A04	15005	1A05	15006	1A06	15007	1A07	15010	1A08
6665	15011	1A09	15012	1A0A	15013	1A0B	15014	1A0C	15015	1A0D

DEC	0/5 OCT	HEX	1/6 OCT	HEX	2/7 OCT	HEX	3/8 OCT	HEX	4/9 OCT	HEX
6670	15016	1A0E	15017	1A0F	15020	1A10	15021	1A11	15022	1A12
6675	15023	1A13	15024	1A14	15025	1A15	15026	1A16	15027	1A17
6680	15030	1A18	15031	1A19	15032	1A1A	15033	1A1B	15034	1A1C
6685	15035	1A1D	15036	1A1E	15037	1A1F	15040	1A20	15041	1A21
6690	15042	1A22	15043	1A23	15044	1A24	15045	1A25	15046	1A26
6695	15047	1A27	15050	1A28	15051	1A29	15052	1A2A	15053	1A2B
6700	15054	1A2C	15055	1A2D	15056	1A2E	15057	1A2F	15060	1A30
6705	15061	1A31	15062	1A32	15063	1A33	15064	1A34	15065	1A35
6710	15066	1A36	15067	1A37	15070	1A38	15071	1A39	15072	1A3A
6715	15073	1A3B	15074	1A3C	15075	1A3D	15076	1A3E	15077	1A3F
6720	15100	1A40	15101	1A41	15102	1A42	15103	1A43	15104	1A44
6725	15105	1A45	15106	1A46	15107	1A47	15110	1A48	15111	1A49
6730	15112	1A4A	15113	1A4B	15114	1A4C	15115	1A4D	15116	1A4E
6735	15117	1A4F	15120	1A50	15121	1A51	15122	1A52	15123	1A53
6740	15124	1A54	15125	1A55	15126	1A56	15127	1A57	15130	1A58
6745	15131	1A59	15132	1A5A	15133	1A5B	15134	1A5C	15135	1A5D
6750	15136	1A5E	15137	1A5F	15140	1A60	15141	1A61	15142	1A62
6755	15143	1A63	15144	1A64	15145	1A65	15146	1A66	15147	1A67
6760	15150	1A68	15151	1A69	15152	1A6A	15153	1A6B	15154	1A6C
6765	15155	1A6D	15156	1A6E	15157	1A6F	15160	1A70	15161	1A71
6770	15162	1A72	15163	1A73	15164	1A74	15165	1A75	15166	1A76
6775	15167	1A77	15170	1A78	15171	1A79	15172	1A7A	15173	1A7B
6780	15174	1A7C	15175	1A7D	15176	1A7E	15177	1A7F	15200	1A80
6785	15201	1A81	15202	1A82	15203	1A83	15204	1A84	15205	1A85
6790	15206	1A86	15207	1A87	15210	1A88	15211	1A89	15212	1A8A
6795	15213	1A8B	15214	1A8C	15215	1A8D	15216	1A8E	15217	1A8F
6800	15220	1A90	15221	1A91	15222	1A92	15223	1A93	15224	1A94
6805	15225	1A95	15226	1A96	15227	1A97	15230	1A98	15231	1A99
6810	15232	1A9A	15233	1A9B	15234	1A9C	15235	1A9D	15236	1A9E
6815	15237	1A9F	15240	1AA0	15241	1AA1	15242	1AA2	15243	1AA3
6820	15244	1AA4	15245	1AA5	15246	1AA6	15247	1AA7	15250	1AA8
6825	15251	1AA9	15252	1AAA	15253	1AAB	15254	1AAC	15255	1AAD
6830	15256	1AAE	15257	1AAF	15260	1AB0	15261	1AB1	15262	1AB2
6835	15263	1AB3	15264	1AB4	15265	1AB5	15266	1AB6	15267	1AB7
6840	15270	1AB8	15271	1AB9	15272	1ABA	15273	1ABB	15274	1ABC
6845	15275	1ABD	15276	1ABE	15277	1ABF	15300	1AC0	15301	1AC1
6850	15302	1AC2	15303	1AC3	15304	1AC4	15305	1AC5	15306	1AC6
6855	15307	1AC7	15310	1AC8	15311	1AC9	15312	1ACA	15313	1ACB
6860	15314	1ACC	15315	1ACD	15316	1ACE	15317	1ACF	15320	1AD0
6865	15321	1AD1	15322	1AD2	15323	1AD3	15324	1AD4	15325	1AD5
6870	15326	1AD6	15327	1AD7	15330	1AD8	15331	1AD9	15332	1ADA
6875	15333	1ADB	15334	1ADC	15335	1ADD	15336	1ADE	15337	1ADF
6880	15340	1AE0	15341	1AE1	15342	1AE2	15343	1AE3	15344	1AE4
6885	15345	1AE5	15346	1AE6	15347	1AE7	15350	1AE8	15351	1AE9
6890	15352	1AEA	15353	1AEB	15354	1AEC	15355	1AED	15356	1AEE
6895	15357	1AEF	15360	1AF0	15361	1AF1	15362	1AF2	15363	1AF3
6900	15364	1AF4	15365	1AF5	15366	1AF6	15367	1AF7	15370	1AF8
6905	15371	1AF9	15372	1AFA	15373	1AFB	15374	1AFC	15375	1AFD
6910	15376	1AFE	15377	1AFF	15400	1B00	15401	1B01	15402	1B02
6915	15403	1B03	15404	1B04	15405	1B05	15406	1B06	15407	1B07
6920	15410	1B08	15411	1B09	15412	1B0A	15413	1B0B	15414	1B0C
6925	15415	1B0D	15416	1B0E	15417	1B0F	15420	1B10	15421	1B11
6930	15422	1B12	15423	1B13	15424	1B14	15425	1B15	15426	1B16
6935	15427	1B17	15430	1B18	15431	1B19	15432	1B1A	15433	1B1B
6940	15434	1B1C	15435	1B1D	15436	1B1E	15437	1B1F	15440	1B20
6945	15441	1B21	15442	1B22	15443	1B23	15444	1B24	15445	1B25
6950	15446	1B26	15447	1B27	15450	1B28	15451	1B29	15452	1B2A
6955	15453	1B2B	15454	1B2C	15455	1B2D	15456	1B2E	15457	1B2F

	0/5		1/6		2/7		3/8		4/9	
DEC	OCT	HEX	OCT	HEX	OCT	HEX	OCT	HEX	OCT	HEX
6960	15460	1B30	15461	1B31	15462	1B32	15463	1B33	15464	1B34
6965	15465	1B35	15466	1B36	15467	1B37	15470	1B38	15471	1B39
6970	15472	1B3A	15473	1B3B	15474	1B3C	15475	1B3D	15476	1B3E
6975	15477	1B3F	15500	1B40	15501	1B41	15502	1B42	15503	1B43
6980	15504	1B44	15505	1B45	15506	1B46	15507	1B47	15510	1B48
6985	15511	1B49	15512	1B4A	15513	1B4B	15514	1B4C	15515	1B4D
6990	15516	1B4E	15517	1B4F	15520	1B50	15521	1B51	15522	1B52
6995	15523	1B53	15524	1B54	15525	1B55	15526	1B56	15527	1B57
7000	15530	1B58	15531	1B59	15532	1B5A	15533	1B5B	15534	1B5C
7005	15535	1B5D	15536	1B5E	15537	1B5F	15540	1B60	15541	1B61
7010	15542	1B62	15543	1B63	15544	1B64	15545	1B65	15546	1B66
7015	15547	1B67	15550	1B68	15551	1B69	15552	1B6A	15553	1B6B
7020	15554	1B6C	15555	1B6D	15556	1B6E	15557	1B6F	15560	1B70
7025	15561	1B71	15562	1B72	15563	1B73	15564	1B74	15565	1B75
7030	15566	1B76	15567	1B77	15570	1B78	15571	1B79	15572	1B7A
7035	15573	1B7B	15574	1B7C	15575	1B7D	15576	1B7E	15577	1B7F
7040	15600	1B80	15601	1B81	15602	1B82	15603	1B83	15604	1B84
7045	15605	1B85	15606	1B86	15607	1B87	15610	1B88	15611	1B89
7050	15612	1B8A	15613	1B8B	15614	1B8C	15615	1B8D	15616	1B8E
7055	15617	1B8F	15620	1B90	15621	1B91	15622	1B92	15623	1B93
7060	15624	1B94	15625	1B95	15626	1B96	15627	1B97	15630	1B98
7065	15631	1B99	15632	1B9A	15633	1B9B	15634	1B9C	15635	1B9D
7070	15636	1B9E	15637	1B9F	15640	1BA0	15641	1BA1	15642	1BA2
7075	15643	1BA3	15644	1BA4	15645	1BA5	15646	1BA6	15647	1BA7
7080	15650	1BA8	15651	1BA9	15652	1BAA	15653	1BAB	15654	1BAC
7085	15655	1BAD	15656	1BAE	15657	1BAF	15660	1BB0	15661	1BB1
7090	15662	1BB2	15663	1BB3	15664	1BB4	15665	1BB5	15666	1BB6
7095	15667	1BB7	15670	1BB8	15671	1BB9	15672	1BBA	15673	1BBB
7100	15674	1BBC	15675	1BBD	15676	1BBE	15677	1BBF	15700	1BC0
7105	15701	1BC1	15702	1BC2	15703	1BC3	15704	1BC4	15705	1BC5
7110	15706	1BC6	15707	1BC7	15710	1BC8	15711	1BC9	15712	1BCA
7115	15713	1BCB	15714	1BCC	15715	1BCD	15716	1BCE	15717	1BCF
7120	15720	1BD0	15721	1BD1	15722	1BD2	15723	1BD3	15724	1BD4
7125	15725	1BD5	15726	1BD6	15727	1BD7	15730	1BD8	15731	1BD9
7130	15732	1BDA	15733	1BDB	15734	1BDC	15735	1BDD	15736	1BDE
7135	15737	1BDF	15740	1BE0	15741	1BE1	15742	1BE2	15743	1BE3
7140	15744	1BE4	15745	1BE5	15746	1BE6	15747	1BE7	15750	1BE8
7145	15751	1BE9	15752	1BEA	15753	1BEB	15754	1BEC	15755	1BED
7150	15756	1BEE	15757	1BEF	15760	1BF0	15761	1BF1	15762	1BF2
7155	15763	1BF3	15764	1BF4	15765	1BF5	15766	1BF6	15767	1BF7
7160	15770	1BF8	15771	1BF9	15772	1BFA	15773	1BFB	15774	1BFC
7165	15775	1BFD	15776	1BFE	15777	1BFF	16000	1C00	16001	1C01
7170	16002	1C02	16003	1C03	16004	1C04	16005	1C05	16006	1C06
7175	16007	1C07	16010	1C08	16011	1C09	16012	1C0A	16013	1C0B
7180	16014	1C0C	16015	1C0D	16016	1C0E	16017	1C0F	16020	1C10
7185	16021	1C11	16022	1C12	16023	1C13	16024	1C14	16025	1C15
7190	16026	1C16	16027	1C17	16030	1C18	16031	1C19	16032	1C1A
7195	16033	1C1B	16034	1C1C	16035	1C1D	16036	1C1E	16037	1C1F
7200	16040	1C20	16041	1C21	16042	1C22	16043	1C23	16044	1C24
7205	16045	1C25	16046	1C26	16047	1C27	16050	1C28	16051	1C29
7210	16052	1C2A	16053	1C2B	16054	1C2C	16055	1C2D	16056	1C2E
7215	16057	1C2F	16060	1C30	16061	1C31	16062	1C32	16063	1C33
7220	16064	1C34	16065	1C35	16066	1C36	16067	1C37	16070	1C38
7225	16071	1C39	16072	1C3A	16073	1C3B	16074	1C3C	16075	1C3D
7230	16076	1C3E	16077	1C3F	16100	1C40	16101	1C41	16102	1C42
7235	16103	1C43	16104	1C44	16105	1C45	16106	1C46	16107	1C47
7240	16110	1C48	16111	1C49	16112	1C4A	16113	1C4B	16114	1C4C
7245	16115	1C4D	16116	1C4E	16117	1C4F	16120	1C50	16121	1C51

DEC	0/5		1/6		2/7		3/8		4/9	
	OCT	HEX	OCT	HEX	OCT	HEX	OCT	HEX	OCT	HEX
7250	16122	1C52	16123	1C53	16124	1C54	16125	1C55	16126	1C56
7255	16127	1C57	16130	1C58	16131	1C59	16132	1C5A	16133	1C5B
7260	16134	1C5C	16135	1C5D	16136	1C5E	16137	1C5F	16140	1C60
7265	16141	1C61	16142	1C62	16143	1C63	16144	1C64	16145	1C65
7270	16146	1C66	16147	1C67	16150	1C68	16151	1C69	16152	1C6A
7275	16153	1C6B	16154	1C6C	16155	1C6D	16156	1C6E	16157	1C6F
7280	16160	1C70	16161	1C71	16162	1C72	16163	1C73	16164	1C74
7285	16165	1C75	16166	1C76	16167	1C77	16170	1C78	16171	1C79
7290	16172	1C7A	16173	1C7B	16174	1C7C	16175	1C7D	16176	1C7E
7295	16177	1C7F	16200	1C80	16201	1C81	16202	1C82	16203	1C83
7300	16204	1C84	16205	1C85	16206	1C86	16207	1C87	16210	1C88
7305	16211	1C89	16212	1C8A	16213	1C8B	16214	1C8C	16215	1C8D
7310	16216	1C8E	16217	1C8F	16220	1C90	16221	1C91	16222	1C92
7315	16223	1C93	16224	1C94	16225	1C95	16226	1C96	16227	1C97
7320	16230	1C98	16231	1C99	16232	1C9A	16233	1C9B	16234	1C9C
7325	16235	1C9D	16236	1C9E	16237	1C9F	16240	1CA0	16241	1CA1
7330	16242	1CA2	16243	1CA3	16244	1CA4	16245	1CA5	16246	1CA6
7335	16247	1CA7	16250	1CA8	16251	1CA9	16252	1CAA	16253	1CAB
7340	16254	1CAC	16255	1CAD	16256	1CAE	16257	1CAF	16260	1CB0
7345	16261	1CB1	16262	1CB2	16263	1CB3	16264	1CB4	16265	1CB5
7350	16266	1CB6	16267	1CB7	16270	1CB8	16271	1CB9	16272	1CBA
7355	16273	1CBB	16274	1CBC	16275	1CBD	16276	1CBE	16277	1CBF
7360	16300	1CC0	16301	1CC1	16302	1CC2	16303	1CC3	16304	1CC4
7365	16305	1CC5	16306	1CC6	16307	1CC7	16310	1CC8	16311	1CC9
7370	16312	1CCA	16313	1CCB	16314	1CCC	16315	1CCD	16316	1CCE
7375	16317	1CCF	16320	1CD0	16321	1CD1	16322	1CD2	16323	1CD3
7380	16324	1CD4	16325	1CD5	16326	1CD6	16327	1CD7	16330	1CD8
7385	16331	1CD9	16332	1CDA	16333	1CDB	16334	1CDC	16335	1CDD
7390	16336	1CDE	16337	1CDF	16340	1CE0	16341	1CE1	16342	1CE2
7395	16343	1CF3	16344	1CE4	16345	1CE5	16346	1CE6	16347	1CE7
7400	16350	1CE8	16351	1CE9	16352	1CEA	16353	1CEB	16354	1CEC
7405	16355	1CED	16356	1CEE	16357	1CEF	16360	1CF0	16361	1CF1
7410	16362	1CF2	16363	1CF3	16364	1CF4	16365	1CF5	16366	1CF6
7415	16367	1CF7	16370	1CF8	16371	1CF9	16372	1CFA	16373	1CFB
7420	16374	1CFC	16375	1CFD	16376	1CFE	16377	1CFF	16400	1D00
7425	16401	1D01	16402	1D02	16403	1D03	16404	1D04	16405	1D05
7430	16406	1D06	16407	1D07	16410	1D08	16411	1D09	16412	1D0A
7435	16413	1D0B	16414	1D0C	16415	1D0D	16416	1D0E	16417	1D0F
7440	16420	1D10	16421	1D11	16422	1D12	16423	1D13	16424	1D14
7445	16425	1D15	16426	1D16	16427	1D17	16430	1D18	16431	1D19
7450	16432	1D1A	16433	1D1B	16434	1D1C	16435	1D1D	16436	1D1E
7455	16437	1D1F	16440	1D20	16441	1D21	16442	1D22	16443	1D23
7460	16444	1D24	16445	1D25	16446	1D26	16447	1D27	16450	1D28
7465	16451	1D29	16452	1D2A	16453	1D2B	16454	1D2C	16455	1D2D
7470	16456	1D2E	16457	1D2F	16460	1D30	16461	1D31	16462	1D32
7475	16463	1D33	16464	1D34	16465	1D35	16466	1D36	16467	1D37
7480	16470	1D38	16471	1D39	16472	1D3A	16473	1D3B	16474	1D3C
7485	16475	1D3D	16476	1D3E	16477	1D3F	16500	1D40	16501	1D41
7490	16502	1D42	16503	1D43	16504	1D44	16505	1D45	16506	1D46
7495	16507	1D47	16510	1D48	16511	1D49	16512	1D4A	16513	1D4B
7500	16514	1D4C	16515	1D4D	16516	1D4E	16517	1D4F	16520	1D50
7505	16521	1D51	16522	1D52	16523	1D53	16524	1D54	16525	1D55
7510	16526	1D56	16527	1D57	16530	1D58	16531	1D59	16532	1D5A
7515	16533	1D5B	16534	1D5C	16535	1D5D	16536	1D5E	16537	1D5F
7520	16540	1D60	16541	1D61	16542	1D62	16543	1D63	16544	1D64
7525	16545	1D65	16546	1D66	16547	1D67	16550	1D68	16551	1D69
7530	16552	1D6A	16553	1D6B	16554	1D6C	16555	1D6D	16556	1D6E
7535	16557	1D6F	16560	1D70	16561	1D71	16562	1D72	16563	1D73

	0/5		1/6		2/7		3/8		4/9	
DEC	OCT	HEX	OCT	HEX	OCT	HEX	OCT	HEX	OCT	HEX
7540	16564	1D74	16565	1D75	16566	1D76	16567	1D77	16570	1D78
7545	16571	1D79	16572	1D7A	16573	1D7B	16574	1D7C	16575	1D7D
7550	16576	1D7E	16577	1D7F	16600	1D80	16601	1D81	16602	1D82
7555	16603	1D83	16604	1D84	16605	1D85	16606	1D86	16607	1D87
7560	16610	1D88	16611	1D89	16612	1D8A	16613	1D8B	16614	1D8C
7565	16615	1D8D	16616	1D8E	16617	1D8F	16620	1D90	16621	1D91
7570	16622	1D92	16623	1D93	16624	1D94	16625	1D95	16626	1D96
7575	16627	1D97	16630	1D98	16631	1D99	16632	1D9A	16633	1D9B
7580	16634	1D9C	16635	1D9D	16636	1D9E	16637	1D9F	16640	1DA0
7585	16641	1DA1	16642	1DA2	16643	1DA3	16644	1DA4	16645	1DA5
7590	16646	1DA6	16647	1DA7	16650	1DA8	16651	1DA9	16652	1DAA
7595	16653	1DAB	16654	1DAC	16655	1DAD	16656	1DAE	16657	1DAF
7600	16660	1DB0	16661	1DB1	16662	1DB2	16663	1DB3	16664	1DB4
7605	16665	1DB5	16666	1DB6	16667	1DB7	16670	1DB8	16671	1DB9
7610	16672	1DBA	16673	1DBB	16674	1DBC	16675	1DBD	16676	1DBE
7615	16677	1DBF	16700	1DC0	16701	1DC1	16702	1DC2	16703	1DC3
7620	16704	1DC4	16705	1DC5	16706	1DC6	16707	1DC7	16710	1DC8
7625	16711	1DC9	16712	1DCA	16713	1DCB	16714	1DCC	16715	1DCD
7630	16716	1DCE	16717	1DCF	16720	1DD0	16721	1DD1	16722	1DD2
7635	16723	1DD3	16724	1DD4	16725	1DD5	16726	1DD6	16727	1DD7
7640	16730	1DD8	16731	1DD9	16732	1DDA	16733	1DDB	16734	1DDC
7645	16735	1DDD	16736	1DDE	16737	1DDF	16740	1DE0	16741	1DE1
7650	16742	1DE2	16743	1DE3	16744	1DE4	16745	1DE5	16746	1DE6
7655	16747	1DE7	16750	1DE8	16751	1DE9	16752	1DEA	16753	1DEB
7660	16754	1DEC	16755	1DED	16756	1DEE	16757	1DEF	16760	1DF0
7665	16761	1DF1	16762	1DF2	16763	1DF3	16764	1DF4	16765	1DF5
7670	16766	1DF6	16767	1DF7	16770	1DF8	16771	1DF9	16772	1DFA
7675	16773	1DFB	16774	1DFC	16775	1DFD	16776	1DFE	16777	1DFF
7680	17000	1E00	17001	1E01	17002	1E02	17003	1E03	17004	1E04
7685	17005	1E05	17006	1E06	17007	1E07	17010	1E08	17011	1E09
7690	17012	1E0A	17013	1E0B	17014	1E0C	17015	1E0D	17016	1E0E
7695	17017	1E0F	17020	1E10	17021	1E11	17022	1E12	17023	1E13
7700	17024	1E14	17025	1E15	17026	1E16	17027	1E17	17030	1E18
7705	17031	1E19	17032	1E1A	17033	1E1B	17034	1E1C	17035	1E1D
7710	17036	1E1E	17037	1E1F	17040	1E20	17041	1E21	17042	1E22
7715	17043	1E23	17044	1E24	17045	1E25	17046	1E26	17047	1E27
7720	17050	1E28	17051	1E29	17052	1E2A	17053	1E2B	17054	1E2C
7725	17055	1E2D	17056	1E2E	17057	1E2F	17060	1E30	17061	1E31
7730	17062	1E32	17063	1E33	17064	1E34	17065	1E35	17066	1E36
7735	17067	1E37	17070	1E38	17071	1E39	17072	1E3A	17073	1E3B
7740	17074	1E3C	17075	1E3D	17076	1E3E	17077	1E3F	17100	1E40
7745	17101	1E41	17102	1E42	17103	1E43	17104	1E44	17105	1E45
7750	17106	1E46	17107	1E47	17110	1E48	17111	1E49	17112	1E4A
7755	17113	1E4B	17114	1E4C	17115	1E4D	17116	1E4D	17117	1E4F
7760	17120	1E50	17121	1E51	17122	1E52	17123	1E53	17124	1E54
7765	17125	1E55	17126	1E56	17127	1E57	17130	1E58	17131	1E59
7770	17132	1E5A	17133	1E5B	17134	1E5C	17135	1E5D	17136	1E5E
7775	17137	1E5F	17140	1E60	17141	1E61	17142	1E62	17143	1E63
7780	17144	1E64	17145	1E65	17146	1E66	17147	1E67	17150	1E68
7785	17151	1E69	17152	1E6A	17153	1E6B	17154	1E6C	17155	1E6D
7790	17156	1E6E	17157	1E6F	17160	1E70	17161	1E71	17162	1E72
7795	17163	1E73	17164	1E74	17165	1E75	17166	1E76	17167	1E77
7800	17170	1E78	17171	1E79	17172	1E7A	17173	1E7A	17174	1E7C
7805	17175	1E7D	17176	1E7E	17177	1E7F	17200	1E80	17201	1E81
7810	17202	1E82	17203	1E83	17204	1E84	17205	1E85	17206	1E86
7815	17207	1E87	17210	1E88	17211	1E89	17212	1E8A	17213	1E8B
7820	17214	1E8C	17215	1E8D	17216	1E8E	17217	1E8F	17220	1E90
7825	17221	1E91	17222	1E92	17223	1E93	17224	1E94	17225	1E95

	0/5		1/6		2/7		3/8		4/9	
DEC	OCT	HEX	OCT	HEX	OCT	HEX	OCT	HEX	OCT	HEX
7830	17226	1E96	17227	1E97	17230	1E98	17231	1E99	17232	1E9A
7835	17233	1E9B	17234	1E9C	17235	1E9D	17236	1E9E	17237	1E9F
7840	17240	1EA0	17241	1EA1	17242	1EA2	17243	1EA3	17244	1EA4
7845	17245	1EA5	17246	1EA6	17247	1EA7	17250	1EA8	17251	1EA9
7850	17252	1EAA	17253	1EAB	17254	1EAC	17255	1EAD	17256	1EAE
7855	17257	1EAF	17260	1EB0	17261	1EB1	17262	1EB2	17263	1EB3
7860	17264	1EB4	17265	1EB5	17266	1EB6	17267	1EB7	17270	1EB8
7865	17271	1EB9	17272	1EBA	17273	1EBB	17274	1EBC	17275	1EBD
7870	17276	1EBE	17277	1EBF	17300	1EC0	17301	1EC1	17302	1EC2
7875	17303	1EC3	17304	1EC4	17305	1EC5	17306	1EC6	17307	1EC7
7880	17310	1EC8	17311	1EC9	17312	1ECA	17313	1ECB	17314	1ECC
7885	17315	1ECD	17316	1ECE	17317	1ECF	17320	1ED0	17321	1ED1
7890	17322	1ED2	17323	1ED3	17324	1ED4	17325	1ED5	17326	1ED6
7895	17327	1ED7	17330	1ED8	17331	1ED9	17332	1EDA	17333	1EDB
7900	17334	1EDC	17335	1EDD	17336	1EDE	17337	1EDF	17340	1EE0
7905	17341	1EE1	17342	1EE2	17343	1EE3	17344	1EE4	17345	1EE5
7910	17346	1EE6	17347	1EE7	17350	1EE8	17351	1EE9	17352	1EEA
7915	17353	1EEB	17354	1EEC	17355	1EED	17356	1EEE	17357	1EEF
7920	17360	1EF0	17361	1EF1	17362	1EF2	17363	1EF3	17364	1EF4
7925	17365	1EF5	17366	1EF6	17367	1EF7	17370	1EF8	17371	1EF9
7930	17372	1EFA	17373	1EFB	17374	1EFC	17375	1EFD	17376	1EFE
7935	17377	1EFF	17400	1F00	17401	1F01	17402	1F02	17403	1F03
7940	17404	1F04	17405	1F05	17406	1F06	17407	1F07	17410	1F08
7945	17411	1F09	17412	1F0A	17413	1F0B	17414	1F0C	17415	1F0D
7950	17416	1F0E	17417	1F0F	17420	1F10	17421	1F11	17422	1F12
7955	17423	1F13	17424	1F14	17425	1F15	17426	1F16	17427	1F17
7960	17430	1F18	17431	1F19	17432	1F1A	17433	1F1B	17434	1F1C
7965	17435	1F1D	17436	1F1E	17437	1F1F	17440	1F20	17441	1F21
7970	17442	1F22	17443	1F23	17444	1F24	17445	1F25	17446	1F26
7975	17447	1F27	17450	1F28	17451	1F29	17452	1F2A	17453	1F2B
7980	17454	1F2C	17455	1F2D	17456	1F2E	17457	1F2F	17460	1F30
7985	17461	1F31	17462	1F32	17463	1F33	17464	1F34	17465	1F35
7990	17466	1F36	17467	1F37	17470	1F38	17471	1F39	17472	1F3A
7995	17473	1F3B	17474	1F3C	17475	1F3D	17476	1F3E	17477	1F3F
8000	17500	1F40	17501	1F41	17502	1F42	17503	1F43	17504	1F44
8005	17505	1F45	17506	1F46	17507	1F47	17510	1F48	17511	1F49
8010	17512	1F4A	17513	1F4B	17514	1F4C	17515	1F4D	17516	1F4E
8015	17517	1F4F	17520	1F50	17521	1F51	17522	1F52	17523	1F53
8020	17524	1F54	17525	1F55	17526	1F56	17527	1F57	17530	1F58
8025	17531	1F59	17532	1F5A	17533	1F5B	17534	1F5C	17535	1F5D
8030	17536	1F5E	17537	1F5F	17540	1F60	17541	1F61	17542	1F62
8035	17543	1F63	17544	1F64	17545	1F65	17546	1F66	17547	1F67
8040	17550	1F68	17551	1F69	17552	1F6A	17553	1F6B	17554	1F6C
8045	17555	1F6D	17556	1F6E	17557	1F6F	17560	1F70	17561	1F71
8050	17562	1F72	17563	1F73	17564	1F74	17565	1F75	17566	1F76
8055	17567	1F77	17570	1F78	17571	1F79	17572	1F7A	17573	1F7B
8060	17574	1F7C	17575	1F7D	17576	1F7E	17577	1F7F	17600	1F80
8065	17601	1F81	17602	1F82	17603	1F83	17604	1F84	17605	1F85
8070	17606	1F86	17607	1F87	17610	1F88	17611	1F89	17612	1F8A
8075	17613	1F8B	17614	1F8C	17615	1F8D	17616	1F8E	17617	1F8F
8080	17620	1F90	17621	1F91	17622	1F92	17623	1F93	17624	1F94
8085	17625	1F95	17626	1F96	17627	1F97	17630	1F98	17631	1F99
8090	17632	1F9A	17633	1F9B	17634	1F9C	17635	1F9D	17636	1F9E
8095	17637	1F9F	17640	1FA0	17641	1FA1	17642	1FA2	17643	1FA3
8100	17644	1FA4	17645	1FA5	17646	1FA6	17647	1FA7	17650	1FA8
8105	17651	1FA9	17652	1FAA	17653	1FAB	17654	1FAC	17655	1FAD
8110	17656	1FAE	17657	1FAF	17660	1FB0	17661	1FB1	17662	1FB2
8115	17663	1FB3	17664	1FB4	17665	1FB5	17666	1FB6	17667	1FB7

	0/5		1/6		2/7		3/8		4/9	
DEC	OCT	HEX	OCT	HEX	OCT	HEX	OCT	HEX	OCT	HEX
8120	17670	1FB8	17671	1FB9	17672	1FBA	17673	1FBB	17674	1FBC
8125	17675	1FBD	17676	1FBE	17677	1FBF	17700	1FC0	17701	1FC1
8130	17702	1FC2	17703	1FC3	17704	1FC4	17705	1FC5	17706	1FC6
8135	17707	1FC7	17710	1FC8	17711	1FC9	17712	1FCA	17713	1FCB
8140	17714	1FCC	17715	1FCD	17716	1FCE	17717	1FCF	17720	1FD0
8145	17721	1FD1	17722	1FD2	17723	1FD3	17724	1FD4	17725	1FD5
8150	17726	1FD6	17727	1FD7	17730	1FD8	17731	1FD9	17732	1FDA
8155	17733	1FDB	17734	1FDC	17735	1FDD	17736	1FDE	17737	1FDF
8160	17740	1FE0	17741	1FE1	17742	1FE2	17743	1FE3	17744	1FE4
8165	17745	1FE5	17746	1FE6	17747	1FE7	17750	1FE8	17751	1FE9
8170	17752	1FEA	17753	1FEB	17754	1FEC	17755	1FED	17756	1FEE
8175	17757	1FEF	17760	1FF0	17761	1FF1	17762	1FF2	17763	1FF3
8180	17764	1FF4	17765	1FF5	17766	1FF6	17767	1FF7	17770	1FF8
8185	17771	1FF9	17772	1FFA	17773	1FFB	17774	1FFC	17775	1FFD
8190	17776	1FFE	17777	1FFF	20000	2000	20001	2001	20002	2002
8195	20003	2003	20004	2004	20005	2005	20006	2006	20007	2007
8200	20010	2008	20011	2009	20012	200A	20013	200B	20014	200C
8205	20015	200D	20016	200E	20017	200F	20020	2010	20021	2011
8210	20022	2012	20023	2013	20024	2014	20025	2015	20026	2016
8215	20027	2017	20030	2018	20031	2019	20032	201A	20033	201B
8220	20034	201C	20035	201D	20036	201E	20037	201F	20040	2020
8225	20041	2021	20042	2022	20043	2023	20044	2024	20045	2025
8230	20046	2026	20047	2027	20050	2028	20051	2029	20052	202A
8235	20053	202B	20054	202C	20055	202D	20056	202E	20057	202F
8240	20060	2030	20061	2031	20062	2032	20063	2033	20064	2034
8245	20065	2035	20066	2036	20067	2037	20070	2038	20071	2039
8250	20072	203A	20073	203B	20074	203C	20075	203D	20076	203E
8255	20077	203F	20100	2040	20101	2041	20102	2042	20103	2043
8260	20104	2044	20105	2045	20106	2046	20107	2047	20110	2048
8265	20111	2049	20112	204A	20113	204B	20114	204C	20115	204D
8270	20116	204E	20117	204F	20120	2050	20121	2051	20122	2052
8275	20123	2053	20124	2054	20125	2055	20126	2056	20127	2057
8280	20130	2058	20131	2059	20132	205A	20133	205B	20134	205C
8285	20135	205D	20136	205E	20137	205F	20140	2060	20141	2061
8290	20142	2062	20143	2063	20144	2064	20145	2065	20146	2066
8295	20147	2067	20150	2068	20151	2069	20152	206A	20153	206B
8300	20154	206C	20155	206D	20156	206E	20157	206F	20160	2070
8305	20161	2071	20162	2072	20163	2073	20164	2074	20165	2075
8310	20166	2076	20167	2077	20170	2078	20171	2079	20172	207A
8315	20173	207B	20174	207C	20175	207D	20176	207E	20177	207F
8320	20200	2080	20201	2081	20202	2082	20203	2083	20204	2084
8325	20205	2085	20206	2086	20207	2087	20210	2088	20211	2089
8330	20212	208A	20213	208B	20214	208C	20215	208D	20216	208E
8335	20217	208F	20220	2090	20221	2091	20222	2092	20223	2093
8340	20224	2094	20225	2095	20226	2096	20227	2097	20230	2098
8345	20231	2099	20232	209A	20233	209B	20234	209C	20235	209D
8350	20236	209E	20237	209F	20240	20A0	20241	20A1	20242	20A2
8355	20243	20A3	20244	20A4	20245	20A5	20246	20A6	20247	20A7
8360	20250	20A8	20251	20A9	20252	20AA	20253	20AB	20254	20AC
8365	20255	20AD	20256	20AE	20257	20AF	20260	20B0	20261	20B1
8370	20262	20B2	20263	20B3	20264	20B4	20265	20B5	20266	20B6
8375	20267	20B7	20270	20B8	20271	20B9	20272	20BA	20273	20BB
8380	20274	20BC	20275	20BD	20276	20BE	20277	20BF	20300	20C0
8385	20301	20C1	20302	20C2	20303	20C3	20304	20C4	20305	20C5
8390	20306	20C6	20307	20C7	20310	20C8	20311	20C9	20312	20CA
8395	20313	20CB	20314	20CC	20315	20CD	20316	20CE	20317	20CF
8400	20320	20D0	20321	20D1	20322	20D2	20323	20D3	20324	20D4
8405	20325	20D5	20326	20D6	20327	20D7	20330	20D8	20331	20D9

APPENDIX III

SHORT-FORM CONVERSION TABLES

The use of the short-form tables is probably best illustrated by looking at some examples.
1. Convert 2,147 on the base eight to the base ten.
From the short-form table for octal to decimal conversion, it can be seen that 2,000 on the base eight is equal to 1,024 on the base ten, 100 on the base eight is equal to 64 on the base ten, 40 to the base eight is equal to 32 on the base ten, 7 on the base eight is equal to 7 on the base ten. Expanding 2,147 on the base eight one gets

$$2147_8 = \sum_n a_n 8^n = 2 \times 8^3 + 1 \times 8^2 + 4 \times 8^1 + 7 \times 8^0$$

$$= 2 \times 512 + 1 \times 64 + 4 \times 8 + 7 \times 1$$

Thus, we see that it is only necessary to add the decimal numbers that we have found, i.e. 1024 plus 64, plus 32, plus 7 gives

$$2147_8 = 1127_{10}$$

2. Convert 425 on the base ten to the base eight.
From the decimal to octal short-form conversion table it can be found that 400 on the base ten is equal to 620 on the base eight, 20 on the base ten is equal to 24 on the base eight, and 5 on the base ten is equal to 5 on the base eight. Adding the octal values that have been found, it can be seen that

$$425_{10} = 620_8 + 24_8 + 5_8 = 651_8$$

Conversion of binary numbers to other bases and other bases to binary numbers are not included in these tables because binary numbers may be converted to either octal or hexadecimal numbers by inspection.

SHORT-FORM CONVERSION TABLES (Continued)

Decimal to Octal Conversion

Units		Tens		Hundreds		Thousands		Ten Thousands	
Base 10	Base 8	Base 10	Base 8	Base 10	Base 8	Base 10	Base 8	Base 10	Base 8
1	1	10	12	100	144	1,000	1,750	10,000	23,420
2	2	20	24	200	310	2,000	3,720	20,000	47,040
3	3	30	36	300	454	3,000	5,670	30,000	72,460
4	4	40	50	400	620	4,000	7,640	40,000	116,100
5	5	50	62	500	764	5,000	11,610	50,000	141,520
6	6	60	74	600	1,130	6,000	13,560	60,000	165,140
7	7	70	106	700	1,274	7,000	15,530	70,000	210,560
8	10	80	120	800	1,440	8,000	17,500	80,000	234,200
9	11	90	132	900	1,604	9,000	21,450	90,000	257,620

Octal to Decimal Conversion

Units		Tens		Hundreds		Thousands		Ten Thousands		Hundred Thousands	
Base 8	Base 10	Base 8	Base 10	Base 8	Base 10	Base 8	Base 10	Base 8	Base 10	Base 8	Base 10
1	1	10	8	100	64	1,000	512	10,000	4,096	100,000	32,768
2	2	20	16	200	128	2,000	1,024	20,000	8,192	200,000	65,536
3	3	30	24	300	192	3,000	1,536	30,000	12,288	300,000	98,304
4	4	40	32	400	256	4,000	2,048	40,000	16,384	400,000	131,072
5	5	50	40	500	320	5,000	2,560	50,000	20,480	500,000	163,840
6	6	60	48	600	384	6,000	3,072	60,000	24,576	600,000	196,608
7	7	70	56	700	448	7,000	3,584	70,000	28,672	700,000	229,376

SHORT-FORM CONVERSION TABLES (Continued)

Decimal to Hexadecimal Conversion

Units		Tens		Hundreds		Thousands		Ten Thousands	
Base 10	Base 16	Base 10	Base 16	Base 10	Base 16	Base 10	Base 16	Base 10	Base 16
1	1	10	A	100	64	1,000	3E8	10,000	2,710
2	2	20	14	200	C8	2,000	7D0	20,000	4,E20
3	3	30	1E	300	12C	3,000	BB8	30,000	7,530
4	4	40	28	400	190	4,000	FA0	40,000	9,C40
5	5	50	32	500	1F4	5,000	1,388	50,000	C,350
6	6	60	3C	600	258	6,000	1,770	60,000	E,A60
7	7	70	46	700	2BC	7,000	1,B58	70,000	11,170
8	8	80	50	800	320	8,000	1,F40	80,000	13,880
9	9	90	5A	900	384	9,000	2,328	90,000	15,F90

Hexadecimal to Decimal Conversion

Units		Tens		Hundreds		Thousands		Ten Thousands	
Base 16	Base 10	Base 16	Base 10	Base 16	Base 10	Base 16	Base 10	Base 16	Base 10
1	1	10	16	100	256	1,000	4,096	10,000	65,536
2	2	20	32	200	512	2,000	8,192	20,000	131,072
3	3	30	48	300	768	3,000	12,288	30,000	196,608
4	4	40	64	400	1,024	4,000	16,384	40,000	262,144
5	5	50	80	500	1,280	5,000	20,480	50,000	327,680
6	6	60	96	600	1,536	6,000	24,576	60,000	393,216
7	7	70	112	700	1,792	7,000	28,672	70,000	458,752
8	8	80	128	800	2,048	8,000	32,768	80,000	524,288
9	9	90	144	900	2,304	9,000	36,864	90,000	589,824
A	10	A0	160	A00	2,560	A,000	40,960	A0,000	655,360
B	11	B0	176	B00	2,816	B,000	45,056	B0,000	720,896
C	12	C0	192	C00	3,072	C,000	49,152	C0,000	786,432
D	13	D0	208	D00	3,328	D,000	53,248	D0,000	851,968
E	14	E0	224	E00	3,584	E,000	57,344	E0,000	917,504

APPENDIX IV

PDP-8 INSTRUCTION SET

The following is a list of instructions for the PDP-8
family of computers. Along with each instruction is given a
verbal description of the action that results from executing
the instruction. The instruction set is not complete in that,
with one exception, it does not include the input/output instructions that are assigned to various peripherals and options.
The one exception is the instructions for the Teletype terminal, because they have been used several times throughout the
book; these are the instructions TSF, TCF, TPC, TLS, KSF, KCC,
KRS, and KRB.

Mnemonic	Description
TAD	TWO'S COMPLEMENT ADD. The contents of the memory lo-cation specified by the address portion of the instruc-tion is added to the content of the accumulator in two's complement arithmetic. The result of this addition is held in the accumulator and the original contents of the accumulator is lost.
ISZ	INCREMENT AND SKIP IF ZERO. The contents of the mem-ory location specified by the address portion of the instruction is incremented by one in two's complement arithmetic. If the resultant content of the memory location equals zero, the content of the program counter register is incremented by one and the next instruction in the program is skipped. If the re-sultant content of the memory location does not equal zero, the program proceeds to the next instruction in the program.
DCA	DEPOSIT AND CLEAR ACCUMULATOR. The content of the accumulator is deposited in the memory location spec-ified by the address portion of the instruction and the accumulator is cleared, i.e. set equal to zero.
JMS	JUMP TO SUBROUTINE. Suppose the address portion of this instruction specifies address Y. Then the con-tent of the program counter register is deposited in memory location Y and the next instruction executed is the one of memory location Y+1. The content of the accumulator is not affected by the execution of this instruction.

PDP-8 INSTRUCTION SET-(Continued)

Mnemonic	Description
JMP	JUMP TO Y. Y is the memory location specified by the address portion of the instruction. Address Y is set in the program counter register so that the next instruction executed is that of address Y. The original content of the program counter register is lost. The content of the accumulator is not affecte by the execution of this instruction.
NOP	NO OPERATION. This instruction causes a one instruc tion delay in the program, and then the next sequen- tial instruction is initiated.
IAC	INCREMENT ACCUMULATOR. The content of the accumula- tor is incremented by one in two's complement arith- metic.
RAL	ROTATE ACCUMULATOR LEFT. The content of the accumu- lator is rotated one binary position to the left wit the content of the link register. The contents of accumulator bits 1 through 11 are shifted to the nex greater significant bit, the content of accumulator bit zero is shifted into the link register, and the content of the link register is shifted into accumu- lator bit 11.
RTL	ROTATE TWO LEFT. The content of the accumulator is rotated two binary positions to the left with the co tent of the link register. This instruction is log- ically equal to two successive RAL operations.
RAR	ROTATE ACCUMULATOR RIGHT. The content of the accumu lator is rotated one binary position to the right wi the contents of the link register. The content of accumulator bits zero through 10 are shifted to the next less significant bit, the content of accumulato bit 11 is shifted into the link register, and the co tent of the link register is shifted into accumulato bit zero.
RTR	ROTATE TWO RIGHT. The content of the accumulator is rotated two binary positions to the right with the content of the link register. This instruction is logically equal to two successive RAR operations.
CML	COMPLEMENT LINK. The content of the link register is complemented.
CMA	COMPLEMENT ACCUMULATOR. The content of the accumu- lator is set to the one's complement of the current contents of the accumulator. The content of each bi of the accumulator is complemented individually.
CIA	COMPLEMENT AND INCREMENT ACCUMULATOR. The content o the accumulator is converted from its current value to two's complement of its current value. This con- version is accomplished by combining the CMA and IAC instructions.

PDP-8 INSTRUCTION SET-(Continued)

Mnemonic	Description

CLL   CLEAR LINK. The content of the link register is cleared to contain a zero.

STL   SET LINK. The link register is set to contain a binary 1. This instruction is logically equal to combining the CLL and CML commands.

CLA   CLEAR ACCUMULATOR. The content of each bit of the accumulator is cleared to contain a binary zero.

STA   SET ACCUMULATOR. Each bit of the accumulator is set to contain a binary 1. This operation is logically equal to combining the CLA and CMA instructions.

HLT   HALT. Execution of this instruction halts the computer.

OSR   OR WITH SWITCH REGISTER. The inclusive OR operation is performed between the content of the accumulator and the content of the switch register which is a series of 12 toggle switches on the operator's console of the PDP-8. The result is left in the accumulator, the original content of the accumulator is lost, and the content of the switch register is unaffected by this instruction. When combined with the CLA instruction, the OSR performs a transfer of the content of the switch register into the accumulator.

SKP   SKIP, UNCONDITIONAL. The content of the program counter register is incremented by one so that the next sequential instruction of the program is skipped.

SNL   SKIP ON NON-ZERO LINK. The content of the link register is sampled, and if it contains a 1 the content of the program counter register is incremented by one so that the next sequential instruction of the program is skipped. If the link register contains a zero, no operation occurs and the next sequential instruction of the program is executed.

SZL   SKIP ON ZERO LINK. The content of the link register is sampled, and if it contains a zero the content of the program counter register is incremented by one so that the next sequential instruction of the program is skipped. If the link register contains a 1, no operation occurs and the next sequential instruction of the program is executed.

SZA   SKIP ON ZERO ACCUMULATOR. The content of each bit of the accumulator is sampled, and if each bit contains a zero the content of the program counter register is incremented by one so that the next sequential instruction of the program is skipped. If any bit of the accumulator contains a 1, no operation occurs and the next sequential instruction of the program is executed.

PDP-8 INSTRUCTION SET-(Continued)

Mnemonic	Description

SNA   SKIP ON NON-ZERO ACCUMULATOR. The content of each
bit of the accumulator is sampled, and if any bit
contains a 1 the content of the program counter register is incremented by one so that the next sequential instruction of the program is skipped. If all
bits of the accumulator contain a zero, no operation
occurs and the next sequential instruction of the
program is executed.

SMA   SKIP ON MINUS ACCUMULATOR. The content of the most
significant bit of the accumulator is sampled, and
if it contains a 1, indicating the accumulator contains a negative two's complement number, the conten
of the program counter register is incremented by
one so that the next sequential instruction of the
program is skipped. If the accumulator contains a
positive number, no operation occurs and the next
sequential instruction of the program is executed.

SPA   SKIP ON POSITIVE ACCUMULATOR. The content of the
most significant bit of the accumulator is sampled,
and if it contains a zero, indicating a positive
(or zero) two's complement number, the content of th
program counter register is incremented by one so th
the next sequential instruction of the program is
skipped. If the accumulator contains a negative num
ber, no operation occurs and program control advance
to the next sequential instruction of the program.

TSF   SKIP ON TELEPRINTER FLAG. The teleprinter flag is
sensed, and if it contains a binary 1 the content of
the program counter register is incremented by one
so that the next sequential instruction of the program is skipped.

TCF   CLEAR TELEPRINTER FLAG. The teleprinter flag is
cleared to zero.

TPC   LOAD TELEPRINTER AND PRINT. The Teletype output reg
ister is loaded from the contents of bits 4 through
11 of the accumulator; then the Teletype character
just loaded is selected, and punched and/or printed.

TLS   LOAD TELEPRINTER SEQUENCE. The teleprinter flag is
cleared; then a Teletype character code is transferred from the content of bits 4 through 11 of the
accumulator into the Teletype output register, the
character is selected and punched and/or printed.

KSF   SKIP ON KEYBOARD FLAG. The keyboard flag is sensed,
and if it contains a binary 1 the content of the
program counter register is incremented by one so
that the next sequential instruction of the program
is skipped.

PDP-8 INSTRUCTION SET-(Continued)

Mnemonic	Description
KCC	CLEAR KEYBOARD FLAG. Both the accumulator and the keyboard flag are cleared in preparation for transferring a Teletype character into the accumulator.
KRS	READ KEYBOARD BUFFER STATIC. The content of the Teletype input register is transferred into bits 4 through 11 of the accumulator. This is a static command in that neither the accumulator nor the keyboard flag is cleared.
KRB	READ KEYBOARD BUFFER DYNAMIC. The accumulator and the keyboard flag are both cleared, then the content of the Teletype input register is transferred into bits 4 through 11 of the accumulator.

THE ASCII CODE

The following table is devoted to the USA Standard Code for Information Interchange (ASCII). The code is given in four different forms. Only seven bits are required to uniquely define the code. This form is shown in the column labeled 7-BIT ASCII.

Many times eight bits per character are used with the eighth bit serving as a parity bit for validity checking. As always one can choose to use either odd or even parity. Columns two and three of the table are the eight bit odd and even parity forms of ASCII respectively.

Finally, some have chosen to use an eight bit form of ASCII where the eighth bit is arbitrarily always a logical one. This is the form shown in the table under the heading 8-BIT ASCII (8th LEVEL).

All entries in the table are octal.

Various Forms of the USA Standard Code for Information Interchange (ASCII)

CHAR-ACTER	7-BIT ASCII	8-BIT ASCII (ODD PARITY)	8-BIT ASCII (EVEN PARITY)	8-BIT ASCII (8th LEVEL)
0	60	260	60	260
1	61	61	261	261
2	62	62	262	262
3	63	263	63	263
4	64	64	264	264
5	65	265	65	265
6	66	266	66	266
7	67	67	267	267
8	70	70	270	270
9	71	271	71	271
A	101	301	101	301
B	102	302	102	302
C	103	103	303	303
D	104	304	104	304
E	105	105	305	305
F	106	106	306	306

THE ASCII CODE (Continued)

CHAR-ACTER	7-BIT ASCII	8-BIT ASCII (ODD PARITY)	8-BIT ASCII (EVEN PARITY)	8-BIT ASCII (8th LEVEL)
G	107	307	107	307
H	110	310	110	310
I	111	111	311	311
J	112	112	312	312
K	113	313	113	313
L	114	114	314	314
M	115	315	115	315
N	116	316	116	316
O	117	117	317	317
P	120	320	120	320
Q	121	121	321	321
R	122	122	322	322
S	123	323	123	323
T	124	124	324	324
U	125	325	125	325
V	126	326	126	326
W	127	127	327	327
X	130	130	330	330
Y	131	331	131	331
Z	132	332	132	332
!	41	241	41	241
"	42	242	42	242
#	43	43	243	243
$	44	244	44	244
%	45	45	245	245
&	46	46	246	246
'	47	247	47	247
(	50	250	50	250
)	51	51	251	251
*	52	52	252	252
+	53	253	53	253
,	54	54	254	254
-	55	255	55	255
.	56	256	56	256
/	57	57	257	257
:	72	272	72	272
;	73	73	273	273
<	74	274	74	274
=	75	75	275	275
>	76	76	276	276
?	77	277	77	277
@	100	100	300	300
[	133	133	333	333
\	134	334	134	334
]	135	135	335	335

THE ASCII CODE (Continued)

CHAR- ACTER	7-BIT ASCII	8-BIT ASCII (ODD PARITY)	8-BIT ASCII (EVEN PARITY)	8-BIT ASCII (8th LEVEL)
↑	136	136	336	336
←	137	337	137	337
EOT	4	4	204	204
W RU	5	205	5	205
RU	6	206	6	206
BELL	7	7	207	207
Line Feed	12	212	12	212
Return	15	15	215	215
Space	40	40	240	240
ALT MODE	175	375	175	375
RUB OUT	177	177	377	377

PUNCH CARD CODES

There are two codes currently in wide use for punch cards. There is some ambiguity in designating the respective codes. Originally Herman Hollerith developed a means of encoding punched cards by which each column of a card contains one alphanumeric character. Until recently only one code was in wide use, and as time passed this came to be referenced as the Hollerith Code. However, a second code was added recently and is known as the Extended Binary-Coded-Decimal Interchange Code (EBCDIC). This raises a point of confusion because both codes use the Hollerith Technique of coding. In keeping with conversational usage the older code is labeled Hollerith in the following table and the newer code is labeled EBCDIC.

The Hollerith Code and the EBCDIC code for punch cards.

Character	Rows Punched		Character	Rows Punched	
	Hollerith	EBCDIC		Hollerith	EBCDIC
.	12,8,3	12,8,3	H	12,8	12,8
)	12,8,4	11,8,5	I	12,9	12,9
]	12,8,5		J	11,1	11,1
<	12,8,6	12,8,4	K	11,2	11,2
←	12,8,7		L	11,3	11,3
+	12	12,8,6	M	11,4	11,4
$	11,8,3	11,8,3	N	11,5	11,5
*	11,8,4	11,8,4	O	11,6	11,6
‐	11,8,5		P	11,7	11,7
>	11,8,6		Q	11,8	11,8
&	11,8,7	12	R	11,9	11,9
-	11	11	S	0,2	0,2
/	0,1	0,1	T	0,3	0,3
,	0,8,3	0,8,3	U	0,4	0,4
(	0,8,4	12,8,5	V	0,5	0,5
"	0,8,5		W	0,6	0,6
#	0,8,6	8,3	X	0,7	0,7
%	0,8,7	0,8,4	Y	0,8	0,8
=	8,3	8,6	Z	0,9	0,9
@	8,4	8,4	0	0	0

PUNCH CARD CODES (Continued)

Character	Rows Punched Hollerith	EBCDIC	Character	Rows Punched Hollerith	EBCDIC
↑	8,5		1	1	1
'	8,6	8,5	2	2	2
\	8,7		3	3	3
?	12,0		4	4	4
A	12,1	12,1	5	5	5
B	12,2	12,2	6	6	6
C	12,3	12,3	7	7	7
D	12,4	12,4	8	8	8
E	12,5	12,5	9	9	9
F	12,6	12,6	←	All Other	Codes
G	12,7	12,7	;	0,8,2	
			↑	11,0	

GLOSSARY OF TERMS

ABSOLUTE ADDRESS. The complete address of an actual memory
    location, as opposed to a partial address such as a page
    address or a base address.

ACCESS TIME. Some peripheral devices, such as disks, magnetic
    tape transports, and drums, vary as to the time required to
    read or write data on a specific position because of the
    relative location of the desired position and the recording
    mechanism. Magnetic memorys, on the other hand, have a
    fixed time to read or write in a location. The time to
    read or write the first data word is the access time.

ALGORITHM. A step-by-step procedure for obtaining a result.
    In programming, the procedure by which a given program
    solves a problem.

ALPHANUMERICS. A group of characters usually made up of the
    letters of the alphabet, the digits zero through nine, and
    other special characters such as =, +, (, etc. typically
    found on typewriter and Teletype unit keyboards.

ANALOG TAPE TRANSPORT. The electromechanical unit used to
    read and write analog tape. Analog tape has continuous
    (analog) signals recorded on it as opposed to digital tape
    transports which record discreet (digital) signals.

AND. One of the three basic logical operations. In digital
    electronics if the signals A and B are fed to the input of
    an AND gate and the output of the gate is C, then C is true
    if A and B are true and false if A and/or B is false. See
    also OR and NOT.

APPLICATIONS SOFTWARE. Those programs written to specifically
    accomplish the utilization of a computer for a specific
    task. Applications software is to be opposed to systems
    software which is exemplified by assemblers and compilers.

431

ASCII. The USA Standard Code for Information Interchange.
Often pronounced ask-ē. A code for representing the alphanumeric characters.

ASSEMBLER PROGRAM. A program that converts computer instructions as written by a programmer into the equivalent binary
numbers required by the computer to execute the instruction

ASSEMBLY LANGUAGE. An assembly language is a particular class
of programming language. It is composed of computer instru-
tions which are defined to the assembler program and which
normally have a one-for-one relationship to the actions tha
can be executed by the computer.

BASE. The base is the smallest tally of a number system, i.e.
the smallest grouping of a number system. For example, the
base of the decimal number system is ten and the octal number system is eight.

BATCH OPERATION. A method of operating a computer system
whereby a serial string of programs are fed to the computer
to be executed. This method of operation is common at central computer facilities and uncommon at on-line computer
facilities.

BAUD. A unit used in telecommunications to specify transmission rates. A baud is one pulse per second. Until
recently bits per second and baud were synonomous, but
present techniques permit transmitting more than one bit
per pulse.

BCD. See BINARY-CODED-DECIMAL.

BINARY-CODED-DECIMAL. A term commonly given the codes of a
character set. Any means of grouping binary bits to represent decimal digits. The ASCII representation of the
digits zero through nine is an example.

BINARY NUMBER. A number represented on the base two. The
binary number system uses only the integers 0 and 1.

BOOTSTRAP LOADER. A very short and simple program used to
read a more sophisticated loader program into the computer
memory. See also LOADER.

BRANCH TABLE. A series of branch instructions in a computer
program which directs the further action of the program
based upon predefined conditions.

BUFFER. Normally a contiguous group of memory or register
locations used for temporary storage. In the case of registers often there is only one register and it is called a
buffer register, e.g., memory buffer register.

BYTE. A group of binary bits. In present usage often meaning, eight bits.

CAMAC. A standard for on-line computer interfacing. The standard is achieved by fixing the physical dimensions of interface modules, the signal busses, and the signal characteristics.

CATHODE-RAY-TUBE DISPLAY. A cathode-ray-tube is a device used to generate and control a stream (beam) of electrons which impinge on a fluorescent coating on the face of the tube producing light. Several such light "spots" constitute a displayed picture.

CENTRAL PROCESSING UNIT. A subunit of a computer. It is difficult to define precisely as the design of computers evolve, but is often thought of as the control and arithmetic sections of a computer.

CLOCK. A computer clock is somewhat different than a wrist watch. Normally it does not keep track of absolute time like the wrist watch, but accounts for elapsed time. If at some point the computer is "told" the time then absolute time is determined.

CLOSED-LOOP CONTROL. If one device in controlling another, not only gives directions, but can sense the state of the controlled device and take appropriate steps to maintain the desired state, then closed-loop control is being exercised. See also OPEN-LOOP CONTROL.

CODE. In the computer sciences there are two common meanings for code. In programming, a program or series of computer instructions is often referred to as a code. In representing alphanumeric characters, a given convention is often referred to as a code, e.g., the ASCII code.

COMPILER. A compiler is a computer program which translates the instructions of a higher level language, such as FORTRAN, into assembly language instructions for a particular computer. See also ASSEMBLY LANGUAGE.

COMPILER COMPILER. A computer program that is used to generate compilers for a particular computer or family of computers. See also COMPILER.

COMPILER LANGUAGE. A higher level language, such as FORTRAN, which requires a compiler to translate its instructions into a form usable by the computer. See also COMPILER.

CONFIGURATION. A grouping of computer(s) and peripheral devices interconnected and functioning as a system.

CONTROL LANGUAGE. A programming language designed specifically
for on-line applications, and which can respond quickly to
the requests of peripheral devices. It should also have the
characteristic of being easily applicable to non-standard
computer peripherals.

CONVERSATIONAL LANGUAGES. A type of computer language, primarily run from Teletype terminals, and noted for their
English-like instructions and ease of use. Example languages are AID, BASIC, CAL, ESI, FOCAL, JOSS, and TELECOMP.

CPU. See CENTRAL PROCESSING UNIT.

CRT DISPLAY. See CATHODE-RAY-TUBE DISPLAY.

DATA CHANNEL. One type of input/output port to the memory of
a computer. This type of port is characterized by two facts
The data does not pass through the central processing unit
arithmetic or program control registers; and two memory
registers are used to direct the data flow to or from the
desired memory locations and to keep account of the amount
of data to be transferred. See also DIRECT MEMORY ACCESS
CHANNEL.

DEBUGGING. The activity of finding and correcting errors in
a computer program.

DECIMAL NUMBER. A number represented on the base ten. The
integers of the decimal number system are: 0,1,2,3,4,5,6,
7,8, and 9.

DEVICE DRIVER. See DEVICE HANDLER.

DEVICE HANDLER. A block of programming associated with one
type of computer peripheral, e.g. magnetic tape transports
and disks. Any program may access a peripheral by simply
calling for the appropriate handler. Device handlers normally perform the formatting of all data passing to and
from the peripheral.

DIAGNOSTICS. Assembler programs normally print messages which
describe errors found in the user's program during assembly.
These messages are referred to as diagnostics.

DICTIONARY. In assemblers dictionary is synonymous with table
e.g., symbol table. Sometimes used more generally to mean
an index to a list of program or data files.

DIGITAL TAPE TRANSPORT. The electromechanical unit used to
read and write digital tape. Digital tape has discreet
(digital) signals recorded on it as opposed to analog tape
transports which record continuous (analog) signals.

DIRECT MEMORY ACCESS CHANNEL. One type of input/output port
  to the memory of a computer. This type of port is characterized by two facts: the data does not pass through the
  central processing unit arithmetic or program control registers; and two hardware registers external to the computer
  memory are used to direct the data flow to or from the desired memory locations and to keep account of the amount of
  data to be transferred. See also DATA CHANNEL.

DISPLAY PROCESSOR. A special purpose computer designed to
  control a cathode-ray-tube display.

DMA. See DIRECT MEMORY ACCESS CHANNEL.

EBCDIC. The Extended Binary-Coded-Decimal Interchange Code.
  Often pronounced ebb-sĕ-dick. An 8-bit code for representing the common alphanumeric characters.

EVEN PARITY. See PARITY BIT.

EXCLUSIVE OR. In digital electronics if the signals A and B
  are fed to the input of an EXCLUSIVE OR gate and the output
  of the gate is C, then C is true if A and B are logically
  different and false if A and B are logically alike. See
  also OR, AND, and NOT.

EXECUTIVE SYSTEM. A program(s) which controls the general operation of the computer. For example, an executive system
  permits the user to carry on most of his activities, such
  as loading, assembling, executing, and debugging programs
  from one control device, typically a keyboard.

FILE. An arbitrary grouping of data or information in storage
  for example, a block of data on a magnetic tape or disk.

FLOATING POINT ARITHMETIC. Performing arithmetic with numbers
  that may have both integer and fractional parts, i.e.,
  arithmetic computation keeping track of the decimal point.

FLOW CHART. A chart using defined symbols to indicate flow.
  In programming a flow chart shows the sequence of steps
  performed by a program.

FLOW DIAGRAM. See FLOW CHART.

GENERIC INSTRUCTION. A general family of computer instructions
  that primarily control the action of central processing unit
  registers. See also MEMORY REFERENCE INSTRUCTION and
  INPUT/OUTPUT INSTRUCTION.

GLOBALS. A mechanism which permits programs and/or subroutine assembled at different times to be linked at the time they are loaded so that they can access each other and so that arguments can be transferred back and forth.

GRAY CODE. A binary code in which sequential numbers are represented by binary expressions that only change one bit in succeeding numbers.

HARDWARE. Referring to actual equipment as opposed to programming (software).

HARDWARE REGISTER. See REGISTER.

HEXADECIMAL NUMBER. A number represented on the base sixteen. The integers of the hexadecimal system are: 0,1,2,3,4,5,6, 7,8,9,A,B,C,D,E, and F.

HIT. See LIGHT PEN HIT.

INCLUSIVE OR. See OR.

INCREMENTAL TAPE TRANSPORT. See STEPPING TAPE TRANSPORT.

INDIRECT ADDRESSING. In _direct_ addressing a memory reference instruction utilizes the contents of the memory location addressed. In _indirect_ addressing the content of the memory location addressed is taken as a second address, the contents of which are to be utilized.

INPUT/OUTPUT INSTRUCTION. A computer instruction which is utilized in the passage of information to or from the computer. See also MEMORY REFERENCE INSTRUCTION and GENERIC INSTRUCTION.

INTERFACE. The electronics which electrically connect a peripheral device or process to the computer.

INTERRUPT. A process by which an on-going computer program is stopped, the computer is caused to execute a program segment related to the interrupt, and finally the computer returns to continue executing the original program.

INVERTER. See NOT.

LABEL. See TAG.

LATENCY TIME. See ACCESS TIME.

LEADER. A particular code used to indicate the front portion of a paper tape.

LIGHT BUTTON. An area displayed on an oscilloscope screen. When any portion of this area is detected by a light pen the computer program executes an action prespecified to be associated with that area.

LIGHT PEN. A device resembling a pencil or stylus which can detect a fluorescing spot on an oscilloscope screen.

LIGHT-PEN HIT. The detection of a fluorescent spot on an oscilloscope screen.

LINKING LOADER. A loader program that can read several programs into the computer memory which have been assembled at different times. The linking loader establishes communication (links) the programs as they are loaded. See also LOADER.

LITERAL. A means of reserving a memory space for the storage of a program variable without designating a specific memory location.

LOADER. A program which is used to load other programs into the computer memory. See also LINKING LOADER and BOOTSTRAP LOADER.

LOGICAL DEVICE ASSIGNMENT. A means whereby a program can access different peripheral devices by changing a variable(s). For example, logical device one might be a magnetic tape transport whereas logical device two might be a disk. See also DEVICE HANDLER.

LOGICAL OPERATIONS. The three basic logical operations are AND, OR, and NOT. See also AND, OR AND NOT.

MACRO-INSTRUCTIONS. An assembly language instruction which is expanded into two or more computer instructions by the assembler. Also used to denote those computer instructions which combine several operations into one instruction.

MEMORY CYCLE TIME. The cycle time of a magnetic core memory is made up of two subcycles; the read cycle and the write cycle. The combined time for the read and write cycles is the memory cycle time.

MEMORY INTERLEAVING. A means of increasing total data flow to or from magnetic core storage accomplished by using more than one memory bank and storing or retrieving sequential data words in succeeding banks. The average time required to store or retrieve a memory word becomes less than one memory cycle time.

MEMORY PAGING. A scheme which breaks computer storage into
   subunits called pages. In the case of smaller on-line computers a memory page is often related to the number of memory words that a memory reference instruction can address.
   Pages may be fixed, refer to specific memory locations; or
   floating, refer to locations relative to some register content such as the program counter register.

MEMORY REFERENCE INSTRUCTION. A computer instruction that
   accesses the computer memory during its execution. See
   also GENERIC INSTRUCTION and INPUT/OUTPUT INSTRUCTIONS.

MEMORY REGISTER. See REGISTER.

MODEM. A unit which is used to attach a digital device, such
   as a computer or a Teletype terminal, to a telephone line.
   The term is a contraction of modulator-demodulator.

MONITOR, FOREGROUND-BACKGROUND. An executive system which permits two activities on a time-shared basis. The foreground
   activity is of higher priority, e.g., the control of a
   process. When the process does not require computer time,
   the background activity, such as a program assembly, is
   conducted.

MONITOR PROGRAM. See EXECUTIVE SYSTEM.

MULTIPLEXER. An analog multiplexer is a device which sequentially switches continuous (analog) signals to a single
   terminal, e.g., an amplifier input. A digital multiplexer
   sequentially switches discreet (digital) signals to a single
   point, e.g., a computer port such as a data channel.

MULTIPLEXOR. See MULTIPLEXER.

NOT. One of the three basic logical operations. In digital
   electronics if the signal A is fed to the input of a NOT
   gate (also known as an inverter) and the output of the gate
   is B, then B is true if A is false, and false if A is true.
   See also AND and OR.

OBJECT PROGRAM. An assembler program after processing a user
   program produces the computer instructions in a code,
   usually binary. This code is the object version of the program; it is the paper tape, deck of cards, etc. that is
   loaded into the computer for execution. See also SOURCE
   PROGRAM.

OCTAL NUMBER. A number represented on the base eight. The
   octal number system uses the integers: 0,1,2,3,4,5,6, and
   7.

ODD PARITY. See PARITY BIT.

OPEN-LOOP CONTROL. If one device in controlling another only
    gives directions and cannot sense the state of the con-
    trolled device, then open-loop control is being exercised.
    See also CLOSED-LOOP CONTROL.

OPERATING SYSTEM. See EXECUTIVE SYSTEM.

OR. One of the three basic logical operations (also known as
    an INCLUSIVE OR). In digital electronics if the signals A
    and B are fed to the input of an OR gate and the output of
    the gate is C, then C is true if A and/or B is true and
    false if A and B are false. See also EXCLUSIVE OR, AND,
    and NOT.

OSCILLOSCOPE DISPLAY. See CATHODE-RAY-TUBE DISPLAY.

PAGING. See MEMORY PAGING.

PARALLEL-TO-SERIAL CONVERSION. Taking a group of bits, such
    as contained in a register, and feeding them to another de-
    vice or unit serially one bit at a time. See also SERIAL-
    TO-PARALLEL CONVERSION.

PARITY BIT. A bit appended to a group of bits to make the
    sum of all the bits, with a value of one, always odd or
    always even. If the sum of one bits is odd, then odd par-
    ity is being used; if the sum is even, then even parity is
    being used.

PERIPHERAL DEVICES. Auxiliary equipment attached to a computer,
    e.g., oscilloscope display, card reader, paper tape equip-
    ment.

PRINTOUT. A loosely used term referring to almost anything
    printed by a printer attached to a computer.

PROGRAM INTERRUPT. See INTERRUPT.

PSEUDO-INSTRUCTION. An instruction placed in a computer pro-
    gram which directs the action of the assembler at the time
    the computer program is assembled. A pseudo-instruction
    does not result in any code being produced in the object
    version of the program.

RADIX. See BASE.

READ-ONLY MEMORY. A particular type of memory, the contents
    of which are permanently encoded. Therefore, information
    can only be read from such a memory and not written into it.

REAL-TIME. An ill defined term usually meaning that a computer or other device can respond to a given circumstance with sufficient speed to provide the desired results.

REAL-TIME EXECUTIVE SYSTEM. An executive system that operates with sufficient speed to permit the control of all peripherals on the computer. See also EXECUTIVE SYSTEM.

REENTRANT PROGRAM. A program which still completes execution properly after being interrupted and executed as a result of the interruption.

REGISTER. A device for holding and/or manipulating a group of bits. Sometimes broken into two categories: hardware registers, e.g., those constructed from flip-flop circuits; memory registers, those which are divisions, such as words, of magnetic core memories.

ROM. See READ-ONLY MEMORY.

SERIAL-TO-PARALLEL CONVERSION. Taking a serial sequence of bits as they arrive from another device or unit and collecting them into a group of bits, e.g., as the contents of a register. See also PARALLEL-TO-SERIAL CONVERSION.

SOFTWARE. Referring to the programs for a computer as opposed to the actual equipment (hardware).

SOURCE PROGRAM. A programmer writes a program, using the instructions of the programming language. This list of instructions is the source program. See also OBJECT PROGRAM.

STEPPING TAPE TRANSPORT. A tape transport that operates in a discreet rather than a continuous manner. A stepping motor advances the tape under the read/write heads, the read or write pulses are generated, the tape is again advanced by the stepping motor, etc.

STROBE. To strobe the contents of one register into another register is to transfer the contents of one register to another register. The transfer action is initiated by a strobe pulse.

SUBROUTINE. A self-contained portion of programming which may be accessed by another program.

SYNTAX. The structure of expressions in a programming language, or the rules governing the structure of a programming language.

SYSTEMS SOFTWARE. A term used to distinguish programs more
    intimately associated with the operation of the computer
    than computer applications. Examples are compilers,
    assemblers and loaders.

TABLE. A collection of data, each item being uniquelly iden-
    tified either by some label or by its relative position.

TABLE OF COMBINATIONS. See TRUTH TABLE.

TAG. In assembly language programming any instruction can be
    associated with a name called the tag for that instruction.
    This permits the programmer to reference the instruction by
    its tag and also relieves him from having to know the mem-
    ory word in which the instruction will eventually reside.

TAPE DRIVE. See TAPE TRANSPORT.

TAPE TRANSPORT. See ANALOG TAPE TRANSPORT and DIGITAL TAPE
    TRANSPORT.

TIME-SHARING. To use a device for two or more interleaved
    purposes.

TRAILER. A particular code used to indicate the end portion
    of a paper tape.

TRUTH TABLE. A table which describes the operation of a log-
    ical circuit by listing the state of the output for all
    possible combinations of the inputs. Also referred to as
    a table of combinations.

UNBUNDLING. A practice whereby a computer manufacturer does
    not sell computer equipment and programs under one price
    structure, but sells each separate from the other.

UTILITY PROGRAMS. Programs used to assist in the operation
    of the computer, e.g., floating-point arithmetic, print
    programs, ASCII-to-binary conversion.

VIRTUAL MEMORY. A method of organizing an executive system in
    such a way that all storage on the computer is addressable
    from a user program, giving the user the illusion of having
    almost limitless memory.

INDEX

Access time, 258, 259, 261
Accoustic coupler, 375. See
    also Modem
Accumulator register. See
    Register
Adder circuit, 209
  full adder, 210
  half adder, 210
Address bits, 73
Address block. See Address
    bits
Address, memory. See Memory
    address
Algorithm, 18
al-Khuwarizmi, 17
Alphabetic number system.
    See Number system
Analog-to-digital converter
    (ADC), 290
  programming, 293
  ramp, 292
  successive approximation,
    291
AND gate, 190
Arithmetic section. See
    Computer organization
ASCII. See code
ASCII-to-binary conversion,
    328
Assembler program, 164
  definition, 67, 174
  diagnostics, 174
  equipment requirements, 181
  features, 175
  format, 165
  macro-assembler, 176

off-line, 181
one-pass, 165
operation, 164
purpose, 164
relation to loaders, 175
two-pass, 165

Base
  concept, 18
  to represent a number, 19
  two, eight, and sixteen, 23
Bid procurement, 369
Binary number system, 23. See
    also Number system
Binary-to-decimal conversion,
    338. See also Conversion
Bit, 50
Boolean algebra, 197
  theorems, 199
Branch table, 118
Break point, 185
Byte, 58

CAMAC concept, 319
Card duplicator, 305
Card punch, 304
Card reader, 305
Card verifier, 305
Cathode-ray-tube display. See
    Oscilloscope display
Central Computing Facility
  batch operated, 3
  off-line assembly, 157
Central processing unit (CPU),
    56, 60. See also Computer
    organization